# Hill Rat

# HILL RAT

## BLOWING THE LID OFF CONGRESS

## John L. Jackley

REGNERY GATEWAY
Washington, D. C.

Library of Congress Cataloging-In-Publication Data

Jackley, John L., 1955–
    Hill rat : blowing the lid off Congress / John L. Jackley.
        p.   cm.
    Includes bibliographical references and index.
    ISBN 0-89526-529-X
    1. United States.   Congress—Ethics.   I. Title.
JK1140J33   1992
    328.73'07'09048—dc20                                    91-43739
                                                                                  CIP

Published in the United States by
Regnery Gateway
1130 17th Street, NW
Washington, DC 20036

Distributed to the trade by
National Book Network
4720-A Boston Way
Lanham, MD 20706

First Edition
1992 printing
Printed on acid free paper
Manufactured in the United States of America

99   98   97   96   95   94   93   92       5   4   3   2   1

This book is dedicated to Janet
and the promise of her silent toast;

And to the women and men of the American news media,
who for all their supposed faults are really
the only ones we have that keep the big boys
from stealing everything in sight.

# ACKNOWLEDGEMENTS

This book could not have been written without the help and encouragement of many people along the way.

Special thanks are due Deborah Davis, who assisted greatly with innumerable drafts of my book proposal as well as with agents while I made the jolting transition from Capitol Hill press secretary to writer; she is the first, to my knowledge, to have used the phrase "death of the genuinely public man." The same to David McMichael, who provided so much thought and perspective to events involving the contra war in Nicaragua, as did journalist John Canham-Clyne, who along with Joe Pichariello of the *Washington Post* and myself are among the last of the Iran-contra junkies.

Tony Nagle kept my spirits up during the long, dark years on the Hill when we were groping for a way out without success.

My agent, Jay Acton of Acton and Dystel, Inc., gave me a great deal of encouragement at the critical early going when the book was little more than an idea; one could not wish for better representation.

Perhaps more than anyone, I am deeply grateful to Al Regnery at Regnery Gateway, who saw the possibilities of this book before anyone else and was able to make it happen, as well as the assistance of Megan Brockey, Jennifer Reist, and the rest of the great staff at Regnery Gateway. I will always be grateful to John Fund, the book's godfather, for all his help, support, and advice.

The opportunity to work with an editor as talented, tolerant, and thoughtful as Patricia Bozell was a special experience. Her calming and sensible influence can be found throughout the book. Thanks, too, to Martin Wooster, whose keen eye not only for detail but also coherence strengthened the work immeasurably.

Special thanks for intellectual sustenance and support go to the classics gang at Portland State University, and especially to Dr. Michael Reardon, who will recognize (probably alone) the tradition and techniques against which this book is written, as well as the rest of the History department and its chairman, Dr. Bernard Burke. I am forever in the debt of the intellectual and honor traditions of Washington and Lee University in Lexington, Virginia; Capitol Hill is a moral free-fire zone, and my years there were an invaluable guide in helping me regain my way when the path was at best uncertain.

Special thanks, of course, to Larry and Jo Jackley, my father and mother, and the rest of my family for all their love and support over the years; the same to Jim and Mary Plummer, on whose kitchen table this book began, and also to Robert and Renée Plummer for keeping me focused on the truly important issues of windsurfing, skiing, mountain biking, and hiking.

I will never forget the friendships and bonds I forged on the Hill over the years; they were all very, very helpful and supportive, and there were far more people than I can or should list here for obvious reasons. To them along with heartfelt thanks I truly wish good luck and success in the future.

And perhaps most of all, I am grateful for inspiration from the children: Julia and Bobby Jackley; Ben, Emily, and Zachary Plummer; Sean and Kelly Baskin; Will and Sarah Kuckro; Rebecca Brown; Peter and Danny Cook; and all the rest of the next generation who must live with the uncertain legacy of this one.

Finally, this book could not have been written without the moral, practical, and loving support of my wife Janet, who truly does make it all happen.

West Linn, Oregon
January 1992

# CONTENTS

# ACTUAL CONSTITUENT POSTCARD

Dear Congressman:

This morning I watched a little segment on TV about a place called Bullfeathers (if I remember correctly). It is supposedly Washington DC's "Cheers." According to the report, the staff members of a lot of congressmen congregate there. They are not elected. Few, if any, of them ever earned a nickel from manual (let alone, menial) labor. And yet they have a great deal of influence in making our laws. I'd venture to guess that many of them actually WRITE our laws. A lot of them probably read the proposed law and advise the congressman which way to vote. They, no doubt, open and read the letters and determine which, if any, the congressman sees. From the answers I get, I am sure they choose the form answer. One of the ninnies sent me a "thank you" for a teabag from you. I never sent a teabag to anyone.

I doubt that my congressman sees this, but some postmen and other people might. I hope.

Here's to life, liberty and the pursuit of happiness!

# INTRODUCTION

I listened with awe and admiration on March 2, 1989, when the distinguished historian David McCullough addressed a joint session of Congress celebrating the institution's bicentennial. McCullough spoke of current strong criticism of Congress, adding, "But what should be spoken of more often, and more widely understood, are the great victories that have been won here, the decisions of courage and vision achieved, the men and women of high purpose and integrity. . . . It was Congress, after all, that provided the Homestead Act, ended slavery, ended child labor, built the railroads, built the Panama Canal, the Interstate Highway System. It was Congress that paid for Lewis and Clark and for our travels to the moon." McCullough went on to underscore other congressional triumphs such as the Marshall Plan, Social Security, the GI Bill, and the Voting Rights Act.

He received thunderous applause from the assembled members, who were grateful for any praise at a time when the Jim Wright scandal was about to peak amid severe criticism of the institution's conduct in general.

I felt no elation, only despair as I pondered my own decade working on Capitol Hill and thought: He said nothing of Congress in the 1980s. Something happened here, didn't it, something of which those of us on the Hill dare not speak.

But we all reach our crossroads in life, and with me it really did come down to the children.

I will never forget how the joy over the birth of our son Bobby on Christmas Eve 1988 turned to terror. He stopped breathing twice and was rushed in a pediatric ambulance across the Potomac River to Children's Hospital in Washington, D.C., to have an immediate and life-saving operation. Would he live? How long? What was wrong? How bad was it? As we packed to leave the hospital a few days later, we were stunned by the possibility of facing emergency heart surgery. With equal suddenness, Bobby's condition stabilized, and we took him home the following day.

Your life changes after truly dark times. At some point after Bobby's birth—I cannot remember exactly when, those first hours and days and weeks and months are still blurry and difficult to probe—I promised myself what I would do about a longstanding problem.

I would simply write the truth.

It would be a big change. I had been a Democratic press secretary on Capitol Hill for most of the 1980s, charged with the care and feeding of a congressman's most precious asset: his public image. If truth is the first casualty of war, as Winston Churchill asserted, then it never even makes it to the front lines in politics. Truth to a politician is like a coin that has been rubbed down, passed around, its image reduced to flat metal; it is a flexible reality, something to be molded, cajoled, purchased, and sold in the marketplace of public opinion.

It was my job to do it—our job, I suppose, us Hill rats, who run the House of Representatives on a daily basis, keeping some sense of sanity amidst the chaos.

I first heard the expression Hill rats—political slang for congressional staff members—while sitting in a Capitol Hill bar late one afternoon in 1983 with some friends. A man on a barstool next to me appeared despondent.

"What am I going to do?" he asked.

"Have another drink?" I suggested.

"Phil is dead."

"Have another two drinks?"

It turned out that he had worked for the late Rep. Phil Burton of California, one of the smartest, toughest hardballers ever to play the game.

"I can't do anything else," the man went on, ignoring me. "I work on the Hill. I'm a Hill rat, that's what I am, a fucking Hill rat, pure and simple. I can't do anything else, and I don't want to, either."

Few do.

When my wife and I sit down to drink whiskey and tell lies, we laugh about those crazy times when we first came to Washington, scrambling to get ahead, eating our dinners at Hill receptions and lobbyists' soirees to save money, partying all night with the rest of the young hustlers, riding whatever wave happened to come along. The times were more direct, more immediate and more meaningful.

Now I don't know. Maybe it's age. Maybe it's crossing the line of thirty and hurtling toward forty. Maybe the questions come from growing up: I grew up on the Hill just as surely as anywhere else; my years there were the longest I spent in any one place in my life. We can laugh about the questions over the whiskeys but that doesn't mean they go away.

The Hill can be a heady place. It is easy to glamorize the climactic votes, the clashes of lords, the exercise of raw power, and the feelings you get when words you write are spoken on the House floor or are quoted on the front page of the *New York Times* or *Washington Post*. But it carries a price: the dark side of influence and the human corruption in its shadow.

I used to think I could separate what I did in Congress from the rest of my life. Politics and power and running the country were just something you did, like making widgets or automobiles.

But having children creates an awareness that your life is a single piece, not a collection of easily separated fragments. As I entered the late '80s, I labored under crushing doubts about the legitimacy of my work. I realized, deep in my heart, that my job was to manage the fiefdom, protect privilege, expand power, and along the way do whatever was necessary to keep my boss in office.

America was catching on, too. By the end of 1988, when my daughter Julia was three and Bobby's birth approached, the House of Representatives was becoming known by its misdeeds: Backdoor pay raises. Ethical scandals. Jim Wright. Bribes and payoffs. PACs and campaign contributions and favors in return. Sexual misconduct. Inability to govern.

"So where you from?" a man asked me in a bar in Roanoke, Virginia; where my wife and I were visiting friends. The bar was smoky, Lynyrd Skynyrd soared from the jukebox.

"Washington, D.C.," I replied, and added without thinking, "I work in the House of Representatives."

The man's eyes narrowed dangerously and he took a hit from his beer. "That so?" he snapped. "Sure as hell wish I could vote *my*-self a goddamned pay raise. Buncha' fuckin' assholes." He slammed the empty longneck on the table and moved away.

And no wonder. Public fury is at an all-time high toward an institution that has voted itself every perquisite imaginable while failing to deal with issues of historical importance. When Congress should have provided stability and leadership to help the nation come to terms with issues such as the Iran–contra scandal, the widening gap between rich and poor, or our changing role as a superpower, its members were placing the highest premium on personal political survival.

Members of the House had lost their sense of common purpose. In the decade that celebrated private values over public ones, when the most affluent fifth of all households saw their wealth rise 14 percent between 1984 and 1988 *after* inflation, the House of Representatives became a dark mirror for the worst of America. Its inabilty to solve the nation's problems seemed to stem directly from this change in character; we presided over the death of the genuinely public man.

I recorded these days in private hardbound journals, started in 1983 when I was press secretary to then-freshman U.S. Rep. Ronald Coleman of Texas, a House Majority Whip At-Large and lieutenant of Jim Wright, who would shortly succeed Thomas P. "Tip" O'Neill as Speaker of the House. I had just turned twenty-seven, and had spent the previous two years working for Dallas Congressman Jim Mattox, who in November 1982 won the race for Texas attorney general. After his own election to the House, Coleman promptly won a seat on the Armed Services and Government Operations Committees; he would soon became a member of the coveted

Appropriations Committee, which funds every federal department and agency.

I had other reasons to keep my journal: the tensions and dynamics of the congressional office were such that an accurate written record of when something was done, by whom, and to whom, was vital to my survival in the Coleman operation. Staff director Paul Rogers spent the first year purging the staff of anyone with independent links to Coleman, including his secretary of seventeen years in El Paso. The long knives were out and the night had just begun, and Rogers, an experienced political hack from Jimmy Carter's White House, had the infuriating but effective habit of denying to Coleman that he had ever told an underling to say, do, or write something when a deal turned sour. So I worked as a secret journalist, recording events and conversations I could not afford to forget.

My conscience developed broader reasons for keeping a journal. As the House changed for the worse, and our office along with it, I became angry. I expanded my journal to address my children, calling it in 1985 *Julia's Sunday Journal.* Each Sunday, amidst the scatter of toys and books and other objects of early childhood, I weighed and measured the nitty-gritty of American democracy as we Hill rats fought it out issue by issue, mailing by mailing, and dollar by dollar. I was determined to write and record while events were still fresh, while the swinery of the culture of influence swilled around me. I wanted to understand what we were doing and why, and I wanted to be able to explain it to my children.

It became the story of an institution ruled by the adage "money talks and bullshit walks," characterized by members who acted like demigods and debased by the deliberate and flagrant abuse of the taxpayers' money for political and personal purposes. I wanted desperately to tell about the Capitol Hill that affected the average American, not the Hill of the textbooks or the political science monographs about committee voting behavior. This was the Hill from the gut level, inward, bared and glistening, the soul, the driving force behind the veneer of issues and the puffery of policy. More than anything else, I did not want the varnish of time and distance to dull my memory of the members' arrogance and contempt for the average citizen, of the grasping, clutching, calculating, take-no-prisoners approach of the modern congressional office of our time.

The greatest single influence on written history today (no matter how historians argue over his merits) is still the nineteenth-century German, Leopold Von Ranke. He revolutionized the emerging professionalization of history by insisting that slavish documentary evidence was the best possible way to recreate the "essence" of historical experience. But because the House of Representatives produces an annual torrent of written material—hundreds of millions of letters and newsletters, tens of thousands of pages of committee and subcommittee hearing transcripts and reports, thousands of pages of the *Congressional Record*, and countless internal office memoranda and documents—a framework of meaning must be imposed to produce a comprehensible story. I have chosen to illuminate that part of Capitol Hill that Von Ranke would have termed the essence: those tense, often dark inside moments of power where public hope collided with private appetite, and political considerations danced nakedly around their apologia of legislation, position papers, debates, amendments, hearings, investigations, and high-sounding rhetoric.

But these are only signs of what I call the political beast: the barely restrained appetite for power for its own sake, an obsession with its acquisition and consolidation.

The public record vanishes at the end of the official paper trail. To rely on it solely would be to define the entire ocean by its whitecaps, ignoring the more powerful undertow. Official public records can be very misleading, too: without the political graffiti from Capitol Hill's back alleys and secret passageways, they become little more than empty books in a barren land. Accordingly, I have supplemented the public record with accounts from my private journals and collection of letters, as well as from news accounts, confidential memoranda, declassified national security and intelligence documents (including a complete copy of Lt. Col. Oliver North's personal notebooks), court transcripts, internal studies, General

Accounting Office reports, Congressional Research Service products, and other primary source material.

Besides, far too many books about Washington politics toss up a shield of impenetrable jargon of acronyms, legislative terms, and specialized vocabulary. But the American people need fewer theoretical discussions of MX basing modes and more descriptive accounts from the belly of the political beast, where members and Hill rats talk privately:

"So how many missiles *you* want?"

"Speaker says fifty."

"Fuck the Speaker. He has no primary [opponent]."

"Someone said the committee could live with less."

"Enough to nuke the Russians?"

"Hell yes."

"So how many you going for?"

"Shit, I don't know. How many's half?"

And so on. The language of the House behind closed doors is locker-room rough, like most language of power today; I have reproduced it faithfully.

For a decade I had a ringside seat at the greatest human circus in America. We squandered more money than Wall Street ever dreamed of. We made Jim and Tammy Faye Bakker look like amateurs. We had more scandals in a week than the Pentagon had in a year. We made the public forget about the hundreds of Reagan-era officials accused of misconduct. And, amidst the bumbling and the buffoonery, we made real decisions that determined the future of American health, trade, education, and transportation, not to mention, every now and then, war and peace.

My House was many things:

It was watching in frustration as complicit Democratic and Republican Intelligence Committee leaders deliberately suppressed the Iran-contra scandal for six months before it finally burst open in November 1986.

It was the rise of the holy trinity of PACs, honoraria, and campaign contributions as members raised money with the desperation of a hooker trying to make cab fare home.

It was the rise and fall of the Texas crowd, and I'm not just talking Jim Wright.

It was the refinement to a high art form of the use of public resources for reelection purposes. In 1987 alone, we produced 595 million pieces of *unsolicited* newsletters, postcards, and letters. It worked. In 1988, only six of 408 members running for reelection were defeated, a turnover rate less than that of the Soviet Politburo. The election year of 1990—the first post-Jim Wright, postcongressional scandal election—saw 96 percent of all incumbents reelected.

It was perks and privileges to the tune of $2,044,288 per member per year, making the House the world's most expensive legislative body.

It was the cult of the incumbent, a place where members no longer worked to make the laws but to stay—literally.

It was brutal trench warfare on a thousand fronts as the Reagan administration launched a determined attack on the legitimacy of representative government itself. While Visigoths and Vandals howled at the gates of the city, House Democrats focused their energies on making the Democratic party their private preserve, ignoring the collapse of many of their cherished programs.

It was a time, as Hunter Thompson wrote, when the hogs were in the tunnel. Money and greed called the tunes of the day, as members stole everything that was not nailed down before they went looking for the hammers.

Worst of all, perhaps, it was losing some semi-serious money in all three of my betting pools on Jim Wright's resignation.

And throughout the mess was the intertwined dance of madness of the great pulsating beast of the House and my vantage point for this window into Capitol Hill's political mysteries: Democratic leadership member U.S. Rep. Ronald Coleman, a lazy, talented, lonely, intensely partisan Texas figure from the U.S.-Mexico border city of El Paso, and his staff director, Paul Rogers, who became the ultimate Hill rat as he came to assume and exercise the powers of an elected member. Over the years, my job gave me a unique view of the universal changes that enveloped Capitol Hill in the 1980s. Coleman, as one of the 435 Gods Who Walk, symbolized everything that was right and wrong about the House of Representatives; he was someone whose intimate political secrets I knew for eight years without ever truly knowing the man.

By 1983, the House had become a political casbah, a playing field of legislative operations with no rules, and Coleman, Rogers, and I hit the ground running. We crushed every political challenger back in Texas, shook down the PACs, dodged two federal indictments, almost died together in a near-plane crash, played Wheel of Fortune with the public's money through the Appropriations Committee, and rose and fell with the tides of the town. "If you're gonna run with the big dogs, you gotta learn to piss in the tall grass" is a favorite Texas expression. Coleman ran, he learned, and in the end he nearly pissed it away.

My Capitol Hill journal had grown to thirty-five volumes and over four thousand pages by the time I resigned in June 1990. Along with my collection of files, newspaper clippings, photographs, correspondence, memoranda, confidential documents, and other material, the journal helped bring my decade in the House into focus.

The picture that emerged opened up a world largely unknown to Americans beyond the Washington Beltway. When President Bush, for example, asked Congress in 1991 for action in one hundred days on crime and transportation bills, many on Capitol Hill were genuinely perplexed. Did he mean one hundred calendar days? One hundred legislative days? One hundred days of the "Union calendar" or the "Calendar Wednesday?" It was not a silly discussion. Frustrated in 1988 at Republican opposition to budget reconciliation legislation, former Speaker Jim Wright used arcane parliamentary maneuvers to create singlehandedly another legislative day in the same day to pass the bill. As political expert Doug Bailey has pointed out, Washington and America live in different worlds and speak different languages.

This, then, is a book for the rest of the country.

Why should people care? John Adams stated that the American people have "an indisputable, unalienable, indefeasible, divine right to that most dreaded and envied kind of knowledge, I mean, of the characters and conduct of their rulers." And despite today's rampant abuses, the promise of the House remains as extraordinary as the genius of the Founding Fathers who conceived it. This account is the story of what happened when that extraordinary promise met the 1980's "Me Decade" generation of men and women who were willing to pay any price, bear any burden, and oppose any foe to assure their personal political survival. That price included the institutionalization of their own worst instincts—a price paid, ultimately, by the nation.

I made another rash promise on that desperate Christmas Eve of 1988. If Bobby lived, we would have the children baptized. I have little taste for organized religion, but it means the world to my wife. Besides, there are few atheists in pediatric intensive care wards and I had precious little else to offer. I am skeptical of miracles, but I made the promise in the car on the way to Children's Hospital. When I arrived in the surgical recovery room, I learned that not only was the operation successful, but all the baby's insides were there and in some semblance of working order. We would have a long road ahead of us—more operations, more panics, more problems—but the little guy was out of immediate danger.

Would I have written the book anyway? Probably. Would Bobby have been okay anyway? Sure. I think. But I'm taking no chances. The definition of honesty in politics is staying bought once you're bought, and on Capitol Hill we are, after all, honorable men.

# Hill Rat

## CHAPTER ONE

# PAST AS PROLOGUE

How DID THOSE of us on Capitol Hill come to wield the kind of power we have? Solving the riddle of how Congress in the 1980s produced the crisis of the 1990s requires a look into the past at a now-legendary, yet completely true, incident that took place in the late 1970s.

The participants were hardened professionals in America's ugliest participant sport: Capitol Hill politics. These "Hill rats" prided themselves on their ability to do anything in the name of the cause.

The contract "hit" had been issued in between votes on the House floor by a widely respected Midwestern congressman. The crimes of the condemned victim included disruption of personal property and destruction of domestic tranquility. In the Capitol Hill culture, it had become "a political problem," code words for termination with extreme prejudice.

After laying the ambush, they struck with terrible swiftness—an ordinary pillowcase wrapped around the victim's head, the body shoved into the backseat of a car, a flash of white over the 14th Street Bridge, and the final splash in the Potomac River below.

The two Hill rats looked at each other with grim satisfaction— but not for long. Inexplicably tortured by conscience, the actual

3

murderer was driven to confess. After agonizing, he decided to seek an audience with the congressman's wife.

"We killed your cat," he was reported to have muttered.

To appease his wife's wrath, the congressman summarily fired both men, who, unlike the unfortunate cat, landed promptly on their feet and found other employment. The wife bought another animal.

To the uninitiated, the moral of the story is elusive. Yet to those of us who understand the Byzantine ways of the Capitol, the incident reveals sacred truths. The members, those 435 Gods Who Walk, always come first. Hill rats may be the currency of the place, but they exist to be spent. (On October 10, 1991, House Foreign Affairs Committee aide George Warren was struck by a heart attack and had to wait eighteen minutes for a public ambulance. A block away, the ambulance reserved exclusively for members of Congress sat unused. Warren died.)[1]

The confession in the infamous cat hit also taught one of the Hill's most rigid tenets: never give your conscience an even break, and never, never, *ever* compound a simple mistake with an utterly complete disaster.

We are, after all, professionals.

This is the story of a breed, and these are my people.


Go ahead, ask anyone in town. There is something about this special species of Washington political operative that makes them instantly detectable on the subway, at parties, anywhere. They are smug. They are arrogant. They believe they work on a political Mount Olympus from which they survey the rest of the planet. It shows, and they do not seem to care. The god of this town is power and its currency is power, defined a thousand ways.

Power: the twenty-three-year-old legislative assistant on the down elevator in the Cannon House Office Building at 6:20 P.M., flush with success from jerking around some GS-12 in the Department of Agriculture. "I told that sonofabitch that if he didn't have that letter *on my desk* by ten tomorrow morning, I'd have my boss slap the assistant secretary in Thursday's hearing in front of the press . . . you could hear his asshole pucker all the way over here."

Power: veteran lobbyists called hall sharpies prowl the corridors of the office buildings, darting in and out of the legions of out-of-towners (the dreaded Constituents) with their nametags and slick briefing materials produced by their trade or professional association. In contrast, hall sharpies travel light. Very few briefcases, mostly a few shards of paper folded into a jacket pocket of a dark suit. They smoke a lot, too, and their eyes seem to be permanently narrowed into the flitting, searching look of the professional hunter. They don't amble and they don't second-guess. They know who and what they're looking for and they know where to find them. They're either waiting for someone or they're on their way somewhere—the hushed meeting, the whispers under the stairwell, the furtive trading of confidential paper and gossip—this is the stuff of the House.

Power: the lunchtime talk drifting from the Longworth Building cafeteria, the Being In The Know clatter from the gaggle of staff, members, lobbyists, constituents, and visitors milling around the *Washington Post* vending machines by the front door: ". . . got to make sure the *key* staffers are on board before we go to the committee. . . . And I said, can you believe the balls on that guy? We ought to leak a totally wrong story and fuck him good. . . . Just between you and me, there's no way she can get away with it without . . . And then the computer went down and we lost every targeted letter. . . ."

Power: once you're in, you're in. You're here. You're happening. You're part of the biggest, baddest, greatest show on earth and you damn well know it.

Most true Hill rats work in the members' personal offices, the political equivalent of a big city emergency room on a hot Saturday night. It is showtime the minute the Hill rats walk in the door to plug the wounds and perform meatball surgery on the body politic.

The members? Many Hill rats consider them bothersome necessities that come and go; Hill rats endure and prevail. I once joked in a 1983 staff meeting about a newsletter and said it "usually took me a member or two to get this thing right." Freshman Congressman Ron Coleman was not amused.

The play's the thing on the Hill. And the true Hill rat's credo is: "Ask not what your member can do for the issue, but rather what the issue can do for your member."

The message is clear: get the job done and do whatever you can get away with. If you crash and burn, if the sin is not too egregious, maybe you can turn the situation to your advantage. If not, you might have to resign or go through a ceremonial firing so that the member can go through the obligatory cleansing process in the press and the public consciousness.

Employment is granted and withdrawn with equal suddenness. When Rep. Tony Hall (D-OH) was appointed to succeed the late Rep. Mickey Leland as chairman of the House Select Committee on Hunger, the staff director of the committee found she had been replaced by reading a newspaper article; twenty-four hours after Hall's appointment, Miranda Katsoyannis was gone. *Roll Call*, Capitol Hill's house organ, pointed out that "the abrupt firing of important Hill aides is business as usual in the rough-and-tumble self-styled macho culture of Congress. This sort of commonplace brutality hurts the institution; it encourages cynicism and discourages long-term commitment."[2] Those with their ears to the ground, however, discovered that Katsoyannis had supported a rival member's attempt to be appointed chairman by the Speaker. And so the game goes . . .

Once in, it is not all easy going; pitfalls lurk for the unwary or those blinded by hubris. Elwood Broad, a former Hill rat who worked for U.S. Rep. Gus Yatron (D-PA), sued Yatron in May 1991 for restitution for alleged forcible kickback payments to the congressman. Broad claimed he was required to pay Yatron's wife $700 a month from his congressional salary. Yatron, in turn, called Broad a disgruntled employee who had some questions of his own to answer about missing campaign funds. The Federal Bureau of Investigation has taken up the matter.

Another case had an even stranger twist. In 1984, the *Washington Times* reported that documents seized during the 1983 U.S. invasion of Grenada revealed that Carlottia A. Scott, an aide to Rep. Ron Dellums (D-CA), had developed a personal relationship with Grenada's late Marxist prime minister, Maurice Bishop. Scott, in her letters to Prime Minister Bishop, addressed him as "My Sweet," "My Dearest," and "My Darling Comrade Leader." Following a "fact-finding" trip to Grenada by Rep. Dellums, Scott, and Dellums's administrative assistant Barbara Lee, Ms. Lee hand-carried Dellums' official report on the trip to Grenada to clear it with the prime minister. Scott wrote on House of Representatives letterhead, "I still love you madly."[3]

Hill rats are a special breed, all right.

Where else can $18,000-a-year legislative assistants in their early twenties make life miserable for civil servants at the peak of their careers, some of them confirmed by the United States Senate?

Where else can young press secretaries twist Cabinet secretaries in knots, or gleefully and shamelessly spearhead rumor campaigns against the highest officials in the land?

Where else can a Hill rat like R. Spencer Oliver, chief counsel to the House Foreign Affairs Committee, get profiled in a national newspaper for his skill at political "war-by-investigation" and be criticized in the Republican minority report in the Iran-contra affair for conducting a "wide-ranging fishing expedition into irrelevant political issues"?[4] Oliver probably uses that line to buff his resume.

This is the place. The Twilight Zone. Powertown personified. Derivative power, of course, but the incredible time demands on the members stretch them so thin that each staff member has become the deputy congressman for Press, deputy congressman for Defense and Foreign Policy, and so on. As one of my friends put it, "Lord Acton was only half right. Power might corrupt, but absolute power is a blast."

Jonathan Yates, a former Hill rat writing in *Newsweek* about his experiences, observed, "Just 23 and fresh out of college, I was dealing daily with generals, ambassadors and business executives."[5] This kind of power disturbs some people. In the 1989 *Blanchard v. Bergeron* decision, Supreme Court Justice Antonin Scalia wrote in a concurrence, "What a heady feeling it must be for a young staffer to know that his or her citation can transform into the law of the land, thereafter dutifully to be observed by the Supreme Court." Scalia took a narrow view of so-called legislative intent, by which the judiciary attempts to divine the meaning of many of the laws passed by Congress, and criticized current practice: "As anyone familiar with modern-day drafting of congressional committee reports is well aware, [the references] were inserted, at best by a committee staff member on his or her own initiative, and at worse by a committee staff member at the suggestion of a lawyer-lobbyist, and the purpose of those references was not primarily to inform the members of Congress what the bill meant . . . but rather to influence judicial construction."[6] Scalia went on to state that the judiciary should only consider language in the actual law, language that was voted on and passed, and not the parenthetical comments in committee reports that were not voted on by the whole Congress.

I called a friend of mine, a former Hill rat and now one of those lawyer-lobbyists excoriated by Justice Scalia. He scoffed. "Great. I'm all for doing it by the statute. Who do you think writes those bills anyway? We write the bills, not the members. Screw 'em. That's what I'm doing right now, trying to get something into the Science and Tech report. You wait and see. What would Washington do without lawyer-lobbyists?"

"It would work," I suggested with a laugh. He chuckled in return and said, "We'll talk about it over lunch."

Hill rats are also important because of a procedure called a "staff mark," another one of Congress's secrets. Before a major piece of legislation is "marked up," or changed and then voted on in committee, Hill rats who work for the committee members commonly divide up the spoils. Each Hill rat is trained, of course, to represent the member's best political interests. And since the staff knows what the member needs—probably better than the member himself—it saves the elected official from any unduly burdensome thinking.

Several years ago, when the nation's patent and copyright laws were being overhauled, the House received from the Senate a huge comprehensive bill that had taken three years of painstaking legislative craftsmanship to complete. But the Senate had not bothered to consult the House while writing the bill, and the bill was sent over with only five weeks left in the session in the expectation that the House would comply meekly with the Senate's wishes.

The size, complexity, and late arrival of the bill meant that it was headed for a staff mark. The legislative assistants assembled at the office of the committee staff director, who asked, "Okay, who really wants to do this shit?"

Everyone groaned. The various staffers were up to their ears in their bosses' end-of-the-session political fights. No one wanted to spend an inordinate amount of time, probably weekends and nights, learning the arcana of copyright and patent law, no matter how much money was at stake.

"Well, how much do we really have to do?" one staffer finally asked.

The staff director replied that a bare-bones version would only involve two or three items, and he could take care of it in a day or so.

Heads began to nod. U.S. copyright and patent law had fallen into the hands of overworked Hill rats, and the deal was done.

Much of Capitol Hill in the summer of 1989 was consumed, among other things, with something known as Section 89. Added onto the 1986 Tax Reform Act, it forced businesses to prove they did not discriminate between management and labor in providing benefits. Businesses complained about the huge amounts of paperwork and costs this requirement entailed. After some investigation, it turned out that Section 89 had been inserted into the bill solely by a few staffers of the House Ways and Means Committee without the knowledge of the members (or so they said).

In a statement titled "Section 89: What Staff Hath Created, Congress Should Take Away," Rep. Chuck Douglas (R-NH) deplored what these Hill rats had done. Douglas quoted a legal analysis that said, "It is undisputed that two staffers, Harry Conaway and Kent Mason, created Section 89 between them. No bill was ever filed in Congress. . . . [R]ather, it was inserted by Messrs. Mason and Conaway at some point during the closed sessions of the tax-writing committee. . . . They are virtually invisible . . . [and] they are unassailable—being unelected and beyond recall even if identified by a victimized citizenry. They are all-powerful—deferred to as 'experts' by Congress, they are licensed to act in its name as the law of the land.[7]

Others agree with Rep. Douglas. "Congressional staff are our invisible governors," wrote the president of the Cleveland Council on World Affairs in the *Christian Science Monitor*. "The congressman becomes dependent. . . . [V]irtually no constituent knows who his representative has running committees."[8] Congressional staff has indeed grown with the increased power of Congress itself. There were 992 congressional staffers in 1934; by 1989, that number had grown to 9,683, and the total number of congressional employees was more than fifteen thousand.

Former Hill rats Mason and Conaway, no fools, are now high-priced fixers with Washington law firms.

As Rep. Douglas lamented, the town pays homage to the power of Hill rats. People fork over fees upwards of hundreds of dollars to attend seminars that teach how to deal with us. "What do Members expect of these staffers that you should know about that help the staffer, and in turn yourself, to succeed?" an advertisement for one such seminar read. "Where do you fit into competition for Members' attention? The KEY: Learning the right touch. . . . And doing it quickly without wasting their time."[9] Remember: Hill rats are the currency of power. One of the bitterest complaints of House Republicans against the Democratic leadership, in fact, is that they do not receive a fair allocation of staffers on the various committees. In March 1990, the problem became so acute that Republicans threatened to vote against administrative funds for all committees if more Republican Hill rats would not work for them. As one of the many Congressional Research Service analyses of this issue pointed out, "Although the number of employees allocated to each committee has grown . . . the allocation of staff [to Republicans] has not necessarily kept pace."[10]

Perquisites follow closely behind power. Pay for Hill rats increases each time the members vote themselves a raise (and they never vote pay cuts). In 1991, the House voted 275 to 139 to delete a proposed $50,000 increase in congressional staff pay, but the House Administration Committee issued a letter stating that, the vote notwithstanding, it would fund the raise. As of July 1991, at least 130 House staffers were making from $100,000 to a maximum of $115,092 in salary.

Power offers the perquisite of genuflection, which in one form or another is pervasive. Theodore Mathison, administrator of the Baltimore/Washington International Airport, sent a letter on February 24, 1987, to every congressional office offering free valet parking to members and Hill rats: "We guarantee the availability of spaces for you . . . [and] we will make every effort to have your car started and warmed up by the time you arive to pick it up."[11] Washington associations also treat them well; every year the American League of Anglers and Boaters holds a champagne breakfast exclusively for Hill rats, and the Eastern Professional River Outfitters invites selected staffers to spend a day white-water rafting in West Virginia to "talk issues."

The Hill rat also enjoys countless lavish receptions. If you could freeze-frame your standard Capitol Hill reception, you would have a poster of a pond, complete with scum at the top. Let's say the event is sponsored by the National Association of Manufactured Widgets. Young people crowd the room, which means someone in Restaurant Supply passed the word that the NAMW bought the "A" menu. Forget cheese and crackers. We're talking two open bars, a live jazz band, and a long table in the middle of the room piled high with fruit, vegetables, and fine food. Across from the band sits another long table covered with ice on which are stacked fresh stone crab claws, shrimp, raw shucked oysters, and clams.

The NAMW's Washington representatives are slick. Whenever a member enters the room, the band pauses while he or she is escorted by the NAMW's president to a stirring round of applause. All eyes in the room rivet on the demigod who deigns to step down from Olympus to shake hands with mortals from Memphis and Tacoma and Dubuque. The rich food, of course, is only a loss leader. Buying, selling, trading, copying, and borrowing influence—all these are the universal spice at the banquet of politics.

The emphasis, moreover, placed on staff by the reception circuit and favor-seeking lobbyist is not misplaced. I once had breakfast with some Appropriations buddies, and the morning's topic was the book *Liar's Poker*. "The name comes from an incident in which a Wall Street bigwig bets one million dollars on a single hand of liar's poker," I explained.

One staffer hunched over his sausage and eggs and peered at me. "A mil? One lousy mil?" He grinned. "I can do *ten* mil with report language and not even have to ask the chairman." That may or may not have been true, but his disdain was palpable.

"But you don't get to keep it," I protested.

"Keep what?" he countered. "The money? Who cares about keeping the money? I'd rather be the one with the stones to power it through. They can keep their lousy one mil. It's a lot more fun to shove a *hundred* mil up someone's ass and then knock off for the rest of the day for a cold one."

Even the Internal Revenue Service pays tribute to the power of the Hill Rat. Every tax season, it opens an office in the Cannon House Office Building to personally assist members and staff to prepare their income taxes. It can get complicated; one newspaper survey in 1989 found that at least eighty-five members, including Democratic Majority Leader Richard Gephardt and Republican Minority Whip Newt Gingrich, dramatically raised the pay of their key Hill rats just before or just after they had gone on leave to work on the members' reelection campaigns.[12]

Foreign governments get in the act, too. Philip Mosely, the Republican staff director of the House Ways and Means Committee, accepted trips from both the Taiwanese and the People's Republic of China in 1988. His wife Norah was, and is, his $41,624-a-year assistant. Expecting sympathy instead of raised eyebrows, Mosely described his overseas schedule to the *Austin American-Statesman* as "brutal."[13]

Like their members, many Hill rats actively sought out speaking fees, or honoraria. In April 1989, Richard Sullivan, chief counsel of the House Public Works Committee, was paid $2,000 by a toxic waste disposal company to visit a plant. In 1989, Kevin Gottlieb, staff director of the Senate Banking Committee, made approximately thirty speeches at $600 apiece for an organization called Washington Campus. Gottlieb, in fact, earned more money in speaking fees in 1989 than U.S. senators were allowed to make. "I'm not shortchanging the committee," he told the *Washington Post*. "I'm good at what I do."[14]

They are all good at what they do. Check out Capitol Hill at a quarter to nine on any given morning. The dark blue K cars are already appearing, each one chock-full of supplicants from the executive branch. Corporate lobbyists are popping out of their limos and taxicabs, $400 briefcases in hand. Concerned and earnest citizens wander about aimlessly as the subway disgorges its human cargo in waves.

In the midst of this great flotsam of democracy, the Hill rats truck in. They come in all shapes, sizes, races, sexes, and income brackets. But they have one thing in common. They all sport that "Christ-please-no-constituents-today" sneer, and they have that knowing walk, that here-I-come, ready-or-not, three-piece-suited swagger that says here be Hill rats, and they be bad.

But sometimes their Hill rat persona drops, and I see haunted, driven eyes as they scurry through the halls. We are the apprentice shamans of America's civic religion, hurling lightning bolts of fear and authority that bear the names of Founding Fathers, constitutional doctrines, and national saints. We legitimize the fundamentally irrational behavior of politicians by manipulating hallowed symbols and stories. So I wonder: Do they think inside? Are they like me? Do they think about these things as I do?

We pass looking, never seeing. I never ask, either, because Hill rats do not exist in a vacuum. Our behavior and attitudes take place within Capitol Hill's political culture in which, despite protestations, all of this is considered perfectly normal.

## CHAPTER TWO

# TASTE OF THE TOWN

I HAD this haunting dream.

Suddenly I am all the people who exist on America's margin—forty-year-old parking lot attendants, the elderly couple down the block who sweep lint out of apartment laundry rooms, people who write their congressmen about lost government checks without which they cannot eat. It is very cold and I have a baby in my arms. I have no blankets. Desperately, I tear through the closets, but they are empty. The baby shivers. Its cries weaken. I am helpless, overwhelmed by frustration, clawing against unseen enemies and cursing a God who could let this happen . . .

I know from where the dream comes but I do not know why I only seem to remember it when I go down the Hill to the Democratic Club to find out what has happened to our heroes after the battles of the day.

The Democratic Club is three-and-a-half blocks away from the Capitol, adjacent to the Democratic National Committee complex and across the street from the power plant that provides electricity exclusively to Congress. There is steady foot-traffic up and down the Hill's slope between the club, congressional office buildings, and the Capitol itself.

The Democratic Club is private. But it opens its door to the greater Democratic community—members of Congress, Hill rats, lobbyists, political consultants, campaign officials, and similar species. Journalists are prohibited from joining or entering. No photographs can be taken, ever.

It is a place where the bar talk—if remembered or recorded—could be called the exercise of power by history. You can drop in for a hamburger and see people the public believes are leaders, or get from the lobbyists what Ernest Hemingway called the "true gen"—the inside skinny, the real score—on everything from the prospects of legislation to the latest rumors of leadership maneuverings. Later in the day, you can rub shoulders (from a respectful distance) with the floor managers of the day's legislation. If you strain to listen, you can hear their frontline reports of the debate and the voting: who stood with them, who betrayed the cause, who knuckled under to whom and for how much, how the powerful performed. Names like Gephardt and Panetta, Fazio and Murtha, Bonior, Obey, Wilson, and other temporary deities dominate the conversation. On one typical day, former Speaker of the House Thomas P. "Tip" O'Neill held court at the table in front of the wine rack. To his right, a man complained to a woman about "the goddam commies giving up and sending all the defense contracts to hell." Two tables away, a black-suited short man stuck a large, equally black cigar between his teeth and smiled.

At the Club you sense that for all their sophistication, these hardened political operatives have a superstitious fear that something beyond the walls and out of their control might be "playing in Peoria"—that an issue or idea might be making an impact Out There. I have seen grown men—tough, no-nonsense fixers who deal regularly with the highest officials in the nation—become despondent over newspaper headlines or reports from congressional sources about a flood of "real mail" on some issue. In Washington parlance, "real mail" comes from "real" people, those without a Washington-based political stake in the issue. Outside the Beltway, it is called public opinion.

You can tell the Democratic Club is an insider's place as soon as you walk in past the coat-check and manager's office: soft lighting, the coarse laughter of cronies, ironed dinner napkins and good silverware, darting eyes scanning the entranceway from every angle. Experienced Washington hands can eat an entire meal without looking each other in the eye, one person covering the front entrance and the other the dining area as they hold lengthy conversations, speaking past each other yet remembering it all. The seating is arranged expressly for this purpose. Photographs of all current Democratic committee chairmen are on the walls. Across from the entrance to the dining room and in front of the elevator are signs telling political action committee representatives and lobbyists which members are holding fundraising receptions in which rooms. The signs are changed daily.

The usual crowd of lobbyists will be at the bar, hidden from immediate view while they watch the House floor proceedings on C-SPAN, news on CNN, or a ball game. If the House is in session, members will take up positions at the bar or at tables in the dining room. Outside, their cars and drivers wait to take them to the floor if a vote is called. For those who cannot see the television behind the bar, a voice breaks onto the intercom, "Two bells recorded votes, two bells recorded vote, members have fifteen minutes to vote on . . ." The regulars' table, full at lunchtime, thins out later; stragglers head for the bar around 2:00 P.M. to play liar's poker. Years ago, at this bar, I learned from an accomplished lobbyist the Hill's ancient admonition: "Money talks and bullshit walks."

Three-and-a-half blocks away, House Speaker Thomas Foley presides, a modern monarch unruffled by the intrigue of the restless lords below. More than geography separates us. The Speaker is praised, and rightly so, for restoring stability and ethics to an office badly tarnished by the Jim Wright scandal. But no one asks the Speaker what he had to do to earn $555,140 in political action committee contributions for election year 1988 alone.[1] When Speaker Foley responded to President Bush's 1990 State of the Union message by proclaiming, "Let's be blunt about it: don't we all know there's too much money being raised and spent in American politics?" no eyebrows were raised.[2] This is a town, after all, where you still have to hit all the right notes even when they give you an easy melody to sing for your supper.

But the Speaker has to understand, as I do, that at the end of any journey into the heart of politics lurks a Captain Kurtz—the emotive, irrational beast one rides at one's peril, but also, for those of us who have chosen the political path, general and foot soldier alike, because one must. This is one of the Hill's secrets: that all the fine latticework of policy elevated to the public spotlight is somehow hostage to one of the dark, eyeless, pulsating beasts of politics in the shadows below. Policy is interest, interest is politics, and politics is appetite in its rawest form imaginable.

I have always been struck by political scientists who search for statistical clues in voting patterns and computer-generated correlations of interest group support. They yearn to dehumanize politics, to pretend it is bloodless and has nothing to do with deals and anguish. But the political world in which I lived was a world of shadows and uncertainty, a place where right and wrong became genuinely as well as deliberately confused; it was a constant walk along a precipice where you were buffeted by fate as well as favor.

One day at the Democratic Club I recognized someone who had stood in front of me in the Cannon Building cafeteria carryout line that morning. He was talking to a fellow Hill rat. Their conversation went like this:

"Hey, how you doing?"

"Fine, just fine."

"You still doing some Liberia?"

"Yeah. See the paper this morning?"

"Not yet."

"Government forces attacked the United Nations compound and kidnapped thirty people."

"Hmmm. Still doing Angola?"

"Yeah, Angola, Zaire, Liberia."

"My neighbor works for [U.S. Rep.] Jim Cooper. He's off on that Angola trip, Savimbi, UNITA, you know?"

"Sure. How good is that ham and egg?"

The speakers had learned their Hill lessons well: you have to keep score. You win some, you lose some. Revolutions, revolts, bloody civil wars carried out by Cold War surrogates—all are added up at the end of the day like so much ham and egg. Victories— amendments to American policy, successful speeches in debate— are advertised, and losses are forgotten.

The author Ward Just once remarked to an interviewer that Washington is a town where "everybody had everybody's hand on everybody else's leg. . . ."[3] In the summer of 1990, Speaker Foley's private words on the savings and loan crisis indicated it was often a two-fisted grip. The Democratic "Whip," or leadership, organization met regularly on Thursday afternoons to go over the upcoming week's legislative schedule and to thrash out any political problems.

On Thursday, June 14, 1990, the Democrats had a big one.

The party had enjoyed headlines the week before. The top stories told how leading Democrats, such as Senator Bill Bradley and New York Governor Mario Cuomo, were winning political points by labeling the savings and loan crisis the fault of the Republicans. That Thursday, after discussing an appropriations bill and the politics of the constitutional amendment on flag burning, the talk at the Whip meeting turned to the savings and loan crisis.

But despite the success of Bradley and Cuomo, concern was voiced that the "S&L crisis is going to engulf the Congress." The Speaker warned, "There will be an attempt to personalize and make this an anti-Democratic issue in the fall election."

Rep. Byron Dorgan, a tough populist from North Dakota, argued that the party was allowing a Republican failure to become a Democratic liability. Other members made the point that the Democrats should "nail the Republicans and bring Neil Bush back to the witness panel." Tempers were rising as Speaker Foley entered the fray.

But instead of agreeing to help the party score partisan points against the Republicans—or even to search out the truth—Speaker Foley darkly reminded the activists that "any congressional investigation will allow the Republicans to call witnesses." He pointed out that the Justice Department indictment the previous day of Texas S&L operator Donald R. Dixon of Vernon Savings and Loan included illegal congressional campaign contributions. Foley also knew that the indictment named Rep. Jim Chapman (D-TX), an Appropriations Committee member and leadership supporter, as a recipient of those contributions. Dixon had also been on intimate terms with former Majority Whip Tony Coelho, evoking pictures of Coelho's money machine at the Democratic Congressional Campaign Committee; it would be dangerous to encourage any digging into that particular black hole.

"We will not be able to avoid being called into this imbroglio," Foley warned. "The record will include both sides of the political aisle. Those calling for a special investigation like Iran-contra should remember that Iran-contra was only a question of the actions of a Republican president and his staff."

In case anyone missed the point, Foley stated directly, "The S&L crisis affects both parties."

Any chance of a blue-ribbon congressional investigation into the S&L crisis had been killed. Already, Donald Dixon alone had been found responsible for losses of $1.3 billion, the tip of the iceberg in a disaster estimated by the party's own Democratic Congressional Campaign Committee (DCCC) to cost from $300 to $500 billion. Even the administration, which tended to downplay the numbers, estimated in June 1990 that the cost would go beyond $132 billion.[4] Foley's argument that the political price was too high nevertheless won; there were too many dirty fingers, too many marked decks, too many ugly things were waiting to scurry out from under too many rocks. Foley had said, in effect, the price is us.[5]

Without missing a beat, the Democratic National Committee issued a statement from Chairman Ron Brown on June 19: "Democrats Call for More Investigators—Demand Prosecution of S&L Crooks."[6] The DCCC continued Foley's hand-on-the-leg approach three days later in a June 22, 1990, document titled "The Politics of the S&L Crisis." "Perception may become as important as reality," the committee argued in several opening paragraphs excoriating Republicans for causing the crisis and brushing aside Foley's private but candid admission of Democratic complicity.

Then the campaign committee got down to the real business of perception: a checklist to shield Democratic incumbents from the S&L issue. It identified *twenty-three* possible areas in which Democratic members of Congress might have implicated themselves in the scandal. They ranged from accepting political action committee (PAC) contributions from S&Ls to personal payments for speeches, personal investments and financial holdings, floor votes, meetings with lobbyists, public statements, and criminal or fraudulent activities. *"We strongly urge you to work closely with your most trusted campaign staffers to undertake a comprehensive review of your potential exposure on the thrift issue* [emphasis in original]," the document continued.[7]

The political culture never blinked. Our response was muted, but grateful. Oh. Thanks. What's next? Congressmen exist in a moral free-fire zone, devoid of commonly accepted definitions of right and wrong. They manage issues. They do not stand for principles, and they will certainly not lose their seats over them.

Speaker Foley's tacit implication was that the S&L loan crisis affected both political parties because of money, or more precisely, the thirst for it and what it took to get it. "These guys raise money with the desperation of a hooker trying to make cab fare home at dawn," a friend once observed. As a lobbyist, she spoke with admiration.

The Founding Fathers assumed a certain amount of self-interest when they constructed the legislative system. But in the House today, self-interest *is* the system. "The candidate who proclaims himself the 'issues' candidate is usually losing the fundraising race," a political consultant commented. He was correct. Constitutional checks and balances no longer have meaning; the only checks that count are the ones you can cash.

Modern campaigning is hideously destructive and unbelievably expensive. The negative advertising that dominates the electoral landscape is conducted by an army of slick-faced consultants whose loyalties go as far as their clients' bank accounts. Private detectives report a booming business during campaign season.[8]

Campaign culture has become a separate and distinct entity. A campaign trade magazine points out that "Technology, money and timing have coincided to create a $6 billion-per-cycle marketplace for politics." Like Capitol Hill, this political culture believes in its elevated status. An advertisement for a company called Nordlinger and Associates claims that it—not the candidates—has been "undefeated in federal general elections since 1978." The membership of the American Association of Political Consultants has risen from fifty in 1980 to seven hundred in 1990.

Incumbent reelection rates of 98 percent in 1988 and 96 percent in 1990 suggest that the high-tech continual campaign is efficient, but the price may be very high: Political clout is now defined as cold, hard cash. After Democratic Chief Deputy Whip David Bonior (D-MI) won reelection with only 54 percent in 1988, he did not search for new and better ideas, but for more and more money. The man who as head of the Whip Task Force on Nicaragua had stymied President Reagan's contra policy in the 1980s through sheer intellectual tenacity turned his talents to another object: raising money. By March 1990, he had amassed $505,000, 65 percent of which came from political action committees.[9]

Lately, members have begun to pursue political action committees for purposes other than reelection. The cash culture has become such that money is now the key to advancement within the institution, and money talks loudest in the vitally important contests for leadership positions.

Florida Democrat Larry Smith hustled political action committees as part of his ultimately unsuccessful strategy to head the Democratic Congressional Campaign Committee in 1990. In a letter to PACs, Smith wrote, "An incredibly helpful way that I can establish my bona fides even more . . . would be to get you to purchase a block of tickets to this year's DCCC Summer Dinner—and have your contribution credited to me."[10]

So-called "leadership PACs" have become decisive factors in races, and members can contribute up to $10,000 per election cycle to other members. As of January 1, 1990, Majority Leader Richard Gephardt had handed out $240,708 to fellow Democrats; Ways and

Means Committee Chairman Dan Rostenkowski had disbursed $154,921; and Speaker Thomas Foley, $73,832.[11] Most of these funds originated from special PACs representing business and labor, thus doubling their influence. House leaders now owe not only their existence to PACs, but their leadership positions that allow them to be called statesmen as well.

According to Common Cause, thirty-two "leadership PACs" raised at least $25,000 each from January 1987 to December 1989.[12] The uses of the money became more sophisticated as the members themselves became the middlemen; they not only accepted money from PACs, they became them. In many cases, contributions from these personal PACs were made to state and local candidates to increase the member's political base at home. Appropriations Subcommittee on Defense Chairman John Murtha (D-PA), for example, distributed $16,475 to nonprofit groups in his district in 1989 and another $13,000 to local Democrats.

It is little wonder, then, that the principal obstacle to campaign finance reform has been the House Democratic leadership itself. As Speaker Foley confided on the S&L scandal, the price of reform is all too often us.

The impact on government of the great gush of cash was deleterious, but it was not a one-way street. In 1988, certain Democrats on the House Energy and Commerce Committee advocated product liability legislation solely to attract campaign contributions from concerned lobbyists and industries. The game has gone international, too. The Congressional Research Service identified 102 foreign-owned corporate PACs that contributed $2,362,338 to congressional candidates in the 1985–1986 election cycle alone.[13] As Democratic leadership member and unofficial "Mayor of Capitol Hill" Vic Fazio (D-CA) told the *National Journal*, cash is the "basic conflict we live with around here." Fazio, like his Democratic and Republican colleagues, simply assumed that accepting money for services rendered was not inherently wrong, that instead it was a legitimate subject for discussion and accommodation.

Contrary to popular opinion, the actual transmission of funds from the pocket of the PAC to the hand of the politician is, like the end of a played-out love affair, drearily ordinary. There is no smacking of the lips, no leering look at the tinkle of silver.

In the summer of 1990, I walked to lunch with a friend who was a legislative assistant to a Democratic House member.

"I have to meet Dick Cook from GTE on the corner of New Jersey and C Street," he told me as we left the Cannon House Office Building.

"What for?" I asked.

"He called to see if there was anyone around who could receive a check from his PAC. He said he had hurt his leg so I said I'd meet him on the corner."

We stood at New Jersey and C Street for a few minutes, right across the street from the United States Capitol, whose dome rose above the trees in the foreground. The lobbyist showed up right on time and pulled his car over to the curb. He rolled down his window, reached into his jacket pocket, and pulled out an envelope containing the PAC check. My friend took it.

"In the shadow of the Dome," I cracked to my friend. "Isn't America great?"

There was nothing sinister about this rendezvous. In this busy business, that day the lobbyist had too many checks and not enough time. One lobbyist profiled in the *Washington Post* attended forty-six fundraising receptions in a single week to distribute some of his $768,820 annual giveaway.[14]

The numbers reveal another Washington truth: professional money does not support the power of ideas; it supports the idea of power. According to Common Cause, in 1988 PACs gave $82 million to incumbents and only $9 million to challengers. That same year, as the *Wall Street Journal* pointed out in 1990, incumbents had $63 million left after the elections—money they could not even spend.[15] All told, challengers had raised only half that amount. In the election process, self-preservation has superseded all other goals. Members are no longer on the Hill to make the laws. They are here to stay—literally.

The case of Rep. David Obey (D-WI), one of the brightest and meanest members of the House, reveals how official resources can be taken advantage of by even the most outspoken reformers.

Adversaries mistake Obey's constant blinking as a sign of slowness or inattention as he sits in the chairman's seat of the House Appropriations Subcommittee on Foreign Operations, thick glasses perched on a hawk nose—until he launches a petty personal attack on a witness. Obey, who writes the multibillion dollar foreign aid bill, dismisses the Foreign Affairs Committee as a debating society because it cannot back its policies with money. A relatively young fifty-three, he will probably become chairman of the House of Lords, as the Appropriations Committee is known. It is no exaggeration to say that Obey holds the future of nations in his hands; nations such as Israel rely on him and the money he controls for their very existence.

Obey, who is fond of denouncing demagogery in the press, was one of the most outspoken advocates of the 1989 congressional pay raise. When questioned about his view, he would actually bridle. Obey's attitude was all the more unusual because he had made his mark early in his career as a reformer by writing the landmark 1977 House ethics regulations that limited income and gifts members could accept from persons with an interest in legislation. But by the late 1980s, with an added ten years' seniority and more than $1 million in PAC money, Obey's idealism had faded. Seven years after authoring comprehensive ethics reform, Obey formed his own personal political action committee. He has since voted for free parking, a government-issued Diners Club card, and a free gymnasium, to name just a few of the House's vast perquisites; and he has helped exempt the House from the Equal Pay Act, the Age Discrimination in Employment Act, the Occupational Safety and Health Act, and the National Labor Relations Act, among others.

Obey apparently sees no contradiction between these votes and his liberalism. After all, the American Civil Liberties Union and Americans for Democratic Action rated him 91 and 90 out of 100, respectively. Defense of congressional privilege, in his view, should have no bearing on the public's judgment of members. It is a sign of today's Congress that a man like Obey can accept $308,399 from

PACs for his 1988 campaign[16] and in the same breath ask, as he did, in a recent speech, "Is American politics so brain-dead that we are reduced to having political shysters manipulate symbols?"

No eyebrows were raised when the Democratic Congressional Campaign Committee blamed the Republicans for the S&L scandal one week after Speaker Foley had admitted privately that his party was knuckles-deep in the scandal. So too, none was raised when David Obey made his statement. Washington worships at the altar of power, not consistency. We learn not to expect answers in a town of no questions.

The advantages of today's House incumbents are so great that many political scientists refuse to analyze their campaigns. Writing in *Congress and the Presidency*, Susan Welch noted that races with incumbents were not part of her research because "it is only through open seats that major changes in the composition of Congress will occur."[17]

But the political culture cannot bring itself to acknowledge this situation. Minutes into his first speech as Speaker-elect on June 6, 1989, with the political corpse of Jim Wright still quivering in the well of the House, Thomas Foley launched into a defense of the old congressional order, claiming that the House "is not, as many have suggested, a fixed, unchangeable body. . . . in the years since 1980, fully 55 percent of the House has changed its membership."[18] But turnover is not the same as competitiveness. According to the Congressional Research Service (CRS), incumbents seeking reelection in the two campaigns previous to Foley's assertion were successful 98 percent of the time and over 90 percent for the rest of the 1980s, a higher winning percentage —95.45 percent— of incumbents than any other decade in the House of Representatives since the founding of the republic. CRS also found that turnover almost never resulted from defeat, but from retirement, death, seeking other offices, or criminal conviction. In 1790, only slightly more than half of all House members sought reelection; in 1988, 94 percent did so.[19]

These reelection rates do not occur by accident, and in large part they are charged to the public purse. In the first three months of 1990, House incumbents mailed over 130 million letters, postcards, calendars, and newsletters. Members received $178,775 per year for office rent (it is adjusted regularly), but House "rules" allow them to divert much of this money into mail, salaries, and other perquisites. U.S. Rep. Gerry Sikorski (DFL-MN), nationally known for requiring staff members to assist his wife in taking her dogs to be artificially inseminated, shifted $43,339 to buy mailing lists, newsletters, and postcards. Rep. David Dreier (R-CA) bought laser printers and computers with his rent money. Most congressional offices, in fact, maintain detailed computer profiles of every voter in their district. Names are cross-analyzed against a voter registration tape for age, sex, and party affiliation; against a drivers license tape for ethnic background; and finally against church, business, and civic lists of all kinds to identify religious beliefs, occupations, and political opinions. These profiles are so complete that in some cases they resemble top-notch counterintelligence files.

From the members' of Congress perspective, the data are put to good use. In fiscal year 1987, they sent out 595 million unsolicited letters, newsletters, and postcards as part of this shotgun marriage between the taxpayers' money and campaign-style tactics. Caucasian women over the age of sixty, for example, selected out of the data banks by the computers, might receive personal letters three times a year portraying their congressman or woman on the correct side of issues that concern elderly white women in certain income brackets and neighborhoods. The process is repeated for every possible demographic combination. It is the federal government's largest propaganda campaign, and it costs taxpayers hundreds of millions of dollars in staff, computers, printers, paper, and other official resources. As Rep. John R. Rowland (R-GA) said in a rare moment of candor, "Let's face it. You have to be a bozo to lose this job."[20]

Few do, and the 96–98 percent who win acquire what many observers term an arrogance of power.

In October 1989, millions of needy Americans suffered cuts in their federal benefits by the Gramm-Rudman deficit reduction process, triggered by Congress's inability to reduce the federal deficit below $110 billion by the October 15, 1989, deadline. Members of Congress could afford to procrastinate. Earlier in the year, they had voted to exempt congressional pay from the automatic cuts under Gramm-Rudman. On November 16, 1989, they voted themselves a pay raise of 33 percent. Five days later, they agreed to let the rest of the country suffer from automatic cuts until February 1, 1990.

Capitol Hill underscores Lord Acton's observation that there is no worse heresy than that the office sanctify its beholder. The kind of news that really stirs the political culture was the announcement in March 1990 that Sergeant-At-Arms Jack Russ would change the special parking privileges of members at the Washington, D.C., National Airport. Russ told members that the excuse of "official business" would no longer allow them to tear up parking tickets in no-parking zones or in the airport's main traffic circle. Even worse, since the metal license plate tags issued to every member were being lent to staffers and lobbyists, Russ said he would substitute plastic stickers that were nontransferable. My own boss, Congressman Ron Coleman, routinely lent his congressional license plate to his father-in-law to use at the airport. The new policy lasted only days; in the ensuing uproar, the nontransferable stickers were revoked.[21]

By the same token, news broke later that summer that Hill rats— not members, but their staffers—were *cutting back* on accepting personal payment for speeches and appearances. The issue was not whether they should be indulging in the practice in the first place. William Pitts, floor assistant to Republican Minority Leader Robert Michel, reported taking $17,500 in such payments in 1988, but none in 1989. Pitts was also involved in one of the more celebrated cases of staff following their boss's footsteps and cashing in on their access and influence. Press reports revealed that he and John Mack, his Democratic counterpart, had earned $28,000 from lobbyists in forty-eight hours. Among other transactions, they received $2,000 upon being picked up at an airport, $2,000 on arriving at the corporation's office, $2,000 for speaking with company officials, and $2,000 for being guests of honor at a dinner.

Our crowd's reaction was not outrage, but grins and exclamations ("Damn!"), as if someone at the gym had just performed a 360-degree double-pump slam dunk. In contrast, this personal enrichment is accompanied by disinterest and irresponsibility concerning policy and individual actions. A housing project in Chicago pushed by Ways and Means Committee Chairman Dan Rostenkowski (D-IL) defaulted on a $170.8 million Federal Housing Administration loan. The project had been exempted from low-income set-asides and received a lucrative break on its federal mortgage. As it turned out, at one time one of the developers had managed Rostenkowski's blind trust, which received $50,000 from a no-risk investment arranged by the developer.[22] Rostenkowski denied any connection or conflict of interest—as he did when news surfaced that he had spent 30 percent of his time in the winter of 1981–82 as the beneficiary of corporations, trade associations, and wealthy individuals at resorts in Florida, California, and Hawaii while receiving gifts of golf clothes, luggage, and other valuables.[23]

In a similar incident, Rep. Robert McEwen (R-OH) took to the floor of the House in early 1990 to declare that "home rule in the District of Columbia is a disaster" because traffic on Interstate 395 had made him late for work. "The total incompetence of the D.C. government in Washington, D.C.," he said angrily, "has become an embarrassment to our entire nation. . . ."[24]

This overweening self-importance imbues members with a certain shamelessness about the whole endeavor.

On September 2, 1989, former Congressman Billy Lee Evans sent a letter to my boss, Congressman Ronald Coleman. Billy Lee had shut down his own lobbying firm, where he represented tobacco companies and the Great Western Financial Corporation, and landed a job with Fleishman-Hilliard, a public affairs and lobbying firm in Washington. Former members routinely become lobbyists—the *National Journal* identified seventy-four in 1989[25]—and Billy Lee was anxious to let us know about his personal contribution. "I have enjoyed our past association," he wrote, "and hope to continue our productive working relationship on matters of mutual interest." He then offered to assist with Rep. Coleman's campaign and enclosed a news release about his new job.[26]

Billy Lee's letter was especially brazen because he had lost his seat in 1982 in an election in which the main issue had been his fine for accepting illegal campaign contributions and various loans in his

1980 campaign. But as a former member, Billy Lee had access to the cloakrooms and the House floor where, under current rules, he could lobby his former colleagues on behalf of any special interest willing to pay his fee.

It's there for the taking . . . the House Supply store bought its flag cases exclusively from a company owned by the Sergeant-At-Arms, the third-ranking officer of the House[27] . . .

Democrat and Republican leaders kept secret the details of the 33 percent pay raise in 1989 until twenty-four hours before the vote, then agreed not to make the pay raise a campaign issue . . . concurrently, $124,984 in members' personal accounts at the House Dining Room were more than 120 days overdue[28] (and this was two years before the dining tab scandal of 1991) . . . 581 checks were bounced by 134 members for over $1,000 or more, according to the General Accounting Office . . . Rep. Arlen Stangeland claims all 341 calls he made to and from the home of Eve Jarvis, a female lobbyist and "friend," and charged to his House credit card, are for business . . .


I once gave a tour of the Capitol to a visiting Russian who was struck by the differences between our two systems. He pointed to members. "Do they have a car and driver?" he asked.

"No," I said. "Only the leadership."

"Dacha?"

"No."

"House?"

"No."

"The Congress gives them none of these things?"

"No," I replied. "They have to steal them fair and square."


The concept of the federal government as a contest to see who can remain the longest at the public trough is so ingrained that it has become institutionalized in the literature of the political culture; the Congressional Research Service churns out handbooks such as the one titled "Grants Work in a Congressional Office." The report "discusses the grants process and varying approaches and techniques congressional offices have developed in dealing with grants. . . ."[29] There are no comparable publications by the Congressional Research Service on how to advance one's *ideas*.

Money is pursued for personal gain as well as for political impact. In one case, former Rep. Dan Mica (D-FL) was allowed to stay on the House Foreign Affairs Committee payroll while working as a lobbyist for a law firm representing foreign clients in order to attain twenty years of government service and collect pension checks at age fifty instead of sixty.[30] This is not scandal in the political culture, but gratitude.

The relentlessness with which money is chased is shown by the check-accepting schedule of Rep. Willis Gradison (R-OH) in early 1988:

| | | |
|---|---|---|
| 2/3 | $1000 | American Venture Capital Association |
| 2/10 | 500 | CASE |
| 2/11 | 2000 | American Physical Therapy Association |
| 2/15 | 500 | Center to Promote Health Care Studies |
| 2/23 | 500 | Washington Campus |
| 2/24 | 300 | Brookings Institution |
| 3/2 | 500 | Washington Campus |
| 3/4 | 2000 | American Psychological Association |
| 3/7 | 500 | Washington Campus |
| 3/11 | 2000 | American Association of PPOs |
| 3/17 | 2000 | Paine-Webber |
| 3/21 | 2000 | National Health Lawyers |
| 3/21 | 1000 | Touche Ross |
| 3/23 | 2000 | American Hospital Association |
| 3/28 | 2000 | SMS Financial Health Executives |

(Federal Election Commission data reprinted in the *Washington Post*)

In eight short weeks, he had pocketed $18,800, or a check nearly every third day.

Power and money are the first two parts of Capitol Hill's holy trinity; media attention is the third. It is a town where public relations is everything, the beginning and the end, the ying and the yang. According to the General Accounting Office, even the executive branch of the federal government spends more than $100 million a year for "congressional affairs," which includes lobbying and getting the media's attention. During the height of the legislative season, the Hill becomes a "visual" battleground—PR stunts competing for camera coverage and the twenty-two minutes of network news available each evening. One Washington public relations firm owned by Pamela Kostmayer, former wife of U.S. Rep. Pete Kostmayer (D-PA), specializes in "visuals"; one of her advertisements carries the endorsement: "Pamela Kostmayer, a veteran Washington PR woman, is the queen of the Capitol Hill visual, which is a major PR art form in this era of photo-op politics."[31]

The image-mongering extends to the venerable *Congressional Record* itself. U.S. Rep. Jack Brooks (D-TX)—the self-styled meanest member in Congress—has a reknowned sense of the institution. He served on the Iran-contra special committee, and in one of his finest moments accused former National Security Advisor Admiral John Poindexter of a crime against history, charging that by making "the historical record conform to what you wanted it to be by tampering with that record . . . is to steal from . . . future generations." But he did not object to Congress or himself manipulating its own *Record*. On April 25, 1990, during debate over the Price Fixing Act, the Republicans tried to offer an amendment to bring up a different crime bill. Brooks argued against the Republican crime bill, mainly because he had bottled it up in his Judiciary Committee for nearly a year. The House vote was on party lines, and the Republican attempt was defeated. Brooks then tampered with his own words. He had the sentences—"And all of us have voted for crime bills almost every year for the past few years. We have almost as many crime bills passed as they have crimes committed."—deleted. The offending words were not published the next day. The political culture, naturally, never missed a beat.

The ability to change or delete what has been said pales in comparison to another arcane House rule involving the *Congressional Record*. On May 3, 1990, for example, I reviewed a *Record* statement for Congressman Coleman for the budget debate that preceded the vote on the national budget on May 1. How a statement written on May 3 can be part of the *Record* for May 1 is an interesting question.

At the very end of every debate on an important issue, a predesignated member will rise and ask unanimous consent for "all members to have five legislative days to revise and extend their remarks." Then the professionals take over. Assume, for example, the debate and vote took place on a Thursday, when major votes often occur. The House is out of session on Friday. The *Record* arrives that morning, which allows a congressman (or more likely his or her staff) to pore over the debate, read the newspaper coverage, and construct a perfect *ex post facto* defense of his position, one that ripostes every argument offered by the opposing side as well as any from the Monday morning press quarterbacks in the press. If it is a vote of major national importance—a strategic weapons system, Social Security, or, in this case, the national budget—a member can think about it during the weekend and mull over the commentary in the Sunday newsmaker talk shows and the op-ed pages of the *Washington Post* and the *New York Times*.

The statement is then delivered to the Democratic Cloakroom for insertion into the *Record*—the *Record* for the day of the vote, not the day of submission—and the published version bears the date of the vote. As far as the official proceedings of the House of Representatives are concerned, a member can send a floor statement back into time and have it appear in the past although it responds to the arguments of the future.

One recurrent criticism of the House from all political strata is the lack of contrition.

In a statement titled "Reinvigorating the Congress," Rep. Lee Hamilton (D-IN), one of the most respected members of the House, offered solutions to the ethics crisis raging at that time,[32] which included the Barney Frank scandal, where the House Ethics Committee investigated allegations of the congressman's involvement with a male prostitute; the Jim Wright scandal, which brought about the Speaker's resignation; the personal financial dealings of Majority Whip Tony Coelho, which forced his abrupt resignation; and a swirl of allegations of misconduct by members of both parties.

Yet Hamilton found no room to mention any of these scandals. Instead, he called for a pay raise to keep members from accepting personal payments for speeches, demanded sanctions against internal critics who made "distorted and demeaning statements about the Congress," and tried to lay the blame for Congress's misdoings on congressional red tape and bureaucracy, as if the creations of the members were somehow separate from the members themselves, thus allowing them to accept blame without any acknowledgement of individual responsibility.

Hamilton later argued in a private letter that it was entirely within the rights and regulations of the House to impose disciplinary action on members who made "distorted, demeaning statements" about Congress, such as the assertion that "members of Congress are spineless."[33] (See Appendix I) Like most of his breed, Hamilton simply could not bring himself to admit that individual actions color the public's perception of the institution. (The public impact of bringing legislative business of the House to a halt for a lengthy trial of a member for stating that "members of Congress are spineless" can only be imagined.)

Tempers are wearing thin under the strain, and bitter partisanship has split the institution. On March 29, 1990, it spilled onto national television on the House floor over a dispute about a restrictive rule on child care that allowed no Republican amendments, a most unusual situation.

"If you want to know how bad this rule is . . . ," began New York Republican Gerald Solomon.

"Oh, yeah? How bad is it?" interrupted Tom Downey (D-NY).

"I am going to tell you right now," replied Solomon as he began to lose his temper. "You should not be a smart aleck about it because you ought to be serious about it." Solomon then threatened to draw an X, voodoo-fashion, through a picture of Speaker Foley.

Republican Robert Walker struck back. "Come on, guys. Somewhere along the line, admit the fact that you have decided to run this House like a petty little dictatorship, that you have the votes and you are going to use the votes to muscle whatever you want, whenever it is important to you."

Republican Minority Leader Robert Michel attacked the Democrats' "craven fear of real debate . . . a mockery of the democratic process . . . We have no glasnost in this House. The majority has turned this House into a den of inequity."

Democratic Rules Committee Chairman Joe Moakley (D-MA) replied laconically, "I hope he doesn't take me off his Christmas card list."

The Republicans cheered lustily. Walker and Rules Commitee member Martin Frost (D-TX) got into a shouting match over whose statements were true. The bill passed on the largely party-line vote of 246 to 176.


And yet . . . and yet, despite it all, part of me loved this town and this Hill. Part of me sensed that the 1980s was our time for that luckiest sliver of the most affluent generation in history that found itself in the middle, to paraphrase a popular bank commercial of the time, of working for the most important people on the most important Hill in the most important city in the most important country in the world. We laughed at our vaunted insider's status, joked about it, dismissed it when necessary, but deep down, deep down we *knew* that for better or worse, this is where it was happening—and we were part of it.

And perhaps that is why I only remembered dreams of dying babies when I was at the Democratic Club. We were insiders to the point of losing touch with the outside and all the people in the "provinces," as one congressman termed it. Political battles are bloody only in an abstract sense. Those who wield the sword and shield of press release and fax machine never see the human consequences of their exertions. The Hill insulates and protects. There is no room in this inn for real flesh and blood, and certainly no stomach. The soul of Washington's political culture may well reside in places like the Democratic Club and countless other hideouts in this town—a soul slick and darting, and truly without mercy.

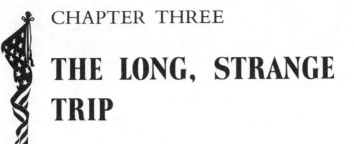

CHAPTER THREE

# THE LONG, STRANGE TRIP

In the beginning, of course, there were no questions, only the Word. And the Hill—that great, glorious beacon so many thousands of us so desperately wanted to belong to—was the Word.

I did not see the town then the way I do now. The days were younger, and brighter with promise and ambition. Like all would-be Hill rats, I had long dreamed about the first Hill job that would propel me into the corridors of power. And then, just like in the dream, a Hill job was mine. The power was real, I discovered, but the reality was somewhat unexpected.

"Get in here," the voice on the intercom snarled.

My heart jumped. "Batter up," someone called from the back of the legislative shop. It was my first time up to brief the Duke on a piece of legislation. The older hands couldn't hide their glee.

"*Grease* up, buddy," laughed my best friend on the staff, who had arrived from Cincinnati a few weeks ago, fresh from the successful 1978 reelection campaign of Democratic U.S. Rep. Thomas A. Luken, known to his staff as the Duke. It was now January 1979, and although I had been hired as press secretary and legislative assistant a month and a half before, I had barely met the congressman, who, after his victory, had not returned to Washington until recently.

Luken was a brilliant politician. Much sooner than his contemporaries, he had sniffed out the rumblings of the antitax hysteria about to sweep much of the country and, in a remarkable feat of political double-jointedness for a Democrat, had joined forces with conservative crusader Howard Jarvis, of Proposition 13 fame in California. Luken had introduced a national version of Proposition 13 before the 1978 election to blunt his Republican opponent's campaign charges that Luken was a high-tax, big-spending liberal. Now, after his victory, one of my missions was to keep Howard Jarvis and his henchmen at bay and figure out how to avoid introducing the legislation again. If unsuccessful, our follow-up plan was to introduce a watered-down version and then quietly and anonymously kill it in committee.

At the same time, Luken had been supported heavily by organized labor, which had known all along that the antitax bill was not designed to be passed in the first place; even in 1988, Luken's AFL-CIO rating was 78 percent. Luken had support in another area, too; he claimed to have cast the final and deciding vote for Jim Wright's one-vote victory in 1976 for House Majority Leader over Californian Phil Burton, earning him special points with Wright's staff. But because Luken's Cincinnati district was heavily Republican, he did everything in his power to appear conservative, and he would not allow himself to be outflanked on the right, as his most recent Republican opponent had just discovered.

Now Luken was back in Washington and the House was about to go into session. The opening day's legislation was to make the tune, "Our Merchant Marine Hymn," the official merchant marine song of the United States of America.

I thought I was ready.

Luken was first elected to Congress in a 1974 special election, but he had lost in the fall to Willis Gradison, his local Republican nemesis. After his defeat, he moved from the 1st Congressional District to the 2nd, both of which were in Cincinnati and surrounding Hamilton County, and won that seat in 1976. Luken, born of modest circumstances, served in the Marines in World War II, earned a J.D. from

Salmon P. Chase Law School, and in due course served as U.S. district attorney for the Southern District of Ohio until 1964, when he entered electoral politics and won a seat on the Cincinnati City Council. He was mayor of Cincinnati from 1972 to 1973.

Somewhere, somehow along that journey, "it" happened—that instant when his staff speculated that Congressman Luken for all intents and purposes left the human race.

To many staff members, the Duke was evil incarnate. He had an oversized, fleshy head and large, peering eyes that sat on top of dark and forbidding puff bags. The head dominated and defined his persona, allowing him to show off what recipients called his "evil" eye. The head would cock itself up and to the left, like a bloated Civil War mortar, partially obscuring the left eye, and the right eye would bear down on its prey like a cyclops because it looked like there was as much of his head from his right eye to his ear as there was between both eyes.

With a minotaur's bellow fused onto a legendary temper and an equally legendary appetite for human flesh, the effect would be terrifying, particularly on new employees, who before being put on the House payroll would have been courted extensively. Then, as a former staff member observed, "It was like sticking a blowtorch up your wazoo and turning it on to full rock 'n roll." People reacted in different ways. One staff member simply froze into silence, unable to speak or even whisper. A former television reporter from Cincinnati who had joined the staff regularly threw up after Luken's tirades.

Luken had a lot of the bully and the swagger in him and he liked it. His behavior only went on behind closed doors or on the telephone, like child abuse or obscene phone calls. To the outside world, he was always the charming, dynamic congressman. To those of us who worked for him, he was a Fifth Horseman of the Apocalypse who had just killed and eaten the original four and wanted *you* for dessert.

New employees were subjected to a six-week version of boot camp, cloistered in his office for hours and subjected to unending lectures, diatribes, accusations, and taunts—all at maximum volume. Luken sought to own them, break them apart mentally, spit on the pieces, and sell them back, still dripping, one shard at a time. He would hurl accusations at staff members of conspiring with his opponents on the Cincinnati City Council. He would accuse them of trying to break into his safe, of doing everything possible to undermine his personal and political agenda. We dreaded having to go into his lair and ask him about anything because he was never interested in the answer, only in your hide.

I had heard vague rumors about the Duke from my labor lobbyist buddies at the Democratic Club (I shared a Georgetown townhouse with one of them at the time) who had arranged the initial interview for me, but the thought of actually having "Hill experience" checked my doubts. Luken was dangerous, ugly, and everyone on the outside thought they could handle him.

I know I sure did.

Army brats who move all over the world usually become pretty quick on their feet. You get used to meeting new people, making new friends, leaving old ones, sizing up situations, and taking advantage of opportunities. In Paris in 1964, I played a choir boy in the Elizabeth Taylor-Richard Burton movie *The Sandpiper*. After attending three different high schools and eight elementary schools from Kansas to Europe to Panama, I went to Washington and Lee University in Lexington, Virginia, with my eyes set on a journalism career. By my junior year I had discovered history, the true intellectual love of my life, and was concentrating on post-World War II U.S. diplomatic history. My father, a Defense Department member of the U.S. Panama Canal treaty negotiating team, was able to make an arrangement with the U.S. ambassador to Panama for me to work in the political section of the embassy in the spring of 1976. The job was undefined and unpaid, but the experience was priceless. I was twenty years old and had a Top Secret security clearance, which allowed me to spend the first couple of weeks perusing the classified files on Panama's leaders, including then-colonel and intelligence chief Manuel Noriega, who at one time was little more than one of the two-bit hoods in uniform that populate the governments of Central America with irritating frequency.

But to obtain college credit for my time in the embassy, I had to write a paper that my professors would be allowed to read. I soon turned to more usable areas of study.

I was no stranger to Panama. My family had lived there from 1969 to 1971, and then again from 1974 to 1975, when my father commanded the Seventh Special Forces Group at Fort Gulick. Those guys played for keeps; the command office once had a golden plaque simply inscribed "MTT 416," or U.S. Military Training Team #416; its CIA/Special Forces members had nailed Che Guevara in Bolivia in 1967.

I had spent the previous summer of 1975 as a laborer at the canal's Gatun Locks on the Caribbean side, and I had many friends who were "Zonians," the nonmilitary American residents of the Panama Canal Zone who actually ran the canal operation.

Well, I asked myself, why not concentrate on the Zonians in my paper? No one really seemed to give a damn about them in the treaty negotiations. So by default I became an unofficial liaison to the Zonian community. I gave speeches all over the Canal Zone on behalf of the negotiations and my efforts received a lot of local media attention.

The right-wing press back in the United States had other ideas. The fate of the Zonians in the treaty negotiations was becoming a political issue in the Republican presidential primaries, and my paper had suggested, among other things, that the U.S. government direct its propaganda and communications resources at them to calm them down. Someone leaked the paper to the press. Right-wing newsletters across the country denounced me and my paper; Lester Kinsolving's *Panax Washington Weekly* ran a splashy headline on October 13, 1977, "CANAL ZONE AMERICANS CALLED EXPENDABLE PAWNS," and the newspaper printed a picture of my college freshman photograph. The story eventually became the subject of a Jack Anderson column.

Throughout the episode, I became sharply aware of the power not only of the press but of the written word to transform human perceptions. It was my first excursion into Perceptionland—a not entirely welcome one—but it opened up a new realm of knowledge that I would use, for ill or otherwise, on Capitol Hill a few years later.

Despite the media free-for-all, the State Department experience led to a job in 1977 with David Rockefeller's Council of the Americas, where I lobbied to ratify the Panama Canal treaties.

A year later I was twenty-two, not a year out of college, and we had *won*, passing the treaties by the skin of our teeth. I had personal letters of commendation from President Carter and Secretary of State Cyrus Vance, and with the arrogance of youth and inexperience, I thought I owned this town.

More than that, though, both Panama jobs taught me about the Inside Deal. When I lobbied for the treaties, the staff of Senate Majority Leader Robert Byrd loaned me a spare desk in the Steering and Policy Committee office. Like the embassy, the Senate was another looking glass to the inside deal. I first learned that people actually did trade favors for votes. People really did get leaned on politically and personally—real things, real people, just undamnbelievable, and I was in the middle of it. It felt good the first time you leaned on someone older and smarter and heard the crack of bone over the telephone.

After a year at the Council of the Americas, I moved to the American Council on Education. By that time, I had learned that Capitol Hill was the center of Washington's universe, and in November 1978, I used my labor buddies' connections to land a job on Congressman Luken's staff.

"Our Merchant Marine Hymn" was a ridiculous little bill. But knowing the Duke's reputation, I treated it like a declaration of war. His legislative system was designed to produce maximum chaos. Instead of one person responsible for defense, another for trade, and so on, Luken assigned legislation depending on where a particular bill stood. That meant one legislative assistant would handle it in subcommittee, another in full committee, and a third on the House floor. The further a bill progressed, the less the staff member in charge knew about it. Luken liked it that way.

I handled all floor legislation in addition to press relations. So I ran all the political traps, in this instance calling the Majority Leader's office, the shipping industry, and the maritime labor unions. I wanted to leave no stone unturned. By the time I was finished, I had a floor file half an inch thick for a bill that would pass unanimously on voice vote in about ten seconds.

The chair stood in front of his desk and I sat down without waiting to be ordered.

"What's on the floor today, John?" he asked much too politely, like a hangman who asks if you had enjoyed a good night's sleep.

"One bill, Congressman, to designate 'Our Merchant Marine Hymn' as the official U.S. merchant marine song," I replied crisply. Earlier impressions of the Duke faded. Wow! Here I was! On Capitol Hill! Briefing a congressman! And he's listening!

"Who's for it and who's against it?"

"Everyone's on board, sir," I said in my best Capitol Hill briefing tone. "The leadership has no problems with it, and I'm informed that it will be adopted by unanimous consent."

"Says who?"

"The leadership."

"How the hell do you know?"

"I asked, sir."

"Who'd you ask?"

"The Majority Leader's floor assistant."

"What the hell does she know?"

"She schedules the bills, sir."

"So how the hell do you know that?"

"That's what the Majority Leader pays her to do."

"So you think you fucking know it all now, don't you?"

Uh-oh, I thought, here we go. "Pardon me, sir?"

"You think that just because you talked to one goddamned staff assistant you can run this whole fucking Congress?"

At this point I knew it was going to be a long morning. Even

though I had steeled myself for the ordeal, my heart began to pound
and I had stage fright.

"Answer me!"

My throat had tightened and I couldn't respond.

"So you don't have an answer to that one, do you, smartass?"

"Congressman, I . . ."

"God-DAMN-it!" he yelled. He slammed his glasses on his desk
as he leaped to his feet. "I ought to kick your ass right here and now.
You want me to go out on a limb, vote yes with my eyes closed on
some goddamn sellout bill just so you can get free drinks from your
labor buddies at the Democratic Club tonight, not giving one
goddamn whether I sink or swim!"

"But Congressman . . ."

"I'm asking the questions around here," he yelled, jabbing his
finger at me, still on his feet. "Let's just see how far you were willing
to screw me."

He came out from behind the desk—according to leading Duke-
ologists, the opening move of the classic Duke treatment. He stood
in front of me for a moment, then turned his back—the ultimate
sign of contempt—and paced like a district attorney with the prize
catch on the witness stand.

"The unions?" he demanded.

"No problem, sir. I checked with their lobbyists and with their
political action committees, and they all support it." Money, especially campaign money, was very important to Luken, and he actually murmured a positive sound.

It lasted only a second. "Business!" he exclaimed as he whirled
around, hurling the word like an accusation.

"No position either way. The Chamber of Commerce told me it
was such a minor bill that it wasn't worth taking a position on."

"The district?" He meant Cincinnati.

"Nothing. No letters, no calls, no telegrams."

Even though I could sense his frustration at not being able to
catch me off guard, I thought for a minute I might escape relatively
unscathed. The last question had been somewhat gentle in tone, and

I thought I remembered that he was supposed to attend a meeting shortly.

Silence. More silence. Then, almost mildly:

"How's it go?"

I furrowed my brow, looked at him, and without thinking, stepped off the edge:

"Uh, it's going just fine, sir, how about you?"

"No goddamnit, how's it *go go go!*" he exploded. "How's it go? *How does it go?* Which word don't you understand? Which one? *Which one?* How does it fucking go? *Go!* Dumdee dum dum dum! *Go! Go!*"—almost choking out and screaming the final syllable. "De deedum go go dum dum dee dum de *fucking go!*"

Luken gurgled unintelligibly, his face red and purple. Veins emerged in the stumpy neck and the head assumed its feared position, cocked up and to the left. All I could see was the evil cyclops eye bent on my destruction.

"Well? *Well? Well?* How's it go, smartass, how's it go?" He had regained control of his breathing, and his eyes were gleaming.

"Well . . . sir . . . I guess I really don't know how it actually goes."

"Aha!" was the only English word I could make out of the torrent of gibberish that followed.

Roughly translated, he had me.

"So you don't know how it goes! Don't know how it goes! How it goes! Little smartass doesn't know how anything goes! Doesn't know how his job goes! How the Hill goes! How anything goes! Go go go go goes!"

I thought that the spit must by now be cutting off some of his words before they could fly through his lips.

Trying to buy time, I took a step back and held out my file as a sacrificial offering. "Look in here, Congressman, you'll see that this legislation is no big deal . . ."

"Here's what I think of your files and your deals!" he shrieked, snatching it out of my hands. "*You're outta here!* Go home and don't come back until you know how it goes!" He threw the file to the top of the eighteen-foot ceiling and whirled around at me through the shower of white paper and pink telephone messages like a crazed bull elephant in a confetti parade.

Forewarned, I made a desperate dash—and I mean desperate dash—for the door to the main office. I beat him to the reception area, where by the grace of God two visitors from his district were waiting for him.

He was booming cheery hellos to the constituents as I raced down the corridor.

I left Luken's office for good six months after this incident. By the time I quit in June 1979, the months under Luken's guns had worn me down. I was broke and had no immediate job prospects. My fiancee was paying the apartment bills, and my confidence was at an all-time low. I had hit Capitol Hill and been knocked back on my heels. I had learned several important lessons, though. First of all, no job and no boss ever seemed too bad after Luken. Second, you have to take the Hill on its own terms—to succeed you have to use its power instead of fighting it. And third, after countless episodes like "Our Merchant Marine Hymn," I have to admit that Congressman Luken did teach me in his own inimitable way how to investigate anything down to the smallest lead and the most infinitesimal point. Thanks to Congressman Luken, I would never again not know how it goes.

After a brief stint of unemployment, I spent two years off Capitol Hill in the wilderness, working for a Democratic political consulting firm with a Washington-based confederation of street-smart political hustlers who had more letterheads than cash and more chutzpah than principle. My title sounded great—"Executive Vice President" of two of the companies, Public Interest Opinion Research and Democratic Victory Group Associates—but the pay was less than terrific. Still, the education was invaluable, especially the opportunity to become intimately familiar with the dark craft of running American political campaigns and its mechanics of polling, fundraising, direct mail, media manipulation, radio and TV scripting, voter targeting, and the rest of the real tools of democracy.

It was as if I lived in a seedy Washington novel. Our office was at the corner of 9th and F Streets, and in 1979 the area still bore the scars of the 1968 riots. The building was old, and the elevator cage had to be banged shut.

Every afternoon at 6:00 P.M. sharp the walls would vibrate as the punk rock band at the 9:30 Club next door warmed up. Our doorway was a favorite place for junkies and winos to pass out, frequently leaving a morning smell of fresh urine. One of my duties was to arrange meetings with prospective clients downtown—restaurants, offices, bars—anywhere we didn't know the neighborhood hookers by their first names.

The ringleaders of our letterhead nest were Vic Fingerhut and Jim Rosapepe, two of the most accomplished if unsung political operatives of our time. Vic, fortyish, with a Ph.D. in political science, was a compassionate, understanding, old-line labor Democrat. He was the resident genius, the one with true creative and analytical talent for discerning the poll numbers and crafting the media messages that won campaigns. He had been Hubert Humphrey's media advisor in 1968 and had worked for Senator Lloyd Bentsen's presidential campaign as well as scores of successful congressional candidates and labor unions along the way.

Vic tells a story about Capitol Hill I'll never forget.

"So I'm in my hotel room, right? And I really don't want to see this guy, but I end up doin' it. The guy says, 'Hi, I hear you're good. I want to know how much it's going to cost me to make my boy Nick Joe Rahall a congressman.' So I need to get rid of this joker, okay? So I say something wild like $400,000, and that's only to start. The guy looks at me and says in all seriousness, 'Do I make the check out to Vic or Victor?'"

"So did you take the check?" I asked the first time I heard the story.

"Fuckin' right I took the check," Vic chortled, although the amount tended to change with each rendition. "*And* we won the election."

That was in 1976. Today, Nick Joe Rahall represents the 4th District of West Virginia and is the chairman of the House Interior Subcommittee on Mining and Natural Resources. Vic Fingerhut owns a beautiful condominium in the exclusive Watergate-at-Landmark complex in Northern Virginia.

Jim Rosapepe was the salesman, the front man, the promoter, the guy with a million angles and all of them for sale. Rosapepe drew upon both his Italian and Irish heritage for his temper. After prep school, he spent a semester at Yale, only to decide he was too smart for the place and quit to enter politics full-time, working for liberal candidates and causes. First and foremost, Jim was a talented writer and produced some of the most effective direct mail in the business; I learned from him much of the promotional craft I would later use on the Hill. Jim moved to Maryland after commissioning a targeting study to determine which area would be most likely to elect him to something, anything. Rosapepe is now a member of the Maryland House of Delegates and is married to ABC White House correspondent Sheila Kast.

It was fun for a while. I made all kinds of contacts, especially in the Democratic political community. I learned neat campaign tricks and became somewhat knowledgable in running a campaign. I also learned that these talents were more valuable on Capitol Hill than anything learned in graduate school. The Hill was entering the 1980s with a vengeance, and its incumbents were starting to go high-tech. The era of modern campaigning with computers had just begun, and the machines would revolutionize politics as much as television had a generation before. Although in control of the House, Democrats in 1981 were running scared, still shocked by the 1978 Senate victories of sophisticated right-wing campaigns. Ronald Reagan's election in 1980 jolted Democratic incumbents into searching out newer and better ways of staying elected.

By the summer of 1981, I was ready to return to the Hill. A steady paycheck was attractive, and I hated chasing business. My break came, of all things, in a *Washington Post* classified advertisement for a press secretary on Capitol Hill. A Texas Democrat from Dallas with big dreams was looking for a good political writer, someone who knew how to handle the media, and above all, someone with good campaign instincts.

For a second time, I thought I was ready.

So did Texas Congressman Jim Mattox.

"Let me tell you what this job is all about," he said as he brandished an envelope during my job interview. "I'm in a district full of Republicans and the newspapers hate my guts. The TV stations are out to get me. I'm always barely a step ahead of the political undertakers and I win by a couple of percentage points if I'm lucky. The only chance I have is mail." He paused for a moment and waved the envelope bearing his personal signature, or frank, which means that it can be mailed at taxpayer expense. "We are going to mail, mail, mail and then mail some more. You're going to mail until you run out of ideas. Then you're going to talk to the rest of the staff and mail until they run out of ideas. After that you're going to come to me and mail until *I* run out of ideas. And when that happens, we're going to staple my picture to pages of the goddamn Yellow Book and mail them out, too, and lemme tell you, you cain't *ever* run out of them sons of bitches."

We laughed, and the job was mine. I had already successfully interviewed with Don Buford, Mattox's administrative assistant, and the interview with Mattox was the final hurdle. It was August 1981, and I was back on the Hill to stay.

Jim Mattox remains the best and most complex politician I've ever worked for. Personally warm, fair, and understanding, he is probably the most ferocious campaigner in the history of the state of Texas, including Lyndon Johnson. Jim's sister Janice discovered that John Hannah, Jim's opponent in the runoff election for Texas attorney general in 1982, had never been to law school. He had read for the law as a member of the state legislature and had passed the bar exam, but as Mattox said, "Let him do the explaining." Not only did Mattox pronounce Hannah unfit to hold office, but he charged him with a coverup. Shoved on the defensive, Hannah, a stellar

United States attorney but a first-time campaigner, backpedaled his way to defeat.

Growing up in a poor, broken family in affluent Dallas made Jim a populist. He was driven by his past and by a determination of shocking depths to succeed at any cost, overcoming dyslexia and poor high school grades to graduate near the top of his law school class.

Jim had a true appreciation of chaos and his political organization reflected it. He had no single chief of staff; the heads of his Dallas office (Tom Green) and Washington office (Don Buford) were on equal footing. In practice, Don had the upper hand concerning all things in Washington, and Tom called the shots concerning campaigning, fundraising, and grub-politicking back in Texas.

Don Buford was in his midthirties, tall, beefy, a great guy to work with and for. The Washington staff was divided into two camps: Don's, on whose side I was because he had hired me; and the rest, whom Don disliked for one reason or another but couldn't get Jim to fire because he rarely fired anyone.

A woman named Karen was an exception. On my first week on the job, I received a call from Rudy Maxa at *Parade*.

"I want to know why Jim Mattox sent an official observer to the meeting of the Palestinian National Congress in Beirut, Lebanon," he barked, getting straight to the point.

"I think you've got bad information," I replied with a laugh. "The congressman has done nothing of the sort." It would have been crazy, even political suicide, to do something like that. Mattox was an ardent defender of Israel, and he counted on the Jewish community for a significant part of his financial base.

"Wrong," said Maxa, relishing being right. "A woman from your office is in Beirut, Lebanon, attending the meeting of the Palestinian National Congress as your boss's official observer."

"Hold on a second," I said. I called Don. "Where'd Karen go?"

"She's somewhere down south visiting her sick grandmother," Don answered.

"Well, I got Rudy Maxa from *Parade* on hold on line two. He says she's in Beirut, attending the Palestinian National Congress as Jim Mattox's official observer."

"Arggh!" Buford exploded. I was unaware that Karen had had a Palestinian boyfriend and had become somewhat of a convert to the Palestinian cause.

"I don't fucking believe this!" Buford yelled. "I'll check it out. Tell the guy we'll get back to him."

I punched line two. "Mr. Maxa, our information is that she went to visit her sick grandmother," I said. "But I'll double-check and call you right back. Can I have your number?"

Rudy Maxa was right. She was indeed attending the Palestinian National Congress.

Mattox knew he had a potential firestorm on his hands, and he moved quickly. He fired Karen on the spot and then made a series of calls to national and Texas Jewish leaders, explaining that he was completely unaware of her involvement. He had always been a staunch friend of Israel and was anxious to remain so. I called Rudy Maxa and told him that Karen had lied to Mattox and had been summarily fired.

Anything can happen on the Hill, and will.

On another occasion, I had the pleasure of spending the Thanksgiving week of 1981 in Dallas to help Jim raise money for the upcoming campaign for either his House seat or Texas attorney general.

"Jim, you can't call now, people will be eating dinner and watching the Cowboys game," I protested after we had finished a wonderful belly-buster of a meal at his sister's house.

He grinned. "Hell, boy, it's the *best* time to call. That way you can catch 'em at home. They'll want to get me the hell off the phone and we'll do 50 percent better than we might normally would." We were in his downtown office. I sighed and picked up another stack of oversized index cards to place another call. "Good afternoon, can you hold a second for Jim Mattox?" I would ask for the fiftieth time that day.

What was out of the ordinary was the way we went about doing it. Jim had written a highly regarded booklet on fundraising, and he had a round-the-clock approach. It was an obsession with him. He had total and instant recall of his contributor list, and he knew by name who had pledged how much and whether or not it had been paid.

Once a check came in for $5,000. I handed it to him and he scowled. Tossing the check on the desk, he told me to get the man on the phone. I did.

"Billy? Jim Mattox here. That's right, that's right, just came in the mail today. And I want to let you know I just tore up that sumbitch and pitched it where it belonged. Listen, you and me go back a long way. I know you can do better than that. I *know*. I know you're good for ten at least. Shit, I read about that deal in the paper. Maybe you good for a hunnert!" Jim laughed loudly. "So I figure you musta just made a mistake, or maybe your secretary did it or somehow it got fucked up. Now can I count on you for the ten? Is that dog gonna hunt?"

More often than not, Mattox got his ten thousand. And when the poor bastard on the other end of the line would hem and haw and finally agree, Jim would say, "Great! Tell you what. John here in my office was heading over there anyway to pick up a few other checks, I'll just have him stop by and get yours too. He don't show up in twenty minutes, you give me a call."

Money was Mattox's obsession; the Randall Christian case was mine.

Randall Christian was a Dallas Marine recruit, a champion high school swimmer who drowned in boot camp in San Diego on August 27, 1981. Despite numerous eyewitness accounts that his drill instructor deliberately prevented Christian from saving himself when he began to struggle in the training pool, the "informal" investigation, as the Marine Corps called it, concluded that the death was an accident and that no one was at fault except, by implication, the dead young man.

Mattox, a former assistant district attorney in Dallas, was acquainted with the boy's father, an investigator in the DA's office.

From his training, Artie Christian knew that the Marine Corps' investigation was a sham, and he asked Mattox for help.

It was a politician's dream: a nonpolitical issue that had sparked the black community in Dallas, a made-for-order crusade in which we would be on the right side all the way. I took over the case as one of my first assignments, and away we went. Even a cursory glance at the "informal" report showed that something stank. Then Artie Christian received several calls from Randall's fellow recruits, telling him off the record that the drill instructor had drowned his son. We began to push the investigatory process amidst screaming headlines all over Texas, and asked U.S. Rep. Richard White, chairman of the House Armed Services Committee Subcommittee on Oversight and Investigation, to request that the Marine Corps conduct a formal investigation.

We did our own digging, too, especially as a spate of news reports on additional training deaths began to surface. Thanks to Luken's investigatory training, I uncovered more bombshells. Several Marines present at the drowning reported a chilling story of official coverup, intimidation and threats to witnesses, and destruction of evidence.

Prodded by Mattox, the Marine Corps convened a formal Board of Inquiry that only refined the original whitewash. On January 25, 1982, Mattox wrote Navy Secretary John Lehman to use the powers of his office to get justice for the Christian family. "After carefully reviewing the report of the Board of Inquiry, I have regretfully concluded that we are faced with an official whitewash . . . and a glaring abuse of the military system of justice by the Marine Corps."

The Board itself termed the drill instructor's testimony "inconsistent, confused, and lacking in adequate information," and the transcripts revealed a running commentary aimed at discrediting the eyewitness testimony that showed how the drill instructor prevented Randall Christian from saving himself.

PVT. SHANNON: Christian reached the wall and Rodriguez pushed him back.

PVT. RICHIE: Christian reached for the wall and Rodriguez pushed him back.

PVT. DAHN: Christian grabbed the side and another instructor pushed him under.

PVT. CONNER: Christian grabbed the side and an instructor forced him away from the wall.

PVT. YBANEZ: Christian was on the wall and an instructor pushed him away.

PVT. WASHINGTON: Christian was on the side and an instructor pushed his hand off with his feet.

PVT. ELSTAD: A black private was pulled off the side.

PVT. POTTS: Christian reached for the side of the pool and was pushed away.

But, in the end, the Board of Inquiry exonerated the drill instructor. Under the military system of justice, without high-level intervention, the case was over.

Incredibly—I still believed in justice back then—Navy Secretary John Lehman refused to reopen the case. Frustrated, we wrote President Reagan, but to no avail.

With no new developments, media attention soon died off, and our interest along with it. Mattox was embroiled in the political fight of his life for the Democratic nomination for Texas attorney general, and we were beginning to hear rumblings from the Hispanic political community because the drill instructor accused of causing Christian's death was Mexican-American. Naturally, we were disappointed. We had been making headlines all across the state for months, leaking and announcing each new step or development.

Mattox never forgot the political and media value of the case. At one particularly difficult point in the attorney general race, he took off his glasses, rubbed his eyes wearily, and said, "Sure could use me another dead Marine right about now." He did not mean it literally, of couse. Jim's personal compassion for the family and his deep Christian beliefs were too great for that. What he wanted was An Issue, a crusade, something to galvanize public emotions and turn them into a tidal wave of victory.

What could I do? Capitol Hill had collided with the real world, and I didn't like the sight. Faceless issues in black ink on white paper were far preferable. In one sense, I was shamefully relieved that the case had gone away after spending haunted nights wondering if Randall Christian had had the same sad eyes as his father. Now it was over. Like every Hill rat, I was learning to keep score. Add 'em up at the end of the day, advertise the ones you win, and forget the rest.

Mattox went on to win the Democratic nomination in the runoff and the general election in a walk. A victorious campaign carries a sweet finality. You helped change something, even if it was only the face behind the desk. That represents progress in politics.

After the November victory, I set my own course. I knew I didn't want to move to Austin. Washington was my town. I was here to stay, but I needed a job. Luck intervened. U.S. Rep. Mickey Leland's press secretary put me in touch with a guy named Paul Rogers, slated to become the top staffer to newly elected Congressman Ronald Coleman from El Paso. It was an exciting possibility; in the state legislature, Coleman had the reputation of being a fearless progressive scrapper against special interests. He would, I felt, bring this driving force to Washington.

It all happened fairly quickly. After meeting with Rogers, I saw Coleman on January 25, 1983. It was a lecture more than an interview. Coleman gave me a rundown of the press situation in the 16th Congressional District of Texas and his political relationship with each newspaper and station.

"The *El Paso Times* hates my guts," he pointed out several times. Naturally, I agreed enthusiastically. Politicians are the center of their known universe and, accordingly, they reason that they are at the center of everyone else's as well.

We shook hands, and Rogers told me they would be in touch. *Oh well*, I thought. *You never know*.

It was late afternoon and I wandered over to the Democratic Club for a drink, yukking it up with the labor boys and getting ready to watch the State of the Union address.

"Telephone for John Jackley," the pager intoned. "Telephone for John Jackley."

I ordered another round and made my way to the telephone. "Hel-lo," I said jovially.

"John Jackley?" a voice asked.

"That's me."

"This is Jose Sanchez with Congressman Coleman. The congressman wanted to know if you could come to the office and help prepare his press response to President Reagan's State of the Union message tonight."

"Uh, sure, I'll be right there." I had a job! I gulped a cup of coffee, grabbed my coat, and stepped out into the frigid air. When I reached First Street, I looked up. The Longworth House Office Building, a cockroach hotel that housed Coleman's new office, was right across the street. Beyond it rose the magnificent white dome of the United States Capitol, bathed in light and awaiting the arrival of the president. I shivered in the cold but didn't mind because it helped clear my head.

I took in the scene for a moment: helicopters circling with their searchlights, hordes of motorcycle cops, SWAT teams getting into place, security goons everywhere, Republicans in real fur coats scurrying about.

My mind flashed back to a scene eight months before during Mattox's Texas attorney general campaign. I was in a car driven by another aide with thinning hair and aviator sunglasses. We were on our way to lunch with a third aide, who sat in the back seat. We approached a set of railroad tracks. The lights began to flash. Slim (not his real name) chortled without slowing down.

"Hey, man," Tex (not his real name, either) pointed out nervously from the back seat, "train's coming."

"So are we," Slim laughed. He accelerated.

"No, man, you don't understand, the train's coming," Tex persisted.

"Watch this."

I figured Slim would never try to beat the train, so I leaned back to enjoy the scam. But when Slim hit sixty-five (in a residential district), I began to feel the adrenaline.

"Are you fucking crazy? Slow down and stop!" Tex demanded.

"Do I look crazy?" Slim grinned as he gunned it.

"The train's coming!" Tex yelled.

"The train's coming!" I yelled.

"No, man, you don't understand, THE FUCKING TRAIN'S COMING!" Tex shrieked.

The guard rail dropped seconds after we burst across the tracks. I turned around and saw the train.

"Hell of a rush, eh?" Slim chuckled. "Do it all the time where I come from in Texas." My breathing was hard, shallow, rapid.

"You're fucking crazy," Tex told him, still shaking.

"Hey man," Slim replied softly. "It's the Eighties. Go for it."

The image passed and I saw the Capitol again. I crossed the street. I took a deep breath and paused in front of the entrance to the Longworth Building. Then, with a shrug and a smile, I winked at the Capitol Dome and entered the world I was so determined to embrace.

## CHAPTER FOUR

# DESPERATELY SEEKING SURVIVAL

*"I feel confident that we've assembled a top-notch team . . . to serve the residents of the 16th District of Texas. We have that necessary combination of Washington experience and familiarity with the district that every Congressman needs to give his constituents the representation they deserve."*

U.S. REP. RONALD COLEMAN,
February 3, 1983, press release

A SPECIAL KIND of hell is reserved for fools who drink cheap tequila all night long in Mexican bordertowns and develop hangovers without ever having gone to bed.

It starts with a dread sinking sensation that perhaps everything is not going to be all right, that you cannot knock down "coscarones"—tequila and 7-Up in a tall shot glass that is slammed onto the table to create a deadly froth—with impunity. The hangover begins to play with your head, which spins slowly and queasily. *I'm going to be fine . . . Oops, no, I'm not going to be fine. Well, maybe we can just slip through the next few hours without the hangover noticing . . .*

Then you realize in a panic it's 6:30 in the morning and you still haven't crossed the border and in thirty minutes you're supposed to be taking off in a hopelessly overloaded twin-engine aircraft with the congressman and his new young wife to visit small towns in the West Texas desert as part of the newly elected representative's victory lap of the district.

The trip had started off well enough. I had flown to El Paso two days before with Congressman Coleman's staff director, Paul Rogers, and our legislative director, Jose Sanchez, and checked into our hotel. Jose and I were stuck into one room for budgetary reasons; Rogers, being the boss, had his own.

We were unpacking when the phone rang. "Hey," Rogers laughed, "I did you guys a big favor."

That made me nervous. "What is it?" I asked cautiously.

"El Paso County Commissioner _____ offered to send one of his favorite girlfriends to me as a welcoming present. Said she was very clean, very friendly. So being thoughtful, I naturally gave out your telephone number instead of mine."

I chuckled. One more deal on the border. Besides, I thought, all we needed was a sordid little local sex scandal and the commissioner would have something on us for the rest of the time Coleman was in office (which was, of course, the real purpose of the offer).

Still, I could never tell when Rogers was leading us on, but I figured this was one of them. "Oh, sure," I replied. "Thanks for the help."

I explained the matter to Jose.

"Sure, sure," Jose replied nervously. Jose was one of the nicest, most straight-arrow guys you would ever meet in your life. He also did not have a liberal sense of humor. He was the Felix Unger of our operation, the deputy congressman for decorum, and we loved him dearly.

He was also a prime target. "I'm not kidding," I added. "She could be here anytime."

But after several variations on that theme, I finally let him off the hook and told him, no, I had not called her and had no intention of doing so.

He glared at me and then went to sleep nervously, one ear cocked for a knock on the door.

We had spent the next day in Congressman Coleman's El Paso

office and the night across the border. Now, terrified that we might miss the plane, we dashed out of the bar into the early sunlight and the sweet stink of the dawn streets of Ciudad Juarez, right across the Rio Grande from El Paso. By the time we lurched into the private-aircraft section of the airport, small demons were poking my head with sharp sticks and Jose Sanchez was turning a particularly bilious shade of green.

"Well, boys, you ready?" Coleman boomed. He was feeling good. A few months earlier he had been just one more state representative. Then came the surprise retirement announcement of Rep. Richard White, which created a scramble. After knocking off a few early opponents, Coleman won the 1982 general election with 54 percent of the vote over a Republican city councilman.

Coleman had repeatedly promised in his 1982 campaign not to neglect the sparsely populated rural areas of Texas's 16th Congressional District, whose geographical area is roughly larger than Massachusetts, Rhode Island, and Connecticut. This March 1983 trip—his first back to Texas since Congress convened in January—was part of the fulfillment of that promise. We would hold "Congressional Town Hall Meetings" to encourage the locals to meet their congressman in person. This practice establishes "accessibility" and "accountability" in political parlance, but the real dividend comes from being allowed by the rules of the House to send out postcards bearing Coleman's name and photograph to every mailbox in the congressional district.

Don't laugh. A quarter of a million postcards each time means that incumbent reelection rates of 98 percent don't happen by accident.

"Gonna be a little jumpy out there," the pilot remarked about the wind as he checked the engines.

Jumpy? It was a frigging sleigh ride. Our first stop was Van Horn, Texas, ninety long miles east of El Paso. A delegation of local notables met us at the airport. I could not help but notice world-class tumbleweeds, big as Volkswagens, flying through the air.

"State police just closed the highway to big rigs," a man remarked.

I didn't like the sound of it. "Closed the highway?" I asked Jose Sanchez. "Whaddaya mean, closed the highway!"

"The wind can blow them right over during these March windstorms," Jose whispered.

March windstorms? I felt as if everyone knew something I didn't know. "March windstorms?" I hissed.

"Windstorms," Jose repeated matter-of-factly. "We get windstorms in March out here." Jose is from El Paso and knows these things.

Then I began to relax. If they're closing the highway because of the wind, there's no way in hell we're going to be flying out of here.

Wrong again. "It's close to ninety miles an hour on the gust," the sheriff told us after the Congressional Town Hall meeting. Coleman only laughed and made some stupid-sounding crack about flying into the face of death.

The next stop was Marfa, a small town outside Coleman's district but with the nearest airport to Fort Davis. We landed after another sleigh ride. The Town Hall meeting went fine, but I would learn quickly that the aerodynamics for landing are slightly different than those for taking off.

The pilot's knuckles began to whiten immediately after takeoff, and even Coleman became quiet. We cleared the edge of the runway but needed to gain enough altitude to clear the mountain in front of us. The mountain loomed closer—we would need a lot more altitude. The plane began to shake violently. We all became quiet and still. The mountain grew larger. We did not have enough altitude.

Suddenly the pilot stood the plane nearly on its starboard wing and cleared the mountain. "I was praying that the starboard engine wouldn't cough," he said later. "Unequal pressure on one wing makes the plane flip."

White-faced and shaken, we all let out small sighs of relief and even began to banter a bit. We hit violent turbulence thirty seconds later.

This was not normal commercial jetliner turbulence. This is when objects fly around the inside of the plane, when you have to reach down and grab the metal seat supports to keep from being battered against the cabin wall, which is shaking as much as you are.

We hit another big one and Tammy, Coleman's wife, helpfully screamed in her Texas twang, "We're all gonna DIE!!"

Somehow we leveled out above the turbulence and flew relatively smoothly toward Pecos.

"We're getting ready to land," the pilot said.

"Where?" I asked. I couldn't see anything below us.

"Oh, that's a sandstorm," the pilot replied. "We just get on top and drop down like an elevator." Drop down? So your insides whoop up to your nose and your sinuses begin to boil and you land in Pecos, Texas, home of the Western World's oldest rodeo. Once again, the Town Hall meeting was the easiest part of the trip. Coleman had been the first candidate in memory not to have segregated campaign rallies and meetings in Pecos, and he insisted that his Anglo and Hispanic supporters meet under the same roof, an act of courage that eventually won him the admiration of both camps.

We ate, then started to go to the airport until we realized that Coleman was actually going to fly back to El Paso.

"He's out of his mind," someone protested. The grumbling grew louder. Finally the pilot told us that the winds die down at night.

The lights of El Paso twinkled smoothly in front of us as the pilot radioed to the airport tower of our approach. The tower told him to circle, that a commercial jetliner was approaching and had prior clearance.

"We've got the United States congressman aboard," the pilot answered sharply. Without hesitation, the tower—run by federal air traffic controllers—ordered the jetliner to change course and cleared the way for our tired little bunch.

Congressman Coleman was exultant. Forget the near-death experience, the stress, the fatigue. Paths were being cleared for him in ways he had never imagined. The skies themselves had been parted for him: orders were issued and jetliners diverted, along with hundreds of passengers. The rolling-out of the technological carpet carried the unmistakable smell of power. We liked it.

As our plane made its unencumbered final approach, this spontaneous bending of the knee cemented in his mind that he had, at long last, arrived.


A Democratic Club joke:

An explorer was heading upriver in the heart of the jungle. After a day of paddling his canoe, with the sun low on the horizon and the shadows lengthening, he spied a settlement and, before long, he tied up at the dock and sat down at the restaurant, surrounded by the usual mix of other explorers, smugglers, mercenaries, and the like. But one glance at the menu told him he was in cannibal country. The menu read:

| | |
|---|---|
| Explorers | $ 5.25 |
| Missionaries | $ 6.00 |
| Doctors | $ 5.75 |
| Members of Congress | $49.95 |

Puzzled at the extraordinarily high price for members of Congress, the explorer motioned to the maitre d' and said, "The prices for the first three seem reasonable, but why in the world are congressmen so incredibly expensive?"

The maitre d', taken aback, replied, "Ever tried cleaning one of them things?"


We were off to a good start in 1983. We pored over lengthy memoranda produced by the higher-ups on how to handle constituent mail, prompting one written response, "Have you been watching old re-runs of Lost in Space?" And Paul Rogers spent most of his time consolidating his position as Coleman's Nancy Reagan, cutting off the congressman from any staff member other than himself and ordering on February 23 that everything that needed the congressman's signature must be cleared by him *before* it went to the congressman.

Like many Hill rats, Paul Rogers represented the Hill's contradictions. He could be personally compassionate; I was allowed to take as much time as I needed, even during working hours, when the kids were sick. He treated me well—big Christmas bonuses, yearly pay increases, six weeks' vacation each year. But at the same time he deliberately cultivated the attitude that he was the "real" congressman. He set up a private office with the same flags that flanked the congressman's desk, and commissioned his own official stationery with a gold-embossed seal. He also adopted Coleman's scotch, told his jokes, and even started reading the same terrible pulp detective novels.

Paul was the ultimate broker and middleman. He never really "did" anything. He never wrote anything, never handled specific projects other than fundraising, never produced anything. But he decided which constituent would receive what level of attention—a letter, a call, a gift bearing the congressional seal. These were Matters of State to him, and he treated his decision-making with the same reverence as he fought Conspiracies.

He was in charge of access, too, which he brokered with lip-smacking relish, often in front of the rest of the staff as he discussed a supplicant's most personal and private problems, chuckling and snickering. He decided who got what piece of the congressman and what the price would be.

Personal power plays aside, immediate priorities were legislative bandaids for local problems. We needed them quickly. Coleman had come to Congress in 1983 under a cloud created by a last-minute campaign mailing that used retiring Rep. White's congressional letterhead—a potential federal offense. The FBI conducted an investigation, and Coleman blamed it on an overzealous aide named Rob Ambrose (whom he would later help become an important leadership staffer in the House as floor assistant to Democratic Caucus Chairman Rep. Steny Hoyer). No charges were filed against Coleman or the aide, although dark rumors persisted about what had been said and done by the individuals involved in order to avoid prosecution.

So we hit the legislative ground running—the more we talked about the future instead of the past, the better. Nor was it the time for political niceties. Coleman had campaigned as a strong environmentalist, but he decided our first priority was to stop the U.S. Environmental Protection Agency from cutting off federal highway funds because of El Paso's noncompliance with the Clean Air Act. Being Democrats did not stop us from using the Republican rhetoric of the times; in January 1983 we called the Environmental Protection Agency an "out-of-control bureaucracy" while, in other areas, we shored up our support among environmentalists.

Antidrug legislation was equally fashionable, and the race was on between congressional Democrats and the Reagan administration to see who could draft a bill first, then accuse the other of being virtually pro-heroin.

But for an individual member to garner attention, a platform was needed. Congressman Coleman had been put by the leadership on the Government Operations Committee (the equivalent of a beauty pageant's Miss Congeniality award) because he had lobbied furiously and successfully for a choice seat on the powerful House Armed Services Committee. Committee assignments in the House are sought by freshmen for one reason—money.[1] Entire freshmen classes in the 1980s would list the Energy and Commerce Committee as their top choice because, according to Common Cause, members on that committee received more PAC money than those on any other committee. Outside the Big Three—Energy and Commerce (which regulates the big money), Ways and Means (which taxes the big money), and Appropriations (which spends the big money)—the outlook for a Congressman is bleak. As New York Democrat Tom Downey remarked to *Congressional Quarterly* in 1987, "Life outside those committees can be pretty dreary. It's like a coal mine—only the people in the car have access to the coal."[2] As a member of the Ways and Means Committee, Downey was in the front seat of the car.

Still, Government Operations was worth a headline every now

and then. One of Coleman's subcommittees was headed by Democrat Glenn English of Oklahoma, an ambitious, press-hungry chairman who had honed the art of accusation to a science. Coleman participated in the February 24, 1983, announcement of a "border-to-border" drug interdiction program into which we tossed as much high-tech babble as we could. I was working on the press release when I noticed that the information from the subcommittee mentioned that drug-fighting airplanes would use "F-15 look-down radar."

"What the hell does that mean? It looks down but not up? What about sideways?" I asked our legislative expert who handled anti-drug legislation that week.

"Beats the shit out of me. Sounds great, though, doesn't it?"

"Can't wait to use it."

The fact that not a single drug-laden aircraft was ever caught by F-15 look-down radar was totally immaterial. *Action, action, action* was the name of the game, and we knew exactly what we were doing. From the night of their first victorious congressional election to the night of their second, congressmen spend every waking hour working to get reelected. Every step, every statement, every political and legislative move is calculated to snuff out opposition, answer potential critics, and create a tidal wave of incumbency. Incumbency also increases one's standing in the House. It is one thing to join the pack, another entirely to claw your way to the front. Power within the institution begins with raw political strength at home; the leadership will not waste its time on those who are not "keepers."

Unfortunately, winning elections is solely up to you: the demise of the party system has spawned the age of political entrepreneurship. Our polls from the 1982 campaign told us that being a Democrat meant nothing to the public. Hamilton College's Arthur Sanders accurately pointed out in 1988 that over one-third of the nation's population had no image or feeling whatsoever about either political party.[3] The same was true in 1983; our own poll told us that Congressman Coleman, in fact, meant nothing to the public, either.

But far from being fearful, we took on the ultimate political challenge. We would embark on a grand adventure into the dazzle of

Perceptionland—that modern mass media experience of radio, television, newspapers, magazines, and direct mail. Paradoxically, although Perceptionland is formed by everyone, not everyone has access to it. There are relatively few gatekeepers, and most of them are called reporters. Perceptionland, like politics, has no rules other than to equate success with survival. My job as press secretary was to translate the gyrations of our particular political beast into gravitas and acclaim. We would build, from scratch, a congressional persona.

"All business is local," House Speaker Thomas P. "Tip" O'Neill admonished the Class of 1982. We made every attempt to convince the public and the media that Coleman personified the district, that each piece of pork he snatched was a victory for the district.

So in 1983 we began a journey to develop an attitude in Perceptionland about the congressman: A step for the congressman is a victory for the district. The Congressman benefits personally, the district wins. Using computers, mass mailings, radio actualities, video press releases, news statements, speeches, staged events, C-SPAN broadcasts of floor debates, and other modern media techniques, we repeated this message over and over in a thousand different ways to drive home a single concept: the man *is* the district.

We argued constantly that the federal government was or should be paramount in the voters' lives. If the federal government appeared inconsequential, voters might not care who their congressman was (a major no-no). This is the fundamental problem of all politicians: getting the attention of people who don't care.

Besides, these were dangerous political times; we had parachuted into a maelstrom of national and global issues. The Reagan Revolution was on the march—"boots on the cobblestones," the liberals muttered darkly—and the House of Representatives was the bastion of Democratic resistance on issues such as taxes, the economy, jobs, Central America, the military buildup, school prayer, and abortion.

But the tide was slowly starting to shift our way. With unemployment hovering at 10.4 percent in January 1983 (the postwar high was the previous month's 10.8 percent), Democrats had won 26 new seats, which allowed Speaker O'Neill to regain control of the House from a coalition of Republicans and conservative Democrats. Lots of partisan elbows were being thrown, to the extent that Minority Leader Robert Michel charged in early 1983 in a fight over proposed new rules for the House, "Mr. Speaker, you are converting this body of representatives into robots in a glass-covered dome, who come only when they are called, speak only when they are told, and cast their vote only when it is unavoidable."

*Great,* I thought. *Things are finally returning to normal.*

Pundits never fail to quote English member of Parliament, Edmund Burke, who proclaimed in his speech to the Electors of Bristol in 1774, "Your representative owes you, not his industry only, but his judgment; and he betrays instead of serving you if he sacrifices it to your opinion."

Members, on the other hand, never forget the modern Democratic committee chairman's trenchant observation that in the very next election, "Burke got his ass sent packing home," which in fact he did. All policy, all issues, all debate for first-term members are seen through the dark glass of that first reelection campaign. And I learned one thing immediately: we were going to *talk* Democratic, but we were going to *do* survival.

Shortly after returning from the March trip to Texas, I received a telephone call from a local television producer in El Paso. His voice was low and somber.

"John, I . . . I don't know who else to take this to," he began right away. "It's weird and someone's life might be at stake. Can I have your word that this will stay just between us?"

"Us and Coleman."

"Uh . . . okay. Here's the deal. I have a friend who works at William Beaumont Army Medical Center at Fort Bliss. A trauma specialist. He's scared, frightened, and doesn't know who to turn to, so he came to me. A short while ago, he was drinking across the border in Juarez with a bunch of his buddies. Then the MPs roar up and grab him and take him back across the border. The next thing he knows, he's in a U.S. military jet transport with a bunch of other trauma specialists and they're heading south. A few hours later, he's near a provincial capitol in rural El Salvador. Some kind of field MASH unit? I don't know. Anyway, he found himself treating all kinds of casualties."

He paused. "They were *American* dead and wounded. None of them in regular uniforms. He says CIA and maybe some military. What happened was that the FMLN had ambushed the government's elite Atlacatl Battalion and wasted a bunch of our guys along with the Salvadorans."

"Jesus," I said.

"Yeah. So he does what he can. Gets 'em ready for sending back to the States—some of them to Beaumont or the big U.S. army trauma center in San Antonio. Now he's back and his conscience is bothering him. We're not supposed to be fighting in El Salvador, right? We're only supposed to be helping the government. And isn't there some kind of legal limit on military advisors? Anyway, he comes to me and I come to you. What can we do for this guy? He was ordered by his superiors never to speak about the incident again."

"Let me talk to Coleman right away," I said. "I'll get back to you today."

El Salvador, not Nicaragua, was the principal hemispheric foreign policy issue in 1983. With the Salvadoran rebels gaining victory after victory, Democrats were skittish; Rep. Dan Mica (D-FL) commented to the press that we did not want to be labeled the party that lost El Salvador. On February 22, Defense Secretary Caspar Weinberger told the White House that the El Salvador government was so shaky that the administration was planning to use the president's emergency authority to send $60 million in aid.

The heat was on, but by this time, I knew the score: no one talked to Congressman Coleman except through Paul Rogers. Paul was very concerned about the report, but not for the same reasons I was.

"We're not in the story, are we?" was the first thing he wanted to know.

"No," I replied, puzzled by his reaction. We had a potential national story here. Why was he so defensive?

"Good," he said, sounding relieved. "We'll handle it from here."

He conferred with Jose Sanchez about the matter, and they decided to place a routine query to the Department of the Army.

I was furious. What was the army supposed to say? Yo, army—are you violating the law by fighting covertly in El Salvador with a lot of help from your buddies at Langley? The response was predictable. Oh no sir, the Army replied. Nothing like that around here.

That was the extent of our involvement. For the next few days I rationalized that, hell, maybe the soldier was wacked out or something, and his story, maybe his story had been fabricated.

Then, leafing through the daily report put out by the CIA's Foreign Broadcast Information System (FBIS), an unclassified compendium of media reports from every country in the world, I turned to the El Salvador section and froze. FBIS reported intercepting and transcribing a transmission from Radio Venceremos, the voice of the FMLN insurgency, that reported a victory in an ambush of the Atlacatl Battalion. The trauma specialist's account of the engagement had been verified.

I sighed. Oh well. I had already learned to keep score, but I couldn't tell if this one was a run, a hit, or an error. Later in the year and on steadier political ground, Coleman did blister Reagan on Central America. But not now, not when the congressional persona and its vital "moderate" core was still being molded. Survival was the name of the game, and in this operation it meant keeping your head real low.

To be successful, politicians need more than a message; they need muscle, and in this town, muscle means money. Lots of it. Within weeks of his swearing-in, Coleman scheduled two fundraisers, a March 26 event in El Paso and an April 7 reception at the Democratic Club in Washington (a mere $250 a head). Early fundraisers allow PACs who bet on the wrong horse—your opponent—to ante up and jump on the caboose before the train leaves the station. They also let you take advantage of your new committee assignments before you have to cast votes that might antagonize one interest group or another. PAC money is not accepted reluctantly and only after a great deal of soul-searching. It is seized with abandon, and bragged about to colleagues and cronies. It is a measure of your political manhood.

Coleman's seat on the Armed Services Committee meant that we were going after defense contractors (and vice versa). A few like Rockwell International, with a plant in El Paso that made a pro-Rockwell vote a local jobs issue, were natural allies. It took money for the rest to become the congressman's close personal friends.

By March 10, lobbyists like Pratt and Whitney's Mel Good-weather were meeting privately with Coleman on matters before the Armed Services Committee and, at the same time, helping with the April 7 fundraiser, a situation that was by no means confined to Coleman. Washington sees no conflict in this arrangement, nor do those Members who enlist lobbyists to raise money for them while they consider legislation that affects the lobbyists' interests. Ways and Means Committee Chairman Dan Rostenkowski, for example, not only obtained money from Shearson Lehman/American Express to help underwrite the $500,000 gala celebration of the committee's 200th anniversary, but he allowed an American Express lobbyist to use a desk and telephone inside the Ways and Means Committee while the same person was lobbying Rostenkowski and the committee on a major tax bill. Lobbyists need the access, Members need the money. As top lobbyist Robert Gray once wrote with a straight face, "Access is an earned, essential raw material."

By the time of the April 7 fundraiser, Coleman was meeting with an average of two to three PAC people per day, and with no soul-searching over its propriety. It was simply the way things were done in Washington. His personal schedule cards, in fact, specifically pointed out contributors and PAC people. House Speaker Thomas Foley might downplay the selling of access in 1990 by sniffing, "Many Americans believe that their elected representatives are more responsive to campaign contributors than to constituents. Regardless of how accurate that view really is. . . ."[4] But in the real world Coleman did not intend to challenge the system, but to make the most of it instead.

Being a new member can be a heady experience. In a few short weeks, Ronald Coleman had gone from being a bordertown lawyer to participating in a March 9 afternoon classified codeword session of the House Armed Services Committee's Research and Development Subcommittee on strategic nuclear systems and a briefing on the same subject that evening in the White House. (His schedule read: "PRESIDENT BRIEFING ON DEFENSE. HIGHLY CLASSIFIED. Cocktails and finger sandwiches.") In this rarified atmosphere, voting your conscience could mean losing the next election. No longer in the game. Off the circuit and out of the loop. And if politicians are good enough and lucky enough, they're ready by the time they take office to do anything and say anything to keep their hand in the game. As former member Dan Marriott noted in *Roll Call* in 1990 when contemplating a comeback election, "The fever's got me. And the only cure is Congress."

Votes on the nuclear freeze and MX missile would give us our first major tests in this year of seeking survival. We pulled out the 1982 campaign bible—a poll by Peter Hart and Associates— showing that Coleman's congressional district opposed the freeze by 48 percent to 40 percent. Consequently, Coleman leaned against the freeze despite his liberal inclinations.

Then President Reagan went on national television and questioned the loyalty of Democratic freeze supporters. Coleman reacted with partisan emotion and switched. "Have a thirty-second speech ready for the critics," he barked at me. "Get some *good* reasons to vote for it." That was my job: to dress up the political beast in store-bought finery, to add policy and intellectual cachet to the demands of its appetite. I wrote the speech, but having done so, Coleman flip-flopped again and voted to release $625 million for MX engineering and flight testing.

When the press pointed out the apparent inconsistency between Coleman's support for both the freeze and the MX, Coleman said they were "separate steps to achieve the same goal of arms control. A nuclear freeze is a supportable goal for nuclear arms negotiators, while the MX in the meantime is a step toward interim stability." My private reaction to Coleman was: you are not making sense. But what counts in Perceptionland is not logical consistency but smoothness of style. When confused or cornered, sound authoritative. Besides, we had no monopoly on lame logic. Then-Democratic Rep. Phil Gramm demonstrated his own intellectual strength by arguing that our current missiles with three warheads were "dangerous" and thus should be replaced by one with ten warheads which were presumably less so.

We also learned another painful lesson: be consistent within any given issue. After voting for MX flight testing, Coleman turned around yet again on July 20 and voted against producing the missiles.

"He did what?" the legislative staff screamed. Congressman Coleman had simply followed his fundamental political instincts to be all things to all people and split the difference, thereby enraging MX supporters (whom he sided with on testing) without assuaging MX opponents (who still didn't trust him). *Harper's Magazine,* in fact, gave him its "Dunce of the Month" award for the flip-flop. Hell, we finally decided, it's probably time to start talking about drought relief.

Something else bothered me. A Rockwell lobbyist (Rockwell builds the MX) later gave our office a beautiful photograph. The scene was dusk, and light from the dying sun streaks through darkening clouds. A small chunk of brilliant light at the top of the photograph is shooting streaks of white light down and across this peaceful image. The chunk was the MX distribution bus, descending from space and breaking up in the upper stratosphere. The streaks of light were the test reentry vehicles, zooming to their targets on earth. We named this picture, understandably, the End of the World.

It is a sobering image. The MX missile can carry up to twelve Mk-21 reentry vehicles without stacking, all with W87 nuclear warheads that can be retargeted while in flight. The maneuverable W87 is extraordinarily accurate and allows for targeting of super-hard Soviet control centers and fourth generation ICBM silos. With each warhead carrying the equivalent of 300,000 to 475,000 tons of TNT, it packs a hell of a blast.

Serious stuff, in other words. But there was something disturbing about the way our decisions were made with little thought that maybe this one was different, that too much money and too many lives were potentially at stake for fundamentally political judgments. We were, after all, talking about the beginning of the end of the world. But these doubts on my part were momentary. I was still learning to keep score on the Hill. The MX might have been serious, but like those Hill rats discussing civil wars in Africa, it was still so much ham and egg.

Let me make it clear: broad issues like the future of America are not high on the agenda of freshmen members; local projects with high reelection value are. In fact, many Hill offices employ people who do nothing but bird-dog federal grants to make sure the cash keeps sloshing in. Those with special aptitude can take courses to improve their skills at springing federal dollars.

Our own program was simple: Sniff out any and all opportunities for federal money. Threaten civil servants in Washington to approve grant applications from your district. Vote for the money, take credit for it by plastering the district with your taxpayer-funded newsletters, and don't forget to rail, rail, rail against the deficit.

When the political culture discovers someone who does not subscribe to this creed, the reaction is one of amazement. Later in the 1980s, after Congressman Coleman won a seat on the House Appropriations Committee, we investigated the extent of federal projects in the Pennsylvania district of Republican Robert Walker, a parliamentary master who gave the Democratic leadership fits on the House floor.

"So whatta we got on the guy?" I asked a staff member.

"Nothing."

"Nothing. What do you mean, nothing?"

"I mean nothing. The guy doesn't hustle projects. Is he crazy or something?"


Lying low and staying local was the name of the game for us as the great issues swirled above our heads. I felt as if we were in a front-line trench, with artillery shells and missiles blasting over our heads and just out of sight while we went after lesser game with knives and shovels. It was 1983, the year the Supreme Court struck down the legislative veto; the national holiday for Martin Luther King passed. Bipartisan agreements were struck on the budget and Social Security. And, slowly but surely, the twenty-six seats picked up by the Democrats were allowing the leadership to outmuscle the conservative coalition that had triumphed with the Reagan tax cuts.

But a member's first term is spent insulated, almost in hibernation from the great issues of the day except when he dashes out of his cave to vote and dashes back into the shadows of obscurity, hoping no one noticed.

Coleman understood, if only intuitively, the sharp distinction between himself as a person and the congressional persona I was in charge of creating. He was able to step back and see his persona and evaluate it critically. When I told the press in October after the massacre of U.S. Marines in Beirut that Coleman was "gravely concerned," he complained, "I'm tired of being gravely concerned. That sounds like shit." And he was right: it was time to stop being "gravely concerned," and time to be something else.

But unrehearsed exposure can hurt. Coleman found himself in the Speaker's chair one day, presiding over routine business (freshman leadership prospects get to take their turn at the wheel every now and then) when Rep. Robert Walker suddenly asked for unanimous consent to bring up *the* Republican school prayer bill.

On national television. Coleman's eyes looked this way and that for a Democrat—someone, anyone—to object. No one objected. Coleman looked again and realized that there was no Democrat on the House floor at all, a potentially fatal mistake by the leadership. Walker knew it, and he was moving in for a sneak shot-on-goal.

Finally Coleman said in a strained voice, "The Chair will not recognize the gentleman for that purpose."

"It is in order," Walker replied.

"The Chair has the same right to object as any Member, and I do so object."

Within days, the New Right had printed a bumper sticker that read: "COLEMAN HASN'T GOT A PRAYER."

CongressSpeak is never used in casual conversations or in deals. It is an artificial and translated language. For example, my boss might say the following:

Before a private meeting with the Republicans: "No-good bastards. Caught 'em with their pants down. Now they owe me big time."

In the meeting: "Now look, we ought to be able to handle this . . ."

On the House floor: "My distinguished colleague on the other side of the aisle has graciously agreed to enter into a colloquy on the meaning of Section 12 of this amendment . . ."

You get the picture.

On days like those, I had no choice but to head for a notorious grease pit up Pennsylvania Avenue called the Tune Inn, maker of the best bacon cheeseburger in the entire Free World.

It has also become the adopted home of every professional Texan in Washington, D.C., so I guess you could call it a wash.

You know the type. They haven't lived in Texas for more than a decade, but it takes barely half a beer to get them misty-eyed about the hill country of Austin, which I understand is somewhat akin to those ravines in Africa where elephants go to die. These professional Texans run into each other on Capitol Hill receptions and immediately begin to blather about Texas arcana that no one ought to have to listen to.

The conversations go like this:

Lobbyist and former presidential advisor (B.A. Columbia, Harvard Law School): "Wayll har thar. Har U?"

Legislative director to a congressman (B.A., M.A. Georgetown, Ph.D. Johns Hopkins): "Jist fahn, Jimbo, jist fahn. How's it hangin?"

Lobbyist: "Purty good. Cold and deep, buddy, cold and deep."

Congressman (member of House leadership): "Wal looky har. Dadn't thank that old dog got out to hunt no more."

Lobbyist: "Sheeeet."

Grins and chuckles break out fiercely on all faces like a bad rash.

Texas acknowledged, Texas affirmed, Texas uber alles.

Late one morning Paul Rogers walked past a non-Texan staff

member's desk. His nose twitched like a bloodhound's. His eyes narrowed. He stopped. He looked down at the staff member, who was eating an early lunch brought from home.

"Figures," Rogers said in a disgusted tone.

"What's your problem and why won't it wait until I'm done?" the staff member asked, munching on a piece of cold barbeque chicken.

"The sauce," intoned Rogers, as if revealing biblical truth.

"What sauce?"

"On your chicken."

"What about the sauce?" the staff member demanded nervously, thinking that maybe Paul or I had snuck into the refrigerator and laced it with ExLax or pee or something.

"You put it on while you were cooking, didn't you?" Paul accused.

"When the hell else do you do it?"

"After you take it off the grill, idiot, after you take it off the grill! Nothing but a waytbrush while it's on the fire. Nothing!" Paul jabbed the air for emphasis. He was born in Missouri but moved to Texas at an early age and continued to embrace the culture with a convert's fervor.

"Waytbrush," by the way, is Texan for "wet brush."

"You're fucking crazy," my friend said. "Go away. Shake down a lobbyist. Cop a headline. Just leave me alone. All I want is to eat in peace and not listen to bullshit about fucking chicken sauce and wet brushes. Why don't you take your tape player and put on some of that wagonwheel-shit you listen to and leave me alone?"

"Jesus," muttered Paul, stalking away toward his private office we called the Clubhouse. "No waytbrush. Sauce on the fire. What's the goddamn world coming to?"

Texas is a walking contradiction. It is at once the most self-confident of religions and the most terribly insecure. Texans are proud, boastful, and brash, and yet they wonder why the rest of the nation takes such sweet delight in kicking them when they're down (an old Texas political expression, by the way).

Texans love to lord over others what they consider to be their power. Walk up to a batch of them at a party and pull out your stopwatch. How long will it take one of them to tell you that Texas was the only state to enter the Union after having been a sovereign and independent nation? And furthermore—a comment usually presaged by a practiced sniff—the terms upon which Texas allowed the Union to admit it gave them the right to split into five states?

"Yeah," I replied when it happened to me at a Capitol Hill reception, "but if there had been a back door at the Alamo, there never would have been a Texas."

"Wahll," flounced the North Dallas blonde as she pointed her surgically correct pug nose at the ceiling. "You certainly don't know your history." The guy who had the monogram of his family's ranch on his shirt pocket gave me one of those "told you, buddy" looks and followed her dark-rooted, frosted mane back to the bar.

It is no mistake that CBS did not place Southfork Ranch and J.R. Ewing in Aroostock, Maine.

People love to hate Texans. Almost as much as Congressmen. Part of it is a feeling that maybe they did not completely earn it. Most of the state was stolen from Mexico and then they used the Texas Rangers to throw Hispanics off their land by any means possible. If you really want to get a rise out of a Texas patriot, say "Let's face the truth: for most of its history, Texas was a place where northern cattle barons sent their sheep to shit for the summer." Unfortunately, some grizzled old wildcatter stuck a pitchfork in the ground out in East Texas in the 1920s and hit what became known as Spindletop, the world's single greatest proven oil reserve. Texas would ride high forever—and hopefully on the backs of the rest of the country. Who can forget the Texas bumper stickers of the late 1970s that said "Drive Fast—Freeze A Yankee"?

And today, Texas precipitated the nation's savings and loan crisis, and then in true frontier spirit, won a Texas-sized, taxpayer-funded bailout. At the same time, they stuck a multibillion supercollider down the nation's throat and laughed all the way to the bank despite attacks by lawmakers from other regions. "Texas has a cavalier attitude toward a project that is going to cost the federal taxpayer $5 billion before cost overruns," Reps. Silvio Conte (R-MA) and Sherwood Boehler (R-NY) pleaded in an April 1990 letter to all House members. "We can't let Texas back away from its commitment and leave the federal taxpayer holding the bag."[5] Conte and Boehler wanted an amendment requiring Texas to ante up its share of the cost. The amendment was not adopted.

The latest bumper sticker in Washington read: "Don't Wait: Hate Texans Early."

But don't laugh too quickly. They might pull it off.

They had a Texan as Speaker for a while, but the ethics scandal some called an oil slick brought him down hard. Texas's political fortunes were jolted, but there were still a whole lot more where that one came from. The chairman of the Judiciary Committee was a Texan, as was the chairman of the Agriculture Committee. And there was good money in it. In 1983 the average Texas member had an income of between $156,000 and $213,000, and average assets of between $664,000 and $1 million. (The ethics rules are deliberately written to create artificial categories such as these, with no apparent rhyme nor reason; there is no reason a congressman cannot simply report that "I made this much and here's how.")

Please understand where most of these Texas politicians come from: the Texas legislature is perhaps the most notorious public assemblage in America. Lobbyists pass out $10,000 checks on the Senate floor. And the state has a wide-open, take-no-prisoners style of campaigning. Party affiliation aside, Texas pols know that if you can't give 'em a good show, you don't belong in the race. Texans expect their politics to provide a certain amount of comic relief, too. In the 1990 race for the Republican gubernatorial election, candidate Jack Rains, the secretary of state, announced a ten-point plan to improve education. When he released the plan's details, it had nine points. Rains blamed the discrepancy on aides educated in the faulty school system.

Texas is oil and gas. "Ulngs"—one-syllable Texan again. "It's an 'ulngs' vote," Congressman Coleman would tell our legislative staff as he dismissed eight hours of research and analysis that backed a recommendation on a vote. If anything even remotely resembled an "ulngs" vote, all debate was over and we were for it in the biggest and baddest way possible.

★  ★  ★

We had supported the important compromises of 1983 on Social Security, jobs, and the War Powers Act. We had dodged the deficit debate—but so had Ronald Reagan, and that meant we were covered. We had danced around hard substance such as broadcast and cable deregulation and interest and dividend withholding. We had voted to raise the debt limit from $1.389 trillion to $1.49 trillion. By the end of 1983, our fundamental building blocks were set.

Above all, we looked for nonpolitical, nonpartisan, *local* issues to champion by playing on El Paso's historical sense of powerlessness, by becoming, in a sense, "the voice of the border." Coleman had formed and chaired the bipartisan Congressional Border Caucus, whose first rule was to take up only issues its members had already agreed upon. Its impact was summarized neatly by Scripps-Howard's Bob Duke, who observed that when Coleman stood in the House chamber to lecture his colleagues about the border, ". . . Congressmen yawn. Some use the time to answer nature's call. Few listen." True, but not important. What counted was the ability to repeat the words "bipartisan Border Caucus" as part of our political mantra, over and over and over again as we tried to make local projects the definition of Coleman's job performance rating. The mantra worked. Although by February 4, 1984, no members were attending meetings personally, we would promote the image of the Caucus to the point where one newspaper, in its 1984 endorsement of Coleman's reelection, said that the caucus "gives us a much more compelling voice in a place where our existence was all but forgotten."

To paraphrase football personality John Madden, we were moving Perceptionland's political pile forward. And most importantly, we had made no lasting mistakes. Run right on defense, run left on social programs. Duck on Lebanon and Grenada. Everything was in place. We had not yet been thrown from the political beast, which can prove to be a politician's undoing. (Former Speaker Jim Wright was not brought down by grand national issues, but by his dealings with dubious characters from his district.)

We ended 1983 with a real kick, a Christmas scare letter to thirty thousand senior citizens about President Reagan and Social Security, claiming the president wanted to cut cost-of-living adjustments (COLAs). And with a good showing in the 1984 election, we envisioned ourselves rocking and rolling with the best of them. We would, as the Texans say, be pissing mightily in the tall grass and be ready to run with the big dogs.

All we had to do now was get through the Silly Season first.

# CHAPTER FIVE

# THE SILLY SEASON

"OBVIOUSLY," then-U.S. Rep. Phil Gramm (R-TX and currently a U.S. Senator) thundered in a National Republican Congressional Committee press release, "Ronald Coleman chose to support communism rather than the people of this country."

We were actually supporting President Ronald Reagan, who wanted to use international loans to help wean countries such as Poland and the People's Republic of China away from the Soviet Union's influence (remember, the Cold War was very icy back then). The legislation "will provide critical development resources for countries of strategic importance to the United States," the president wrote Congress on the eve of the vote. But his fellow Republican Phil Gramm offered an amendment to forbid the United States from participating in loans through the International Monetary Fund to "communist dictatorships." The Republican White House opposed Gramm's amendment, and President Reagan had called Congressman Coleman personally to ask him to vote against Gramm's amendment.

That's supporting communism.

Welcome to the Silly Season.

The Silly Season is not fun. It is ugly and putrid and disgusting. It is also where true Hill rats earn their money.

How any politician blunts an attack such as Rep. Phil Gramm's is an art, not science. Amazingly, the media do not dismiss such charges out of hand. Instead of reporting something along the lines of "in a raving that would land someone who was not a United States congressman in jail, and possibly the psycho ward, frothing right-winger Phil Gramm today babbled uncontrollably that . . . ," they will state with a straight face that "Phil Gramm today accused Ronald Coleman of supporting communism." If, in a fit of self-righteousness, you do nothing, they will write "and Ronald Coleman had no comment." If you deny it, they will write, with equal aplomb, "which Ronald Coleman denied"—almost as bad. This is not the kind of story politicians want to see. So you drop everything, make dozens of telephone calls telling reporters that Coleman was *supporting* President Reagan and that the loans would be used to wean transitional nations *away* from communism, not towards it, and when you are finished faxing your paper tracks all over town, you have only proven that Congressman Phil Gramm is still as crazy as everyone knew he was in the first place.

This particular episode took place in 1983, but it foreshadowed what freshmen offices would have to endure in the reelection year of 1984. Democrats, of course, do the same thing to Republicans, only not as well. The Silly Season is a political bacchanal. It is the season of Anything Goes, of wild claims and counterclaims. There is no charge too wild, no assertion too crazy not to capture media attention. In Texas, for example, Republicans attempt to convince whoever will listen that they will win a majority of the state's twenty-seven congressional seats, something they have not done since Reconstruction and something they probably never will do until the Apocalypse. Democrats embark on fantasies that culminate in nominating people like Michael Dukakis to run for president. The Silly Season is a time of intoxicating madness, when everything around you in the nation's legislature seems ready to burst.

There are ways to deal with the Silly Season, though, and it starts with hitting first.

In Coleman's office, to inoculate ourselves against such attacks, we planned to send roughly 2.3 million pieces of congressionally franked mail for 1984. These letters would not only continue to cement Ronald Coleman's persona in the minds of El Paso voters but, equally important, allow us literally to publish more about the congressman than the local newspapers if they should run negative stories.

An offensive posture was necessary because 1984 was our pivotal year. The big events of the 1980s were still to come: Congressman Coleman's original investigation of Lt. Col. Oliver North's secret contra operation, for which North and former National Security Advisor John Poindexter were indicted; his emergence as a prime-time wheeler-dealer on the House Appropriations Committee; his role as a national spokesman on U.S.-Mexico relations and the border; his national radio addresses in response to President Reagan's Saturday talks; his internal maneuverings as one of Speaker Jim Wright's lieutenants; in 1983 we were just one more freshman office, fighting to get reelected.

It was a year to turn inward, to ignore national issues even further, to concentrate solely on the political survival of a single member of Congress.

We also had an attitude problem, and unfortunately it started with me.

Most congressmen are press hogs. It is the nature of their egos as well as of their business. They live and die by their coverage; the quickest way to perish, as they say on the Hill, is to walk between the voracious Rep. Ron Wyden (D-OR) and a television camera. But Congressman Coleman was curiously different. He had a remoteness to him that came across in the press; some called it arrogance. He did swagger a bit, I have to admit. But his attitude toward the news media was largely the result of ten years of being a leading liberal in a town whose largest newspaper was run by old guard conservatives. And the congressman's natural defensiveness was bolstered by our staff director, Paul Rogers, who still carried his Jimmy Carter White House posture with him.

As a result, my role became quite different from that of most Capitol Hill press secretaries. I was not simply to "get" press for Coleman, I was to be his spokesman in name as well—"Coleman press secretary John Jackley charged today that . . ." It violated every norm of congressional news management. It also meant that I had to take all the personal hits. A final, and possibly deciding factor, was that Paul Rogers purposely and successfully limited Coleman's accessibility to the media—the *Dallas Morning News*, the Associated Press, the *New York Times*—take your pick. He could not control what Coleman said, but he could control me. His power became such that he could even decide whether or not Coleman would be told about a call from the press. From the standpoint of Coleman's own good, I might add, that was mostly advantageous.

Paul specialized in press wars. At any given moment, we might have two, three, or more separate vendettas underway against offending members of the media. Nearly all were fomented by Paul, who felt he did not need the congressman's permission to start a Press War. I often had to make lists to remember who I was allowed to speak to. Paul was in charge of Conspiracies, which of course were Everywhere. Unfortunately, the only brake on his paranoia toward the media was me. And not having the courage to confront reporters himself, he ordered me to do it.

I usually made sure something got lost in the translation.

A typical conversation would invariably begin with "Chickenshit motherfuckers!!!" booming from out the inner depths of Paul's private office. I would place my head in my hands. Paul would storm out, offending clip in hand.

The next sentence would be one of two things: "I want you to get this sorry bastard on the telephone . . ."; or, "It is hereby the policy of this office not to speak with this sorry bastard . . ."

And so on.

The opening skirmish began in May 1983 when Coleman himself ordered me to prepare a memorandum detailing the high crimes and misdemeanors of the Gannett-owned newspaper in El Paso, the *Times*. Coleman thought it was outrageous that the paper would run a story on his personal finances titled, "Coleman Owes El Paso Banks," even though it was perfectly true, having been culled from Coleman's own disclosures. Admittedly, the *Times* had not run stories on five press releases we had recently issued. In any case, I never did discover what happened with the memorandum. Perhaps the congressman and Paul kept it on their desks for muttering purposes only.

Here is a sample dialog from a typical staff meeting (May 23, 1983) on how to avoid being tagged as anti-environment for opposing federal sanctions against El Paso for noncompliance with the Clean Air Act:

The congressman (somewhat agitated at the loss of dignity from having to explain why opposing compliance with the Clean Air Act was not anti-environment):

"Get a letter or column published to clear up the Clean Air situation. Maybe the *Herald-Post* will run an opinion piece."

"OK," I replied. (Fat chance.)

"What about a Bob Duke [Scripps-Howard reporter] story?"

"What about one?"

"*Get* it."

To politicians, newspaper stories are not something nice, or even useful. They are essential to this sense of self-image. They are trophies, something to be seized, something to be *gotten*, not asked for. Like scalps, they do not count for much if offered freely.

Politicians also believe that they and they alone have the right to decide what is news and what is not. Members of Congress become crazed when their hometown papers run Associated Press summaries of key votes on national issues, which are usually not the ones they want to draw attention to. The worst reactions, though, can come not from information dug up by reporters but from what members themselves disclose. In August 1983, for example, our staff director Paul Rogers became apoplectic over a newspaper story back in Texas that broke down how much each person on our staff was being paid—all from public records.

"You get them on the phone and let them know that this does not help me run this office," Rogers ordered.

*Great*, I think. *Tell the media that it is their duty to help this Hill rat run his office as conveniently as possible.* A Hill rat like me is being told by an immediate superior to do or say something that clearly goes against the member's best interests. When this happens, you punt, and try to buy time. I think I might have "left a lot of messages on their desks" before he forgot about it and went on to other Conspiracies.

In 1984 a true imperial attitude emerged in our congressional office that still persists, and it began with the use of language itself. I wanted to use a slightly more literary style in our official communications—press releases, statements for the record, and so on—a style sprinkled with elements of friendly conversation and history to make Congressman Coleman appear warm and understanding. Ronald Reagan superbly used this approach throughout his career. But Congressman Coleman, at Paul Rogers's urging, wanted a *Congressional Record* approach—rigid, arms-length pronouncements. I heard the phrase "not congressional enough" frequently in 1984, meaning that my drafts did not communicate the congressman's own sense of his majesty.

Buffing a member of Congress's image doesn't just take place through words alone. In a crisis, Paul Rogers's first reaction would be to order a position paper; mine would be to go on television or do a video, and the congressman would usually agree with me. The intellectual violence of today's modern campaign warfare means that incumbents use video to crush an opponent who relies on words alone. Written forms of communication are important to shape the opinion of educated elites and print media, but images make the difference between victory or defeat.

Tactics or strategy can be questioned, of course, but you can never raise doubts about the legitimacy of the mission—to protect the congressional persona and beat back any challenge to his or her divine right of reelection. No legislative aide would ever suggest that a member take a position simply on the merits of the case if it should create a "political problem," and no aide would really want to. Congressmen are living proof of the ancient Greek philosophical concept of metensomatosis, the migration into one body of many different souls.

With this sense of burning mission, you can easily get carried away with yourself on Capitol Hill; its very surroundings are designed to invoke a hushed and reverential atmosphere that, not uncoincidentally, extends to the members who populate it.

Nearly every American has seen, at one time or another, a stand-up television interview of a member of Congress reacting to a national or world event. Next time, look closely at the visual background. These interviews, particularly after a State of the Union address, are usually done in a place called Statuary Hall, a wing of the House adjacent to the floor. It started in 1864 as a local hall of fame to which each state could send its favorite citizen. Statuary Hall, like every other part of the Capitol open to the public, is tall, shadowy, and imposing.

This sense of imperial surroundings is consciously extended to the members' offices. They are set up as inner sanctums— protected by an imposing outside office from the voters—and they all have unmarked doors that open to outside hallways in case the member needs to make a quick getaway.

Many offices have delicate crystal chandeliers, or the huge brass version at no extra charge. Each member is assigned a "Member's Desk," a solid chunk of cherry or mahogany that members can buy for $50 when they leave the House. The Member's Desk always sits in the middle of the room. An American flag is behind and to the right, with the appropriate state flag behind and to the left. Both flagpoles have solid brass eagles perched on top, with the most luxurious gold tassels hanging down at an elegant angle.

Between the flags and behind the desk sits solid mahogany or some other dark, wall-hugging furniture, the perfect spot for framed pictures of the adoring spouse, kids, and dogs, the adroitly placed human touch midst the symbols of might and legitimacy.

To complete the symmetry of the room, tall mahogany or cherry bookcases with beveled glass can be ordered from Property Supply and set up on either side of this arrangement. And while you're at it, you might want to tell the U.S. Botanical Garden to double-time over with some nice healthy green plants, another service provided free of charge. Just make sure the plants match the hue of the crushed velvet drapes you have selected from the House's inventory, fabric which you've already coordinated with brand new, wall-to-wall carpeting that each member is entitled to install—again, free of charge (to them, at least)—every two years.

Tired of the color of your office walls? Get 'em painted any color, any time—gratis—by the House painting crew.

Need another cable TV hookup for the free color sets provided to each office? You know where the phone is.

Does the member or the staff need new bookshelves? Call and have them custom-made by the House Carpenter Shop. Same thing goes for the upholstering on your chair or sofa or overstuffed leather couch. And in case you're thirsty after all this shopping, buckets of ice for cold drinks are delivered to members' offices by 10:00 A.M., Monday through Friday—for constituents, of course, in case they stop by.

The leadership does even better. In July 1987, a House Administration subcommittee approved $7,595 for twelve pieces of furniture for the Democratic leadership, including four custom-made wooden chairs and tables for then-Majority Leader Thomas Foley, at a cost of $4,432. Then-Majority Whip Tony Coelho spent $1,765 for two other chairs and tables. Press reports indicated that Republicans on the subcommittee threatened to object to the spending, which had been approved unanimously by all of two members, both Democrats. But when the Democrats approved $2,425 in new carpeting for Republican Minority Leader Robert Michel, the threat was withdrawn.

If the manipulation and brandishment of national symbols is the primary concern of the entire Capitol, each individual member has his own personal obsession as well—stroking and stoking local mythology. Each and every office feels compelled to engage in the most shameless boosterism, far beyond the boundaries of good taste. Stick your head in the door of any office and you'll be assaulted by home-town posters, knick-knacks, maps, products on display, and photographs of local note. Ours was no different. Photographs of the West Texas desert hung on the walls alongside posters celebrating Hispanic cultural events. Native American pottery adorned the bookshelves, and one year Paul Rogers returned from El Paso with a bag of gaudily-colored tourist trinkets with which he proceeded to cover virtually every flat surface in the reception area.

But there is more at work here than simple Chamber-of-Commerce-itis. The images of the art and architecture of the Capitol and, indeed, the members' offices themselves, symbolize and reinforce a simple message: The member *is* the district.

Politics can take a toll on your personal life, too. "You never give me a straight answer about anything," my wife complained once, and with some justification.

"I'm not paid to give straight answers," I replied without thinking. "And that's exactly my point."

What's the matter with people, I would sulk to myself. Don't they know how important a skill that is? Don't they understand how the Hill *celebrates* this behavior? But the moment passed and I let it fade into the shadows, losing the chance to learn. I was young and still early into the Game. It was not only the wrong time for straight answers, but for questions as well.

Preliminary evaluations in early 1984 of our congressional persona were high. The conservative *El Paso Times* noted a "curious blend of liberal and moderate positions," while in Washington, *Congressional Quarterly* reported that the congressman had supported conservatives 48 percent of the time and opposed them 49 percent of the time. "Right on the money," Coleman grinned. Freshman members seek balance above all and avoid any extreme like the plague. Success was not the outcome of the votes on the issues themselves, but their cumulative impact on the congressional persona.

The pleasant lull did not last long.

Reps. Coleman, Tom Luken and Pat Schroeder were the only Democrats on the House floor on January 24, 1984, when out of the blue, conservative Republicans requested unanimous consent to bring up constitutional amendments banning federally funded abortions, permitting prayer in public schools, and requiring a balanced budget. Republican Reps. Newt Gingrich, Robert Walker, and other young Turks had undertaken a sort of guerrilla theater to embarrass House Democrats.[1] Coleman was forced to object.

The day before, Gingrich had asked for four hours a day for special orders—lengthy speechifying sessions after legislative business was over for the day—for every day the House was in session in 1984, presumably to continue Republican attacks on House Democrats. House floor proceedings were now televised, and C-SPAN was rapidly developing a national audience.

It may seem strange to read today that politicians were once afraid of these issues, but Democrats in the mid-1980s were still smarting from the 1978 and 1980 Republican victories. We held one of our innumerable Crisis Meetings immediately after the smoke cleared that afternoon. Coleman's normal position in a staff meeting was as horizontal as the physics of his chair would allow. Today he was hunched over his desk, lips pursed, chin twitching, eyes narrowed.

The only thing noisier than a politician squealing for credit is one running for cover. "Figure out why it was different from the Equal Rights Amendment," he snapped, referring to legislation passed by the Democrats the exact same way. "We'll call it a smokescreen to hide Reagan's deficits. Plus I'm gonna move in the Whip meeting that a member of the leadership should be on the House floor at all times." The Speaker would help the next day when he slapped down Representative Walker by refusing to entertain unanimous consent requests unless cleared by the leadership of both parties, a move that gave the Democrats veto power over Republican requests.[2]

We were still nervous. We had plenty of good excuses, but in the Silly Season it all added up to Congressman Coleman single-handedly killing all those treasured New Right constitutional amendments. So we started another frenzied round of calling reporters and drafting statements claiming that what Coleman was really opposed to was Representative Walker's procedure, not necessarily the substance. Sometimes it worked.[3] The problem, of course, from the Republicans' perspective, was that their bills were being prevented from receiving any legislative consideration at all, thoughtful or otherwise, but all that was irrelevant now that the political battle had been joined.

Strategy in the House is not so much deciding how to vote as what to vote on. Democrats might have opposed those Republican constitutional amendments on abortion, school prayer, and a balanced budget, but they were not about to vote against them.

Like most congressional offices, ours placed a great deal of emphasis on "statements," preferably brandished. A sense of unreality prevails in Capitol Hill crises. Whenever we pressured someone, we would hint darkly that "the Congressman is prepared to issue a statement," reacting in much the same fashion as New Guinea aborigines who shake painted tree bark at a threatening presence. The Hill pretends that its version of reality is the world's. You learn to define your problems and your solutions by House rules; you give House answers to real world questions, House solutions to real world problems. This was our biggest blind spot. The country wanted its problems solved, not tabled in committee or in conference. But those are the tools of the House, and members react with anger and disgust when We The People refuse to express their gratitude upon being granted a member's attention.

Members of Congress are capable of doing anything when a challenger yips at their heels. Since we were running hard to the right on defense—always a good bet in an election year—our summer defense newsletter was strongly influenced by our opponent's charges of being too liberal. At the same time, our campaign polling revealed that Coleman should not be seen as merely anti-Reagan, but as someone with his own defense platform. Coleman's potential weakness was with Anglo male voters in certain middle-class neighborhoods. Since we had a tape of every registered voter in the district in our congressional computer, identifying those Anglo males was easy. In the part of a newsletter that focused on the Middle East, I sharpened the strategic picture, writing, "We cannot afford to allow the Syrians, a puppet regime with the strings coordinated from Moscow, to gain another strategic foothold in the eastern Mediterranean. . . ."[4] Then I highlighted the congressman's support for defense projects at Fort Bliss, our local army base, turned scattered votes on strategic systems into something approaching a coherent philosophy, and voiced support for beefed-up conventional forces.

This sort of rhetoric was deplored by the foreign policy types on our legislative staff, who knew that the Middle East and U.S. defense policy were a lot more complicated than that. But in times like these on our Hill, those of us who have to get things done prevail over those charged with uncovering the truth.

"But this isn't the Council on Foreign Relations," I would tell the foreign policy experts. "It's a typical congressional in-your-face newsletter. Three points and a cloud of dust. Besides, it's the Eighties. Ronald Reagan versus the Evil Empire. The Cold War works." His Democratic party allegiance aside, Coleman himself had no personal concept of strategic or diplomatic affairs; that was left to me. Our position evolved, without direction on the part of the congressman, into a middle-of-the-road internationalist approach that gave us plenty of ways to get through the Silly Season.

If the Silly Season makes us dance, the Numbers call the tune. The Numbers are the holy entrails of public opinion read and interpreted by your pollster or political consultant. The Numbers run everything. There is nothing more pathetic than seeing a previously politically healthy member of Congress, pasty-faced and clutching his stomach, knowing that no matter how he votes, his Numbers will drop. When you've got a Numbers problem, word spreads quickly in funereal tones. Walking through the Rayburn Room, a massive mahogany-paneled open meeting room just off the House floor, you'll hear conversations like this:

"Hey, you hear about poor Jim?"

"Sinking like a fucking rock, that's for sure."

"Has he flatlined yet?"

"Might not be that bad."

"Yeah. I heard BIPAC [a business political action committee] isn't going to downgrade him into the marginals for another week."

"Probably nothing a couple hundred grand couldn't cure."

"No shit."

Unfortunately for members, campaign contributions follow Numbers. PACs and other handicappers keep lists of every congressional race in the country. "The marginals" mean incumbent members who might not win hands down. PACs do not place bets—

campaign contributions—on long shots. They back winners who can produce for them. Bad Numbers are hard to hide. Members with good Numbers spread them all over town, even, I sometimes suspect, on bathroom walls. So when a member does not brag about his Numbers in an election year, the handicapping crowd not only gets suspicious—it gets tight.

Numbers tell you more than who is winning or losing; they tell you how to get the other guy. When our Numbers specialist argued in October 1984 that it was time to attack Coleman's Republican opponent, he looked at the man's "negatives"—special-interest support and "inexperience." The inexperience charge would work with "Coleman Target Voters, Hispanics aged 18–49, Working-Class Anglos, and Rural Voters." Accusing our opponent of being tied to special interests would shore up "Weak Coleman Voters, Anglos aged 18–49, and White Collar Anglos." As our specialist concluded, "this information should allow us to tailor these charges against [the opponent] to the particular audience that is being addressed. Moreover, we need to make the special interest charge against [the opponent] before he raises it with us."[5] Coleman had raised $136,692 from political action committees in 1982 and was on his way to taking $200,860 in 1987.

Silly Season Numbers can produce a special form of insanity in a congressional office. Two of our staff members once fell into an argument over whether or not a newsletter should be in English or Spanish. "It's *got* to be bilingual," demanded a woman I'll call Mariana. "More than half the women in the entire congressional district are Hispanic. I mean, don't we want to reach the people who need this information the most?"

"It's symbolic crap that we don't need," retorted our Numbers guy. "The Numbers say we've got to reduce Coleman's gap with Anglo females. And there's some racial antagonism out there. We all know that. So what are we going to do? Is this mailing supposed to make us all feel warm inside or is it supposed to get the job done?"

Mariana had her "growing up on the picket line" look so I interrupted quickly.

"Look, why don't we do this," I offered. "Let's do a computer sort for females only. We'll divide that list into two parts, Anglo and Hispanic. We can put all *your* shit"—I pointed to her—"in a Hispanic newsletter. We'll double the size, make it bilingual. For the Anglos it'll be English only and cut out the welfare talk. Maybe we'll do something for Yuppie housewives worried about their IRAs. If anyone complains we'll tell 'em we're just trying to be responsive to the entire community. I can handle that part with the press if it goes public. Whaddya say?"

"What the hell, why not?" they both agreed.

The meeting had, on the whole, gone well. Everything on the Hill becomes an "issue," manageable, malleable, and massageable. The message loud and clear from Paul Rogers was that the "women and family" train was leaving the station and we had better get on board. Congressman Coleman's congressional persona was thus to be further defined in yet another newsletter. It would need a little day care, some child support enforcement, maybe a paragraph or two about spousal IRAs. And, oh yeah, don't forget missing kids, what with those pictures popping up on the shopping bags and all that. Throw in some health and nutrition tips, a couple of hot-line numbers, a few photos of the congressman with a grandma or two, and presto! the Congressman has now become a caring, "pro-family," politician. A hundred thousand copies later and the odds are that most people will think so too.

June brought us two interesting highlights. The first was a reelection endorsement by the *El Paso Herald-Post*. Rogers wrote me on a copy of the clipping: "Bronze or otherwise frame." We were reaping what we had sowed; all our hard work of the last year and a half was beginning to pay off. The second, unfortunately, was what the legislative staff thoughtfully termed the "SheepNoFuck" issue.

Valentine, Texas, is a sparsely populated town east of El Paso. It is in the middle of the desert, which makes it a good place for the Air

Force to train jets. So good, in fact, that the flyboys wanted several hundred flights a month.

"So what's the big deal?" I asked.

"Sonic booms," our staff expert-of-the-week said.

"So what?"

"Scares hell out of the sheep."

"Scares hell out of me too," I replied.

"Yeah, but they don't keep you from fucking."

"What!?"

"That's what the local ranchers are claiming."

"Is it true?"

"I think so. But so what? It's their best shot. How can you prove it doesn't? What are they going to do, get a bunch of Air Force uniforms out there with clipboards and pencils to count how often sheep fuck or don't fuck when the F-15s are zipping around?"

The Air Force officially announced on September 13 that it would fly up to three hundred flights per month. The ranchers enlisted Congressman Coleman's help and the battle was on. In the years ahead, we would redefine constituent service in a most unusual way.

Paul Rogers's fear of Coleman talking to the press on his own was finally borne out in February 1984 when the congressman told reporters after a budget meeting that Stealth fighters might have to be cut. We had no idea where he came up with that one. Upon reflection, neither did he. His announcement started quite a scramble, particularly among the panicked defense lobbyists, but fortunately no one is ever held to his budget predictions on the Hill, or else we all would have long since been on the unemployment line. The lobbyists soon discovered that Coleman had just been running at the mouth, and they thankfully let the matter drop.

Floor confrontations earlier in the year over conservative issues and liberal ratings popping up like weeds led Coleman to be buffaloed on the school prayer issue. On March 10 he came out in favor of a moment of voluntary silent prayer, which he no more believed in than he did Buddhism. It was the political beast's way of slicing the salami between advocates of a constitutional amendment for school prayer and the issue itself.

Paul Rogers privately advised our staff at around that time to start "holding your noses," that the Silly Season would soon pass. This is a window into the soul of a modern politician: belief does not come from within. Belief is what works, and one says and one does what one must in order to make it work.

We continued to lurch. First Coleman announced he was opposed to abortion but would not support legislation or a constitutional amendment to outlaw it. Then he veered left and signed a letter to Speaker Tip O'Neill, endorsed by sixty-seven other liberal Democrats urging additional aid to the government of El Salvador only after the House and Senate confirmed that the government would crack down on the death squads, enter into negotiations with the rebels, and prosecute the murderers of U.S. citizens. That was fine until the second week of May when Coleman heard that his Republican opponent was hammering away at his liberal stance. With his patron Majority Leader Jim Wright and fifty-five other Democrats backing the administration, he abruptly shifted to the right and supported President Reagan on a 212–208 vote to authorize $120 million to El Salvador with no conditions whatsoever. [6]

At the time, the situation in El Salvador was ugly even by that country's standards. A Congressional Research Service analysis pointed out that reform-minded officers had seized power in 1979 after the military-controlled political party had resorted to fraud in the 1972 and 1977 presidential elections. Political killings had reached eight hundred per month by 1980 when right-wing death squads assassinated Archbishop Romero, raped and killed four American nuns, and, in January 1981, murdered two U.S. land reform advisors. The left-wing Democratic Revolutionary Front and the Farabundo Marti National Liberation Front launched a "final offensive" against the junta, which fought them to a stalemate on the military front. [7]

In March 1982, moderate Christian Democrats won 40 percent of the Legislative Assembly elections and the rightist parties 60 percent. The House vote on the $120 million came at the same time that

Christian Democrat Jose Napolean Duarte won the May 1984 presidential runoff election with 53.6 percent of the vote.

The complicated situation in El Salvador involved millions of dollars in U.S. aid, evidence of large-scale murder by the right-wing as well as widespread political violence by the guerrilla insurgency, and hard evidence of Cuban and Nicaraguan support for the rebels. Every side of the issue was supported by strong and compelling arguments. But all such irritants were brushed aside. Our key issue was simple—it was the Silly Season.

Perhaps we were justified in this thoroughly political approach. As the Democratic New Members Caucus advised us at the start of the year, in the Silly Season "you're not a statesman any more and the press won't let you get away with it. You're a political being and are perceived as such. Pick appropriate themes and stick to them." Our theme, more than anything else, was flexibility. One reason we could afford it was that, by May 4, we had raised $170,279 to our opponent's $28,280, and the perks of incumbency were worth at least another million or two. The bottom line was money. Money does indeed talk, and in our case it gave us the power to say anything we needed to say.


Coleman continued to worry about his right flank. "We need to start taking positive angles on liberal, big spending-type issues," Coleman said the next week. "Press releases that say 'Coleman Votes to Reduce Legislative Branch Appropriations'—shit like that." I was mired in busywork that day—getting color slides of the congressman to local television stations, drafting as many newsletters as we could humanly put out before the Labor Day franking cutoff imposed by House regulations, including the defense mailing to white male conservatives.

"But you didn't vote to reduce legislative branch appropriations," I countered, demolishing his fantasy of the perfect headline.

Coleman glared and told me I just needed to figure it out.

I kept putting it off because the congressman was also insisting on a stream of ghost-written letters to editors of local newspapers attacking reporters who criticized him. Such matters are written and handled delicately, but by August, a round of Congressional Town Hall meetings convinced Coleman that we still had to "do something" about the deficit. "We have to show that Coleman voted for less deficit spending than Reagan," Rogers insisted.

I laughed. "That might be hard to do. He's a liberal Democrat. We're all liberal Democrats here. We *love* spending. That's what we're here for."

"Look," Rogers began sternly, "we need the number and we got to figure it out. Let the Republicans argue over the explanation. But we need that number now!"

Thus was born the following official statement attributed to the congressman: "Over the last two years I have voted for $31.5 billion less in deficits than the president requested." Congressman Coleman would repeat this as part of his mantra, saying it out over and over again. This moderate-to-liberal congressman who voted for less deficit spending than President Reagan himself requested— what a ring that had! How did we do it? The answer is deceivingly simple: You take President Reagan's wish-list budget request that comes out at the first of the year, which receives as much serious consideration as a two-year-old who threatens a hunger strike, and you compare it with actual appropriations votes that reflect deep Democratic cuts in defense. Presto! Liberals vote for less deficit spending than Reagan.[8]

The August recess is also the last time to catch your breath before the November election. By August 8, 1984, we had 680,000 computer-targeted letters, postcards, and newsletters in the works. Postage alone for these taxpayer-funded mailings was more than $100,000—nearly half of the $212,892 our Republican opponent would spend for his entire campaign.[9]

If only real defense issues could so easily have been solved. Coleman had free-lanced yet another MX position in May by voting for fifteen missiles, with the funds held in check until April 1985 to see if the Soviets returned to negotiations. The key vote was on eliminating all MX funding, which would have killed the program— and Coleman went with the president on a 218–212 vote. Our greatest worry was appearing to have flip-flopped yet again—not so much with respect to changing positions as to having in mind only the immediate political benefits.

But then, on the day of the vote, President Reagan sent Coleman a letter—paper tracks, armor-plating, hooray!—congratulating him on his support, noting that "you and a majority of the House agreed with me that unilaterally terminating the MX-Peacekeeper at this time would only be rewarding the Soviets for walking away from the negotiating table."

We papered the congressional district with that letter. Our right flank was covered for good, and the left had nowhere to go.

The next one landed in our face. On September 27, Coleman voted instinctively against a crime bill because it was brought up by a Republican. Oops—it turned out to be the president's personal crime bill, a big no-no to vote against in the height of the Silly Season. So within the fifteen minutes allowed for the vote, Coleman hastily switched his vote after "listening to the House discussion," even though debate had ended once the voting began. His Republican opponent in Texas had a field day with the "Great Crime Flip-Flop." Coleman's response was to claim over and over that the record would show he voted not just once for the bill, but twice. By the time our press operation was ginned up again, we were claiming he had voted for the president's crime bill *three* times.[10]

This was not as crazy as it sounded. A freshman member's persona should have jelled earlier; a great deal of turbulence lies between Labor Day and Election Day, a time when the executive and legislative branches of government begin to play a complicated, high-stakes game of chicken with the issues and legislation that have been in the works for the last year and a half. Issues in the Silly Season are massaged, not solved. Massage Therapy, we call it. It is not too hard once you get the hang of it.

In the meantime, other flies were falling into the soup. *Congressional Quarterly* reported that Coleman had supported President Reagan 37 percent and opposed him 61 percent of the time, which combined with a new AFL-CIO rating of 80 out of 100 meant we were going to have to throw some more votes the president's way. The congressional pay raise was raising its tentacles out of the gunk, too. Coleman surprised us by opposing the 3.5 percent cost-of-living increase and sponsoring Rep. Dan Glickman's (D-KS) bill to repeal it. We put out a press release on the Glickman bill and got good coverage. (Coleman, of course, kept every penny of the raise.)

Coleman won the November 1984 election in a relative walk, 57 percent to 43 percent, despite the inner turmoil of the Silly Season and Walter Mondale's forty-nine state loss. Accolades poured in. Richard Estrada, a former Coleman staff member who wrote the Texas political newsletter *Border Politics* before becoming an editorial writer at the *Dallas Morning News*, observed shrewdly that "Coleman is a professional politician, reveling in scenarios reeking tobacco, good scotch, and power, going along to get along to a meteoric first term, wresting the brass ring of national recognition on the way."

We were almost there.

# CHAPTER SIX

# THE FAVOR FACTORY

THE GLAZE-EYE of power.

The eyes seem unfocused at first, then you realize they have locked onto a distant unknown, even though something closer seems to be the object of attention. The pupils widen. The person has stopped using power; he or she has *become* power. The body tingles, and for a brief shimmering moment, the political beast simply *is*. No correlation exists between the glaze-eye of power and actual power. The experience is entirely subjective, an internal political orgasm. The beast is unleashed and can produce fear in those who watch too closely.

I saw the glaze-eye in White House Chief of Staff Hamilton Jordan at the Panamanian Embassy the night the Panama Canal treaties were signed in 1979.

I saw it again in Congressman Jim Mattox the night he won the Democratic nomination for Texas attorney general in 1982.

It is the same look that seared out of the avaricious gaze of Majority Whip Tony Coelho, the Appetite Who Walked Like A Man, and the same that accompanied Coleman's arrogant chuckle when we would sit back with weary satisfaction and sip whiskies, ties and tongues loosened, and contemplate having survived a particularly treacherous day of politics, deals, and compromise.

I saw it shine especially brightly on the day in late January 1985 when, thanks to fellow Texan House Majority Leader Jim Wright, Coleman won a seat on the board of directors of the Favor Factory— the Committee on Appropriations of the U.S. House of Representatives.[1]

The true glaze-eye of power is reserved for the big time. It is not about local school board power, but national power, the ability to say and do things that can alter the course of the country. This power is universally recognized and the ability to manipulate it is hardly the hush-hush stuff of back rooms and shadows; in today's Capitol Hill culture, it is displayed like a prize ribbon. One job-seeking lobbyist inadvertently exposed this attitude in a resume circulated to Capitol Hill offices.[2]

John Howerton's experience was typical. He had been the director of the Washington office of ASARCO for eleven years before getting the axe in a reorganization. His resume reminded prospective employers that his "substantial contact base on the Capitol expands from legislators in areas where we have operations. . . ." He claimed to have obtained a cool $1 million for his company in an appropriations bill. His "Major Lobbying Achievement," he maintained, was how to:

> [s]uccessfully turn around key congressional staff members' negative attitudes by emphasizing corporate credibility through techniques such as by delivering a well-orchestrated on-site tour.

In other words, buying drinks and sending Hill rats on junkets, which go a long way toward changing "negative attitudes." Howerton also spelled out the direct connection between winning appropriations dollars and PAC contributions to members:

> Met our corporate objectives establishing and administering company political action committee (PAC). Raised more than $125,000 over past ten years. Developed philosophy and criteria for selecting

candidates. Organized and managed network of politically knowl-
edgeable local plant managers who keep close contact with their
legislators.

Like many good lobbyists, he raised the money, picked the hits,
and worked a return on his investment by keeping the members' feet
to the fire through local political pressure.

More important than even the kind of campaign contributions
bragged about by John Howerton, however, was the Appropriations seat would allow us to gild Coleman's image by redefining the
fundamental standards by which the congressman's job performance would be judged. We would be beholden no longer to philosophical, moral, or visionary definitions, or even the political and
legislative issues the congressman voted on. Money for the congressional district in the form of specific federal spending projects
would become our measure—a definition that all but guaranteed
success.

When Coleman was reappointed Majority Whip-At-Large seven
days later, we larded the pork, claiming in a news release that
"Becoming Majority Whip-At-Large will . . . maximize the benefits of my recent selection to the House Appropriations Committee.
I can identify and support El Paso's interests in the committee that
has the power of the purse over federal spending, and then take our
case directly to the House leadership."[3] Coleman, from the beginning, would consciously define his own leadership, not by issues,
legislation, or vision, but by how many times he could make the
federal cash register chime.

From the farm bill to South Africa sanctions, Middle East arms
sales, and more, 1985 was the year Congress seized control of the
nation's agenda from Ronald Reagan, but the Favor Factory danced
to its own peculiar tune. Coleman's cash-gobbling attitude was
typical of Appropriations members, rookie and veteran alike. Oklahoma Democrat Wes Watkins bragged to the press in 1989 of his
"master plan" to secure appropriations projects for his rural district,
an effort so successful he needed wall maps to keep track of the
money. Watkins attached amendments and report language to every

possible spending bill for water projects, research, tourism—anything he could get his hands on. As Mississippi Sen. Thad Cochran remarked to the press, "You could look at his district as one massive demonstration project." In the Fiscal Year 1990 Agriculture Appropriations bill, for example, Watkins added $500,000 for "rural industrial incubators," $100,000 for catfish research, and $433,000 for a state public trust. He also won $3 million for an Advanced Technology Research Center at Oklahoma State University, $300,000 for a nonprofit group promoting commercial applications of technology, and a $200,000 down payment on a reservoir.[4] As then–House Majority Leader Thomas Foley told the press in 1988, "One person's pork-barrel project is another person's wise investment in the local infrastructure."[5]

Members of the Appropriations seize federal dollars as a matter of right. The late Rep. Silvio Conte (R–MA) simply added about $1.5 million for Smith College in his home state to the Fiscal Year 1990 Treasury-Postal Service-General Government appropriations bill. Conte even made his move at the last minute—and won the money solely because he was a member of the committee, despite the fact that Smith College already had an endowment of $294.5 million. In the same bill, Maryland Democrat Steny Hoyer took another $1.5 million for a materials research center at the University of Maryland. Both cases operated on the same principle: privilege and prerogative trump any policy, including that of trying to balance the budget.

It is a simple concept to grasp: you sit around a table and divide up the money. Anything that gets in the way of that process—philosophy, conscience, and so on—gets checked at the door. In the Fiscal Year 1990 VA-HUD-Independent Agencies appropriations bill, the members of the VA-HUD-Independent Agencies Subcommittee wallowed in pork. Chairman Bob Traxler (D–MI) hit the jackpot at $990,000 for park improvements in Bay City, $970,000 for a job training center in Saginaw, $600,000 for housing, and $200,000 for Michigan State University. Texas Democrat Jim Chapman, a relatively junior member, was only allowed $800,000 for "economic revitalization" in Marshall, Texas. Bill

Green, a more senior New York Republican, took $1,025,000 for housing.

Like at a poker game, the money is divided up with a minimum of comment. The conversations at these meetings are straightforward; they are of money and power, and the (usually) men who wield them. Traxler's projects get taken care of. So do Bill Green's. There is no partisan talk of Democrat or Republican. Appropriations and its power have created a third party in the House: the party of money.

Appropriations meant prestige, too. Eight days after winning the seat, Congressman Coleman attended a committee meeting on arms control at the White House with President Reagan, Defense Secretary Caspar Weinberger, Secretary of State George Shultz, and National Security Advisor Robert McFarlane. Coleman was now running with a crowd he had previously only been able to watch on television. Strangely, though, he remained consciously aloof except for his recognition of the political benefits. Afterwards, he expressed no sense of history, showed no heightened feelings of gravitas toward great issues and world crises; the glaze-eye of power told him that all this and more was owed him.

The immediate payoff was local. As Coleman would tell the press later in the year, "You're where the funds are and that's how you have an impact on government. You can look out for issues you care about. . . ." Coleman won the seat on January 22. On February 5, he was already promising to get $31.05 million in military construction funds for Fort Bliss, his local military base. That a congressman who had been on the Appropriations Committee for fifteen days could confidently promise $31.05 million—among other things—showed how easlily the committee was able to produce the big money. In 1791, Congress's first appropriations bill was $639,000 for nonmilitary salaries, financial obligations of the government, and pensions of military invalids. A committee member today can simply write that amount into the report that accompanies any particular bill, frequently without a vote. Larger amounts are sometimes fought over, but the Favor Factory wins in the end; even Defense Secretary Richard Cheney lost a $1.3 billion scuffle with

New York Democrat Bob Mrazek over twenty-four additional F-14 navy fighter jets. Mrazek, who represents Long Island communities that depend on the contract, wanted the money. Cheney opposed it. Mrazek won. A seat on the committee is recognized as such a special prize that in the spring of 1991, the strongest immediate public objection to Oregon Democrat Les AuCoin's announcement that he would run for the U.S. Senate was the anticipated financial loss to the state of his leaving the Appropriations Committee.

Coleman, by the way, got his $31.05 million. As he would crack in 1990, "When I come back in a second life, I'm going to be a contractor. Anyone who makes $30 million for putting up bricks is doing okay, and the government will spend it all because they don't know any better."

While Congressman Coleman would plot and vote with the rest of the Democrats, his new power on the Appropriations Committee gave him the strength to define himself by something other than partisan warfare. The symbols wielded by the committee revealed this change in status. Instead of the pedestrian hearing rooms of the Government Operations and Armed Services Committee, located in the far-off House Office buildings, the Appropriations Committee itself was located in the Capitol Building. Ironically, the members sat in between the "Rule of Justice" depicted on the north wall of the meeting room and the "Rule of Tyranny" on the south wall; the committee frequently found itself in a similar position on issues. Elsewhere, opulent frescoes depicted the members' own creation myth of the common citizen called to public service: Cincinnatus leaving his plow, Israel Putnam doing the same thing two thousand years later.

The Appropriations Committee's public meetings are as polite as National Football League linemen. In 1989, while considering a grant of $9 million to Violetta Chamorro during the Nicaraguan elections, Foreign Operations Subcommittee Chairman David Obey did not bother to bring up the legislation before the subcommittee, but bumped it cavalierly to the full committee. Obey imperiously demanded immediate approval from subcommittee members, which included Congressman Coleman.

Our staff director, Paul Rogers, was standing at my desk when he heard the news.

"*I'm* opposed to that," he proclaimed tartly. "This office is opposed to any form of intervention in Nicaragua under any circumstances." The statement was incorrect; the congressman had voted in 1985 for nonmilitary aid to the contras. But Rogers had not informed Congressman Coleman of his decision. Our staff proceeded to communicate Coleman's opposition to the outside, a decision made by the summary decree of a nonelected Hill rat. Such decisions could only be appealed at great peril; under our office's organization structure, Rogers stood between the congressman and the rest of the world.[6]

As it happened, Congressman Obey's deal faced opposition in the Foreign Operations Subcommittee itself by real Members. "That's bullshit," snapped Illinois Democrat Richard Durbin the next day. Durbin was right. Giving $9 million to Violetta Chamorro would be a foreign policy decision of major importance. Durbin wanted his piece of the action.

Obey argued that the leadership had cut a deal with the White House as part of the "big picture." You can do your amendment there, Obey said, but not here. That's still bullshit, Durbin persisted and offered an amendment to eliminate $8.6 million of the $9 million. Coleman, unaware that everyone thought he was opposed to it because of Paul Rogers's decision, ended up voting for Durbin's proposal. After the amendment was defeated, Durbin swore he would offer it on the floor. Obey began to mutter veiled threats, and Coleman, still clueless, left the room.

In the spring of 1985, while Republican walkouts and guerrilla tactics were grinding the business of the House to a halt over a disputed special election in Indiana, Congressman Coleman found out about Rep. Dave McCurdy's upcoming junket to Brazil and Argentina and scrambled to join it. His statement—drafted in case a nosy reporter asked—said he had been "selected" to represent the Appropriations Committee on the House Intelligence Committee's "fact-finding tour of Brazil and Argentina." McCurdy's press release was even loftier: "The future of these countries has become critical to the U.S. We cannot afford to take their fate lightly."[7] The official itinerary for May 26, the day after the congressional delegation (Codel) arrived in Rio de Janeiro, read: "Sunday. Entire day at leisure. Hans Stern, jeweler, will open his shop [at] Copacabana 4–6 P.M. especially for the Codel. Consulate will provide transportation."[8]

Monday, May 27, featured four hours of briefings scheduled at the American consulate before flying to Brasilia, the country's capitol, for a reception and dinner. The congressional delegation left for Buenos Aires the next morning without meeting with any Brazilian leaders, except those who happened to be at the reception and dinner. Similar scheduling demands were imposed during the remaining two days in Buenos Aires. Paul Rogers gave me a three-word order about how much to tell the press: "Nothing in advance."

Or, as Rep. Stephen Solarz's press secretary would claim to the press with unwitting irony in response to a 1989 Ralph Nader report documenting $13 million on congressional travel, "[T]he truly newsworthy story is not those who travel, but those who don't."[9]

Unfortunately, the machinery of government eventually intrudes on the fun. All the individual projects and deals add up to the budget, making Budget Day a Capitol Hill favorite. For starters, the White House always gets the jump on Congress by briefing reporters over the previous weekend and by selective leaks that put the president's request in the best possible light.

That's okay, though, because Congress has some real thorough budget-bashers up here and we always get the last word anyway.

Most congressional offices, ours included, take a first crack at the massive document with an eye toward local impact, unless you're the Speaker or Majority Leader Richard Gephardt, who will invariably intone that the budget presents "tough choices for all Americans," or a similar cliche. For my congressional office, it was border-related activities: the Immigration Service, Customs Service, our military base, and so on. It beats having to read the whole document, which very few staffers and almost no members do. Most staffers, in fact, just read the newspaper headlines and see what happens when the Budget Committee takes a whack at it.

Unlike mornings of military invasions, Budget Day provides members with the unparalleled opportunity to really tee off on the White House. The president has to take the national perspective, which is not always the local one, even for Republicans. Someone, somewhere, is going to get cut. And since the cry of the 1980s was gimme gimme gimme, congressional offices scored hits in the press by finding that one item in the budget to criticize.

Watch the newspapers carefully the next time a president unveils his budget proposals. Two kinds of congressional persona will appear. The current chair of the Budget Committee will offer either a technical comment or a carefully crafted syllogism, followed by the ever-present Richard Gephardt, who after consulting his polls and wizards will say something predictably tiresome about hard times and tough choices. Beneath the big shots, the members provide a local angle—and no one ever seems to stop to ask if cuts are good.

Imagine you're on the Hill on Budget Day morning. Every "policy wonk" is reeling from overload caused by toxic exposure to budget numbers. Legislative alchemists all over the Hill are scrounging through the document, plugging numbers into computers, running analyses and crossanalyses. And press secretaries? We're trying to decide whether to have the roast beef sub or Chinese carryout for lunch. Legislative directors are paid to understand complicated things. Press secretaries are paid to understand complicated people. Give me three things from the budget that I can use and I'll gin up enough quotes to keep us in the news until Friday.

The most accurate description of the process by which the nation's finances are decided is "clusterfuck," as one Hill rat termed it succinctly. A witches' brew involving every committee in the House of Representatives, it is designed to protect and extend the maximum political turf possible for the members. The authority to spend money in the annual "clusterfuck" is separated by law from the actual act of spending it, and both are removed from the appropriations thereof.

On paper, the process works like this. The president submits his budget to Congress early in the year, and usually in January. It is immediately tossed into a computerized Cuisinart at the Congressional Budget Office, which recalculates everything and always comes up with different numbers because it uses different economic assumptions.

Then everyone shrieks and moans throughout February and March as the House and Senate Budget Committees stage hearings. These committees pass budget bills, which then go to the floors of the House and Senate. Conference committees work out the differences by April 15. The budget committees then tell the tax-writing committees how much money needs to be raised and the other committees how much can be spent.

The other committees, known as "authorizing committees," agree among themselves how much money can be spent and for what purpose. Their decisions go to the floor, to conference committee, and then to the president for signature. In August, economic forecasts are revised because changes in the economy may require more or less spending and taxes.

In practice, however, the Appropriations Committee ignores everyone else involved in the process. If we don't like the caps from the budget committee, we take care of business in supplemental appropriations bills. The very first spending bill passed under the Gramm-Rudman deficit reduction process, for example, was the Fiscal Year 1986 supplemental appropriations bill that contained $55.6 million in defense projects at universities in the districts of committee members. "We start," Congressman Coleman told a political scientist in 1990, "from the standpoint that the authorizing committees are not going to get the job done, so we have to run the country." Since we have the money, the reformers always lose. "I feel like a hungry dog," an Appropriations member once said, hefting the four-pound budget document with both hands, "and this sumbitch is *smeared* with meat."

The committee may giveth, but it can also taketh away. "Time to get a new black marking pen," an Appropriations staffer once told me after a floor vote.

I chuckled. What my friend meant was this: any member who votes against an appropriations bill on the House floor stands to lose every project in the bill earmarked for his or her district. Hill rats match projects with congressional districts, and then call up the roll call vote on the bill from House Information Systems on their computers. My friend gleefully went about his task, striking out millions of dollars worth of projects with each flourish of his pen. Most of them were Republicans who wanted to cut the budget and save part for their own district. I did not feel sorry for them.

You wanna play, you gotta pay. Go get 'em, buddy.

Supplemental appropriations bills, called "supplementals," are especially engaging because they are almost always fought out in public on the House floor.

The House of Representatives opens for business with all the grace of a losing minor league baseball team taking batting practice. Complaints and languor fill the air. Members hang around the political batting cage milling about with pages, aides, other members, and other creatures trying to figure out what's going on and when. When the first major league prospect emerges from the Democratic Cloakroom, such as the Majority Leader or Majority Whip, the crowd's egos begin to bloat. Republicans have little power, so no one watches the door to their cloakroom. And when the Speaker himself enters the chamber, a courtier rushes up and inserts a large pole topped by a bronzed eagle into a holder. The Mace of the House has been implanted—let the games begin!

The One Minutes are about to start.

It's showtime.

In a One Minute the right honorable representatives receive, literally and exactly, one minute on C-SPAN to say anything whatsoever. [10] On good days, the one minutes are as polite as sixth-grade dirt clod fights at recess. The Republicans and Democrats take turns, one after another, and when one party is feeling particularly mischievous, it organizes the One Minutes into sustained attacks upon the other, complete with graphs, charts, shocking photographs, and other props. Members treat the Wars of the One Minutes with the seriousness of a nuclear targeting strategist and the skill of a fraternity prankster. Preppie-looking staffers breathlessly man the telephones in the hours preceding the fray, rounding up speakers, distributing talking points, and frantically attempting to convince the press that the fate of the Western world will be determined by their own member's One Minute.

With speeches such as "Protect His Mental Faculties by Flattening His Skull" and "He Who Has the Wits Metes Out the Whacks," the only thing that gets generated is bad blood all the way around. In fact, the One Minutes do little other than exacerbating a sense of panic in the general public over the prospect of the House being in session and gearing up to do things that might actually affect the course of the nation.

That's a terrifying prospect to most people, myself included. "When the House is in session, the smart money puts one hand on their wallet and the other on their gun," my grandfather once told me in his I-mean-it tone of voice.

"He's right," a fellow Hill rat said very matter-of-factly after I had conveyed this comment. "This place is completely out of control." But she also reminded me that if the leadership did not allow One Minutes, the members would have no outlet for their frustrations and would "say all kinds of wild shit during real debate." After all, my friend reasoned, "when you take 435 of the most self-important and egotistical people in the nation and cram them into three office buildings with too much to do and not enough time, you get a situation not unlike a box full of caged gerbils on amphetamines, which is not something to be ignored when you consider the potential for mischief around here."

The mischief factor was especially high early in the summer of 1990 when the House considered an additional spending bill for Fiscal Year 1990, which would end on September 30.

Democrats wanted to talk about funding the war on drugs, Republicans wanted to repeal something called Section 89, and someone or other wanted to bring up China, but the leadership aides talked him out of it. Rep. Roy Rowland of Georgia decried crack cocaine, stating that " . . . within a matter of 8 or 10 seconds the individual is propelled into a feeling of pleasure that is beyond all human experience," prompting Rep. Ben Jones, also of Georgia, to observe that "we are clearly losing the war on drugs."

The final One-Minute hit was by New York Republican Gerald Solomon, who reminded members that the veterans lobby would be all over them if they did not vote for the "clean" veterans supplemental later that day.[11]

Better fill you in about supplementals. Once the budget has been set and funds authorized and money appropriated, the new fiscal year kicks in, and everyone immediately scurries about trying to find ways to get around the spending caps for their favorite programs. One neat trick is deliberately to underfund something that has to be funded as, for example, veterans hospitals. This gives you breathing room to fit in less politically potent programs. After the start of the fiscal year, warnings start coming in from, say, veterans hospitals about to close down, which activates the veterans lobby. They weigh in with their political muscle, and lo and behold, before long that sneaky little creature known as a supplemental appropriations bill begins to start wiggling its whiskers out from under its rock.

Supplementals start out with worthwhile items, but an out-of-control election-year supplemental rampages like a tornado, as members of the Appropriations Committee beef up the sucker like tomorrow will never come. (And in an election year, it might not.)

So your regular old supplemental that started out nice and low at $50 million or so comes waddling out of the Appropriations Committee at three or four *billion*, burping and slopping onto the floor and daring anyone to vote against it. In the media–driven political atmosphere of the 1980s, members lived in fear they might have to "explain." "When you're explaining, you're losing," is Congressman Coleman's favorite expression. He is correct. All the voters know is what the member's opponent tells them: HE VOTED AGAINST OLD PEOPLE, or whatever.

After the One Minutes, the Acting Rules Committee chairman called up the rule for the "Dire Emergency" Supplemental Appropriations Bill. If the rule passes, the supplemental will be brought up for two hours of debate with no amendments permitted. Rules are important. The bitterest debates in the House occur not over which way to vote, but over which votes will be allowed and how. It is like turning over a street fight to a debating society to decide who can throw what punches, how often, and when.

In essence, the Rules Committee controls which ideas will or will not be discussed. It is portrayed to the public as a mechanistic, procedural arena, but it is nothing of the kind. As former Majority Whip Tony Coelho once said, give me process and the other guy substance, and I'll win every time.[12]

While House rules allow members to vote to waive or suspend any of the rules, four main kinds are usually employed. An open rule allows unlimited amendments, which turns the House into a free-for-all. A modified open rule allows a reasonable number of amendments. A closed rule allows no amendments. And what Hill rats call a wacko rule . . . well, a wacko rule will, for the sake of example, allow one motion to recommit but only if offered after the Smith amendment to perfect the Jones substitute, followed by three additional amendments that may be offered in the form of a substitute or separately, in which case the "King of the Hill" procedure is adopted, meaning that the last one that passes is the one that sticks even though the other ones might have been adopted previously . . .[13]

You see what I mean.

Congressman Solomon, a former Marine who served both in Korea and the House Veterans Affairs Committee, started to complain that veterans were being held hostage by the rest of the supplemental. "The veterans package is being used as the engine to drive this monstrosity through the Congress," he exclaimed. (Veterans issues are political heavyweights, and Members go to great lengths to identify with them. After the Persian Gulf War, Rep. Larry Hopkins (R-KY) changed his official biography from "U.S. Marine Corps, 1954–1956" to "served in the Marines in Korea." Unfortunately, he did no such thing, something thoughtfully pointed out repeatedly by his opponent in the gubernatorial primary. Hopkins's explanation was that military service from June 27, 1950, to January 31, 1955, is considered the Korean conflict for the purpose of calculating benefits and pensions, and that was good enough for him.) "The budget process is still being abused," Solomon continued. "Legislative language is still being placed in appropriations bills, and Republicans are still being denied their rights. Defeat this porker of a supplemental!"

Democrats in the front aisles began to make muffled pig noises. Rep. Barney Frank rose to underscore Republican hypocrisy: sometimes they like gag rules and sometimes they don't. The Republicans were outraged. Quoting a member's own words right back at him was an egregious breach of House tradition. Only your campaign opponent is supposed to do that.

Not to be outdone, Republican leader Robert Michel thundered, "This two-headed malodorous swamp monster that the Rules Committee deposited on the floor just yesterday . . . I am reminded of the chant of the carnival barker about the amazing attraction inside the tent: Ladies and gentlemen, it walks, it talks, it chews knives and forks. Somebody let this one out of the tent and if we do not send it back it is going to chew up whatever small shreds of reputation we have."

Frank responded by asking Michel if he paid twenty-five cents to peep under the tent: "Did he see the Republican bearded lady?"

Michel then called the supplemental a "procedural mutant." "The $700 million in the bill is the amount the Democratic leadership is willing to pay for a single vote on the floor of this house to build up a partisan record against incumbents in next year's election."

"Bet your ass," said a legislative staff member standing next to me as we watched the fight on television.

"Is that all we added?" another one asked with a chuckle. "There must be some mistake—I thought I put more in."

When the Budget Committee's commercial was over, Rep. Robert Walker (R-PA) was at the lectern. Some Hill rats call him the Headless Horseman because he resembles Ichabod Crane. He flaps and flails his arms when he gets excited, which is most of the time.

"Cleared for takeoff," somebody said.

The rule passed, 217 to 203, which is a lot closer than most rule votes because they are supposed to be party line votes. So the

Pope—Appropriations Committee Chairman Jamie Whitten, head of the College of Cardinals, as the committee is called—stood up and pulled a slick trick. He offered a "committee leadership amendment"—whatever that meant—to cut a billion or so from the supplemental, which gave the members the opportunity to Vote Against Government Spending and still support the supplemental.

Solomon looked like he was involuntarily passing a kidney stone but Whitten's ploy worked. By giving members the chance to cut a meaningless billion dollars from a supplemental that was larded to the breaking point to begin with, he had provided all the political cover necessary to get the job done.

Right before final passage, Republican John Kyl from Arizona, who was not on the Appropriations Commmittee, said in exasperation, ". . . frankly, I do not have the foggiest notion why we ever vote on budgets around here. . . ."

The Appropriations seat in 1985 provided Coleman a good opportunity to reinforce his congressional persona. As a fitting tribute to his newest elevation, we issued a video release featuring Coleman uttering one of the more amazing political statements of our time: "In 37 out of the last 40 years, the committee has acted as a brake on federal spending."

[The FY 1991 supplemental may have been even better: between the House and the Senate, forty HUD projects were tacked on at the request of specific members to the tune of roughly $30 million. While Congress was bashing HUD Secretary Samuel Pierce over alleged influence peddling, Rep. Bob Traxler (D–MI), a member of the College of Cardinals, snagged $1.59 million for housing and waterfront improvements in Saginaw, Michigan; Democratic Sen. Patrick Leahy teamed up with James Jeffords, his Republican counterpart from Vermont, to get $1.2 million to renovate apartments; two Pennsylvania members, Thomas Foglietta (D) and Lawrence Coughlin (R), hit the jackpot at $3 million for a "ground subsidence program" in Philadelphia, and so on.[14]

Unperturbed and unblinking, the Democratic National Committee blasted the Reagan administration for "HUD SCAM," which the DNC termed "Republican moneygrabbers who scammed the

American public . . . while lining their pockets, protecting their friends, and paying off cronies."

On July 13, 1990, members of the Favor Factory actually sang the chorus of "The Battle Hymn of the Republic" as they passed the $170 billion Labor-Health and Human Services appropriations bill.[15]

Back in March of 1985, the ugly head of the MX missile rose once again, and pressure mounted on Coleman, who because of previous flip-flopping was seen as a swing vote. As with El Salvador, he was unable to extricate himself from the webs of partisanship, and he dithered.[16] Our agony came not from conscience, but rather of politics—which vote would produce the least political pain. We spent our time frantically tallying up telephone calls from the district—six in favor of the missile and sixteen against—and in the mail, which was overwhelmingly in favor.

Besides, the MX debate was an unreal one. Any newspaper reader knew that there was not one chance in a hundred that those missiles would ever be caught in their silos, which made the entire debate over its basing mode preposterous. Like its Trident submarine-based conterpart, the D-5 missile, it is a first-strike missile. Liberals like Oregon's Les AuCoin were muttering that President Reagan had changed the country's nuclear war-fighting blueprint, the Single Integrated Operational Plan, or SIOP, to add a first-strike option, but the plain fact was that every SIOP since Eisenhower had had it, including Jimmy Carter's. The real problem was on the Soviet side: their six hundred new missiles were heavier and more accurate, enough posssibly to threaten our Minuteman missiles, which raised the additional possibility of a first strike on their part. Plus Soviet air and antimissile defenses were improving, which in turn reduced U.S. estimates of how many MIRVed Minuteman warheads would make it through (the MX reentry vehicles and warheads can be zipped around like on a video game).

Since the federal deficit had been in the news recently, Congressman Coleman finally chose the affordability excuse as grounds for his opposition, telling *Time* that "I listened to Max Kampelman

[U.S. arms control negotiator hastily brought back from Geneva to lobby for the MX], but they were the same arguments I heard from the President. I am convinced that we can't afford it."[17] At least this time Coleman was consistent.[18]

Despite these glitches fuzzing his image, Appropriations provided an immediate and stabilizing payback: in the third week of April, we stuck in thirty new U.S. Customs inspectors for the El Paso district. The press coverage was great, and the MX forgotten.

Who cares about frying the world when you can bring home the bacon?

We learned another lesson about Appropriations. The beauty of the House—and why Budget Day can be so much fun—is because the institution really only has to pass one bill per year, a continuing resolution for spending that rolls all thirteen appropriations bills into it. Usually, the thirteen spending bills are dealt with separately, but even thirteen is a far cry from the thousands that are introduced every year.

Technically speaking, of course, no explicit constitutional requirement exists to pass anything. Members are perfectly free to run amok with no legal inhibitions whatsoever (which is what most people suspect they do anyway). On the other hand, if they do not pass the appropriations bills, they will not get paid, so you can count on at least the Legislative Branch Appropriations bill making it through one way or the other.

A second type of bill is called "yo momma." These measures are legislative actions not necessarily required by law, but if they are not acted on, as one legislative aide termed it, "you're a chickenshit." Most "yo mommas" are resolutions of approval or disapproval of actions taken by the White House, such as high-tech arms sales to the Middle East.

The next group of bills fall in the category of "ought to be passed but may or may not be," such as reauthorizations of major bills like the Clean Air Act, the highway bill, and other regulatory legislation.

Then you have the bills that come from individual members of the

House of Lords, the chairman of the major committees such as John Dingell at Energy and Commerce or Danny Rostenkowski at Ways and Means. If their bills don't make it, yours never will. Ever.

The fifth kind could be called "millions of people want this one passed," something which, of course, guarantees nothing of the sort. Immigration control or Pentagon procurement reform are good examples. These bills frequently take years to get action. Finally, the last category, which includes everything else, is known as snowballs, as in "not a snowball's chance in hell of passing."

Suddenly we found ourselves in the missing persons business.

An earthquake had struck Mexico City and thousands of families in El Paso were concerned for the safety of relatives and friends. Paul Rogers decided that the congressional office would serve as a clearinghouse for information, which meant we would give people the same telephone numbers that were being shown on television, only now the congressman could be on television, too.

The mission was worthwhile, and our stated goals laudable. Our hidden intent, however, was somewhat darker. At the time, we had been lurching around issues-wise with no clear-cut entry into Perceptionland except the usual trumpeting of Appropriations projects.

The Mexico City earthquake changed all that. We had an issue, but like most things on the Hill, it quickly turned into a quest for personal credit. In a matter of hours, we churned out a press release with this headline, "COLEMAN LEADS CONGRESSIONAL EFFORTS FOR MEXICO DISASTER RELIEF . . ."[19] Unfortunately, the story developed in a direction that did not include continuous adulation of the congressman, who in fact had not been in the office that entire weekend.

We met on the morning of the 24th. "Disaster relief," Rogers announced. "What needs to be done? How to position ourselves? Where should he be now? Can we resurrect Coleman into the lead somehow?" Our Mexico specialist made the comment that it would depend on how much effort the congressman wanted to invest (which could start by having him show up for work). One of Paul

Rogers's main tasks was to keep up the fiction, even internally, that Coleman was still an active, driving force in the House. It was not an easy one, but he undertook this mission with professional relish.

This episode also revealed how in a matter of nine short months, a congressman had quickly come to rely on an Appropriations Committee-related definition of his office, which to him meant it was on automatic pilot. Nature had struck with terrible ferocity. Thousands of people were dead. Yet the main concern was political ambulance-chasing, "resurrecting Coleman into the lead" of newspaper and television stories on the disaster. The visceral urge for self-renewal through publicity was too strong to overcome.

The seduction of the Appropriations Committee was not the only change underway. Coleman seemed to be withdrawing from the day-to-day operation of the office. His public image was in professional hands and his legislative agenda had been reduced to grabbing federal projects for the district. Paul Rogers, under enormous stress, tried to fill the void. One staffer commented on his management style, "Do you know how much thinner I'm getting from having a piece of my ass chewed out every day?" By now, Rogers was becoming one of the most publicly controversial Hill rats on the Hill; Texas newspapers ran stories at the end of the year that contained harsh criticism of his role as Coleman's "gatekeeper."[20]

Questions came to me, and came again. But no answers materialized. What in the world is going on here? I would wonder in despair. The congressman has turned into a phantom and the operation was veering out of control. By all accounts, the year was ending on a sour, if not despondent, political note. But I was nevertheless personally elated. I was looking forward to something no political hack could diminish: becoming a first-time father.

# CHAPTER SEVEN

# BREAK THROUGH TO THE OTHER SIDE

THE TIME is 3:20 in the morning of December 22, 1985. I am sitting in an ill-lit corner of a large room. A great deal of activity is taking place in the middle of the room, where my wife is on a delivery table. She is exhausted. Four, maybe five—I cannot remember—medical personnel are busily tidying things up in, on, and around her.

No one is paying any attention to me. I find it both strange and disconcerting because I am holding a newborn baby in my lap. I have never done this before, and I feel that someone ought to be watching me to tell me I am doing this properly. I look down. The baby is awake, alert, and trying to figure out what disrupted her perfectly acceptable prior surroundings. She is wrapped in hospital swaddling, with a cotton blanket all around.

I am euphoric. What a wonderful little bundle of life, so small, so perfect . . . so demanding of responsibility on my part. She is the complete antithesis of my life on the Hill—she just *is*—she is not contingent on deals or money or the fixers who wield them. I looked down again. Hey—was that a smile? Couldn't be. Too early. I smile back just in case.

★  ★  ★

Things were not going nearly so swimmingly on the Hill. When I returned to the congressional office after New Year's, I could feel a sense of doom and unease that cut through the usual crackling morning talk of the hallways. The Members had been on a legislative drunk the previous month and passed the Gramm-Rudman deficit reduction bill without thinking through the implications. Rep. Les AuCoin of Oregon could comment to the *Washington Post* that members were anticipating the upcoming session with a sense of "real dread," and no one criticized him privately for saying it. Gramm-Rudman started a process that, by 1990, would lead former Senate Budget Committee Chairman Lawton Chiles to tell the press, "As chairman of the Budget Committee, my main challenge was to keep from pulling a gun on myself while I shaved."[1]

"Incomings," Hill slang for big problems, were sighted everywhere: tax reform, national security, contra aid, Middle East arms sales, South Africa sanctions. Incomings were things to be dodged, deflected, or managed. Only political fools would attempt to solve problems in the Silly Season of a reelection year, and 1986 would be a time to turn inward once again, shove aside the Great Issues, and get down to the real business of preserving our jobs.

To add to the fiscal mess, an announcement came in the second week of January that mandatory cuts of $11.7 billion for the rest of Fiscal Year 1986 (October 1, 1985, to September 30, 1986) would take place on March 1 under the automatic Gramm-Rudman process unless a solution were found. Nor did President Reagan's budget help; it was a reprise of the tired old proposals to cut popular programs such as environmental protection, Medicare, AIDS research, and student aid. Democrats were terrifying Republicans by threatening to bring Reagan's budget to the House floor, intact, for a vote in early March.

But the budgetary problems aside, the political highlight of the year's first legislative session for us was to beef up and mail out an "accomplishments" paper. Virtually all our "accomplishments," of course, were local spending projects we had inserted into various appropriations bills. Most congressional offices prepare some version of this election-year White Paper. In a massive exercise in self-deception, large groups of people huddling in congressional enclaves all over the Hill put three million here or a hundred million there, as if such offerings could actually control the deep rumblings of the earth below the political fault line. Members and Hill rats alike seemed to believe that if the printed money and the position papers that directed them were papered all over the political Mount St. Helens of the world, literally placed on the ground atop the rock and the dirt, and as long as the volcano did not burp, the programs and money would have worked. Members and staff repeat this process year after year until the political earth indeed does rumble. Then they rebuild the same way, reasoning that they must have put the money and position papers in the wrong place; it would have been heresy to contemplate that something was dreadfully wrong with their Congressional answers in the first place.

Election years are not known for their sense of subtlety. A congressional office's atmosphere is increasingly dominated by an obsession with the reelection campaign, and official resources are a primary weapon. On January 6, Paul Rogers directed me, "We should gear up congressional awards and any other 'official conferences' for this year." Within weeks, the congressional office would resemble a war room. Media reports from the district about Coleman's Republican opponent were immediately monitored and responses to opposition campaign charges were prepared by the legislative staff on an instant's notice. The congressional fax machine was worked overtime. Financing the campaign became a nonstop hustle for dollars, and our legislative activities reflected it. At the same time, the congressman and Rogers became more and more convinced that the Texas newspapers were out to end his career. Any press coverage that mentioned Coleman's opponent or that acknowledged that the political contest even existed was deemed dangerous.

Matters would worsen as the November elections drew closer. Rogers went on a verbal rampage on October 22, 1986, yelling in response to yet another press outrage, "Chickenshit press! You tell reporters they're chickenshit and insulting . . . [They don't let you] be a congressman during a campaign, but people don't quit calling because they don't need help. Tell reporters that." He believed that the press should treat our "congressional" news releases with deference and gratitude, that reporters should accept without a murmur our artificial division between a statesmanlike "congressional" persona and a grubby "political" one.

I tried to explain to Coleman and Rogers that reporters simply did not care enough about the congressman to bury cryptic messages in editorials. But they considered my inability to detect these signals to be a professional shortcoming, and I could not convince them otherwise.

Congressman Coleman did not attend any 1986 planning meetings until January 22, when we convened a legislative staff meeting on the session's priorities. Five days later, the *Washington Post* identified him as one of a handful of "swing" votes on the president's contra aid request, which many foreign policy observers called the first public test of the Reagan Doctrine. In an attempt to roll back Soviet power and influence around the world, U.S. military and other assistance was being funneled by the billions to pro-U.S. forces in Ethiopia, Afghanistan, Cambodia, Angola, and elsewhere. Taking a cue from the Soviets themselves, the U.S. supported local insurgencies against established governments virtually wherever the Soviet Union had established a client state or ally.

The Reagan Doctrine was a historic departure from past U.S. foreign policy, if only in its comprehensiveness and muscular implementation. Congress backed the Reagan administration in most instances; one House Intelligence Committee member, Rep. Charlie Wilson (D-TX), singlehandedly pushed the Central Intelligence Agency into providing Stinger ground-to-air missiles to the Afghanistan rebels, and thereby swiftly changed the outcome of the conflict by eliminating Soviet domination of the air.


Yet we were largely removed from this swirl of national and international maneuvering. We experienced no clashing internal debates over the wisdom of the Reagan Doctrine one way or the other; the congressman felt no need to ponder over the changing tides of history. Each piece of the doctrine was considered discretely; a moderate, defendable political balance was our goal. Since we were against the contras, we had to support the Afghan rebels and Jonas Savimbi's UNITA in Angola. As with most members, Democrat and Republican alike, Congressman Coleman's foreign policy menu would have a little something for everyone.

At the same time, the Gramm-Rudman deficit reduction process had everyone on the run. No one, especially Senators Gramm and Rudman, knew how the new mechanism would actually work in practice. On the other hand, you do not need a degree in diesel mechanics to know that you should jump out of the way of a runaway train. The trick, as Paul Rogers observed shrewdly, was to "get ahead of the wave." We paddled fast. In an early February public statement, we claimed that the first Gramm-Rudman vote cut House committee spending by $4 million. "In these times of fiscal austerity and deficit reductions, Congress must set an example for the rest of the nation to follow," the statement read.[2] Spending would not actually decrease from the previous year, of course; what had been cut was the committee's request for new spending. But this was Washington, and no number is considered real until a perception has been spun onto it like sticky threads of golden armor.

In our office as all over Capitol Hill, the year would be dominated by two potentially contradictory themes: that the congressman had voted for Gramm-Rudman and thus was fiscally responsible, and that at the same time he was supporting new spending projects that would help his district. Congressman Coleman began to back away immediately from the impact of his vote for Gramm-Rudman, telling the press in his first January interview that "all those stories assume sequestration [automatic cuts]. It's not going to be easy, but now the talk is of having to cut $11 billion, which is not impossible."

I cringed as he spoke. Cutting $11 billion not impossible? Hell, our own personal projects for the year were roughly $100 million alone, and we had plenty more on the drawing board. Plus what the senior members of the Favor Factory had, not to mention the leadership and committee chairmen . . .

"We should all strive to avoid the teeth in Gramm-Rudman," he continued. "It is more important than ever to work something out."

Ahh, much better. I relaxed when he concluded that what was needed was to "work something out." That was a good response, a political one, and certainly far better than having to cut $11 billion. If you say you can cut $11 billion, you see, the next and troubling question will be: Well, Mr. Congressman, can you please tell us exactly how? No one wants to entertain that kind of question. In politics, it is very important to listen carefully to everything politicians say. It is not what they say at the beginning, but rather at the end that counts. Congressman Coleman might "sound like a conservative as he wails about government spending and borrowing," as one newspaper put it, but at the end of the session what mattered most was how many products we could produce from the Favor Factory.

Democratic leaders seemed confused as well. At the first whip meeting in February, Democrats were warned that President Reagan's budget contained $29 billion in increased revenues. Rep. Bill Gray was given the assignment of proving that the budget was "antifamily," the polls having told us that "family issues" were of primary concern to voters at that particular moment. As usual, Speaker O'Neill offered the most cogent advice, telling members that everyone should know where the budget is cutting them locally and craft one's criticism accordingly.

But where the leadership saw crisis, we saw opportunity. Paul Rogers viewed the upcoming budget debacle and potentially draconian cuts as a prime opportunity to send franked mail opposing those cuts, accompanied by reprints of Congressional Record statements we would write under the congressman's name. While the mailings would not, of course, mention his votes for Gramm-Rudman, the possibilities were endless. After all, the only franked mailing ever officially turned down by a formal vote of the entire House of Representatives was the one to mail a copy of the U.S. Constitution to every household in America. Bleating about the budget was nowhere near as seditious, and our project began immediately.

At this point I was functioning mechanically. New babies mean little sleep, even for fathers. I would watch the congressman and his colleagues with a growing sense of detachment and resignation as they hopped to and fro on the hot coals of Gramm-Rudman and prayed for the Reagan era to end. Congressman Coleman and his fellow Democrats appeared to me as a series of freeze-frame images. I had come to live in two different dimensions, and I saw them as hollow men, stuffed with nothing but the appetite of the Hill.

The difference was that I now had a real flesh-and-blood purpose in life against which my Capitol Hill existence did not measure favorably. A baby—a new person, a new soul, a new world—was something to stand for, to die for, if necessary. More than anything else, my child made me realize that we had come to stand for nothing in the Capitol Hill of the 1980s. We worked for a single purpose—ensuring that our congressman survived and flourished. Issues, ideals, principles, even the Democratic party—all these were of secondary concern.

Even worse, it worked. We had proved that we could not be outflanked on the right. At the same time, our liberal credentials never burned brighter; the Americans for Democratic Action would rate Coleman 70 out of 100 in 1986, and the AFL-CIO's Committee on Political Education would give him an 83. From the MX missile to school prayer, *contra* aid to Gramm-Rudman, we had successfully stormed the Right, slapped around the Left, and bullied the center all at once, a string of political success stories that lacked nothing except any thread of vision or virtue.

So you ask yourself: how much is enough? I look at my daughter, and I wonder what she will think years from now. Will she wonder about my inability to reconcile the dark side of the Hill with the dark side of myself? I used to think I could separate what I did under the congressional aura from the rest of my life. But children give you a greater awareness that your life is whole, not compartmentalized; you learn you cannot turn your inner compass on and off when it suits you.

★  ★  ★

Jump-starting the congressman for the final session of the 100th Congress was not going to be an easy task. He knew that his seat on the Appropriations Committee virtually guaranteed his seat in Congress. Coleman could have used his secure seat to become a driving force in national politics by promoting a national agenda, or even a narrow local one centered on border issues and U.S.-Mexico relations. If he took this road, Coleman could soon be classed with the Gephardts, Panettas, Minetas—a rising Democrat and a potential congressional leader for the 1990s. Instead, for reasons I have never fathomed completely, a deep inner flaw in his character held him back. Instead of seizing the opportunity of a lifetime for true leadership, he was content to lounge about enjoying a comfortable life but not daring to seek the glittering prizes outside his immediate reach.

One possibility Paul Rogers and I hoped might bring Coleman to life was to have him look better on television. In Coleman's case, it meant going to media training class. He and I met on the morning of February 3 in the basement offices of the Democratic Media Center with Michael Sheehan, a Democratic political consultant. Coleman answered a number of questions while being videotaped as if at a real press conference. After Sheehan had monitored the performance intently, the discussion began.

"Well, how'd I do?" Coleman asked with a nervous laugh.

"Terrific, Congressman, terrific," Sheehan answered. "Got a couple of tips for you."

"Sure, shoot."

"First of all, it is more important how you look than what you say. People remember the picture, not the words. Don't forget the answer is always more important than the question. Control is possible: tap into what the viewers already feel, but don't try to educate them."

Coleman looked at him without responding.

"Now, when you get a hot question, chuckle and shake your head," Sheehan continued. "And whatever you do, avoid looking like you're scratching your balls or having an appendicitis attack."[3]

Improved style would be helpful, but we still needed something to say, and aside from Appropriations projects, our official actions were increasingly *reactions* to Coleman's Republican opponent, who had been charging that Coleman was a big-spending liberal and weak on defense. Our opponent, in a radio commercial, charged that Coleman "[v]oted to send our money to communist dictatorships. . . . I'm beginning to wonder whose side Ron Coleman is on."

Someone once suggested to me that a small group of nervous, frightened, and energetic right-wingers is holed up somewhere in the country. They spend their days sitting in a circle, drinking whiskey and loading pistols while they stare at each other and chant, "International Monetary Fund . . . Trilateral Commission . . . the Rockefellers . . ." until one of them stores up enough psychic energy to channel the chanting to a Republican political campaign. The person shrieks, bangs out a few lines of script, and dashes to the fax machine as the drool drips off his cheeks . . .

Well, probably not. But it's the best explanation for the Republican mind anyone on the Democratic side has come up with so far.

When I read the complete transcript of our opponent's radio commercial, I sighed wearily. It was going to be one of those years. Coleman's opponent had hired a political consulting firm named Southern Political Consultants, notorious for their slashing "attack" campaigns. One piece of literature aimed at Majority Leader Jim Wright in 1986 carried the headline, "Jim Wright: Criminals Want Him As Their Next Speaker."

Conspiracy theories aside, the New Right was still on the march. Led by conservative activists such as Richard Viguerie, the New Right was concentrating this year on winning House seats for Republicans by attacking Democrats with sharp, controversial mass media advertisements and political charges. These tactics were "critical to winning," Viguerie would tell the press in October.[4] Rep. Tony Coelho (D-CA), then-chairman of the Democratic Congressional Campaign Committee, had earlier urged Democratic

House incumbents in a "confidential campaign report" to paint Republicans as extremists dominated by the New and Religious Right. "Voters are frightened by the prospect of having these right-wing crazies in control of Congress," he wrote.[5] He was not alone. In *The Decline and Fall of the Liberal Republicans*, Nicol Rae pointed out that the growth of that party's right wing was symptomatic of the decline of party leadership and a growing reliance on political consultants and political action committees, a development mirrored by their liberal Democratic counterpart.[6]

We would successfully adopt Coelho's advice in the 1986 campaign.

Our Republican opponent continued to use antiliberal themes such as our alleged weakness on defense, taxing, and spending, as well as the image of "Tip O'Neill." So Coleman swung right in May, trumpeting his vote on May 15 against the Fiscal Year 1987 budget resolution as "COLEMAN VOTES AGAINST DEMO-CRATIC LEADERSHIP BUDGET BECAUSE OF TAX IN-CREASES . . ."[7]

"Make sure that doesn't find its way into the Capitol Press Gallery," Rogers warned me on the side.

Then, in the same statement, Coleman wheeled left to caution, "A vote against this particular budget should not be construed as support for the automatic spending cuts under Gramm-Rudman."

So far, so good. Run right. Run left. Punch it up the middle, and never let yourself be outflanked. We might not be leading the nation but we sure weren't losing the reelection campaign. Members of Congress will take that choice every time. *And as for our poor Republican challenger*, I remember thinking at the time, *poor bastards like him never have a chance.*

Then raw panic struck on the morning of June 11.

The *Washington Post* broke the story that the United Coal Company had paid fourteen members of Congress $2,000 to tour a Virginia coal mine and discuss energy issues at a dinner.[8] Congressman Coleman was one of the members. "Ah, shit," one of our legislative assistants said in dismay when he saw the story. I knew it was really serious because Paul Rogers, instead of blustering about the press, appeared genuinely worried.

To make matters worse, Virginia Democrat Richard Boucher, who arranged the trip, told the *Post* that "members of Congress . . . expect to get some compensation" for such tours and discussions. We were shocked. Things work in Washington because such obvious truths are never stated on the record. Even more alarming, his statement was perfectly true.

A front-page hit in the *Washington Post* is a political body-blow, and we floundered for the better part of the morning. We had a sense that if we did not handle this one properly, it could conceivably be the beginning of the end. One possibility was to defend aggressively the practice of pocketing personal payments for appearances and speeches, the tack taken by Oregon Democrat Ron Wyden, who had also been exposed by the *Post*. Wyden's nickname on Capitol Hill is "Geraldo" for his tabloid-style approaches to issues and the news media. But we were in an election year with a potentially strong and definitely well-funded opponent, and Wyden's attempt to brazen it out was not feasible for us. To make matters worse, Congressman Coleman was offering no direction; we were going to have to figure it out on our own. (Wyden would later decide not to accept the money.)

Compounding the image problem, *Post* reporter Donald Baker had obtained a copy of Boucher's invitation, which called the coal company's private jet—on which the members flew to and from the visit—"a truly outstanding custom designed aircraft which I think you will enjoy." That meant, of course, an open bar. I knew the deal was going to turn sour when United Coal tried to distance itself from Boucher. Its spokesman was reported as saying, "We didn't have that much to do with it . . . Congressman Boucher really arranged the tour."[9]

Coleman had been invited because the Appropriations Committee was slated to fund a $400 million coal research program that included a grant for United Coal. He accepted because of the $2,000 "H," or honorarium, which unlike a campaign contribution would go straight into his own pocket. Now he appeared stunned, especially because any story broken by the *Post* is a legitimate national story.

Fortunately, a sharp-eyed staffer of one of the other members who went on the trip discovered a way out: the $2,000 checks had not as yet been sent.

"I'm recommending that the congressman not accept the check," he told me over the phone when I called to see how they were dealing with the crisis. "He went on the trip as part of his job, it was proper to tour the mine and learn about the coal industry, but he will not accept the check." My friend was not using that argument, but testing my reaction to the approach.

"Wow. That'll do it. And you're sure about the check?"

"Yeah, as far as we're concerned. I'd check it out from your angle, though."

"Did your boss sign off on the response?"

He sighed. "There's no decision yet." The allure of $2,000 in cold hard cash was still strong, even in this hour of crisis.

"Any tips on how to convince Coleman?" I asked. This would be important. Congressmen are creatures of the herd; a friendly colleague in the same situation turning down the check would carry a great deal of weight.

"Make sure he understands the honorarium *is* the entire issue. Reporters are going to ask, if it's that important and part of your job, why are you taking $2,000 for it?"

Paul Rogers supported the explanation immediately, and we got on the telephone with Coleman. We read him a short statement based on the new information. "Take that tack," Coleman ordered. "It had not been offered. I went on the trip to learn about the coal industry."

I completed the draft and met Coleman near the House floor in the Capitol. He read it and said, "Go with the statement." But he could not resist the temptation to add to his defense when he spoke personally with the *Washington Post* reporter, making the highly unlikely claim that he had not personally seen the invitation that mentioned the honorarium, and in any event would not accept any payment. His comments by this time had taken on an air of out-raged pride that anyone could suggest that he or any other congress-man would accept such an arrangement, an attitude he also expressed to the *Dallas Morning News*.[10]

Because the *Post* had turned a routine payoff into a national story, reporters from all over the country called all through the day and into the next. But the explanation worked; reporters can only criti-cize you once for doing the right thing. Congressman Boucher subsequently commented that he had had no intention of taking any money from the coal company and then reiterated his belief that only other members of Congress—not clean old Rick, mind you—had demanded compensation for personal appearances. To make matters worse, the United Mine Workers Union was furious with its supposed Democratic allies for having accepted payments from one of its arch nemeses.[11]

It quickly turned into one of Capitol Hill's favorite pastimes: the Blame Game. The coal company blamed Congressman Boucher; Boucher groveled in front of the *Washington Post* by saying he was the only one who had not accepted payment; and Congressman Coleman first claimed he had never been offered a payment, then that he would not accept it, and finally implicitly blamed his staff by asserting that he had never personally seen the invitation that men-tioned the $2,000 payment.[12]

"You couldn't drag him out of the Democratic Club unless there was an 'H' attached to it," scoffed one of my colleagues privately.

Not content to leave well enough alone, Coleman told me to prepare a letter for the rural newspapers in his district denying that he had ever received the check. Rumor had it that the National Republican Congressional Committee had sent press releases into the districts of the members who had visited the coal mine, and the congressman wanted to preempt the attack.

In keeping with his escalating sense of outrage, the congress-man's letter read: "The NRCC release states that I received a $2,000 honorarium from the United Coal Company for examining coal mining facilities in Virginia. *This is completely false. . . .* my consistent policy throughout my tenure in Congress has been to reject any outside income for which I have not performed a legitimate service or which presents even the slightest possibilty of a conflict of interest."[13] Three months earlier, his financial disclosure statement revealed he had earned five times as much in honoraria in 1985—$10,000—as he had the previous year,[14] all from lobbyists with direct interests in legislation.

Two years later, in August 1988, we learned by reading splashy newspaper headlines that agents from the FBI's Criminal Division had reviewed personal financial disclosure reports of Coleman and other members. Coleman came unglued. He ranted, he railed, he shouted around the office that the FBI had no business doing that, and besides, they did not have to do it publicly and permanently blacken a congressman's good reputation. Coleman demanded a meeting with FBI Director William Sessions, whom he had known when Sessions was a federal judge in Texas. Sessions would not disclose the nature of the investigation, but he did reveal that Coleman was "not a target." I later learned from press reports that William Weld, the Criminal Division's new chief, had been outraged over press reports of the coal mine junket and wanted to "seek federal indictments" of Coleman and the other members. "This sounded to me," he said, ". . . like a *prima facie* criminal violation." Shocked to learn that the whole affair had been entirely legal, he dropped the matter.[15]

It is good to have a baby around in times like these. I returned home that evening feeling battered. My ears rang. My eyes hurt. I prayed for cold beer. Later, I held Julia in the rocking chair and sighed about the simpler days of the past. Julia, Julia, what are we doing here? Not too long ago I would have been in a bar, celebrating our close victory. Ah, the old days; hundreds of us just recently out of college, all descending upon Washington and the Hill. There were no questions back then. The Hill was there, just there, and we were doing everything we could to get there ourselves.

Maybe the doubts came from maturity, maybe not. My wife and I laughed about them over the whiskey even though they don't vanish. But moralizing doesn't pay the bills, I realized, depressed; politics does.

I looked down at my daughter. She was almost asleep. *We're trying, little one, we're trying.*

Most Democratic incumbents were deathly afraid of right-wing challengers in 1986. We mourned the vanquished Senate liberals of 1978 and 1980. Hell, we still knew their names. Ronald Reagan's bubble had not yet burst, and memories were still strong of his utter destruction of Walter Mondale in 1984.

Our operation was no different. Congressional offices frequently exhibit schizophrenia in reelection campaigns. A great deal of confidence is expressed, privately as well as publicly. Yet great fear simmers just below the surface. Members worry to the point of paranoia that something is going on OUT THERE, something undetected by their political radars.

The main weapon in a member's political defense system is the public opinion poll. Real polling done by real candidates has very little in common with the polls the media trumpets. Public opinion polling is such that a junior in high school stands a reasonable chance of determining a congressman's job rating. But the real skill is finding out exactly who supports the congressman, who opposes him, how strong that support or opposition is, and perhaps most important, what moves the Numbers.

*What moves the Numbers.* You will hear that phrase uttered time and time again in political circles, usually in hushed tones. Through polling, campaigns attempt to discover one or two or three magical factors about a candidate or the opponent that increasess or decreases support when tested on the sample population being polled. Is it voting for the congressional pay raise? A minor legal peccadillo from adolescence that can magnificently be blown out of proportion? The 1988 presidential campaign is a good example. Images of Willie Horton and the flag "moved the Numbers" for Vice President Bush in secretly conducted public opinion polls and focus groups (a small number of people representative of any given electoral population).

So we commissioned a poll by one of Washington's top public opinion specialists, Peter D. Hart Research Associates. Hart had done the polling for the congressman's first election and even more importantly, had credibility with the political action committees. A prime purpose of political polls is not only to handicap the horses but to point moneymen in the right direction. So if the Numbers turn out well, a member will shop around the results to the PACs to prove he is still a blue-chip investment.

Our poll had three goals: to run trial heats between the congressman and his opponent, an ultraconservative Republican accountant named Roy Gillia; to test voters' perceptions of Coleman's personal and political life; and to see what national issues would shape the upcoming race.

The poll results arrived in June. Coleman led in the trial heat, 64 percent to 20 percent, with 18 percent undecided. But later testing brought a warning: fully one-quarter of those who had supported Coleman in the trial heat defected in subsequent trial heats either to his opponent or to the undecided category.[16]

The poll went on to underscore the single most important element in campaigning today: it's not the answers that count, it's the questions you decide to debate. Our opponent wanted a referendum on Ronald Reagan's leadership on social issues and fiscal policy. "In contrast to that national perspective," the poll concluded, "Ron Coleman would prefer a more localized focus on who can best stand up for West Texas . . . and effectively represent . . . voters' parochial concerns in Washington. The outcome in this election may well depend on which side defines the stakes and the issues in this campaign."

The public's general mood was upbeat, especially toward President Reagan. Consequently, the poll suggested:

Considering voters' positive outlook on the nation and Reagan's leadership, Ron Coleman cannot afford to be a naysayer or harping critic of the current Administration. . . . he must not be perceived as an automatic anti-Reagan vote in Congress; instead he should come across as having the interests of West Texas first and foremost on his agenda.

The poll went on to discover that incumbent Texas Governor Mark White was running poorly in West Texas, and as a result we could not rely on his help. Even worse were the implications of a high but soft job rating of the congressman.

The Congressman's job performance rating is respectable but not impressively strong. His mixed ratings among Independents and Anglos are a source of some concern, both scores having fallen since 1984. . . . [V]oters' favorable impressions of Mr. Coleman's job performance are general and lack specificity. To bolster his professional respect and voters' sense of investment in his tenure, the Coleman forces should drive home the idea that the Congressman is working aggressively on two or three key issues. . . .

("By showing up for work in the morning," a legislative assistant muttered after reading this passage.)

The poll uncovered more bad news. Coleman did not have hard-core support, with only 49 percent saying they would vote to reelect him. Hispanics were 61 percent for reelection, but Anglos were only 38 percent with 42 percent adopting a wait-and-see attitude, a situation termed a "major split along racial lines" by the poll. Victory at the current levels of 64 percent would depend on carrying a plurality of Republicans, difficult at best. And because his vote significantly exceeded his positive job performance rating, his totals were "artificially high" and could plummet.

The overall message was clear: KEEP IT LOCAL. As the poll concluded, "If the Coleman forces allow this election to become an ideological showdown . . . the Congressman will be at a decided disadvantage. . . . [T]he Coleman campaign must focus the debate on . . . experience and effectiveness." The poll suggested bringing out "his devotion to family and children." That would be a bit difficult given that he was currently separated from his second wife, but we were not professionals for nothing; the phrase "as the father of an infant son" would be added to nearly every official pronouncement until the end of the campaign.

Some good news also emerged: the poll did not "believe it essential that Ron Coleman have his own comprehensive plan to balance the budget." That really got us off the hook. We would not have to discuss specific numbers, but could remain on the lucrative high plane of principle.

The poll had given us exactly what we wanted: a new strategic plan by which to fine-tune the congressional persona for the Battle of Perceptionland ahead. We did not have to balance the budget all by ourselves. We *did* have to invoke "devotion to family and children" whether the congressman lived with them or not. Stick to the theme of delivering for the district, and above all, avoid (once again) taking on Ronald Reagan directly.

Coleman and Rogers made the conscious decision early in 1986 to avoid any debate on the congressman's record, a deliberation that at no time allowed the public interest to intrude. Members of Congress take a very personal approach to their positions: It is "my" seat that the opponent is trying to "take from me." According to this view, citizens and the press could be allowed to watch the campaign unfold, but under no circumstances were they entitled to have a voice in its conduct.

During the spring and summer of 1986, Coleman had become more and more remote from the press, using me to respond to his opponent's charges. This strategy prompted one Texas reporter to point out to us, "There is more and more disenchantment building up toward Coleman. People think Rogers is isolating him. It's to the point now, when you guys bring in news releases, fuck it. If Phil Gramm can respond, so can Coleman. If Coleman wants something in the paper on an issue or how he voted, let him take out a fucking ad."[17]

The reporter's outburst carried an element of truth of which I was painfully aware. On August 1, for example, the legislative staff suggested getting some press coverage by proposing to cut foreign aid by $1.5 billion. Reasoning that the public did not understand foreign aid and liked it even less, I drafted a statement. The congressman approved it. I telecopied the statement to our El Paso office, from where it would be hand-delivered to the local media. Rogers, who was in El Paso at the time, hit the roof, claiming that his decision had already been made not to do anything on that issue, to play it cool.

"Who did you discuss it with?" I asked. "Neither the congressman nor anyone else knows what you're talking about."

"Goddamnit . . ." he started to reply, but he had no real answer other than to accuse us of playing games, a charge that apparently included the congressman. Like many Hill rats, Paul was brilliant in his own way, but he had convinced himself of his own indispensability; in his eyes he even dwarfed the congressman.

One of our first reactions to the poll was to convene a legislative meeting on July 1 in order to focus on press and mass mailings. Several days later, we mailed an official letter to nearly 50,000 predominantly Hispanic voters in South El Paso on the congressman's opposition to contra aid. The purpose was to cement his base with Hispanics, and it worked. He never saw the letter. I drafted it, Paul Rogers approved it, and the computer did the rest.


The congressman did, however, understand the power of franked mail in general, and he returned from a July 18 meeting with then-Majority Leader Jim Wright full of enthusiasm for a scheme Wright was promoting that involved one of Wright's contributors who owned a computer company.

"Wright sends out a questionnaire to every registered voter," Coleman explained. "Out of 240,000 registered voters, he got 30,000 back. The names are entered into the computer. Within a week, each one gets a personal letter from Wright." Coleman smiled. "See, he's got three automatic paragraphs for the question that asks what's the most important issue facing you today. Phil Duncan [a Wright aide] and Marshall Brockman, who's in the computer business, set it up for Wright. [Congressman] Martin Frost estimates the system'll cost $12,000. Have our guy check it out."

The final days of the summer of 1986 were filled with accelerating lunacy. At the top of the list was the "SheepNoFuck" issue, which was rapidly consuming more of our time than necessary.

Our inquiries had produced no results; the Air Force informed us it intended to continue unrestricted supersonic flights over our constituents' ranches. That meant sonic booms would continue and the sheep would continue to refuse to engage in sex.

Congressman Coleman did not like the Air Force's decision, and he liked its attitude even less. There was only one thing to do: teach the boys in blue a lesson in what the power of the Favor Factory was all about.

Without wasting any more time on letters to bureaucrats, we added a provision to the Fiscal Year 1987 military construction bill that ordered—we on Appropriations do not ask, we order—the Air Force to prepare training plans that did not include flying over our ranchers' sheep. If the Air Force did not do so, *all* military construction funding for Hollomon Air Force base in New Mexico (where the planes originated) would be withheld.

Surprise! The Air Force did indeed begin to pay a great deal of attention to our SheepNoFuck problem, starting with a hat-in-hand visit by Deputy Assistant Secretary for Installations James Boatwright, who offered a compromise whereby they would fly over our area only as a last resort, conduct on-site monitoring of the sonic booms, and agree to meet with the ranchers and local politicians who had given us so much hell in the first place.

Our press coverage was great. "I feel good about it," Coleman told the press afterwards. Apparently the sheep felt even better, because that was the last we heard of the whole mess.

We also did something rarely done at the time, even on Capitol Hill: we managed to send out a computer-generated, "personal" letter to every registered voter—over 100,000 people—in the congresssional district in a matter of days, a monumental feat even by the Hill's standards of excess. Other Hill rats heard the Folding

Room employees complain about its size, and I received congratulatory calls for several days afterwards.

But the real low of 1986 was reached on September 30, when a Scripps-Howard reporter arrived at the office to interview the congressman for the news service's "Take 10" project, designed to promote literacy by urging people to spend at least ten minutes a day reading. Reporters also interviewed members of Congress on their favorite books, and on their recent recreational reading.

"So what's Coleman been reading?" I jokingly asked Paul Rogers a couple of days before the interview. "Danielle Steele? Scotch bottle labels?"

He frowned. "Hell, I don't know," he said. "I'll call him."

He returned a little while later to tell me that Coleman liked history and biography.

"*Liked* history and biography?" I asked. "What good does that do? What has he *read*?"

"Well, he thinks he likes Churchill."

"Look, I know he likes the sound of history, biography, and Churchill, but what's he read—as in the names of the books?"

"Shit, I don't know."

"Okay, okay, I get the picture." This deal could turn real ugly if we did not get a handle on it quickly; we couldn't back out because we'd already committed to the interview.

The only one in the office with a liberal arts degree, I read and collect books on history, literature, classics, and politics, and I had a fairly extensive library at home. I returned the next day with a stack of volumes from which Rogers could choose Coleman's recent readings.

"Solzhenitsyn," I recommended strongly. "Gotta have *The Gulag Archipelago*. Big book, looks impressive, plus it's anticommunist in a big-time way. It'll look great for the conservatives."

"What if he's asked about it?"

"Don't worry. Reporters never read either. Plus I'll do cards."

"Okay. *Gulag's* okay."

"And Churchill. He likes Churchill, right? What about William Manchester's biography? Surely he knows enough about Churchill's life to talk his way out of any problems."

"Yeah, great. What else you got?"

We sifted through six or seven more volumes of history and biography and Paul picked out a couple more.

"Uh-oh," I said when we had finished. "The Bible."

"What about the Bible?"

"Should we include the Bible too?"

Paul hesitated for a moment, then shook his head. "No," he said. "They know him better than that."

I returned to my desk to type up little index card-sized book reports on each volume. *I'm going to burn in hell for this one*, I thought. Dirty deeds, as the song goes, and they're done dirt cheap.

The reporter arrived the next morning. My books were stacked just so on the congressman's desk. She asked him a general question about reading.

"My love of reading began at an early age . . ." he started to say— or read, more precisely, because he had placed a set of general talking points I had written on the desk blotter in front of him. "You know, I can't remember a time when I *wasn't* reading . . ."

I cringed. Then I looked up. The reporter was busily writing down everything the congressman was saying.

"As the father of an infant son, I hope to pass on my own love of reading to him someday . . ."

*Atta boy*, atta boy, I silently cheered. *Use that devotion to family and children*. Now wrap it up . . .

"Reading and literacy are the keys to everything else in life." He smiled, leaned forward, and casually but expertly shuffled the talking points into another stack of papers. "Any questions?"[18]

It was a fitting way to end September; the entire month had been like that. The tidal wave of congressional mailings was behind us.


"Sine die" means that a Congress—the two years between commencement and final adjournment—is over. It is Latin for "the jig is up." *Sine die* is traditionally celebrated by Hill rats with the same consideration for decorum that "straight-leg" soldiers demonstrate when they have won their airborne wings. *Sine die* parties break out all over the Hill; one year we simply shut down the entire hall and filled trash cans with ice and beer kegs.


*Sine die* came on October 16, 1986, but something nagged at me as I finished up a press release and tried to decide which party to go to. Speaker Thomas P. "Tip" O'Neill had banged his last gavel—and what a journey his ten years as Speaker were, the longest continuous term ever. He looked so stately, so large, so steady. He had withstood enormous personal attacks from Republican-financed commercials that made fun of him on national television. To a generation of conservatives, he had come to symbolize everything they believed to be wrong with liberals, Democrats, and Congress.

Yet, at the same time, the failings of his liberal image aside, there was an old-fashioned sense of tradition about O'Neill that I admired greatly. I looked at the naked, dripping appetite of the next generation—Jim Wright, Tony Coelho, Richard Gephardt—and they seemed empty compared to O'Neill, who truly believed in something beyond the deals and the hustle. If you read his autobiography, *Man of the House*, and compare it to the subsequent words and deeds of the new generation, you realize the human soul has gone from Congress. Everything O'Neill spoke about in his book centered on people. There were no abstract "processes" so dear to the heart of a Richard Gephardt, no pure lust for power as embodied in Wright and Coelho.

As O'Neill left the elevated area above the House floor, a sense of sadness swamped me. The old way of honor and belief had passed. A newer, hungrier, shiftier crowd with darker methods was taking over. This new group was slicker, as if the Mob had gone corporate. (When Tony Coelho subsequently resigned in disgrace and joined an investment banking company, a friend cracked, "I'm surprised they could outbid the protection rackets.") I should have been overjoyed—this was Congressman Coleman's crowd of Sunbelt bandits moving in for the kill—but I was uneasy without being able to explain exactly why.

But the moment passed, and back in Texas, Coleman's reelection campaign plodded along to its finale with the usual trading of charges and countercharges. And in this record year of a 98 percent reelection rate for incumbents (including every Texan of either party), we won every single precinct in the entire congressional district except five, running up a margin of 66 percent to 34 percent. [19]

Our experience was typical; 85 percent of our fellow incumbents won by at least 60 percent or were unopposed. So we had indeed broken through to the other side—but not in ways we would have suspected at the start of the upcoming 100th Congress. After four years and the application of some of the slickest, toughest political muscle ever invented in a modern democracy, we had turned a competitive congressional district into a fiefdom. There was a delicious irony; the *El Paso Herald-Post* endorsement termed Coleman a congressman "who thinks for himself," and the clipping was circulated to our entire staff, much to their enjoyment. The district was off the marginal lists forever and the free ride had begun. Congressman Coleman would never again be challenged this decade, either by an opponent, or, sadly, by the job itself.

But it did not matter to me at the time. I was flush with the elation of new fatherhood and all the promise it seemed to foretell. And there was something else, too. A game was afoot in a big, big way, bigger than me or Coleman or any other individual politician on the Hill. The hunt for Oliver North was underway in that fateful summer of 1986, and through a most curious turn of events, I was at the head of the pack.

I had no idea of the enormity of what would happen once we caught him—and catch him we did, dead to rights, no question about it. The fox was treed. Why the members of the hunt abruptly reined in their mounts and turned their backs on the fox, letting him escape to run again, would be another question entirely.

## CHAPTER EIGHT

# THE HUNT FOR OLIVER NORTH

I YELLED WHEN I opened the *Washington Post* one morning in October 1986.

My wife made some comment about disturbing the baby, but I didn't care. American Eugene Hasenfus had just been shot down and captured inside Nicaraguan territory. A momentous chain of events had begun, events that had their roots on one of my very worst days on Capitol Hill.

June 24, 1986, had already turned sour by the time our 2:00 news conference on Nicaragua rolled around.

We had had a tense morning staff meeting over whether fellow Democratic Rep. Leon Panetta's investigation of $27 million in previously appropriated contra aid would overshadow Coleman's digging into secret National Security Council assistance to the contras. "Panetta is on to the $27 million—he wants full accountability of what happened to the humanitarian aid," a legislative aide explained anxiously. "Coleman is on to secret National Security Council assistance and violations of the Boland Amendment."[1]

I groaned. Believe me, there's nothing prettier than politicians squealing for credit, especially if one of them might have been beaten to the punch.

To make matters worse, by late morning constituents were yapping by the dozens on the telephone. Lobbyists were stacking up in our reception area like airplanes in National Airport's holding pattern. Even worse, President Reagan had addressed the nation at noon on Nicaragua. Two days earlier, White House Chief of Staff Donald Regan had called Speaker O'Neill for permission for President Reagan to address the House to lobby for more contra aid. Sensing what he would later term a "cheap political trick," O'Neill offered instead to host a joint session or one that allowed members to question the president. "Having the President appear before only one house to lobby for a legislative proposal would be unprecedented," O'Neill said in a June 23 statement. "The only justification for such an unorthodox procedure would be if the president were to . . . participate in open dialogue with Members of the body."[2]

Donald Regan refused (and with good reason, too, in retrospect, given the avalanche of revelations about how little attention the president paid to the details of his policies). So the president delivered his speech on television, but not before a Republican fool named Al McCandless from California demanded a meaningless procedural vote on the House floor that made most Members miss the speech's opening lines. White House operatives nevertheless took the oppportunity to taunt O'Neill, handing out to the press copies of Article III of the Constitution that allowed the president "on extraordinary occasions, to convene both Houses, or either of them." Republican National Committee Chairman Frank Fahrenkopf, Jr., called O'Neill's refusal "naked political arrogance." President Reagan, however, did not consider the matter serious enough to invoke Article III.

All of this meant, of course, that I could not go out to lunch.

Just another day at the Favor Factory.

So you can imagine my mood that afternoon when a reporter glared at me as though I were wasting his time and threw away our press release. "There's nothing to this shit," he muttered, and left the news conference.

"Who's that?" I asked a bystander.

"Lou Cannon. *Washington Post*," came the offhand reply.

*Lou Cannon! The Washington Post!* Jesus. If someone as famous and savvy as Lou Cannon did not think an obscure Marine lieutenant colonel named Oliver North was providing illegal military and intelligence assistance to the contras with the help of some unknowns named Rob Owen, John Singlaub, and John Hull, then no one would.[3]

I smiled bravely. Maybe I had been wrong. Maybe I had missed something crucial in my investigation. On the other hand, maybe other reporters would not catch it and we could still get some press coverage. *But maybe there was nothing to it.*

The bizarre world of contra aid politics had been handled typically by Congress in fits, lurches, and jerks.[4] It had also begun secretly. In late 1981, Congress secretly approved $19 million in CIA covert military assistance to insurgents fighting the Sandinista government of Nicaragua. Another $19 million was appropriated in 1982 for the next fiscal year, but meanwhile Congress passed the first so-called Boland Amendment, which prohibited the use of those funds to overthrow the Nicaraguan government. Congress shifted to open funding in 1983 with $24 million, but stopped the use of the CIA contingency fund, which had slipped the contras an extra $10 million the year before.

Then the Central Intelligence Agency made a stupid mistake: it directly oversaw the mining of three ports in Nicaragua—an act of war—and Congress cut off aid. At the end of 1984, however, $14 million was appropriated in the fiscal year 1985 continuing resolution for release after February 28, 1985, by joint resolution. The continuing resolution also included the second Boland Amendment, saying, "no funds available to" the CIA, Defense Department, or any other U.S. agency involved in intelligence activities "may be obligated or expended . . . for . . . supporting, directly or indirectly, military or paramilitary activities in Nicaragua." (We had no idea at the time that the Democratic-led House Intelligence Committee was secretly providing huge amounts of money for political and psychological warfare inside Nicaragua and throughout Europe and the Western Hemisphere.)

In April 1985, the Senate passed a resolution to free the $14 million, but the House defeated it. On June 12, 1985, the House approved $27 million for "humanitarian" assistance to the contras, allowing the exchange of intelligence with the contras but prohibiting the Reagan administration from using any funds to support the contras except those specifically approved by Congress. By this time, language itself threatened to become a casualty in the conflict; an executive order in March 1986 defined surface-to-air missiles and training by U.S. Special Forces as "humanitarian aid."

The year 1986 had already seen some firefights. On March 20, the House defeated a $100 million request for contra aid, and we were even able to get Congressman Coleman to participate in the debate, charging that "the course of action followed by this administration has resulted in the entrenchment of the Sandinista regime." (Blaming the success of the Sandinistas on Ronald Reagan would make about as much sense as anything else over the course of this issue.)

The House beat back another attempt at the $100 million on April 16. Meanwhile, Congress and the White House were locked in bitter institutional warfare. The Reagan administration felt that the Democratic-controlled House had blocked key legislative initiatives, while the House saw Reagan partisans as attacking the very legitimacy of representative government. Now the stakes were high and the game was approaching its final move. The House Democratic leadership was fighting desperately with the Reagan administration over the next day's vote of $100 million in contra aid. Since Congressman Coleman was a member of the Democratic Whip Task Force on Nicaragua, we had been working feverishly to defeat the aid request. White House spokesman Larry Speakes said on June 24 that President Reagan still did not have enough committed votes to win. Private Democratic whip counts showed the vote to be extremely close, with our side just a few votes ahead.

Factor in the usual liars and it was a dead heat.

So by June 24, we were fishing for any angle that could move a few more votes. We thought we had a good one. Minutes before the news conference, Coleman had introduced a House resolution of inquiry to compel the Reagan White House to turn over any and all documents relating to the contras and four individuals—marine Lt.

Col. Oliver North, Rob Owen, retired Gen. John Singlaub, and a supposed American rancher in Costa Rica named John Hull.

Our statement went to the heart of the matter:

"Did the National Security Council manage a behind-the-scenes operation, possibly illegal, to secretly aid the contras during last year's congressional ban on military aid?" Coleman thundered. He thundered well, even for a politician. It was a useful talent. "Did this allegedly secret White House operation deliberately break the law?" Coleman placed Oliver North as head of the network, Rob Owen and John Singlaub as middlemen, and the shadowy John Hull as operational assistant.[5]

Until June 1986, Coleman had done little more about the war in Nicaragua than to beat the usual congressional tom-toms: votes against military aid to the contras, occasional *Record* statements, and plenty of hot air for Hispanic voters in El Paso.[6]

Throughout the legislative manuevering, we looked at the polls, and our Democratic and Hispanic voters were overwhelmingly against contra aid and the war. Only fools would try to lead the public, something we never did. After all, we were professionals. (Besides, we had voted for military aid to El Salvador just to show conservatives Coleman was not completely crazy.)

Coleman was extremely partisan. He saw anyone who crossed him—newspapers, columnists, local politicians, cab drivers—as automatically in bed with The Republicans. A month before he introduced the resolution of inquiry, he told Jackie Calms of *Congressional Quarterly*, "I don't intend to vote with the Republicans. . . . I don't see anything wrong with being a Democrat— that's the only label I use."

Despite his snarling anti-Republicanism, we pitched him as a "moderate" because the polls told us to avoid either extreme. He voted once for nonmilitary aid to the contras, and after the usual postering that poses as pondering in politics, he was usually good for a vote in favor of military aid to El Salvador. After his early June trip to Central America, Coleman explained that a compromise legislative package might include increased military aid to El Salvador. "Am I for that? Yes, I am," he told the press. Right-wing elements might run that country, but make no mistake: the Sandinista takeover in Nicaragua was the best thing that could have happened. El Salvador has always been the Democratic moderate's perfect throwaway vote: liberals like Coleman could go ballistic on contra aid and then, because politicians detest imbalance, they could side with the generals and their civilian front men. I am sure the generals appreciated the favor as much as we did.

Meanwhile, I was working on a plan to flood the Hispanic community in El Paso with bilingual franked mail lauding Coleman on anything under the sun. And Paul Rogers was leaning on me to produce a memo to discredit a reporter for the *El Paso Times*. "Something we could share with a lot of people," he suggested darkly.

Coleman had made the requisite trip to Nicaragua and Central America on June 3.[7] The trip was organized by U.S. Rep. Dave McCurdy (D-OK), a member of the House Intelligence Committee who had anointed himself as a leader of "moderate" Democrats on contra aid, but his motives and ultimate intent were murky. Was he trying to kill contra aid, delay it, support it? We were never able to tell, and many members did not trust him. "He's the kind of guy who wakes up in the morning, looks in the mirror, and tells himself that he should be president," a Democratic Hill rat commented.

After the trip, the members held a news conference in the Capitol's Radio-TV Gallery.[8] McCurdy opened by saying, "We don't want to discuss legislation and the drafting of legislation at this point."

Reporters looked incredulously at each other. "So what are we here for?" one of them asked a colleague in disgust.

McCurdy ignored the crowd's reaction and plowed ahead. "I was impressed with the quality of the region's leaders," he intoned, and then detailed his discussions with Nicaragua's Daniel Ortega, Costa Rican President Oscar Arias Sanchez, the contras, and additional heads of state.

"What did the leaders say about contra aid?" a reporter asked.

"Most tried to avoid a position," McCurdy explained, a situation with which he had some familiarity. "No one really knows if it's productive or counterproductive. Nicaragua has food, bread, and economic shortages. To relieve pressure now might be a mistake."

"Something's weird," a nearby reporter whispered to a colleague as McCurdy spoke. "I just can't put my finger on it."

McCurdy closed by saying he hoped to craft a compromise that would combine contra aid in some form with increased economic aid to El Salvador, Costa Rica, and Guatemala.

Then Coleman got the call on Wednesday, June 18, from the big boys in the leadership. As a "Southwestern moderate"—hooray, it worked!—would he be willing to deliver the Democratic party's nationwide response to President Reagan's radio address?

"We need a non-Eastern moderate to make the case against the president's $100 million contra aid request that will be voted on next week," Steve Champlin in Rep. David Bonior's office informed me. Bonior was chairman of the Whip Task Force on Nicaragua, and they had had enough of screaming liberals like Mike Barnes of Maryland. In recent months, Barnes had blistered the administration over its inability to account for $15 million of the $27 million in humanitarian aid to the contras appropriated in 1985. Among other things, an investigation by the U.S. General Accounting Office discovered a $450,000 personal payment to the "commander in chief" of the Honduran armed forces. Republicans accused Barnes of treading on "sensitive matters"—Honduras had never admitted that the contras were operating from base camps within its territory—but they did not deny the substance of the charges. One Republican, John McCain of Arizona, claimed that congressional restrictions on contra aid made accountability impossible. Such a statement may sound preposterous in 1992, but it was plausible enough at the time.

Would Coleman be interested? the leadership wanted to know. "It would be significant because the Democratic leadership has gone to its moderate wing to respond to the president's Central America policy," Champlin explained.

Would Coleman be interested? Would a Double-A utility infielder be interested in being in the starting lineup for the American League playoffs? We lunged at the opportunity. Here it was. The

Break. The Move Out of the Pack. We could see it now: McNeil-Lehrer, the "Today Show," maybe a *New York Times* feature story; it was the stuff of dreams.

By the way, Steve added, Bonior and the Whip Task Force on Nicaragua thought that, Coleman might want to introduce a House resolution of inquiry to stick it to Reagan on Nicaragua.

A resolution of inquiry? What the hell's that? I wondered briefly, and then turned to choreographing the matter at hand.

We House Democrats were running scared in 1986. Not foolish, like in 1990 and 1992, but scared. There were no videotaped depositions of Ronald Reagan forgetting and fumbling, no million-dollar speaking fees from the Japanese, no allegations of astrologers and Nancy Reagan running the White House. As strange as it may seem today, Democratic politicians in the House of Representatives were actually scared of Ronald Reagan. From their perspective, he was demanding blind loyalty to unaccountable executive power. Even worse, he was winning.

"I cannot explain the Constitution in a thirty-second TV spot" was the way one Democratic congressman explained a number of his reluctant pro-Reagan votes to me.

Some of us, however, were willing to take a shot.

Steve Champlin called again at 10:55 A.M. on June 18, 1986, concerned about the press coverage of Coleman's national radio address. "It's a real game," he declared. "And you need a game plan. First of all, no reporter works on a weekend. The Speaker's office has a press list. So you give them the text of the speech on Friday, embargoed until 1:06 P.M. Eastern Standard Time on Saturday. They can write the story on Friday as if they had listened to it on Saturday. The only thing, though, is you can't fuck 'em by changing the text." He laughed at the thought.

"The important thing is to say something that might make news instead of commentary," he finished. "We can beat him [Reagan] bad with a hard news announcement. Just remember two things: don't fuck up the mechanics of getting the word out to the press, and make sure you manufacture a hard news announcement."

The Speaker was to announce the next day that Coleman would

be at bat for the Democrats on Saturday. Bonior's Whip Task Force on Nicaragua met at 3:00 P.M. in Room H324 of the Capitol. Coleman's schedule had it listed as a two-star event, the same rating as Rep. Jim Chapman's fundraiser later in the evening aboard the yacht *High Spirits*, owned by S&L operator (and soon-to-be federal prisoner) Donald Dixon.

Steve Champlin called one more time to reinforce his message. "Pay no attention to the president at all," he warned. "Do your own game plan." Which, of course, meant the resolution of inquiry he had up his sleeve.

Later in the afternoon, Coleman received a signed memorandum from Vic Johnson, who worked for Rep. Michael Barnes's Foreign Affairs Subcommittee on the Western Hemisphere.[9] In the document, Johnson gave a thumbnail sketch of the Boland Amendment, which stated that from October 1984 to November 1985: "No funds available to the Central Intelligence Agency, the Department of Defense or any other agency or entity of the United States involved in intelligence activities may be obligated or expended to support, directly or indirectly, military or paramilitary operations in Nicaragua." In November 1985, the Boland Amendment was revised to permit intelligence sharing, nonmilitary advice, and communications equipment.

Johnson also told us what a resolution of inquiry was: a formal demand from the legislative branch that the executive branch provide specific documents involving specific people.

That out of the way, Johnson discussed some of the scattered press allegations involving a Lt. Col. Oliver North at the National Security Council. North had supposedly "developed a plan for contra funding in the event Congress cut off aid. . . . Israel, South Korea, and Taiwan—who had offered support—were plugged into the network."[10]

Then Johnson put on paper an admission he probably should not have made. "However," he lamented, "when it became clear that McFarlane would not respond adequately to our request in the absence of a subpoena, Barnes abandoned the quest because of the demands of his Senate campaign."

*Because of the demands of his Senate campaign!* That was political dynamite. Worse, it was unprofessional, as the truth normally becomes. I was naturally shocked and appalled.

Johnson hinted at the vicious internal politics that shredded the Foreign Affairs Committee from time to time: "The Committee tries to avoid having such resolutions come to the floor. Because it feels the House has no practical way to compel the provision of the information even if the resolution is passed, the committee prefers to cut the best deal it can and then kill the resolution." He then offered additional insight into the politics behind the selection of Ron Coleman as the leadership's water boy. "[B]ecause of the committee's general hostility toward the whole resolution of inquiry process," Johnson wrote, "it is better for such resolutions to be introduced by someone who is not on the committee."

Translation: Rep. Dante Fascell of Florida, the pro-contra Foreign Affairs Committee chairman, was tired of Mike Barnes's liberal yammering about contra aid. Barnes and the Whip Task Force needed a fresh face. Coleman was it.

In his final comment, Johnson got to the heart of the quagmire. "As a practical matter it could be very difficult to get much meaningful information out of the NSC. If we really want to get it, we would . . . take them to court. But it is a good political issue because it places the administration in a coverup posture."

"Coverup posture." Sock it to 'em. I liked the sound of it already.

Nearly four years later, on March 26, 1990, John Poindexter's legal team desperately attempted to subpoena Vic Johnson and introduce his memorandum into the court record. But the House counsel convinced federal Judge Greene to quash the subpoena. Political motivation, the judge ruled, was not a point of law; the politicians involved could not be compelled to testify, but they could do so voluntarily. The next day, Rick Robinson of the defense team called me at 12:27 P.M. Would Representative Coleman, the one who introduced the resolution of inquiry, be willing to testify? Like many other House members subpoened by Poindexter's defense, Coleman refused. Hours later, the defense abruptly rested its case. John Poindexter was convicted twelve days later.[11]

On the morning of Friday, June 20, 1986, Johnson called me to explain a little hitch he had discovered about the resolution of inquiry. "The Boland Amendment became effective October 1, 1984. The problem is that a lot of the contra funding network was set up by Lt. Colonel North before that time," he said.

"How big a problem?" I asked.

"Well, it would be irresponsible not to pursue allegations of illegal activity." He chuckled. I chuckled. We decided to drop the matter.

Coleman delivered the national Democratic radio address that Saturday without a hitch. "The question before the House is how to best make sure that your taxpayer-funded foreign aid is wisely spent," Coleman told the nation. "When I was at a contra base camp three weeks ago, the troops included ill-fed, poorly clothed thirteen- and fifteen-year-old boys and girls. So where did the taxpayers' $27 million go?"

Most of the radio address touched on the issue of financial accountability, but toward the end Coleman said he would introduce a resolution of inquiry to demand White House documents concerning contacts between the National Security Council and the contras. Afterwards, Steve Champlin told the Associated Press (insisting on anonymity) that Coleman's resolution had the backing of the House leadership and could lead to a confrontation with the White House over the release of documents. [12]

We had press a'plenty. Now it was time actually to introduce the thing and get it over with. No one at the time suspected what we had stumbled across; there was a lot going on in the world that week to occupy our attention—the immigration bill was stalled, President Reagan was threatening to veto the supplemental appropriations bill, Star Wars was cut in committee, a task force had been appointed to study the House restaurant.

I sat at my desk. I wondered who these guys were. Who had ever heard of this Oliver North character? Maybe I should make a few calls. As it turned out, it made no difference. Despite the national radio address, the resolution of inquiry, and the last-minute news conference, we lost the big vote the next day by 221–209. [13] President Reagan would receive $100 million for the contras, $70 million of which would go for weapons, ammunition, and supplies. Once again, the Central Intelligence Agency was to be the administrator of the war. Beyond a number of meaningless grab-bag provisions, the bill left open the question of the use of the CIA's contingency fund.[14]

Oh well, I thought, surveying the "Reagan Wins" headlines the next day. Like every good Hill rat, I knew how to keep score. Add 'em up at the end of the day. Advertise the ones you win and forget the rest. President Reagan had won his contra aid; on to the next battle.

If only it could have been that easy.

On July 8, I called Vic Johnson at the Foreign Affairs Committee for more information about the resolution of inquiry, like what the hell was our official line was going to be and what was it supposed to do, and why did we do it. We might have lost the vote, but Coleman was still stuck with the legislation.[15]

"We had numerous press reports that there was a relationship between the NSC staff and the contras that would have been illegal under the Boland Amendment," Johnson said in that exasperated tone that committee staffers reserve for personal staff members. There is a real difference between us. They see themselves as "issues people"—we call them policy wonks—who do not dirty their fingers in the personal and reelection politics that pay their freight.

"At a minimum," he lectured, "an attempt was made to set up an end-run around the law; at worst, the contacts were ongoing. Mike Barnes tried to get information via a less formal method. The resolution is now pending before the Foreign Affairs Committee, and our subcommittee might hold a hearing next week with Coleman as the witness and then report it out."

Okay, I said. Thanks.

I did not hear from Johnson until 9:27 A.M. on July 11. He dropped the bad news. "The Foreign Affairs Committee's chief of staff has decided not to refer the resolution of inquiry to Mike Barnes's subcommittee," Johnson said. I could tell he was disappointed, even depressed. "Jack Brady doesn't want Mike Barnes causing the administration any more trouble on this issue."

The message from Chairman Dante Fascell, Brady's pro-contra boss, was clear: Back off. Contra aid is a dead issue. We Democrats lost the $100 million aid vote. It's all legal now. The Pentagon and the CIA and Elliott Abrams and everyone else can come out of the closet with whatever they have been doing.

"So what are we going to do now?" I asked. Maybe Brady was right. All we needed was to be branded as true believers. A "true believer" is a term of derision on the Hill reserved for those who believe the substance of an issue is more important than its political framework or partisan permutations.

"We have to press the full committee for action," Johnson insisted. With that comment, I began to realize—and fear—that Johnson was indeed a true believer, and that he wanted to take us down with him. "If we want a hearing, we have to ask for it. A letter to the chairman from Coleman might be best. Coleman should ask to testify, and he should demand that you be consulted on the negotiations with the White House over the provision of the documents. You should also say the committee should be prepared to report the resolution favorably if the White House doesn't respond."

In other words, Ron Coleman, the junior leadership member who needed Dante Fascell on a number of matters of real political importance, should take on the big old bull so Mike Barnes could keep a piece of the action.

I thanked him politely and turned to more pressing duties, like making sure that all 17,030 letters to our voters in rural counties went out on time.

This telephone tag continued on July 15, when Johnson told me the resolution had been referred to Armed Services and Intelligence. "It's a normal referral," he said. "Nothing unusual."

Great, I thought. Les Aspin is running Armed Services and Lee Hamilton is chairing Intelligence. Two good liberals. Terrific. We'll get 'em with both barrels. And Coleman, who was in no frame of mind to take on Dante Fascell, could continue to get mileage out of the resolution of inquiry.

In a late afternoon surprise, Michael O'Neill called. O'Neill was chief counsel for the House Intelligence Committee, one of those guys with an interesting resume for intelligence oversight: he attended the London School of Economics, did not exist for the next twenty years, and then surfaced on the Intelligence Committee staff. You did not need to be a rocket scientist to figure out where he was coming from. I did not trust him.

"Chairman Hamilton has written the president and asked for a response to the resolution," he said smoothly. "He's given the White House a deadline of the end of this week—first of next week. Hamilton suspects they won't do much, but you never know."

On July 21, 1986, John Poindexter wrote the fateful letter which would help indict him and North. In it, he assured the Committees on Foreign Relations, Armed Services, and Intelligence that the administration was adhering to "the spirit and the letter" of the Boland Amendment. "The Administration strongly opposes enactment of the resolution of inquiry. . . . [T]he actions of the National Security Council staff were in compliance with the spirit and the letter of the law."[16] Not the law in general, but the Boland Amendment—a distinction that would become crucial when Intelligence Committee Chairman Lee Hamilton met with him and Oliver North the following month. Rep. Mike Barnes called Poindexter's opposition "stonewalling," and Rep. David Bonior claimed "the administration has now decided to hide the war from public view."

Coleman's press response to Poindexter's letter was, "I am not satisfied."[17] But privately, Paul Rogers and I had doubts about Coleman's grasp of the issue and its enormity. He continued to stumble over a number of key points, such as what it was he had introduced and the names of the people involved. That evening, I did a formal memorandum to spell out the issue for Coleman once and for all.[18] (See Appendix III)

After providing a brief biographical sketch of Lt. Col. North, I told Coleman that our evidence in hand indicated that North, among other things:

• Intervened in October 1985 to negotiate a smooth flow of aid from the Honduran military to rebel units;

- Coordinated the activities of Philip Mabry, a conservative Fort Worth, Texas, security consultant, to raise money for military assistance to the contras;
- Worked with retired Air Force General Richard Secord to purchase short-take-off-and-landing aircraft from Saudi Arabia;
- Helped the contras in early 1985 to obtain SAM-7 ground-to-air missiles.

"From the administration's point of view, and given the nature of North's job, we have essentially asked them for the blueprints of supply networks in the Middle East, Europe, and Latin America for covert operations," the memorandum continued. "The single issue of determining whether North broke the law in helping to obtain SAM-7s in early 1985, for example, would involve a discussion of the European suppliers, the transshippers and middlemen, the methods used to handle financial transactions for operations of this nature, and the intelligence information given to the contras concerning the armor and airframe vulnerabilities of Russian helicopters. A similar situation might be encountered during an investigation of the allegation that North helped obtain aircraft from Saudi Arabia for the contras."

We were all getting a little tired of this resolution business. The reelection Campaign was beginning to suck up nearly every moment in the office. I had statements to write about immigration, education, employment, not to mention the dreaded SheepNoFuck issue. Real political work, not contra aid silliness.

August 5, should have been a key day in John Poindexter's legal defense. We sent Lee Hamilton a set of forty-four questions to ask Oliver North about the secret contra aid network allegations, and urged him specifically to do the following at his meeting with Oliver North (and anyone else at the NSC he might meet with, such as Poindexter):[19] (See Appendix IV)

*Establish the applicability of the Boland Amendment to NSC activities relating to the contras.* This was the central question, and indeed, it became the foundation of Poindexter's defense at the trial. Poindexter had written that the NSC was following the spirit and letter of the Boland Amendment. Did the amendment cover the NSC? In the drafting of the resolution of inquiry, we did not know. Our number one question was: "Is the National Security Council, in fact, involved in intelligence-related activities?" It was the most simple of questions, and the most fundamental. Our second question was: "Are you and were you aware of the Boland Amendment restrictions on U.S. assistance to the contras, as passed by Congress and signed by the president?"

*Establish North's position within the NSC* vis-à-vis *the contra account and U.S. activities concerning military and intelligence information.* Who was responsible at NSC for military and intelligence tasking? Who told the intelligence professionals what to look for and what to get? Did North have that power? Did it change after the Boland Amendment?

*Establish North's ability to initiate actions on behalf of the contras, either personally or through intermediaries.* Dig into Richard Secord's activities. Pin down North about the SAM-7s. And what about Rob Owen, John Singlaub, or any other private individual passing on supply or intelligence information at his direction? Tell us about his negotiations with the Honduran military concerning the flow of contra aid to the base camps.

*Determine if any legal parameters were set concerning the Boland Amendment.* Ask North for a copy of the plan to assist the contras with funding in the event Congress cut off aid. Ask if President Reagan was briefed on the plan.

In retrospect, we had handed Intelligence Committee Chairman Lee Hamilton the keys to the kingdom. The lines of questioning set out in my 1986 memoranda as well as the specific people named— Oliver North, John Poindexter, Robert Owen, John Hull, Richard Secord, John Singlaub—eerily echo the transcripts of the 1987 Iran-contra hearings and John Poindexter's 1990 trial.

We eagerly awaited Hamilton's report of his meetings with North and Poindexter.

The word came softly, like death in the night. Coleman told me privately that Hamilton had caved. He had met North. North had been sitting in the chair normally reserved for the president. In addition to Hamilton, Representatives McCurdy, Kastenmeier, Daniel, Roe, Stump, Ireland, Hyde, Cheney, Livingston, and McEwen were present, along with committee aides Tom Latimer and Steve Berry.

North opened with an overview of what he claimed were his activities. His main mission, he said, was to coordinate contacts with the contras, assess their viability, and explain Boland Amendment restrictions to them. According to a memorandum based on notes of the meeting, North said that "he did not in any way, nor at any time, violate the spirit, principles, or legal requirements of the Boland Amendment."

Incredibly, Hamilton had not asked a single one of the tough questions. He had gone through the motions, but nothing more. He had never pressed them at all. Did you do it? Hamilton asked politely. Oh no sir, no, North replied. We're within the letter and spirit of the Boland Amendment. Gee thanks, Hamilton responded.

Coleman caved, too, in his own way, by refusing to take the matter to the floor—which he could have done under the rules of the House. But he was under heavy political attack back home, and we needed to take contra aid off our front pages; it was time for the Hill rats to clean up the mess. Paul Rogers told me we had to get both Coleman and Hamilton off the hook, so I drafted a letter for Hamilton to send to Coleman stating that no evidence could be found, and thank you for bringing the matter to my attention. Coleman, in turn, issued a public statement on August 7 saying, "I appreciate the Intelligence Committee and the chairman taking the time to pursue the press allegations that prompted the resolution of inquiry in the first place." Naturally, the whole thing was the press's fault. On August 12, Hamilton sent us the final version of his letter, in which he thanked Coleman for his efforts "to remove doubt about United States activities."[20]

(Because of Coleman's political relationship with Hamilton, we would continue to protect him even at the height of the Iran-contra scandal as reporters pressed me for information on why Hamilton dropped the ball.)[21]

The Intelligence Committee, however, did not let the resolution die a quiet death. At the urging of Chief Counsel Michael O'Neill and Rep. Dave McCurdy, the committee voted formally to kill it. Hamilton had cast his lot.

I remained disgusted until the weekend arrived. I woke up with the grubby world of work in my mind and said to my wife, "Sun and water."

"Sun and water?"

"Yes."

"What about them?"

"I need them."

"You make the coffee and pack the lunch. Don't forget milk, crackers, and juice for Julia. I'll get her dressed." What a great wife; I stay up half the night, wake up crazy, change previous plans, and all she says is make the coffee and pack the lunch.

We were at our sailboat's slip on the Chesapeake Bay within the hour. I checked Julia's lifeline and harness, started the engine, pulled out of the slip, and eased past a rusted old dredger stuck in the middle of the marina's channel. Then we veered hard to the left, missing a set of crumbling stakes that marked the silt-shallows in the outlet to the bay. The outlet is tricky even in good weather and good tides, and in a howler the chop gets as high as the bulkheads. When you enter the Slot, as old Johnny the Crabber calls it, only a small square of blue sky and the bay are in your field of vision. Then you clear the mouth of the Slot and the horizon of the bay spreads out before you, way past your vision on both sides.

Julia was still asleep on the cabin floor when we threaded our way past the crab pot buoys and set a course of 60 degrees magnetic, which would take us across the bay to Black Walnut Point on Tilghman Island. My wife was at the helm and the wind was ten knots from the northwest and veering back and forth about fifty degrees either way. No chop and swells at a foot and a half. I raised the jib quickly, then rigged the mainsail. My wife killed the engine, released the boom safety, and then . . . quiet.

I did not say anything until we were in the middle of a bluefish frenzy, with terrified baitfish jumping out of the water all around the boat. I jumped into the cockpit and said, "Screw Hamilton," but I was smiling and my wife knew it without taking her eyes off the telltales on the mainsail.

I felt great. I always felt great after clearing the channel. No matter how many times I headed out, I always got a flash from my teenage years when I had sailed in Panama, clearing the canal and heading 120 degrees toward the Perlas Islands out in the middle of the gulf, the incredible deep Pacific blue rising out of everywhere to meet you as you crossed the hundred fathom line. If you were lucky you might pick up the dolphins halfway to the Perlas . . . then I would shake my head and blink my eyes, and I am back on the Chesapeake Bay, which is not a bad substitute.

Broil and brine and dead butchered baitfish and screw every one of those deal-cutting bastards. They should be so lucky.

# CHAPTER NINE

# THE SECRET LIFE OF THE HOUSE INTELLIGENCE COMMITTEE

THE HOUSE OF REPRESENTATIVES voted to establish a Permanent Select Committee on Intelligence on July 14, 1977. The first paragraph of House Resolution 658 read, "It is further the purpose of this resolution to provide vigorous oversight over the intelligence-related activities of the United States to assure that such activities are in conformity with the Constitution and laws of the United States."[1] But by the mid-1980s, the committee no longer merely oversaw budgets, sources, methods, and results; it had become a forum for creating secret policies as well.[2]

Ever since the Iran-contra scandal broke wide open—starting with the capture of Eugene Hasenfus, followed by the revelations from November 1986 on about selling arms to Iran and the diversion of profits to the contras—Rep. Lee Hamilton has been asked why he did not do more about our resolution of inquiry.

"But what more could I have done? They lied to me . . ." had been his standard response. On April 4, 1990, he told Washington investigative journalist John Canham-Clyne, "When dealing with the government, the custom is to go to the top. We did, and they gave us a flat-out assurance . . . we could not find any witnesses to come forward." Michael O'Neill, the Intelligence Committee's chief counsel, told Clyne, "We had no names; tell me, who could we have asked?"

Coleman's resolution of inquiry, in fact, had named Robert Owen, Gen. John Singlaub, and John Hull, as well as North. The committee made no attempt to question them. On June 13, 1986, Rep. David Bonior circulated a "Dear Colleague" letter that reprinted a June 10 Associated Press story describing in detail the National Security Council-led contra resupply operation. It named two paramilitary trainers of the contras, Tom Posey and Jack Terrell; former contra leader Edgar Chamorro; a Miskito Indian rebel leader named Teofilo Archibald Wilson; the CIA station chief in Tegucigalpa, Honduras; as well as North, Singlaub, Owen, and Hull.

By and large, Hamilton's posture as victim has nevertheless played quite well, and the subject rarely moves out of Iran-contra junkie discussion circles.

If failing to probe more deeply were the only question, Hamilton could be excused for merely making a mistake. It would be a mistake of historic consequences, to be sure, but that is not unusual in this place and would certainly not distinguish him one way or the other in the U.S. House of Representatives.

But the real question is not why Hamilton did not insist on truthful answers, but why Hamilton and committee members did not seem to *want* truthful answers from Poindexter and North.

Until the startling revelations of the Iran-contra scandal and the subsequent trials, I had written it off to politics. Rep. Lee Hamilton was, fundamentally, a politician. And our side had lost—President Reagan had won the $100 million. Contra aid as an issue was history, until the following year's funding cycle, an eternity in congressional politics. You get no mileage around here from pushing principle when nothing more important is at stake. So why bother?

But by the time former National Security Advisor Adm. John Poindexter was convicted in April 1990, a different picture of Lee Hamilton had emerged. Far from being the completely surprised innocent that he claimed to be in June 1986 when our resolution of inquiry was introduced, Hamilton, as chairman of the Intelligence Committee, had been the handmaiden of the Reagan administration's secret war against Nicaragua. From approving anti-Sandinista political operations throughout Central America that were headquartered in Costa Rica to protecting the shadowy activities of Hamilton's constituent, the "rancher" John Hull (later identified as the CIA's operations chief in northern Costa Rica and who ran the contra's southern front in Nicaragua), Hamilton was in the catbird's seat as he watched the covert political, economic, and military operations unfold.

And when Rep. Ronald Coleman introduced the House resolution of inquiry in June 1986 at the behest of the hard-charging Rep. Dave Bonior, Lee Hamilton had a problem.

Lionized by the national press for his thoughtful, considered approach to foreign affairs, Hamilton had been the public conscience of the opposition to contra aid. Twenty-four hours after the introduction of our resolution, he stood on the floor of the House, arguing eloquently against the war and President Reagan's request for $100 million in contra aid: "The choice before us in Nicaragua . . . is whether to pursue a military solution or . . . a regional policy . . . [W]e were wrong to pursue . . . military assistance."[3] Hamilton called for a diplomatic solution and criticized the administration for opposing peace in Central America.

Hamilton needed good reviews for his performance. An enormous political incompatibility existed between his public image— liberal Democrat and potential chairman of the Foreign Affairs Committee—and his private conduct, in which he acquiesced to virtually every single facet of the secret war against Nicaragua except direct U.S. military assistance.

A runaway resolution of inquiry would have uncovered a host of politically damaging revelations about the Democratic managers of intelligence and national security policy. First of all, Hamilton would have been exposed as having already known about Oliver North's role as a storm trooper of the Reagan Doctrine, undermining the Lone Ranger characterization of North that was vital to the House Intelligence Committee as well as to the Reagan presidency. North's personal notebooks reveal a systematic pattern of briefings and contacts with the committee not just on Nicaragua but on a host of intelligence and covert operations and counterterrorism programs around the world.[4] According to the notebooks, his contacts with the Intelligence Committee began as early as January 1984, and possibly much earlier. As a member and then chairman of the Intelligence Committee, Hamilton oversaw and authorized the broader structure under which the Reagan Doctrine was carried out.

The Reagan Doctrine constituted one of the major differences between us Democrats and the Republicans; for better or for worse, they had plans. In his 1985, State of the Union address, President Reagan announced, "We must stand by all our democratic allies. And we must not break faith with those who are risking their lives on every continent, from Afghanistan to Nicaragua, to defy Soviet-supported aggression and secure rights which have been ours from birth."[5]

Translated, the doctrine called for an aggressive rollback of Soviet power and influence around the globe by any means necessary. To accomplish this mission, the United States became involved in or stoked scores of wars the world over, such as helping the Turks fight the Kurdish separatists and other insurgencies; giving enormous CIA assistance to the mujahideen in Afghanistan; and, with the repeal of the Clark Amendment in early 1986, aiding UNITA in Angola (although documents from the Iran-contra hearings suggest that the U.S. had been aiding UNITA in much the same way as it had the contras—through third country funds, private individuals, and intelligence sharing).

All of these operations took place under the nose of the House Intelligence Committee. The Reagan Doctrine, in its essence, meant war, declared or otherwise. Oliver North was in the middle of it, proudly so, and, however reluctantly, so was Lee Hamilton.


Any war involves far more than bullets and money. It must have political support, both at home and abroad. It must rally public opinion by manipulating the media. It must suppress dissent at home. It needs strategic justification.

Lee Hamilton, Dave McCurdy, and their fellow Democrats on the House Intelligence Committee gave the Reagan administration all the prerequisites for war.

They stood by while allegedly politicized strategic assessments provided the justification and set the stage. With no opposition from Hamilton, who could have challenged these assessments, CIA Director William Casey reportedly forced his personal ideology onto professional National Intelligence Estimates (NIEs), including the 1983 "Nicaragua: The Outlook for the Insurgency" and four 1985 NIEs on the Sandinista military buildup, consolidation of authority inside Nicaragua, Soviet support for Sandinistas, and Nicaraguan exportation of communist revolution. In 1984, the CIA's National Intelligence Officer for Latin America, John Horton, resigned in protest of Casey's pressure on him to change his estimates.[6] A 1985 Intelligence Committee report showed the committee was well aware of the controversy, for it stated that the "Committee examined the earlier drafts and the final version of that particular NIE and found that dissenting views were printed at the very beginning of the study, a practice the Committee applauds." The committee report went on to say that "care had to be taken lest analytic thought succumb to pressure to support rather than inform policy."

Even more importantly, Intelligence Committee Democrats authorized the intelligence infrastructure under which the war against Nicaragua was carried out. The action was perfectly legal, of course; it in no way violated congressional restrictions on contra aid. But it was politically incompatible with the image of public opposition by Hamilton and others not just to contra aid but to the overall war. Far from his pretense of having no knowledge of National Security Council participation in intelligence activities, Hamilton knew about the Senior Interagency Group-Intelligence (SIG-I), which was responsible for advising the NSC on intelligence policy. SIG-I was itself established by President Reagan's National Security Council Structure (NSDD-2) on January 12, 1982, and a copy of NSDD-2 is in the House Intelligence Committee files.[7]

No evidence, moreover, exists in the trial documents of Oliver North or John Poindexter, or in any of the Iran-contra hearing material, that these Democrats did anything to block the intelligence system from supporting the war. For example, they did not attempt to stop the National Foreign Intelligence Board's coordination of intelligence community resources to advance the war. A similar absence of evidence indicates Hamilton and Intelligence Committee Democrats did not oppose the Nicaraguan elements of the annual National Foreign Intelligence Program (NFIP), which the NFIB used to allocate specific resources to specific targets. The January 2, 1985, annual report of the Intelligence Committee specifically stated that "one of its most important functions would be to oversee and authorize annually the budgets of the various U.S. intelligence agencies and activities." The report further pointed out that the National Foreign Intelligence Program, which consisted of the resources of the Central Intelligence Agency, the National Security Agency, the Defense Intelligence Agency, and other military and national intelligence activities, were within the "exclusive jurisdiction" of the committee.[8]

When Rep. Lee Hamilton assumed the chairmanship of the committee in January 1985, he vowed in the *Congressional Quarterly* that he would be "very tough" with these budgets.[9] On another occasion, in a March 10, 1985, article in the *Los Angeles Times*, he raised a number of questions about covert action; at the time, in his capacity as chairman, he was authorizing the vital infrastructure that allowed those covert operations to take place.

These same Democrats approved specific operations against Nicaragua. While Hamilton postured publicly about opposing military aspects of the contra war, he approved $13 million in covert political warfare inside Nicaragua—*during the time the 1985 Boland Amendment was in effect.* Later, Hamilton was so desperate to conceal this fact that he had it censored from the public version of former vice presidential National Security Advisor Donald Gregg's Iran-contra deposition. The revelation appeared unclassified in Gregg's Senate confirmation documents on his nomination as U.S. ambassador to South Korea. Hamilton also approved $29 million in covert CIA aid to the contras in Fiscal Year 1982, $29 million in Fiscal Year 1983, and $24 million in Fiscal Year 1984, all under the original Boland Amendment.

Specific operations were authorized as well as money. Hamilton and committee Democrats approved National Security Agency budgets and operations that intercepted Sandinista government and military communications. Nor did they stop the U.S. Signals Intelligence Directives from NSA or the CIA's Communications Intelligence Supplementary Regulations concerning signal intelligence tasking in support of the war. This kind of intelligence was vital to contra military operations. Edgar Chamorro, former member of the political directorate of the contras' Nicaraguan Democratic Force, testified at the World Court on September 5, 1985, that "the CIA, working with United States military personnel, operated various electronic interception stations in Honduras for the purpose of intercepting radio and telephonic communications among Nicaraguan Government military units. By means of these interception activities, and by breaking the Nicaraguan Government codes, the CIA was able to determine—and advise us of—the precise locations of all Nicaraguan Government military units. This type of intelligence was invaluable to us. Without it, our forces would not have been able to operate with any degree of effectiveness inside Nicaragua."

Chamorro added that this intelligence was corroborated by overflights of Nicaraguan territory by U.S. satellites and surveillance aircraft. In fact, Intelligence Committee Democrats approved enormous and secret expenditures by national intelligence agencies to obtain this photoreconnaissance and imagery intelligence from the air and space-based platforms without which the contra war could not have been run. Oliver North's notebooks revealed that on October 19, 1984, for example, an SR-71 spy plane named *Giant Clipper* was scheduled for an imagery and signal intelligence mission for the U.S. Defense Intelligence Agency over Nicaragua, Honduras, El Salvador, and Costa Rica. The next day, a U-2 aircraft named *Olympic Victor* was programmed to fly Track 8Y038, covering downtown Managua, Tegucigalpa, as well as the national territory of El Salvador, Guatemala, and Belize. On the previous Friday, October 26, *Olympic Victor* had flown Track 8Y033 to collect similar intelligence on a circumnavigation of the region.

The following week, North was once again involved in an SR-71 mission. He reported that CIA Director William Casey had asked for "fast track analysis," but his next words were censored. Presumably, they involved imagery from CIA photoreconnaissance satellites such as the KH-11, because the references to SR-71 and U-2 flights were not deleted, and Casey would have no immediate authority over missions controlled by the military. The fast-track analysis was to be coordinated by Robert Vickery at CIA headquarters.

U.S. Rep. Robert Dornan, in fact, confirmed that the contra war involved this sort of sophisticated photoreconnaissance when he stated on the House floor during the June 25, 1986, contra aid debate that he had seen ". . . the fine detail of our KH-11 imagery that most of the time we only see here in top secret session," and then made references to U-2 and SR-21 missions. [10]

Support for the war by committee Democrats did not end with intelligence operations. While posturing with their fellow liberal Democrats, committee Democrats gave the nod to worldwide political warfare against Nicaragua.

They acquiesced to the worldwide political destabilization plan against the Sandinista government authorized in President Reagan's secret February 1984 finding, a copy of which was provided to the House Intelligence Committee. Many of the details of this plan were revealed in an April 14, 1986, story by the Associated Press, which quoted unnamed U.S. officials as stating that political assistance had been provided by the CIA to the contras' political umbrella group, the United Nicaraguan Opposition, to pay officials and supporters and to open offices in Europe and Latin America.

One of the casualties was U.S.-Mexico relations, in which Chairman Hamilton played the political equivalent of "pocket pool," as one observer commented. Meanwhile, William Casey fired the agency's top Mexico expert, John Horton, and rewrote intelligence estimates to "prove" the instability of neighboring Mexico, thereby justifying attempts to stop the communists in Nicaragua. In public, Assistant Secretary of State Elliott Abrams led the Mexico-bashing, straining relations to such a point that they are only now beginning to recover. In private, the U.S. threatened to undermine the ruling

PRI party by throwing support to the rival PAN before the July 1986 elections in northern Mexico. News reports surfaced in 1987 that offers of support were made to the PAN in return for its advocacy of the contras; conversely, U.S. officials warned the PRI that if it tried to support peace initiatives in Central America in conversations with American congressmen, the Reagan administration would lobby in Mexico on behalf of the PAN.[11]

Hamilton and committee Democrats also approved extensive covert political operations inside Costa Rica, the nation used by the Reagan administration as the staging area for the political war against Nicaragua, just as Honduras served as the military staging area, where they authorized the massive growth of CIA facilities at Yamales and the near-doubling of the CIA station in Tegucigalpa. According to intelligence community sources, they registered no objection to the use of the Costa Rican Embassy in Managua as headquarters for the CIA's political warfare operations inside Nicaragua. At the same time, they allowed the CIA to funnel U.S. funds to contra leaders to pay Costa Rican and Honduran journalists to write pro-contra stories, and approved CIA payments to Nicaragua's La Prensa newspaper and other media outlets within the CIA's Propaganda Assets Inventory.

Hamilton and committee Democrats also refused to halt the "secret campaign of threats and intimidation," as press reports such as those of the Miami Herald's Alfonso Chardy described the program run by North, Abrams, and Alan Fiers, head of the CIA's Central America Task Force.[12] The program sought secretly to derail regional peace talks, to end the contra war, and to undermine the participation of Mexico, Argentina, Panama, Costa Rica, and Honduras. The infrastructure of the Democratic-approved secret war—NSA and CIA signals intelligence tasking, the national foreign intelligence data base, and intelligence community-wide resources—was brought to bear on behalf of this program.

These Democrats also protected individuals. Hamilton and committee Democrats were aware of the vast structure of foreign agents paid to prosecute the war. In fact, Hamilton wrote Secretary of State George Shultz in January 1985 to express his alarm that Arturo

Cruz, Jr., was a paid agent of the CIA—in violation of the law—and would appear before congressional committees. Hamilton said he felt "vulnerable." To assuage Hamilton's fears, Shultz arranged a sit-down meeting with him and William Casey at which they arranged a cut-out whereby Cruz would be paid indirectly.

In September 1986, Arturo Cruz, Sr., and Alfonso Robelo, two of the three members of the contra directorate, took time out from their jungle warfare to campaign in El Paso against Ron Coleman, to retaliate for the resolution of inquiry. Both men were on the CIA payroll at the time. And according to Dan Fiske of the now-defunct Office of Public Diplomacy for Latin America and the Caribbean, the CIA paid for their trip to the United States. Hamilton, our supposed ally and fellow opponent of contra aid, did not come to Coleman's assistance.

John Hull, the alleged rancher who was named in our resolution of inquiry, was actually the CIA's coordinator in northern Costa Rica for the war in Nicaragua's southern front. In December 1989, Hull was denounced by an investigating committee of the National Assembly of Costa Rica, which voted to recommend to the judicial authorities that Hull be tried for a variety of offenses, including narcotics trafficking. Hull was arrested. Lee Hamilton then authored a letter, cosigned by eighteen U.S. congressmen, to Costa Rican President Arias on Hull's behalf, and linked the state of U.S.-Costa Rican relations to Hull's treatment. Arias rebuffed Hamilton. Hamilton subsequently explained that he was only trying to assist a constituent, but given his position on the Intelligence Committee, he knew full well who Hull was and feared his appearance in court. (After being indicted, Hull jumped bond and fled to Indiana. He was later indicted for murder in the case of the La Penca bombing, but resurfaced in January 1990 in El Salvador as an "agricultural expert.")

The North notebooks raise an additional question that goes to the heart of the Poindexter case: Can you lie to someone who already knows? And if you do, what is the recipient's responsibility, especially if it becomes a matter of law, as it did in the trials of Oliver North and John Poindexter?

North claimed on July 8, 1987, during the Iran-contra congressional hearings that "the National Intelligence Daily circulated to the Hill gave ample notice of the resupply operations." North's notebooks also show that at least three Republican members of the House Intelligence Committee—Reps. Robert Stump, Robert Livingston, and Henry Hyde—had been briefed by North and then-National Security Advisor Robert McFarlane at the White House on March 4, 1985, on what became elements of the plan to evade Boland Amendment restrictions on contra aid. (See Appendix V) Another Republican, Rep. Bill McCollum, who would later join the committee, also attended.

As Washington journalist John Canham-Clyne has pointed out, what was not indicated on North's notes was that this meeting took place as each element of the contra resupply operation reached a crucial phase.[13]

"The Reagan administration had just communicated the quid pro quo offer to the Hondura government as a means of stiffening their commitment to the contras in the face of a threatened Sandinista mass-border offensive," Canham-Clyne observed. "Assistance from Saudi Arabia, Taiwan, and other sources was petering out, a proposal for aid was before the House Intelligence Committee, and as part of the effort to pressure Congress to aid the contras, Hamilton and the CIA were haggling over 'Cruz control' "—who was going to pay contra leader Arturo Cruz and what lobbying activities he could undertake inside the United States.

On February 7, 1985, the Crisis-Preplanning Group decided to offer increased assistance to Honduras and to release economic assistance despite the absence of economic reforms previously demanded by the United States. President Reagan and Secretary of State George Shultz approved this aid on February 19, and on March 16, 1985, Vice President Bush met in Honduras with President Suazo to seal the deal.

Representative Hyde subsequently claimed that, the North notebooks notwithstanding, "At no time was I ever present at any meetings, including one on March 4, 1985, at the White House with Mr. Robert McFarlane, where I was privy to 'elements of a plan to erode the Boland Amendment.' " Hyde said that the essential purpose of the meeting was to discuss legislative strategy for the upcoming markup on the annual intelligence authorization.[14] (See Appendix VII)

Hyde also termed his reference to Taiwan and Saudi Arabia for possible third-country support a "gratuitous suggestion which McFarlane said he rejected." But those countries were specifically the ones already helping the contras—Taiwan had been asked for help by John Singlaub and North in December 1984, and Saudi Arabia had been giving the contras $1 million per month since 1984. Furthermore, an intelligence finding already existed that encouraged third-country assistance. At a June 25, 1984, National Security Planning Group meeting at the White House, CIA Director William Casey told President Reagan, "The legal position is that the CIA is authorized to cooperate and seek support from Third Countries. In fact, the finding encourages Third Country participation and support in this entire effort . . ."[15] The finding had been sent to Rep. Hyde and the rest of the Intelligence Committee.

Hyde could not say what the $25–50 million mentioned in North's notes was other than it "probably was the amount we were proposing for an appropriations." He also pointed out that Congress appropriated $27 million in humanitarian aid five months after this meeting. But no such amount in military aid to the contras was ever proposed by Hyde or any of the other participants, and no mention was made of any such appropriation in McFarlane's notes of the meeting. Furthermore, a $25 million contra resupply operation was already in effect. And when North wrote his "Fallback Option Plan for the Nicaraguan Resistance," anticipating that Congress would cut off funds completely, there was no mention of any $25–50 million appropriation by Hyde or anyone else; and no legislative option circulated at the time from either party that contemplated the third-country support discussed as part of the March 4 plan. (Third-country support for the contras at the time was one of the Reagan administration's most highly classified secrets. It is highly unlikely that it would have been revealed publicly as part of a routine congressional appropriation and no discussion can be found in the Iran-contra hearings or trial documents about going public with third-country support.)

The North notebooks show that at the March 4 meeting, Rep. Bill McCollum opened the discussion by saying the Hondurans believed that U.S. aid was essential to the contras' success. McCollum did not reveal the extent of his discussions with Honduras or how he knew the position of the Honduran government. Stump cautioned that they did not have the votes for a "covert" program, and Rep. Henry Hyde suggested private, third-country support from Taiwan and Saudi Arabia.

National Security Advisor McFarlane spelled out the elements of the secret plan:

"Plan includes:
  • $25–50 million
  • 3rd country support
  • The CIA to provide the intelligence
  • Center the activity in the White House"

McCollum's response was that he needed a list of "swing voters." Hyde added that there should be a single party line on the issues and mentioned some positive indicators of the public's mood, such as a recent favorable poll by *USA Today*.

Rep. Robert Stump (R-AZ) would come across the issue of third-country funding again on October 29, 1985, when members of a House-Senate conference committee, in a meeting with McFarlane and North, took a secret, apparently nonbinding vote. Rep. Stump, Richard Cheney (R-WY), and others voted yes—as did Democratic Intelligence Committee Chairman Lee Hamilton.

This evidence suggests that Representatives Hyde, Stump, Livingston, and McCollum might have been just as "guilty" of lying to Congress as Admiral Poindexter by not challenging his letter of July 21, 1986, in response to our resolution of inquiry. Poindexter was found guilty of lying to and obstructing Congress—but which "Congress?" Certainly not the Republicans on the House

Intelligence Committee, because they had already been briefed on what became the elements of the plan and had not objected. Stump, Hyde, and Livingston would later attend the fateful August 6, 1986, meeting at the White House with the House Intelligence Committee on the resolution of inquiry, where they were pointedly silent about their prior and ongoing knowledge of the contra resupply operation plans. When North stated that he did not "in any way, nor at any time violate the spirit, principles, and legal requirements of the Boland Amendment," Representatives Hyde, Stump, and Livingston did not say a word.

North's notebooks are equally specific about Democratic Rep. Dave McCurdy. Beginning in June 1985, they strongly suggest that McCurdy was assisting North as he desperately tried to cobble together a program to keep the contras afloat. The notebooks show a regular pattern of meetings and conversations between the two men on a legislative compromise to fund the contras. While North indicated that his relationship with Hamilton was frequently adversarial, and that Hamilton did not know about the secret military aid, he specifically informed McCurdy on at least one occasion, March 3, 1986, of an air drop to the contras from Illopango airport in El Salvador. At the time, of course, such assistance was banned by law. McCurdy's immediate response is not known and he has subsequently refused to answer questions about his knowledge of North's activities. But North did not record any objections by McCurdy, and there is no evidence that McCurdy reported the incident to the Justice Department.

In North's memoir *Under Fire*, he not only confirmed that McCurdy knew about the secret contra resupply operation, but that it was McCurdy who initiated the request to assist the contras (in this case, Miskito Indian units operating on Nicaragua's Atlantic coast). North also suggested that McCurdy should have been grateful to him for not mentioning this fact at the fateful August 6, 1986, meeting: "I was certain McCurdy didn't want me to talk about that, and I didn't."[16]

At the same time, McCurdy's staff was keeping Lt. Col. North secretly apprised of press investigations into the contra resupply network. According to North's notebooks, Steve Patterson, McCurdy's staff director, called North at 9:30 P.M. on August 6, 1985, to warn him that Steve Roberts of the *New York Times* had phoned McCurdy to ask questions about North's involvement in contra fund-raising. "He claims to have Armed Services Committee confirmation that North was raising money and violating the law," Patterson told North. The next day, Patterson called North on the same subject. He later telephoned again to alert North to an upcoming *New York Times* story by Joel Brinkley attacking the administration's position.

The Iran-contra investigations revealed that about $40.3 million went to the contras from sources such as Saudi Arabia, private fundraisers, and Iranian arms sales diversions. But the secret, off-the-shelf funding shrivels in comparison with the billions in legally authorized secret funding and operations against Nicaragua approved by the Intelligence Committee and its Democratic leaders.

Without the active and secret assistance of Rep. Lee Hamilton and the Democratic-controlled House Intelligence Committee, neither the legal nor disputed aspects of the Reagan administration's covert war against Nicaragua could have taken place. It was as if the committee had authorized a swarm of wasps to buzz and circle a target, equipped the wasps with the ability to maneuver and communicate, and then instructed them, daintily and properly, how to deliver their stings. But when some of the wasps stung out of turn, the committee threw up its hands in innocent horror, blaming the entire problem solely on the wasps.

It should be pointed out that this vast array of support activities was legally authorized and funded under the intelligence authorization bill and the intelligence appropriations hidden within the defense appropriations bill. They were carried out by brave, dedicated men and women who, I can personally testify, truly believed in their country and in their mission. It is difficult to fault the professional intelligence community for undertaking operations ordered by the president and funded and authorized by the Intelligence Committees, nor were any of the activities particularly unusual for the trade.

But Rep. Lee Hamilton is another matter; he had been "briefed into a bind," as a former CIA official put it, and by commission or omission, he committed political treachery.

How? Because the controversy over Nicaragua was a fundamental issue for the liberal wing of the House Democratic Caucus as well as the House leadership. Hamilton had dutifully and publicly sided against contra aid and thereby reaped immense political benefits within Democratic party ranks; he was on Democratic presidential nominee Michael Dukakis's short list of candidates for secretary of state. There would have been an uproar had his secret cooperation with the Reagan administration been discovered. He would have had a head-on collision with Rep. Dave Bonior and the rest of the Democratic Whip Task Force on Nicaragua. And he would have been accused by liberals of treason against his own party, of throwing his lot with the very Republicans who delighted in accusing his fellow Democrats of being unpatriotic and procommunist on Nicaragua.

What about Admiral John Poindexter? Any man who could sell U.S. arms to Iranian terrorists and destroy the evidence was no innocent. But the charges involving that segment of his Iran-contra conviction were, in the final result, no different from those of a common criminal—he committed a crime, destroyed evidence, lied about what he had done to criminal investigators, and so on. Every crackhead in Washington, D.C., does the same thing.

But the charges alleging that he lied to Congress about my resolution of inquiry were quite different. They did more than touch directly on the constitutional balance of power; they were dead wrong.

Poindexter stated that the activities of the National Security Council did not violate the Boland Amendment. He believed that the Boland Amendment did not cover the National Security Council, and he had legal opinions to back up that belief, including a 1984 opinion by Bretton G. Sciaroni, counsel to the president's Intelligence Oversight Board at the White House. Hamilton apparently believed the contrary—that the National Security Council was indeed subject to that law. He also had strong legal arguments. But if this question was so important at the time—and even more so today—why did Lee Hamilton not ask John Poindexter or Oliver North directly when he met them face-to-face if they felt the Boland Amendment did or did not apply to the NSC? Why did he not ask, either in person or in writing, when the congressional sponsor of the resolution of inquiry urged him specifically to do so?

Hamilton did not ask North or Poindexter about Richard Secord, Rob Owen, John Singlaub, John Hull, or the others named in the press stories. He did not question Secord, Owen, Singlaub, and Hull himself, or bring them before the Intelligence Committee. After secretly signaling in October 1985 that he would approve Third Country funding for the contras, Hamilton refused to use his power as Intelligence Committee chairman to dig into the activities of Israel, Taiwan, South Africa, South Korea, and others who were allegedly assisting the contra resupply network. Instead, he waited for our resolution to meet with North and Poindexter despite Associated Press stories as early as October 7, 1985, that President Reagan had approved a "secret plan to replace CIA funds with assistance from American citizens and from U.S. allies."

Rep. Dave McCurdy also refused to challenge the response of North and Poindexter to the resolution of inquiry because the resolution would have uncovered his having been notified of a potentially direct and specific violation of the law, his failure to report it, and his extensive secret meetings on political strategy with the hated (from the Democratic viewpoint) Elliott Abrams and Alan Fiers, head of the CIA's Task Force on Nicaragua.

I should make one thing perfectly clear: the resolution of inquiry on which John Poindexter was convicted was purely political. We saw the opportunity for a successful cheap shot at the Reagan administration on Nicaragua that would allow us to snatch some press for our national Democratic radio address in June 1986 and, a few days later, swing a few votes our way on the $100 million contra aid vote. Nothing more. The point on Capitol Hill is not to win on issues, it's to get reelected. Issues are checker chips. You give some away, you take some back.

The resolution's treatment was equally political. It scared Hamilton and McCurdy because it was out of their control, and politicians are notorious control freaks. Killing our resolution was Hamilton's way of keeping score. Like the rest of the House in the 1980s, he had lost his sense of mission. And if the House had become a dark mirror for the worst of America, Lee Hamilton symbolized the death of the genuinely public man. When Rep. David Obey in May 1989 considered delaying foreign aid funding until he could learn why key documents had never been provided to the Iran-contra committees, Lee Hamilton told him there was "no general interest" in the idea. Hamilton would have done well to have pondered Obey's reported reply: "I didn't swear to uphold the Constitution until I got bored."

Lee Hamilton has the reputation of being a kind, even decent man. I would like to believe it despite my knowledge that such reputations are created and burnished by Hill rats. Still, friends I trust tell me that it is true, so I leave the question open, and I hope. Such is Washington and such is the sustenance of myth; no one will ask a man with a reputation like Lee Hamilton what he had to do to earn $152,066 in political action committee contributions for his 1988 reelection campaign.[17]

But he may well have agonized over the demands of his conscience and the pain of his knowledge when he joined the Intelligence Committee in 1983. Perhaps he searched his soul for answers and came up dry; I would like to believe it. We will never know because he has remained silent on these topics. But we do know that when he previously felt tainted by forbidden knowledge—when he learned in January 1985 that contra leader Arturo Cruz, Jr., was on the CIA payroll and testifying before Congress, a violation of the law—he settled for an arrangement that took him off the hook politically without resolving the problem.

Lee Hamilton's secret life was all the more distasteful because he was supposed to have been one of us, the so-called liberal Democrats. The AFL-CIO gave him a 100 percent rating in 1988, and the liberal Americans for Democratic Action were not far behind at 88 percent. In 1986, the year of the resolution of inquiry, Hamilton supported the leadership on party-line votes 83 percent of the time—and he convinced the Democratic Caucus that he was our intellectual and moral leader in the fight against contra aid.

I need to make something else perfectly clear: John Poindexter did not lie to Lee Hamilton, Dave McCurdy, and the rest of the Intelligence Committee. He gave them what they needed. And if that is criminally liable conduct, the House of Representatives will soon be a very empty place.

Because that was the difference between us and Hamilton. We never pretended the resolution of inquiry was anything more than a political chip or that we were anything more than a partisan Texas Ranger with a big iron on our hip. It was a political gunfight and we were betting we could outdraw the administration. Lee Hamilton's protests wounded virtue; we did not. We licked our wounds and we hit back. But Hamilton has presented himself to the foreign policy salons of New York, Washington, Chicago, and Los Angeles as a wise and thoughtful politician. Other governments follow his words and actions closely. He supports processes and mechanisms, and hopes for good will. We will settle for the low road to victory; he prefers the high road to defeat. He has position and stature, and he will act to protect it.


And me? I have learned to keep score too, perhaps even better now than during that fateful summer of 1986. You *do* win some and you *do* lose some. This was one, though, the country lost and cannot win. Meanwhile, life on the Hill goes on. We still armor-plate our incumbency any way we can. We hold elections, and act surprised when fewer and fewer people show up. And if I do not approve of Hamilton's actions, I recognize his duplicity. It is something every Hill rat understands.

# CHAPTER TEN

# HIGH WATER

TEXANS in politics are fond of observing that "if you gonna run with the big dogs, you gotta learn to piss in the tall grass." I once asked a native-born Texan what that saying meant. He was unsure of the literal application, but suggested several other possibilities. One, you need to be a big enough dog yourself. Two, the aphorism was misconstrued somewhere down the line, and it originally said "over" the high grass, i.e., so you wouldn't get it all over yourself when you ran through the grass. Finally, my friend gently reminded me that Texas sayings are immune from literary criticism, especially deconstruction, and if you had to ask what it meant, you probably were not ready to run with the hounds in question. Since he could differentiate with ease the intricacies of Texas barbeque, I took him at his word.

Ironically, like Rep. Lee Hamilton, we were in no mood for questions either. And besides, we had a lot more important things to worry about than wild-eyed Marine lieutenant colonels running Third World wars: political things, real things, like the thousand ways in which the Byzantine exercise of power on Capitol Hill is carried out, beginning with our own.

With the retirement of Speaker Thomas P. O'Neill and the ascension of Majority Leader Jim Wright to the speakership, Congressman Coleman thought he was ready to be a prime-time player in the new 100th Congress that had increased its Democratic majority from 250–180 to 258–187. So did the rest of the Texas delegation—or at least the Democrats.[1] Texas Democrats think very little of Republicans in general, and even less of Texas Republicans in particular. Party-line voting is entrenched in Texas, and the roots of disdain for the other side stretch past Lyndon Johnson and Sam Rayburn all the way back to Reconstruction. (Today, however, it is the Republicans who conduct "ballot security programs" with uniformed thugs standing outside minority polling precincts in what Democrats call an attempt to intimidate them from voting. Republicans claim it is to prevent ballot fraud. Both sides have a good case. Our office once received a list of "newly registered voters" from an organization of community activists. We immediately sent them a franked mailing from the congressman to congratulate them for registering to vote. Nearly two-thirds came back from the post office bearing "no such address." But the precincts turned out heavily on Election Day.)

The most commonly used phrase in our office, in light of our new-found power, would rapidly become "take it to the Speaker." The loyalty of Texas Democrats is as real as the legend, and Congressman Coleman and Jim Wright had been allies back in Texas from the beginning of Coleman's political career. The Armed Services Committee had given Coleman the crucial opportunity to provide for El Paso's local military base. Given the public perception of Democrats as generally weak on defense, it had undercut the most telling charge used by Coleman's Republican opponents in 1984 and 1986.

On the Government Operations Committee, Coleman had simply done whatever fellow Texan Chairman Jack Brooks told him to do, a relationship Coleman repeated as Majority Whip-At-Large under Wright in the leadership system. Wright would profit from this organization, and through the Texas connection Coleman would take on an increasingly important role as Wright moved to gain control of the substance of the Democratic agenda as well as its process in areas as diverse as trade, welfare reform, and the budget.

In a sense, Coleman had paid his dues, especially on budget and fiscal matters, and labor issues. His AFL-CIO rating was 83 out of 100 in both 1985 and 1986. He had also masterminded Wright's preemptive strike on February 2, 1985, of revealing after Tip O'Neill's retirement announcement that he had the support of 184 out of the 267 House Democrats. Now the requests could flow both ways. While Texas newspaper headlines read, "New Speaker A West Texas Friend," Coleman crowed to the press on January 12 that "We now have the ability to have our voice heard by every committee chairman, and that is a tremendous benefit. . . ."

The new Speaker would hear Coleman's voice. I received a frantic call on the morning on October 3, 1988, from Alan Jones at the American Trucking Association. Public Works and Transportation Committee Chairman Glenn Anderson had some amendments to the Motor Carrier Safety Act in the form of a single bill, which had been placed on the suspension calendar. That meant no amendments would be allowed, but it had to pass by a two-thirds vote instead of the usual simple majority. Coleman, however, had a problem with the bill because it would increase the costs of his money people who used Mexican trucks to haul cargo from Juarez, Mexico, to El Paso. The national truck safety legislation therefore came to a screeching halt until a compromise could be found—something that happened because of a single conversation between a junior member and the Speaker, both of whom were Texans.[2]

Not every spotlight focused on Wright; the rise of the Texas delegation was the talk of the town. Sen. Lloyd Bentsen was set to chair the powerful Senate Finance Committee. Republican Sen. Phil Gramm had White House connections. Rep. Jack Brooks was nipping at the Reagan administration's heels at every turn through his Government Operations Committee. Rep. Kika de la Garza chaired the Agriculture Committee. Rep. Martin Frost was Wright's lackey on the Rules Committee. And Reps. Charlie Wilson, Jack Fields, and Ron Coleman were on Appropriations. As Charlie Wilson told *Texas Monthly*, "Ever since I've been in Washington it's been open season on Texas. Now hunting season is over."[3] The cumulative effect was a leveraging one, both for the state and us personally, as K Street lawyers and other fixers began to speak in twangs and learn the names of Mexican dishes.

The fixers did more than change accents. In 1987–1988, Wright's first Congress as Speaker, Common Cause reported that the Texas delegation raked in $765,969 in speaking fees, contributing only $81,709 to charity.[4] Coleman himself made $13,000, although the bulk of it came from Appropriations-related fixers instead of those looking for a pipeline to the Speaker. But even Texans disliked having to talk about the cash machine. Texas Rep. Marvin Leath blamed Ralph Nader, the *Washington Post*, and Common Cause for "making a living beating you over the head." During this time, Leath accepted $73,400 in speaking fees, kept $52,735, and donated the rest to charity, taking a tax break in the process.

This new power could have a personal dimension. One of my best Texas buddies put it succinctly. "I'm gonna eat and drink my way through this town," he stated in his own fake drawl, "and when I'm done I'm not going to be able to recognize what a check looks like." He was kidding—okay, maybe only halfway—but the point was accurate. We were now seen by Washington's players as a pipeline to Wright and, indeed, the tall grass. "Take it to the Speaker" would become useful as a threat, too, with bureaucrats and federal agencies that were not cooperating with our agenda.

Doors we had not dreamed of were now being opened, and we moved rapidly to turn it all to local political advantage. At the end of January, Congressman Coleman directed us to prepare a private briefing paper for the House Democratic leadership on the issue of twin plants—manufacturing facilities that use extremely cheap Mexican labor to assemble products. These factories are understandably as popular with business as they are hated by labor. A U.S. electronics firm could manufacture parts in this country, ship them to Mexico to be assembled for weekly wages lower than a U.S. worker's daily wage, and then return them to the U.S. with import duties levied only on the value added by the assembly operation. In the process, of course, American assembly workers lost their jobs. But since Coleman needed his money people to keep his own job, copies of the briefing paper went to the new leadership: Speaker Wright, Majority Leader Thomas Foley, Majority Whip Tony Coelho, and Chief Deputy Whip David Bonior, all of whom had moved up the leadership ladder following Tip O'Neill's departure.

Like all of us, Coleman relished the thought of Access, much like fans at rock concerts who sport backstage passes that allow them to meet and greet the stars. The most prized pass at such events reads "All Access," the political version of which Coleman now had tatooed across his forehead—and the rest of the Hill knew it. In reality, it would have to be used sparingly, as all true power must be, but it could be used nevertheless. Coleman now lunched with the Speaker every Wednesday at the weekly Texas delegation luncheon, where he could bring anything he desired to the Speaker's attention. Our office immediately began to receive calls from friends we never knew we had who wanted to know every nuance about scheduling of legislation or the Speaker's latest move. Coleman might not have his hand on the wheel, but for the first time he would be inside the bus.

It was a mark of the modern congressman that Congressman Coleman chose to exercise his Access for the first time not on behalf of his Mexican-American constituents (predominantly Mexican-American assembly workers in Texas were losing their jobs as factories headed south) or any other component of his traditional Democratic base, but on the new base of the 1980s—cash constituents. His financial backers were intimately tied to the twin plant industry, and on the border as well as in Washington, money talks.

In the process, we would surf high on the Jim Wright wave. Paul Rogers directed me to start making Coleman's speeches "a little grander, a little more historical—upgrade them," as if the elevation of language could make Coleman appear statesmanlike. Paul had a serious look on his face and sounded as if he really believed it. I reassured him that I would indeed upscale the congressional image.

January 14 was the first legislative session of Wright's reign, and we wondered what bills to cosponsor. There was a lot of momentum from the last Congress, which had rewritten and actually simplified the tax code. Gramm–Rudman had been successfully ignored (Congress had voted $11.7 billion in across-the-board cuts that missed not only every legal deadline but also the target of a $144 billion deficit). Unlike many members, Coleman cosponsored few bills, and the ones he did reflected bones tossed to the foundations of his political constituencies: the Democratic trade bill for labor and the leadership, pay equity and Rep. Pat Schroeder's family and medical leave bill for women, the GI bill for veterans, clean water for environmentalists, a labor bill on disease notification, and three energy industry bills introduced by fellow Texan John Bryant that we had heard were good for raising money.

"What's the impact of the budget on the district?" was the congressman's first question. Even at our new elevation, all business was local. Once we told him about the magnitude of President Reagan's proposed cuts—he considered the task of reading the budget documents as our job, not his—he wanted letters sent to all elected officials in the district to disassociate himself from the budget. Despite the potentially disastrous effect on Coleman's district, the first-ever trillion-dollar budget was a political gold mine because it gave us something to be against. "Like shootin' fish in a barrel," a legislative assistant grinned as he contemplated the mass mailing possibilities.

Politics has many ironies. If Ronald Reagan had given us a completely acceptable budget, we would have been completely out of luck.[5]

Another legislative assistant mentioned that our "truck safety" bill was ready to be introduced. We called it "truck safety" because it would allow Mexican trucks to avoid U.S. safety requirements while chugging back and forth between twin plants in El Paso and Ciudad Juarez. Many of Coleman's influential money people were outraged when the International Trade Commission proposed requiring that Mexican trucks meet such exotic standards as working brakes, and we had hopped to the task immediately. As drafted, the legislation would delay the ITC's ability to impose safety standards for several years.

"Maybe the Teamsters should review it first," Coleman said hesitantly.

Paul Rogers, ever mindful of the fundraising consequences of not introducing something for the moneymen, argued that we could finesse the Teamsters by saying the legislation was only a "vehicle" by which to address the issue. We could ask the Teamsters for their changes later, as well as their money.

A legislative assistant whispered to me, "How many Teamsters does it take to change a light bulb?"

I shrugged and pretended to pay attention to the congressman.

"Twenty at time and a half—you gotta problem with that?"

I tried hard to keep a straight face as Coleman said enthusiastically to no one in particular, "Yeah, yeah. Our intent is to help them make their concerns heard."

"By fucking them with Mexican trucks," someone else whispered. I snickered again. Rogers glared in my direction.


But the first major clash of the season did not occur with Teamsters, or even Republicans, but among fellow Democrats at the pre-1986 Caucus meeting in December 1985. House Armed Services Committee Chairman Les Aspin (D-WI) was facing a determined challenge from conservative Texas Democrat Marvin Leath. Aspin had seized the chairmanship himself in 1985 by jumping over a more senior Democrat, and afterwards had alienated many of his original backers, especially the liberals, by not countering the Reagan defense buildup. Leath, a conservative who was trying to surf the Wright wave in his own way, had won the backing not only of moderates but of leftists like Rep. Ron Dellums from Berkeley. For once in the House, it seemed, the ability to trust a person at his word was running neck and neck with ideology.

The day before the vote, I called around for some skinny; Coleman was going with Leath because he was a Texan. "Is Aspin going to win?" I asked my best source, a Democratic liberal with good contacts in the Hill's defense community.

"I don't know," he replied. "He fucked us on the MX and the

contras. Plus he's an arrogant bastard who makes the mistake of never letting you forget it. He thinks he's there to run the military for himself instead of for the Democrats. On the other hand, I hope he wins because he'll owe the libs big-time and we can start having some fun with some of those programs." He called later in the day to upgrade his assessment of Aspin's chances because "Aspin's conducting a virtual fire sale for votes." He paused to mimic Aspin's earnest speaking style. "What're you selling—whatta ya want? We got it all—bases, programs, guns, grants! Yes, ladies and gentlemen, step right up . . ." Aspin won.[6]

Later in the year, while the defense authorization bill was on the floor, I talked to my friend again. There was a great deal of concern, not all of it politically motivated, that the House was attempting unduly to interfere with the president's ability to negotiate arms controls agreements with the Soviet Union. Some Democrats had expressed concern privately, but most of the public protests came from Republicans. "The Republicans and the White House are screaming about the Constitution," I commented.

"Fuck 'em," he laughed. "Les Aspin won by a small margin on a secret ballot. He doesn't owe them his chairmanship, and they don't run the House.

I needed some talking points for a statement to rebut the Republicans' allegations, so I asked, "But what about negotiating with the Russians?"

"Fuck them too. They don't run the House either. Better yet, tell 'em to form a PAC."


Coleman did a curious thing on January 27: he introduced legislation to repeal the $12,100 congressional pay raise proposed by President Reagan on January 5, and was showered nationally with favorable press.[7] Wow, the media said, a Texan in the leadership, a protege of Jim Wright was standing up against the pay raise! Now there's a story! Studies show that nearly all national press coverage concerns leadership members, especially the Speaker, whenever a particular bill or issue is in the news. National press to anyone else is a political Fountain of Youth—their persona in Perceptionland is renewed and reinvigorated and sparkles like the introductory animation in a Disney film. In most instances, too, receiving national attention is deemed newsworthy in and of itself, beyond the substance of the story; and a member's local press will frequently provide adoring coverage of the member's national coverage.

"Mr. President, you're wrong on the pay raise," Coleman thundered in his press release. He wanted Perceptionland to be aware that President Reagan had made the recommendation to increase congressional pay from $77,500 to $89,500 (having reduced the recommendation of the Presidential Commission on Executive, Legislative, and Judicial Salaries down from $135,000). Under the law, the president's recommendation would go into effect automatically unless Congress specifically voted against it. We did not mention, of course, that the 1985 continuing resolution included an amendment that made presidential pay raises automatic unless rejected by both the House and the Senate within thirty days.

Even so, the legislation was not as noble as it sounded. Coleman had privately told the Speaker that he had been forced to oppose the pay raise in the 1986 election, and he feared disastrous political consequences if he did not oppose it now. Fine, said the Speaker, but do it the right way. The Senate had added an antipay raise amendment to emergency legislation for the homeless, and Wright himself had come under fierce personal pressure to save the raise. Coleman introduced his bill, dutifully testified on its behalf,[8] and breathed a sigh of relief when the deadline of midnight on February 3 passed without a vote. The House did vote to disapprove the pay raise—a day after the deadline. Coleman was joined in his legislation by other members who needed political cover, such as Jim Chapman from East Texas, who called President Reagan's pay proposal "outrageous" and said he would vote to rescind it on the House floor.[9] Like Coleman, Chapman pointedly did not push a vote as the deadline approached; that was, after all, the right way to do it.

Newspaper headlines back home would blare "Coleman Did Try,

But Raises Are In."[10] In the end, he quietly pocketed every penny of the raise, a subject not addressed in my subsequent press releases.

A second curious event took place on February 14: Speaker Wright made a point of telling President Reagan publicly that he thought he was wrong on immigration. Federal regulations had been proposed in the wake of the previous year's immigration bill to implement the legalization process for undocumented persons who had resided in the country for a certain length of time, but the fees for legalization were high and therefore controversial.

February was also the month in which Speaker Wright arrived in El Paso to appear at a fundraiser for Coleman at the El Paso Country Club. On the morning of the 14th, Coleman and Wright held a press conference. Drawing on the material in our earlier briefing paper, Wright defended twin plants, which made Coleman's money people extremely happy. The signal was hard to miss: Ron Coleman had delivered the Speaker of the House of Representatives on the issue of twin plants.

Then Wright turned to the new immigration bill. "If the administration isn't willing to reconsider some of its procedures, Congress may have to write a new law," Wright stated. "Certainly Congress did not mean for exorbitant legal fees to be charged applicants for amnesty."[11]

Something about Wright's tone when he laid down the challenge to the president caught my eye and ear, and those of others, too: Wright was starting to take on the presidency itself. At the time, Wright had been moving aggressively across the board to assert congressional power at the White House's expense. The seeds of the fundamental challenge Wright would later issue to the executive branch were present, although none of us was aware of the extent the challenge would take, nor of the bitterness. Wright deeply believed that the executive branch under Reagan was assuming supraconstitutional powers, and, ironically, Reagan and others felt the exact same way about Congress.

It was not a bad time for Wright to make his move. The Reagan presidency had been permanently weakened by the Iran-contra scandal, which in early 1987 was still unfolding. One newspaper headline after another reduced Ronald Reagan from an invincible political demigod to an ordinary politician his peers no longer feared.

The dean of the media establishment—David Broder of the *Washington Post*—unloaded on Reagan on January 28, 1987, in an article titled, "The Sad State of This Presidency." Broder blamed Reagan's "stubborn insistence" at keeping the autocratic chief of staff, Donald Regan, in office. He said others in the cabinet would follow if Schultz resigned, and then delved into another typical story of Washington intrigue. Four days later, the *New York Times*'s David Shipley weighed in even stronger by claiming that "a sea change has taken place in the press [and] in Congress. . . . [I]f perception is paramount in politics, Mr. Reagan has weakened, opening the way for Congress to take a more confrontational role in foreign policy."

This was the true change on Capitol Hill from the Iran-contra scandal—it had nothing to do with new laws or better oversight of covert operations, and everything to do with the absence of fear. Reagan had been able to shake Democratic constituencies to the bone. That was no longer possible. The impact of Iran-contra had been felt in virtually every legislative area, especially domestic ones that had nothing to do with the scandal or even foreign policy.

As one of my friends commented, "Ronald Reagan can now be fucked with." An earthy observation, to be sure, but strikingly true.

After the Wright visit, we breathed a sigh of relief when we discovered that no issues were appearing in our constituent mail except the congressional pay raise, and we had positioned ourselves on the proper side (oppose the raise and keep the money).

Ah, constituent mail. What kind of mail do members of Congress really receive? I have reproduced faithfully this letter that was sent to Rep. Dan Rostenkowski, which was immediately copied and distributed all over the Hill:

Dear Congressman:

I want to thank you for helping me get my increase in my Social Security payment. I had enough money left last month to buy me a radio. It is so much company to me. I have been here in the nursing home since my dear husband passed away 3 years ago. I had never had any visitors so my new radio means a lot to me. Mrs. _____ who lives in the next room had had a radio since she came here 2 years ago but she would never let me listen to it. She's 85 years old and I will be 83 March 3. Last week her radio fell off the table and broke and she asked me if she could listen to mine and I said fuck you.

Sincerly yours,[12]

From schoolchildren to the nursing home resident above, Americans write their representatives in Congress in great numbers. Our office received on average of between four and six hundred letters a week. Incoming mail is, of course, a mere trickle compared to the torrents we send out, but these letters are from real people with real problems and real opinions. Many of them are quite touching when they express the human toll of unemployment, crime, hunger, and other disgraces. Then there are the high school teachers who instruct their students to write their congressman for a return letter, a photograph, a copy of a bill, which can be quite annoying. Still, most letters are handled with the respect and compassion they deserve.

On the other hand . . .

Well, take "Sgt. Rock, Certified Viet Nam Sniper (Retired) and Gook Killer." That's his name. I know it because it says so in bright black and red crayon on the outside of the envelope and on the letter inside. Each and every time he writes.

In everyday usage, the phrase "write your congressman" has become derogatory, followed by a mocking laugh. You hear it when you complain to the checkout clerk about high food prices or the appliance repairman about an expired warranty.

Curiously enough, though, enough people write enough letters that members hire a significant number of people to answer them. And no, members do not sign their mail personally unless it's a VIP letter or you've enclosed a fat campaign contribution. There's simply too much mail and too little time.

But what actually *happens* when you send a letter to your congressman?

First you sort the letters by political weight. In our office, the staff director went through all the mail and sorted it personally. Postcards in one pile, letters in another, publications in a third, and so on. He was well attuned to Congressman Coleman's personal and political landscape, and so important letters were flagged and tagged for immediate attention.

Now the fun starts.

Remember, this is a town where money talks and bullshit walks. Cash vaults your letter to the top of the pile. It gets your mail opened quicker and answered one hell of a lot faster.

The next priority after money letters is VIPs from the district. You will find a lot of overlap between contributors and VIPs. Every community in America has its own power structure. The elements that make up this network are often at odds with each other, but it is generally a known universe: bankers, community activists, elected officials, and so on.

VIPs from the Washington political community form the next category, a motley group that includes lobbyists who give some money but not enough; the occasional Assistant Secretary of Something or Other; or perhaps a top party official. They are important but not necessarily urgent. The basic attitude with these letters is *yeah, get it done, but anytime this week will be fine.*

We frequently receive letters from all parts of the country on major issues like contra aid or abortion. We throw these away. If you send these letters, I am sorry; the congressman gets reelected by 500,000 people and you are not one of them.

A large percentage of mail from the district comes from people who have a complaint with the federal government. It almost always involves money. The federal government has it; these people think they deserve it; and they want it—now.

Today the average constituent who writes a member of Congress to express an opinion or to urge a course of action receives the response of an organization, not another individual. It is rare to receive a letter on an issue that has not been researched, staffed, overstaffed, understaffed, drafted, corrected, redrafted, massaged, signed off on, memoed, reviewed, maybe even cleared by a committee or the Congressional Research Service, and otherwise screwed, blewed, and tattooed—all before it goes to the Member's autopen machine. No fewer than the legislative correspondent, the legislative assistant for the issue in question, the staff director, possibly the press secretary, the legislative director, and maybe a district staffer or two get their whack at a "text" before it goes to the Member, who on rare occasions may have an independent thought or two. Any changes by the member are then run by each of the aforementioned layers, which takes all the time it suggests.

And the substance of it all?

We adopted the advice quoted in E. S. Turner's account of the fourteenth-century admonition to physicians to maximize the satisfaction of their patients: "Tell the patient that, with God's help, you hope to cure him, but inform the relatives that the case is grave. Then, if he dies, you will have safeguarded yourself. If he recovers, it will be a testimony to your skill and wisdom. If you find the patient dead on your arrival, show no surprise. Say you know from the account of his symptoms he would not recover and inquire the hour at which he died. This will enhance your professional reputation."

By the end of March, things were back to normal. The reception circuit began to get heavy again, and more senior members of our staff were beginning to skip them, much to the annoyance of Paul Rogers. "When's the intern season begin?" wondered one weary staffer. "Let's hire a hundred to do nothing except go to cocktail parties for us."

Coleman's success in the 1986 general election and his influence with the Speaker on the twin plants issue in early 1987 convinced him that he had secured his right flank, that no Republican could ever beat him in a general election. That left open the possibilty of a liberal-left challenge in a Democratic primary, so we moved to shore up the left.

At a March 24, 1987, legislative meeting, Paul Rogers told us, "Get on everything labor's asked us to do." He meant cosponsor all their bills and sign Coleman's name to any letters to the president, federal agencies, or other members that labor's congressional allies might be pushing.

"But we haven't been asked to do all that much," a legislative assistant pointed out.

Rogers, mindful of upcoming fundraisers and the need to secure Coleman's left, barked, "Find something."

Later that day, the congressman graced us with his presence to discuss the next day's vote in the Appropriations Committee of the supplemental appropriations bill. Everyone and his brother was offering amendments, starting with Rep. Norm Dicks, who wanted to impose sublimits on air- and ground-launched cruise missiles under SALT II.

"How'd I vote last year?" Coleman asked.

"For it."

"Okay."

"Green's going to offer the Schroeder-Aspin test ban. You voted for that one, too."

Coleman grunted.

"Plus there's going to be an amendment for $300 million in aid to Central America."

"Who's offering it?"

"No one knows. And the hearing on your Mexican truck safety bill is at ten on Thursday."

"Isn't there some shit about Central America, the Persian Gulf, and the Pacific at 9:30 A.M. in Military Construction?"

"Yeah, but the independent truckers will be testifying at the hearing."

"Oh." Coleman would end up attending the trucking hearing, and for reasons other than the simple fact that it was on a bill he had introduced. Politics trumps national concerns; supporters who are also PACmen trump all.

Then the Taiwanese had to be dealt with. Paul Rogers had met on February 5 with Nathan Mao, a Taiwanese lobbyist, to seal the deal for a junket for Coleman to Taiwan, a trip considered to be the most lavish of all possible junkets. And the Taiwanese footed the entire bill—air fare, top-rate hotels, lavish banquets, and entertainment.

"You do the Taiwan trip yet?" is a standard hall-chatter question in House office buildings. For those who like trips, it is the Hill rat's equivalent of a teenager's first beer: slightly sinful, always available, and nearly everyone tries it at least once. (Alas, I never made the trip myself, but not for lack of trying.)

My assignment was to call the Congressional Research Service to find out what Coleman was supposed to say in his after-dinner remarks once he got there. The Taiwan junket was a well-known one; the specialist did not have to consult her protocol book. "Always recognize the host. Avoid at all costs the word 'China.' " she instructed in a practiced tone. Do not mention the People's Republic. And always use the terms 'Taiwan' and 'the people of Taiwan.' That is in keeping with U.S. policy."

The Taiwanese expected official recognition in whatever form in return for their investment. Like most other members who took these junkets, Coleman became a regular cheerleader for Taiwan in the *Congressional Record*, dropping in a statement whenever Nathan Mao stopped by to make the request. This is the way professionals handle the culture of influence's quid pro quo. Nothing overt, nothing untoward, not even a private wink and a nod. Nathan Mao never had to insist or press his point. He would appear from time to time with sample statements for the *Congressional Record*, usually around the time of year of Taiwan's anniversary or the birthday of one of its leaders. He would be welcomed, and the requisite pro-Taiwan statement would be printed. You could never say in a court of law that a deal had been struck, only that the congressman had accepted an all-expenses paid junket to Taiwan and had subsequently hailed that country in the *Congressional Record*. And again, and again, and again . . .[13]

But the Taiwanese payback is relatively innocuous compared to others. On April 10, Congressman Coleman accepted a personal payment for speaking to the Customs Bonded Warehouse Association at 9:00 A.M. At 9:30 A.M. in the congressional office, our legislative staff met with Timothy Bennett from the U.S. Trade Representative's office about an upcoming trade agreement with Mexico. The first item on the meeting's agenda was the status of the Customs Association.

Some deals are even less subtle. A friend of a friend talked us into meeting with an outfit called National Voter Contact, which was pitching ways to improve "constituent communications."

"It's a great program," explained National Voter's Dave Nuckols as we met in the congressman's office. "Congressmen Frost, Bryant, English, and Daschle have used us, as well as Senators Biden, Baucus, and Hollings." He spelled out the program, which involved calling most households in the congressional district to identify potential supporters, contributors, and important issues.

Then he got to the rub: "Once we identify the important issues, you tie it into franked congressional mail. If you are not willing to do that, the program will not work."

We had no problems with an official marriage between congressional and campaign resources, but National Voter Contact's program proved to be too much even for us, especially at an estimated $100,000 cost.

The rest of the spring and summer of 1987 was disjointed, and the legislative session was particularly frenzied. In congressional politics today you are either moving or losing. You cannot afford to dwell too long on any given issue—the public would soon demand solutions instead of mere attention—so you dart from crisis to crisis as if you were trying to cross a stream quickly, dancing from steppingstone to steppingstone, leaving on each nothing but a wet footprint that soon evaporates in the sunshine. On the rare occasion the politician looks back, it is with the expectation of receiving gratitude for having graced the stone with his presence.

Sometimes it is hard to tell the steppingstones from the incomings. On May 13, we met with Congressman Coleman on the upcoming defense bill. Defense bills present enormous political problems because the legislation is too important and expensive for the Democratic leadership to get away with imposing a closed rule. That means any fool can offer an amendment, and usually does. Three entire weeks had been scheduled for the defense debate, starting May 5, an enormous amount of time to be wasted—from the standpoint of the Favor Factory—on things such as the Strategic Defense Initiative, nuclear testing, antisatellite missiles, SALT II treaty limits, and the rest.

Coleman's main concern was preventing surprise.

"Hertel-Mavroules would knock out the rail-based MX missile," a legislative assistant told him. "The Frank amendment would cut $673 million from the program and reduce the number of missiles from twelve to two."

"How'd I vote before?" Coleman interrupted.

"Dellums would terminate the Midgetman . . . " the legislative assistant tried to continue.

"There's no sense talking about old votes I don't remember anything about," Coleman concluded aloud to himself. The briefing ended, and he jury-rigged his votes by himself from the Democratic Cloakroom. Toward the end of the day, he told me to draft three versions of letters-to-the-editor for the *El Paso Times* that would be sent by political supporters under the guise of spontaneous comments from the public. I did so, and Paul Rogers added a fourth that attacked the journalistic integrity of the paper's editorial writer just for good measure.[14]

Capitol Hill's internal priorities are not always evident. The Iran-contra hearings dominated the public's attention, but to most of us the summer of 1987 was just more of the same nonsense.

A buddy and I were looking at a full-page newspaper advertisement of Lt. Col. North holding up his right hand while swearing an oath before testimony.

"Hey, how about that salute?" he marveled.

"You know," I said, "with a little rubber cement, a pair of scissors, and some air-brushing . . ."

"We could have it done in thirty seconds," he grinned. Our real target was across the hall—Republican Bill Schuette, whose own vanity and self-importance were exceeded only by those of his top staff people. His office was ten feet from ours and the doorway was perfectly aligned.

Oliver North was soon transformed into doing a stiff-armed "Sieg Heil!" and the artwork was taped onto the wall of our legislative compound—in full view of Schuette's reception area. The resulting glares, glowers, and grunts made all things worth while, including living life on the Hill.


By October 1987, the cold war of budget brinksmanship had worn us out. Our staff meetings were hurried, frantic, jumping wildly from one topic to another.

The use of catch-all spending bills called continuing resolutions was over a hundred years old, but their use in modern times dated to 1982 when they began to be employed as omnibus appropriations bills. The Reagan administration, which came to bewail these resolutions, had had no problem with them when it came to passing its own first budget. From 1981 to 1988, more than half of the regular appropriations bills were placed in continuing resolutions, and in 1986 and 1987, all of them were. As one internal House report noted in 1988, President Reagan's style was to stake out uncompromising positions and then refuse to negotiate until the last minute. Given the automatic cuts of the Gramm-Rudman deficit reduction process, final action on spending bills was often delayed to make sure the Gramm-Rudman targets were met.[15]

Ever encounter the Home Repair Project from Hell? You lose a part, add a wire, cut here, paste there, weld something elsewhere, glue something onto something, adjust the motor without reading the handbook, and then plug it in. It works—kind of—but barely, and you haven't the slightest idea where to begin to fix it. You have lost sight of the original intent. Red-faced and furious, you look for someone to blame—your spouse, your kid, your dog. Your focus becomes centered on the repair job, not the original mission.

You have now learned everything you need to know about the fundamental principles of congressional budget management.

Events whirled around us, and the stress became minute-to-minute. No word on budget reconciliation yet? Damn! File folders slammed onto desktops. The realtors' lobby was screaming about caps on mortgage and home equity loans. To complicate matters even more, Paul Rogers told us that "We need to be able to shoot down the attractiveness of a spending freeze." Then he added, "For defensive purposes, do a chronology of the congressman's actions on budget deficits, beginning in 1983 with Rep. Jim Jones's legislation all the way to the present. Use recent speeches and statements."

The overriding goal, like that of worker bees, was to protect the queen: our appropriations projects. On September 9, 1987, the conservative Citizens for America sent us a letter that read:

Dear Congressman:

Congratulations!

You have made the list—the list of Capitol Hill's most brazen and shameless pork-barrel spenders. You are a porker . . . and now everyone is going to know it.

Attached to the letter was the groups' "The Pork Book," which placed Coleman and others in the "Pork Barrel Hall of Shame" and termed them "enemies of fiscal responsibility."[16]

"Comments?" I asked our Appropriations staffer as I showed him the letter and the study.

He read the material and got up quickly.

"Where're you going?" I asked.

"To ask for a raise."

On September 10, we stuck it to Democratic Sen. Dennis DeConcini, with whom we had crafted a $33.4 million deal to upgrade Southwest border crossings and bridges. I released the details a little sooner than the senator might have been led to believe I would, and Coleman—only Coleman—received the first essential wave of credit, the precious lifeblood of politics. Then Sen. Pete Domenici started raising hell, claiming that *he* had been working with DeConcini, too. Texas Sen. Lloyd Bentsen, mad at his staff for getting left behind, issued a press release whining that he, Coleman, and three other Texas members had sent a letter to DeConcini urging adoption of the project. Poor DeConcini, still clueless—or at least his Hill rats were—watched in silence as the hubbub swirled about him.

While we were grabbing all the pork we could find, we were backpedaling from Gramm-Rudman now that real cuts might *really* happen. On October 15, Coleman spelled out potential cuts as determined by the day's estimates released by the Congressional Budget Office, including a 10 percent reduction in military construction and 25 percent in education. Even worse, the automatic timetable was upon us. The White House Office of Management and Budget would make its own determination of cuts on October 20, and meanwhile the president issued some temporary cuts. Congress would have until November 20 to reduce the deficit by alternative means, and the president would enact the cuts.

Again, the first reaction is to manage instead of to solve. "How do you avoid the hit?" is always asked first. Every decision depends upon buffeting pressures—from the leadership, interest groups, and constituents—and its impact on any future election.

Our junior leadership circle expressed a great deal of concern about the lack of Democratic strategy. How could we be taken seriously when the budget reconciliation bill alone included a $5 billion welfare program, still another pay increase to members of Congress, and special tax breaks for pet projects in the districts of Jim Wright, Tom Foley, and Dan Rostenkowski?

Coleman quickly issued a statement opposing the pay increase; fortunately, no one asked him how he opposed the last pay raise and then kept the money. Other things were in the air, such as how to respond to the October 19 Wall Street crash that dragged down the rest of the world's financial markets along with it.

We had yet another budget crisis meeting later in the day. "Why the hell is the welfare reform bill in the budget reconciliation?" Coleman wanted to know. Ways and Means Democrat Tom

Downey had added a $1.7 billion welfare "reform" bill to the reconciliation legislation, which was only supposed to balance the spending totals of the earlier budget bill with current revenue estimates.

"Ways and Means is unconvincing in its explanation," our tax specialist said judiciously. "The Republicans will jump on the numbers discrepancy."

"The Speaker is a total advocate of this plan," Coleman observed.

"The budget says we need a vehicle, if only to substitute for any summit package," the specialist added.

This sort of havoc was commonplace. As a Democratic member once remarked to the Center for Responsive Politics, "It's incredible. I don't know what's going on. Why a bill is pulled from the floor, etc. It's a constant state of confusion."[17] But then, as the writer Hunter S. Thompson has put it, when the going gets weird, the weird turn pro.

On October 29, the pros took over.

After the rule for considering the reconciliation bill was defeated, Wright and the leadership came up with a nifty trick. Because you cannot bring up a defeated rule in the same day, the Democrats adjourned and then immediately reconvened, thus creating a second "legislative day" on the same day.

But even then the budget reconciliation bill did not have enough votes to win when time ran out. The vote was 205 to 206 against. More time went by.

Finally: "Can we lock the damn door?" complained Rep. Trent Lott of Mississippi tiredly. "There ain't nobody coming." He was wrong. Democratic Majority Whip Tony Coelho was running to the front door, indicating that another member had appeared to vote.

But instead of its being a member who had not voted, it was Texas Rep. Jim Chapman who had. He was being dragged down the aisle by John Mack, the Speaker's top aide, who had told him in no uncertain terms to switch his vote from "nay" to "aye." Wright's help was instrumental in Chapman's special election in 1985. Sen. Phil Gramm convinced Rep. Sam Hall to take a federal judgeship, and recruited former Texas A&M quarterback Ed Hargett to run for the seat. Chapman, a former district attorney, performed a professional political evisceration on Hargett on the Social Security issue. Chapman was in the House by the grace of the Democratic leadership, and Mack warned him that he had better not forget it. Chapman dutifully complied. Republicans were screaming and booing.

Wright's personal prestige was on the line, and his ego was enormous. He had lost the rule vote just the day before when forty-eight Democrats defected on a 217-203 vote. It had been a slap in the face to his leadership. When Chapman put the Democrats over the top, our reaction back at the office was to whistle and clap—not for Wright or Chapman, but for John Mack. His performance as a star Hill rat had been seen on national television, and we basked in his glory.

Wright's tricks produced a lot of unnecessary partisan bitterness, and we feared privately that the Speaker's troubles would continue on into 1988. Back on March 23, Jack Anderson had revealed that the Speaker had spent $6,000 on a new fireplace for his office. On the 25th, more stories broke about Wright using his speakership power to keep shaky Texas savings and loans afloat, including the allegation that he made sure that no realistic capitalization requirements survived the House Banking Committee. Another negative story appeared on August 7, this one about Wright putting his daughter on his campaign payroll as a way to funnel campaign money for personal use.

The mounting political pressure on Wright was making us jumpy. When word came on September 29 about a possible amendment to add members of Congress to the jurisdiction of independent counsels—shades of Watergate and Iran-contra—Paul Rogers snapped, "Is this a get-Jim Wright deal?" The independent counsel bill had been kept off the House floor for several weeks because of questions the Republicans were raising over Wright's personal finances. Press reports were alleging that he had made huge profits from Texas cronies on book royalties and other investments, and the *Washington Post* reported that Wright's publisher had received $265,000 in payments from Wright's campaign committee.

Then on December 15, 1987, Republican Rep. Newt Gingrich called for a formal ethics investigation of the Speaker. We dismissed him, but nervously. We saw chinks appearing in the armor as Gingrich claimed, "There has probably never been a speaker whose ethical behavior has been more out of touch with the norms of this society than Jim Wright."

Still, no one took Gingrich that seriously. And besides, what politician could stand really *close* scrutiny?

Wright was our meal ticket. We had backed him on the Reagan-Wright peace plan for Central America and everything else. He, in return, had told the *El Paso Herald-Post* in a profile on Coleman that Coleman was "one of the bright lights. He's dependable, shows a willingness to bite the bullet, and doesn't dodge the tough issues." Later on, in December, Wright had taken Coleman's side in a dispute with the Interior Committee over an amendment to prohibit the West Texas low-level nuclear waste dump site. Coleman had wanted to attach an amendment barring the dump to a groundwater research bill, and Wright obligingly leaned on the Rules Committee to make the amendment in order.

"The subject of the Coleman amendment was under the jurisdiction of the Interior and Commerce Committees," complained Republican Rep. Manuel Lujan. " . . . It should be the duty of the Rules Committee to enforce the rules of the House instead of sweeping them under the table because the leadership has indicated its support of a particular amendment."

"What the hell good is it to have Wright as Speaker if we can't get that kind of shit?" muttered our legislative assistant.

The problem was that the Interior Committee was correct. So we backed off and cut a deal, dropping the amendment in return for a hearing, but not before claiming the hearing was what we had really wanted all along. [18]

We might have had a worldwide financial crisis brought about by the October 27 stock market collapse, but the Favor Factory was not about to let a little federal deficit-cutting get in the way of the December 3 continuing resolution. Frank Wolf (R-VA) snagged an additional traffic lane on the Theodore Roosevelt Bridge over the

Potomac River. Silvio Conte, the Favor Factory's ranking Republican, tossed in an regulation-dodging provision for seven banks in his home state of Massachusetts. Jerry Lewis (R–CA) got $8.5 million for the Loma Linda Medical Center. Our good friend Bob Carr (D–MI) topped the scales with a $28 million highway project (which, frankly, he didn't deserve). And Congressman Coleman won a provision that stopped the closing of our local National Labor Relations Board office; labor was happy again. Not surprisingly, many Republicans with projects were trying to have it both ways by opposing the bill because it did not reduce the deficit enough. (Vic Fazio threatened to cut their projects in conference and many backed off.)

Best of all, we learned that Congressman Coleman would be unopposed in the 1988 election. The Favor Factory had truly paid off. Paul Rogers spent days on the phone telling every fixer in town that it was all due to him, not Coleman. Texas Republicans, buried under the cash avalanche of our appropriations projects, threw in the towel and decided not to run a candidate against him.

Our confidence was high after a string of legislative victories that essentially ended the Reagan Revolution. We had overridden Reagan's vetoes of the highway bill and clean water amendments, and forced him to approve the special prosecutor legislation, which as far as we were concerned declared open season on the executive branch. Catastrophic health insurance was passed, and budget reconciliation contained an $11.9 billion tax increase, something Democrats had wanted for a long time.

By the end of February 1988, House Majority Whip Richard Gephardt was campaigning for the presidency. Gephardt had the curious habit of attacking his Democratic rivals for the nomination on the grounds they did not back the "Gephardt Amendment," which would have imposed heavy trade sanctions on Europe and Japan for unfair trading practices. As an unwitting prisoner of the House, he assumed that "The Gephardt Amendment" in and of itself meant something to the average American. He was wrong. Instead of centralizing his message on the *idea* behind The Gephardt Amendment, he simply thrust it out in a personalized fashion as if the country, like his beloved insiders in the House of Representatives, would shrink in awe and vote him into the White House by acclamation. Issues aside, Coleman backed him on the grounds that first, as a compulsive centrist, no one hated him, and second, even if he lost, he was powerful enough to improve Coleman's position inside the House's hierarchy. Gephardt's reputation as the Cheese Weasel went unchallenged during the campaign. During an early March 1988 swing through Texas, a spokesman was reported to have said, "Gephardt has said Texas is very important to him. He has been in and out of Texas and he will be back again." Hooray for our side, I thought. The oatmeal bubbles.[19]

Other decisions would not be as easy as whom to support for president of the United States. The increased media attention on Speaker Wright's ethics crisis was starting to rub off; the *Wall Street Journal* ran an editorial that listed from the United Press International all members of Congress who had placed a relative on the House payroll—seventy-three, including Coleman, who had put his daughter in the House Postmaster's office the previous summer. Coleman's reaction was startlingly unrepentent—what was government for? Even Paul Rogers threw up his hands in dismay.[20]

Nepotism aside, we needed the Appropriations Committee more than ever because more incomings were sighted every day. May 26 was Financial Disclosure Day, during which every member's honoraria were disclosed and scolded. It produces one of Capitol Hill's worst moods. Four hundred and thirty-five offices file their member's reports and wait for the telephone to ring. By late morning, most of the House has exhaled a collective "Ah, shit" at the prospect of the next day's headlines. Two days later, Philip Stern's book *The Best Congress Money Can Buy* came out, and we took a direct hit: Coleman had taken $257,637—or 50 percent—of his 1985–1986 campaign funds from political action committees, and $10,000 in speaking fees. Fortunately, we were in good company. Financial Disclosure Day also revealed that Jim Wright had taken $45,850 in speaking fees, keeping $32,850 ($167.99 less than the legal limit); eight other Texans had kept the maximum.[21]

The pervasive wailing and gnashing of teeth by members over

these ritual cleansings were accompanied by moans of "Why are they doing this to us? Do we deserve this shameful treatment?" Having to disclose their financial relationships is something "done" to them by enemies; it was not regarded as something they owed the public.

As luck would have it, we had plenty of armor-plating. Coleman and Rogers had approved my plan to mail 1.5 million pieces of franked mail in Political Year 1988, to which Rogers added another 400,000 newsletters and letters as well as more computer-targeted letters to individuals. Two million pieces of mail per year can give a member, if nothing else, a comfort zone from political mistakes.

At the same time, we had an Issue.

In El Paso alone, twenty-eight thousand people lived in shanty-town communities called "colonias" with no access to running water. Over fifty thousand had no sewage. Virtually all were Hispanic and most were U.S. citizens or legal residents. The problem had simmered for years, and even Coleman had not introduced any legislation in his first two terms. Hispanic activist groups across the Southwest decided to make the issue a top priority, though, and by early 1988 Coleman moved to champion the issue.

Coleman went to Speaker Wright in December 1987 and showed him the figures—tens of thousands without water or sewage systems, the entire adult population of the town of San Elizario exposed to hepatitis A, grandmothers pumping water from polluted wells into the converted trolley cars they lived in, *Life* photographs of Americans living in conditions resembling Kurdish refugee camps. Wright spoke with Rep. Jim Howard, chairman of the Public Works and Transportation Committee, and said simply, "I want it fixed." At congressional hearings in El Paso on March 11 a Catholic priest told a water resources subcommittee, "What you have seen and heard today are the sights and sounds of human misery. The situation is so shockingly tragic and profound that most people would presume it not to exist within the borders of this great country."

May 17, 1988, was Congressman Coleman's high water mark in the U.S. House of Representatives: ringed by national leaders such as Wright, Lloyd Bentsen, and a host of committee chairmen, Coleman announced at a Capitol news conference that he was introducing legislation to create a U.S.-Mexico Border Regional Development Commission to authorize water and sewage systems, hospitals, clinics, and other facilities.[22]

As he basked in the glow of national press attention, opposition developed from an unlikely source: South Texas Democrat Kika de la Garza, chairman of the House Agriculture Committee. He felt such programs should be within his jurisdiction—and they were, but he had done little during all his years in Congress other than to grant favors to agribusiness. In September, de la Garza was the sole House member to testify against the legislation, saying at a public hearing that he had seen numerous commissions and "the first thing they do is send an anthropologist to measure our heads."

I blinked. "They what?" I asked a colleague beside me.

"Measure our heads."

"Why would they measure Kika's head?"

"Who knows?"

"Does he realize he's making no sense whatsoever?"

"Who will be able to tell the difference?"

Still, it was the start of a new and different task for us: doing something worthwhile.


But trouble was in the air, and this time it was the real thing. We received a frantic call from a lobbyist at a firm called Cassidy and Associates on May 24, 1988, about the *Washington Post*'s Dan Morgan, who was digging into a notorious little swindle managed by the House Appropriations Committee called the Pirelli Cable project.

Coleman and Cassidy were intimate friends. In April 1988, the firm paid him $1,000 for a five-minute speech plus an all-expenses paid vacation to the NCAA Final Four basketball tournament in Kansas City. In 1987, Cassidy—on behalf of Pirelli Cable and Ocean Spray, Inc.—had paid Coleman and five other members of the House Appropriations Committee $2,000 plus transportation to New Orleans and lodging at the plush Royal Orleans Hotel, *and* tickets to the Final Four Tournament. Better yet, Cassidy and Associates had written the speeches themselves. (The excess to which these lobbyists treated the congressmen was such that their schedule is included in Appendix VI.)

Coleman and Rogers were visibly nervous, and with good reason. Pirelli Cable was up for a $5.6 million installment from the Favor Factory for its environmentally-questionable Hawaii Deep Water Cable Project that would carry geothermally produced electric power from the Big Island to resort developments in Oahu and Maui. Pirelli's share would amount to $400 million in cable contracts, a very good reason to start handing out $2,000 honoraria and perks to Congressmen who would take them, and small potatoes compared to Pirelli's donation of $20,000 to a chair in ranking Republican Silvio Conte's name at the University of Massachusetts.

Most members came a lot cheaper. With the help of Cassidy lobbyists like former aide to Speaker O'Neill C. Frank Godfrey, Pirelli had showered Congress with cash, donating $2,000 to Jim Wright's political action committee, $2,500 to the Democratic Congressional Campaign Committee, and $4,000 to the Democratic Congressional Dinner. Rep. Don Fuqua, chairman of the Science and Technology Committee, got a $2,000 check plus a week in Hawaii for him and his wife. Along with Coleman, Pirelli had taken care of Reps. John Myers (R-PA), Robert Livingston (R-LA), Joe McDade (R-PA), Norm Dicks (D-WA), and the ubiquitous Vic Fazio.

I talked to the *Washington Post*'s Dan Morgan the next day. "What's being paid for? What was the event?" he asked. I told him that the event was hosted jointly by Pirelli and Ocean Spray. Coleman, who was hiding out at his house, refusing to speak to Morgan, had told me the night before, "They do this annually—you speak on national issues. That's one of the draws to get you there. Tell him I'm an avid basketball fan."

Coleman was genuinely perplexed. He saw politics as a way of doing business. You vote for their projects and they take care of your lifestyle. He saw no conflict, had no sense of doing wrong—it was simply the way business was done in the House. As Pirelli Cable

Vice President John T. Barteld wrote to Coleman, "We would like to offer an honorarium of $1,000 for your participation [in two speeches]—Pirelli Cable will, of course, pay the travel and accomodation costs associated with your participation in our meeting."[23]

"It was a wonderful trip," Coleman told the *Dallas Morning News* nearly a year later.[24] If his daughter had not been involved in a car wreck, Coleman told the *News*, he would have gone to the tournament in 1989 as well.

After Coleman spoke to the *News*, he turned to me after the interview and complained, in all seriousness, "God forbid that a member of Congress should be able to go somewhere and have a good time." Spooked by the incident nevertheless, he would publicly foreswear honoraria on July 26, 1988—but not free trips and expenses.

Closer to home, despite the Pirelli flap and other nuisances, we aquired some good political armor-plating. The Associated Press ran a story on June 10 titled, "Coleman Emerges As Leader." The wire service claimed that Coleman was "emerging as a force in Congress who understands the intricacies of a 2,000-mile strand of territory separating the United States from Mexico. . . . the Democrat has the respect of his colleagues [and] a toehold in the House Appropriations Committee. . . ."[25] And what a toehold it was: on June 16, we added $3.78 million for national parks and monuments in his district, and on June 29 yet another $3 million to expand international bridges in El Paso.[26]

Later on, in September, Coleman scored big political points with the Democratic Party when he did the weekly national Democratic radio address. A comical scene developed over the preparations for the script. The Dukakis campaign people wanted to launch thermonuclear war against George Bush. Rogers wanted Coleman to sound "respectful" towards George Bush. And Coleman showed up at the taping session at the last moment without having read any of the drafts.

But like most things in politics, only the result counted. Coleman once again attracted rave national reviews for his strident attack on

Dan Quayle's leadership in the drug war: "How can Dan Quayle be put in charge of the war on drugs when he wouldn't fight in the last one?"[27]

Coleman's political stock was soaring in Perceptionland despite everything. His yearly campaign barbeque had grown into the largest political event in the state of Texas. It was Coleman's time in the sun. The food was rich and the beer was cold, and he had no care for tomorrow.[28]

Tomorrow, however, soon came. By mid-June, the House Ethics Committee had begun looking into the allegations against Speaker Wright, something that Wright in a fleeting moment of idiocy had welcomed, and the Texas delegation was circling the wagons. You could not walk the few steps from my office in 415 Cannon Building to the Longworth Cafeteria without hearing someone—Hill rat, member, lobbyist—carping about Common Cause, which on May 18, 1988, had sent a letter to the House Ethics Committee calling for an investigation of Wright. The Democratic Hill community's response was vicious. Open threats against the organization could be heard on the House floor, in the Cloakroom, and at the bar of the Democratic Club. The political culture's horrified realization that Fred Wertheimer did not see Common Cause as a front group for the Democratic Party came too late.

"They fucked us," Congressman Coleman would mutter over and over again in the summer of 1988, as if he could not comprehend how Common Cause could have instantly legitimized Newt Gingrich and the Republican-led ethics assault on the Democratic leadership.

"From now on, we're against everything they're for," Paul Rogers snarled. Fine, I replied, knowing the practical limitations of his pronouncement, starting with the minor problem that it would turn us into Republicans.

Coleman told the press that the complaints against Wright were "a completely partisan attempt to take the heat off Ed Meese and the administration's sleaze problem." And Government Operations Committee Chairman Jack Brooks accused the Republicans of playing "sack the quarterback." It did not help much when the *Washing-*

*ton Times* spotted Wright, Coleman, and a few other members lurching out of a Capitol Hill restaurant late one night. Wright carried a beer for the road, the paper reported it.[29]

Sensing the gathering storm, Paul Rogers and I, as good Hill rats, were quietly laying the groundwork to distance Coleman from Wright. "We need to get Coleman out front in the ethics issue," he said to me as he observed more and more reporters calling Coleman to get a sense of the depth of Wright's ethics problems.

It was not a good time for a congressman to be in trouble. The Pentagon procurement scandal, which had touched the Hill, was dominating the headlines. Congress's collective tab was beginning to rise. Yet even in this atmosphere, the leadership tried to slip through another pay raise, this one a cost-of-living adjustment. Although defeated on the House floor on June 14, it outraged the populace even further. Then Ways and Means Committee Dan Rostenkowski managed to throw gasoline on the fire by proposing a do-it-yourself pay plan whereby members could choose their own pay from the current $89,500 to $135,000.[30]

Speaker Wright was slipping, badly so, and we were being drawn inexorably into the morass. Ethical issues can become black holes, sucking everything around them into the depths, no matter how irrelevant. In this kind of situation, it is imperative not to stumble on your own.

Wright stumbled.

A reporter asked him at his daily press conference on September 20 if he thought it was true that the CIA was responsible for a demonstration against the Nicaraguan government on July 10 in the town of Nandaime. Wright replied, "We have received clear testimony from CIA people that they have deliberately done things to provoke an overreaction on the part of the government of Nicaragua."[31] He subsequently told the Associated Press that "agents of our government have assisted in organizing the kinds of antigovernment demonstrations that have been calculated to stimulate and provoke arrests."

Republicans immediately launched their attacks in the One-Minutes. House Minority Leader Robert Michel and Rep. Richard

Cheney, ranking Republican on the Intelligence Committee, demanded investigations from both the Ethics and Intelligence Committees into whether Wright had disclosed any classified information about any CIA covert operations to destabilize the government of Nicaragua, a charge denied by Wright on September 22. Someone had to come to Wright's aid, and Coleman decided he would be the one. I did a quick speech for Coleman to defend Wright on the House floor, arguing, "The real question is not what the Speaker did, but what Ronald Reagan did or allowed to happen. Did Ronald Reagan or the CIA once again break the law in Nicaragua?"

To relieve the pressure on Wright, we also sent a letter to the House Intelligence Committee to demand a formal inquiry into the involvement of the CIA in antigovernment activities against Nicaragua, and asked the committee to determine if any laws had been broken.[32] The committee did not respond because, as press leaks suggested and my own sources confirmed, its members had known all along about U.S. political destabilization efforts in Nicaragua, and they had not only not opposed them but had authorized them.

Politics is like pinball: the ball keeps rolling into things even as you save it. Winning $7.1 million to modernize barracks at Fort Bliss helped balance our image and keep Coleman at arms' length from the gathering storm, but it began to appear more and more as if we were going to run out of Appropriations Committee projects before Congress ran out of scandals.

The fallout had begun; the Wright situation had once again brought tough media scrutiny on rank-and-file members. The public-interest organization Congress Watch issued a study at the end of October showing that fifty-eight House candidates who were unopposed in 1988 had nevertheless raised $14.4 million for their campaigns, including $7.3 million since January 1, 1987. Texas Rep. Jack Brooks had raised $312,922, of which $215,262 was from political action committees, Rep. Charlie Wilson had raised $267,994, and Coleman had raised $226,073. "Special interest PACs are giving money to gain access and influence with members of

Congress," Congress Watch charged. "Many members of Congress are piling up huge campaign war chests to discourage viable candidates from challenging them."[33]

In fact, we were stocking our war chest as rapidly as we could. I had just completed work on Coleman's official campaign biography, which in addition to taking credit for all of Western civilization since the fall of Rome included a page titled, "CORPORATE PACS WHICH HAVE CONTRIBUTED TO CONGRESSMAN RON COLEMAN." From Atlantic Richfield's ARCO-PAC to the Zenith Electronics Political Participation Fund, the document listed ninety-two separate corporate political action committees that had anted up. The front-and-back sheet announced loudly, "I play the game."[34]

The public pressure on Congress began to affect us Hill rats. On the morning of November 4, Paul Rogers made the dark announcement that a senior staff meeting would be held later in the day. A staffer asked him for a hint, and he replied it was about an office rule.

"Is it a good rule or a bad rule?" I asked sarcastically.

"It's a goddamn rule, that's what it is, and I'm the only one who's allowed to say if it's a good rule or not!" With which he stalked off. With equal weirdness, the meeting never took place.

No one cared. By this time, we were just praying that democratic presidential nominee Michael Dukakis wouldn't take the party down with him. The results of the 1988 election were predictable: Dukakis lost, and Texas added a few more Democrats in Congress. And we heard more rumblings from leadership sources of a big congressional pay increase in the works . . . .[35]

Once again, though, the fate and fortune of Congress and congressmen had become abstract: my wife and I were going to have another baby on Christmas Eve.

# CHAPTER ELEVEN

# THE SUMMER OF
# OUR DISCONTENT

THE HILL should have been able to look back on 1988 with a sense of pride and near-historic achievement because the 100th Congress had been one of the most productive in recent memory. All thirteen regular appropriations bills had been passed in time to keep the government functioning smoothly. The welfare system had been tuned up. Medicare had been expanded enormously. Trade law had been modernized. At the same time, the Reagan administration was knuckles-deep in the Iran-contra scandal, and its foreign policy frozen. And while Democratic presidential nominee Michael Dukakis did not win, neither did Ronald Reagan. President-elect George Bush did not have the ability to go over the heads of the members and appeal directly to the public; the element of fear was absent.

Instead, Rep. Newt Gingrich entered our lives with a vengeance. He loomed over us like a malevolent force as we considered plans and strategies for 1989, a man who resembled Ted Koppel's evil twin with the energy of a methedrine addict but with less conscience. Congressman Coleman cursed him daily, and loudly, while Paul Rogers prattled vainly about dark retribution, never defined, as if he had the personal power to put it into action. I wished the man

216

would disappear, too, not out of revenge, but so we could turn to the supposedly real business of the House and move the nation forward.

I also sensed a deep, unspoken nervousness, not only for Speaker Jim Wright but for all things congressional. The House of Representatives was, by all accounts, paralyzed. And yet . . . the economy continued to expand, the Russians had not attacked us nor us them, democracy was beginning to stir in Eastern Europe, and our own government had not collapsed. One of the House's great myths was that the government—indeed, the nation—was defined by Congress's actions. By definition, then, the nation's life outside of Washington should not have taken place. That it did so, and apparently with little heed for the great myth, was yet another source of mystery and concern.

The animosity within Congress was as thick and ugly as Washington's summer humidity. Gingrich was trying to drown Jim Wright in a torrent of ethics accusations, and that made the stakes personal. In our worst nightmares, we could see it all slipping through our fingers—years of hard work, sidling up to power, voting the way the leadership wanted, anticipating what Jim Wright as a strong Speaker could do for us. Then, as the story unfolded, we watched with incredulity as Gingrich's own ethical lapses emerged—a sleazy book deal, bonuses from official funds to campaign employees—yet unaccompanied by the opprobrium flung at Wright. As the political orgy intensified, civil war erupted in the House—a war fought within as well as between the two parties. Even Republicans were splitting into cabals; we watched with some amusement as Gingrich's faction, the Conservative Opportunity Society, bickered with the 92 Group, composed of forty moderate-to-liberal Republicans.[1] The people's business was rapidly being set aside. It was time for some real bloodletting, and you could smell it in the air.

But none of this matters when your entire life is reduced to the seconds in between the beep-beep-beep of cardiac and breathing monitors attached to the chest of your hours-old baby who is fighting for life itself. Not political life, or the fulfillment of ambition, or the reach for money, but biological life and death. The beep-beep-beep makes the wailings of the politicals seem irrelevant and small. It is a world in which you cannot cut deals. You become transfixed by these blinking green arbiters of life and death, and you learn that there is little in between except sleeplessness and terror.

The birth went smoothly at 9:40 A.M. on December 24, 1988. The first scare occurred a few hours later when the baby started to choke, turn blue, and stop breathing. The nurses rushed him into intensive care and jump-started him. I remember the scenes vividly: dozens of faces and orders and grim looks, some in focus, some not, people moving with a practiced urgency and desperation. Five hours later and stabilized, Robert was placed in a pediatric life-support unit and taken to Children's Hospital. The immediate prognosis was not encouraging, the diagnosis uncertain.

The Christmas Eve traffic was heavy as I drove to Children's Hospital from Virginia. The weather was cold and damp. I drove deliberately, without speeding, relying on the reassurances of doctors that Robert was not—for the time being—a minute-by-minute question mark. They had said nothing of hours. I glanced to my right as I drove up East Capitol Street and saw the closed shop of a funeral home and coffin company in a row of deteriorating buildings. Neon Christmas lights blinked out of nearby windows, bathing the sign in pale red and green. I shuddered.

A cool wave of relief went through me when I walked into the intensive care nursery and learned that the internal problem that had caused Robert's breathing to stop had been fixed. He would require more permanent surgery when he was older, but he was out of immediate danger. I looked forward to sleep; we had been up most of the night before, timing contractions.

But Robert's medical crises were not over yet. The surgery had required a general anesthetic, which shut down the digestive tract. Robert needed IVs constantly until his digestive system rebounded. Infants' veins are tinier than most needles, and usable veins do not last long. The times began to get scary again and it was real touch-

and-go for a while. But Robert turned out to be a tough fighter, and he started taking fluids by mouth. He was hooked up all the while to blood, heart, and breathing monitors, and it was difficult to hold him. The machines routinely burp and then issue loud alarm signals that can be seen and heard throughout the floor. Nurses and doctors scramble, rushing toward the room with the flashing red lights outside the door. This symphony of terror happened frequently every day and night Bobby was in the hospital. In every case, it was the machine and our nerves that needed resetting, not him.

I would look down at Bobby and I would hurt. His face was covered with abrasions left by surgical tape that had held breathing tubes in place, and his wrists and ankles were black and blue from IV searches. But he wore a bright red Christmas cap with a little white tassle, and he would look up at me with bright inquisitive eyes, for which I had no answers.

More good news arrived: the doctors told us on Wednesday that we could take him home that evening if all went well. We were elated and began to pack.

The roller coaster struck again. It is never good news when large numbers of doctors from Cardiology rush up at the same time with no forewarning and deeply furrowed brows. The team leader did not waste words. "You should prepare yourselves for heart surgery on Bobby as early as this weekend," she said. Or maybe tonight— more tests were needed.

This one just kicked the stuffing out of me. Despair set in, and we listened numbly to words. Bobby's echocardiogram had showed a coarctation of the aorta, a narrowing of the great artery just outside the heart. The cardiologist did not think Robert was getting enough blood to the lower part of his body. He was transferred immediately to the cardiac ward, and we began to panic.

But somehow Bobby improved. Tests showed that plenty of blood was getting through. The ward's cardiologist told us matter-of-factly that while all heart surgery is extremely serious, this kind of defect was correctable. Better still, Bobby would not require immediate surgery.

The night went smoothly, and to our disbelief Bobby was discharged on Thursday afternoon, in time for me to meet my wife's mother at the airport with lots of tears and joy.

By the time New Year's rolled around, Bobby was eating like a lumberjack and looking healthy as hell. He was ours and we loved him and we would not have traded him for the world. Bobby's situation had stabilized enough by early January for me to be able to return to the congressional office, where everyone, Congressman Coleman included, was kind and understanding. I was anxious, however, to get back to work. There is no time after crises to feel sorry for yourself. You simply start moving and doing and pray you do not fall off the edge into the darkness.

But nothing Congressman Coleman did seemed real or important anymore, not even when the *New York Times* mentioned Coleman's U.S.-Mexico Border Commission legislation in a January 3 article about the *colonias* water crisis. I suppose I felt happy for the congressman, but Capitol Hill's standards by which victories were rewarded no longer meant anything to me. When you live with the terror that your baby might die, it is difficult to get too worked up about Congress. To get warmed up for the year, I issued a press release later that afternoon landing the congressman's legislative agenda for the 101st Congress, a menu that included help for the *colonias* and reduction of the federal deficit. The action of writing and thinking about the congressman felt mechanical. I had been wrenched forever from the world where a single politician was the center of my own universe. I would never return.

Pay raises were once again an incoming. As one of the final acts of his administration, President Reagan sought to increase by $45,000 the pay for members of Congress.[2]

The pay raise was one of Washington's typically tortuous issues. Legislation enacted in 1967 established a Quadrennial Commission on Executive, Legislative, and Judicial Salaries to study the relative pay levels of the federal government and the private sector, and to make recommendations to bring federal pay closer to private sector standards. This year's 59 percent increase, according to the liberal Democratic Study Group (DSG), an organization of House members that supported the raise, "merely [sought] to offset the inflation that has occurred since 1969 . . . and to thereby restore federal salaries to their 1969 purchasing power."[3]

As you can imagine, the process by which Capitol Hill convinces itself that its cause is noble does not do us Hill rats a whole lot of good when we try to justify a 50 percent pay raise for an institution splattered by Jim Wright's ethics scandal, budget deficits, and the general inability to govern. Nevertheless, the DSG warned us that the public should be grateful, sniffing that true comparability "would require a considerably larger increase than that which has been proposed."

All that aside, the fix was in. If Congress did not vote to disapprove the raises by February 8, they would become law. Better yet, it was a bipartisan fix. As conservative columnist Pat Buchanan wrote, "And where is that great Wright-baiter Newt Gingrich, paragon of the Conservative Opportunity Society? I'll tell you where Newt is: right in the thick of it, happily endorsing this daylight larceny; Newt will get $90,000 for going along, as does every other Republican who keeps his mouth shut."[4]

I was beginning to feel grateful already.

Congressman Coleman naturally decried this proposed pay raise publicly, but he left the door open by saying that "earning power is more and more becoming the bottom line in attracting top people to public service." That is especially easy to say when you are tasting the prospect of seeing your salary go from $89,500 to $135,000. Personally, I thought it was a big mistake to bring up the entire subject of pay raises, especially since it would not take long for someone with access to Perceptionland to ask him if he intended to keep this one just as he had done last year's $12,500 increase.

But politicians dance to a strange choreography. One must denounce the raise, rail against it without engaging the mechanisms that could actually stop it, and then keep the money. Two Texans were startlingly honest, though. Marvin Leath supported it, albeit somewhat legalistically, while the flamboyant Charlie Wilson took a "hell yes" attitude. A more typical and much safer reaction was that of Steve Bartlett, a Dallas Republican who told the press, "This pay raise is excessive and absolutely insane." Like Coleman and the others, Bartlett kept the money. As the Democratic leadership's chief fixer Rep. Vic Fazio (D-CA) put it, "The leadership is doing what the members want despite the protestations of the members. . . . the only way to tell who is sincere is to see who doesn't accept the pay raise."[5]

The press and the public were outraged, but the Hill appeared not to hear. Editorial opinion nationwide was consistent: the buying should stop.

"You see the paper this morning?" one of our legislative staffer asked me on January 24.

"No, why?" As the congressman's press secretary, I was allowed to see the national newspapers only when Paul Rogers was done with them.

"Pay raise. More than half of the entire Congress—250 out of 435 House members—are already making more than $135,000."[6]

"But I thought we needed to raise members' salaries to that amount to attract talent."

"Bingo."

"Not counting honoraria?"

"Not counting honoraria. Good luck today."

I groaned and braced myself for another onslaught of press calls.

Congress seemed frozen, unsure how to react as it discovered that it was the target of national outrage. The Hill was used to being prosecutor, not defendant. From Viet Nam to Watergate, the CIA hearings, the Reagan administration's "sleaze factor," and the Iran-contra scandal, Congress had become an expert fingerpointer. Surprisingly, it did not know how to dodge.

Majority Whip Tony Coelho made the announcement on January 24 that no vote would be taken on the pay raise.[7] It was pure, sheer arrogance and stupidity—they could not see the gathering storm even though the rain was in their faces and the lightning sizzled overhead. But to believe it you had to see Tony Coelho in those days, the Appetite Who Walked Like A Man, with the burning eyes, seeking to consume and own everything he came into contact with. He would strut down the hall, eyes flashing, emanating power and ooze as he searched for bigger and better political battles.

The pay raise issue exploded, threatening to engulf even rank-and-file members. Even so, Wright confirmed the next day that he planned no action to overturn the raise. For all his vaunted acumen, he still could not feel the country's rage at being forced to put the income of members of Congress in the country's highest 1 percent. The pay raise would also create a class of pension millionaires.[8] According to published reports, the average member would receive $1.5 million to $2.4 million in total retirement pay. Not surprisingly, a mid-January *Washington Post* national poll showed 85 percent of all Americans opposed to the raise.[9]

(At the same time, Congress, much more quietly, was increasing its working budget by 17 percent to $2.5 billion, including an increase in franked mail from $61 million to $114 million, which the *Wall Street Journal* pointed out exceeded all PAC contributions to Democratic incumbents in 1987 and 1988.)[10]

At some point in the secret sweatings of the leadership, they decided to try to take the edge off the deal. *Let us accept the pay raise without further fuss,* they argued, *and we will ban honoraria. Soon. Very soon. Please trust us,* they asked, as members rushed to line up speeches once the word got around. *Pay us, pay us. Stop us before we spend again.*

By the end of the month, the strain was making Coleman more irrational. The Associated Press called on January 31 to ask if Congressman Coleman wanted a vote on the pay raise and if he had communicated that opinion to the Speaker. "That's none of their goddamn business!" Paul Rogers snapped, ordering me not to respond to any more such news queries. I was not to address, by a Hill rat's direct order, the issue which the public was most concerned. Naturally, I disobeyed and simply free-lanced on my own.

The next day Coleman complained to me, "These newspaper editorials opposing the pay raise are right-wing attacks on the representative form of government. Why don't we just abolish the

Congress or adopt a one-party system of government? Don't disagree with the Republicans—that's what they're saying. It's pure, unadulterated horseshit. Fuck 'em."

His remarks worried me. He had never sounded so shrill and unreasonable before; I feared he was becoming as imperially crazy as everyone else around here. Like Wright and Coelho, he was personalizing the attacks, and blinding himself in the process. Paul Rogers was egging him on, too, invoking images of some vast conspiracy of Republicans, the news media, Ralph Nader, Common Cause, the news media again for good measure, and an ignorant citizenry.

Then, with no explanation, the leadership began to fumble. Wright started to justify the pay raise as the only way he could eliminate honoraria. By the time President Bush endorsed the pay raise on January 28, even such a goodwill gesture was seen as betrayal in the paranoic atmosphere of the Hill.[11]

"Treacherous bastard," Coleman barked. "Typical Republican genius—endorse the pay raise and let us take the heat for it." The president was actually taking a little of the heat *off* us, but rationality was dissolving in a bunker mentality in which stupidity, fear, and defiance dominated.

Surprisingly, Jim Wright—the pol of pols—was the first to snap. He revealed on January 30 that he was polling members privately to see if they really wanted a vote on the pay raise.[12]

"Is he out of his fucking mind?" one of our legislative assistants screamed. "That's crazy! He fucked up! Now every reporter in town will be calling to see how members voted!" The heat had been too much for Wright's pride. According to a leadership staffer, he had been deeply angered at the way members were publicly blaming him for blocking a vote on the raise while privately begging him to do so. But the members wanted him to take the heat; they were counting on him to do just that. Instead, as the Brookings Institution's Thomas Mann pointed out, "he was the first to break ranks"[13] on the pay raise issue.

"What are you hearing?" Paul Rogers asked me.

"Nothing yet," I replied carefully. One cannot be too careful in this business. Rogers did not know that I had my own independent contacts in the leadership offices; if he had, he would have ordered me to stop because he considered those places to be his private game preserves. Even worse, he could be challenged on his frequent pronouncements based on nothing but his "leadership sources." But I could quietly double-check most things he told us, and when they were contrary to the truth, or even worse, to Congressman Coleman's interests, I took steps to protect the congressman and my friends on the legislative staff who had to implement Rogers's orders.

There would be plenty to report soon anyway. Pay raise opponents pointed out correctly that Wright's poll was a sign that support for the increase was eroding. Supporters reacted angrily; but these were crazy times. As one anonymous Democrat, who feared for his own political life, told a national newspaper, "There's a firestorm out there. It's a wild kingdom out there in America."

Politicians stumbled about in the hallways of the House office buildings and the tunnels of the Capitol, dazed by the realization that they had completely and totally misread the mood of the country—and the country was letting them know it. Stung and still reeling, the leadership came up with a new scheme on February 2: let the 50 percent pay raise go into effect, then vote immediately to scale it back.

"Now we're cooking with butter," a Democratic buddy told me. "That's the Wright we're paying him to be."

"I don't understand," I said.

"The last thing the public will see is a vote to *cut* the increase, not the fact that we evaded a vote before any of it went into effect. Geniuses! This one might fly."

His hope was misplaced. With typical disregard for the impact of their actions, House Democrats lived it up at the exclusive Greenbrier resort in White Sulphur Springs, West Virginia, the weekend before the vote. Tony Coelho's smug mug graced the front page of the *Washington Post* write-up of the annual retreat; the Saturday night before the big vote on the pay raise saw the nation's top Democrats at a "sock hop."[14] Meanwhile, talk radio stations were going into orbit.

Still not hearing the footsteps, Wright and the leadership brought up a motion on Monday, February 6, to adjourn until Thursday, February 9, which would have kept the House out of session past the deadline for voting to repeal the raise.

The One-Minutes, meanwhile, had been full of jabber about the pay raise. Rep. David Obey used his to flay the hypocrisy of members who spoke demagogically in public against the pay raise while begging for it in private. "Lo and behold," he said, "it is possible for hypocrisy even to reach the floor of the House. . . . Yet one of the gentlemen who spoke within the last ten minutes, and in that speech indicated his opposition to the pay raise, came to me not just two weeks ago and said, 'For God's sake, the Speaker is not going to allow a vote, is he?' "

"It has become known in the public as 'vote no and take the dough,' " chimed in Rep. Robert Walker (R-PA).

Coelho offered the motion to adjourn and the leadership lost, 238 to 88, in a dramatic defeat for Wright. I cheered privately and thought of my babies; for once, the congressional order had been slapped back.

Shaken, Speaker Wright promised a vote the next day.

Rep. Vic Fazio introduced the resolution of disapproval, saying, "This is not a task I enjoy in any sense," and then blasted the news media: "They provided, in some cases, biased coverage. We became cannon fodder for trash television and for talk radio. . . . We fell prey to the deception of the rabble rousers."

Even on the abyss, Majority Leader Tony Coelho was unrepentant. "By voting against a pay raise," he claimed on the House floor right before the vote, "we are voting to delay critical work on AIDS, space exploration, high definition television, or an effective trade policy." His eyes shone with righteous condemnation as he closed with, "The score is easy to read: Ralph Nader 1, National Interest 0. The folly is upon us. Let the march begin." The resolution to kill the pay raise passed 380 to 48.[15]

Someone at the Democratic Club reworked an old joke and cracked, "If Tip O'Neill, Jim Wright, and Tony Coelho all jumped off the Empire State Building at the same time, who would hit the ground last?"

"Who cares?" someone replied to a din of laughter at the bar.

"Coelho," the jokester added, smilingly. "Because he'd stop to spray-paint FUCK YOU on the wall on the way down."

Unrest swept through the ranks as "Foley for Speaker" buttons appeared in the Capitol and members scrambled to save themselves. It was a time when we crawled collectively into the bunker as the shells rained in on our positions. As Rep. Bill Richardson bluntly told the *New York Times*, "I voted no because I think I want to be reelected to Congress."

The next day, Congressman Coleman took to the House floor to deliver what was perhaps the finest speech I ever wrote as a Hill rat. Titled "The Speaker's Uncommon Courage," it likened the tottering Speaker to a Christ-like figure who had sacrificed himself for his beloved members on the cross of the pay raise. Coleman attacked the dishonesty and hypocrisy of his colleagues (not mentioning, of course, that he was one of the most vocal supporters of the pay raise in private and one of its severest critics in public) and praised Wright: "The Speaker of the House exhibited not only courage, but an uncommon courage in the face of mounting odds and rising public ridicule." Decrying the "disgraceful" conduct of members who had publicly assailed Wright for not allowing a vote on the raise while privately thanking him for doing so, Coleman said stridently, "The members of this House ought to be grateful that they have a leader of such uncommon courage and such a high degree of personal loyalty to them. . . . He put his political life, his political fortune, and his political honor on the line, and he deserves far, far better than he has received."[16]

Coleman—the only one to defend Wright that day—glared at the members in their seats and stalked off, unaware of the irony of combining the Declaration of Independence ". . . our lives, our fortunes, our sacred honor . . .") and the final lines of *A Tale of Two Cities*. He was equally unaware, I am certain, that when Sydney Carton nobly stepped into the guillotine and said, " 'tis a far, far better thing I do . . . ," he had his head chopped off. This is one of a Hill rat's few intellectual thrills; the members simply read your speeches, and you have a great deal of liberty with their content.

Coleman had barely left camera range when my phone started to ring.

The first caller was a Hill rat who had moved from our office to another member's where he was rewriting the nation's health care system. "Hey man," he laughed. "You hit a new personal low—I mean personal best—there."

"Thank you, thank you," I replied.

"Yeah," he continued. "If you can write that shit about Jim Wright and get Coleman to deliver it, you can do anything in this town."

I thought about it afterwards and decided I was not sure I wanted the compliment.


Despite the tidal wave of indignation over the pay raise, we had a lot more cooking than trying to line the Members' pockets, even though the general attitude around the House floor and the Members' hangouts was that they would be back for more dough later. The opening shots of the annual budget follies were underway, including Congress's own request of a record $114 million for franked mailings, a $53 million increase for House employee salaries, $16 million for computers, and $3.2 million for a new civics achievement award program in honor of the Speaker of the House. Wright was trying to stake out new ground for the "speakership" to compete with the presidency, and this program was a step in that direction. Insanity reigned.

With emotions ricocheting over the pay raise and the growing dread that Jim Wright's ethics troubles were bottomless, petty bickering broke out throughout the Democratic ranks. The real rats fled the ship of state. Arkansas Democrat Tommy Robinson, peering around, decided the roof was about to cave in on the liberals and announced a fund-raising effort to oust the dastardly "national Democrats" from office and replace them with "fellow Boll Weevils." (It is a mark of our time that people voluntarily name themselves after destructive insects.) "I intend to go to all my defense industry friends, being a member of the House Armed Services Committee," he told the *Washington Times*. "I think a lot of them are going to give money if they know it's not going to be used to elect more liberal Democrats."[17] New Hampshire Republican Chuck Douglas took the opportunity to point out Rep. Barney Frank's self-acknowledged homosexuality as an example of liberal bias on the Judiciary Committee, which Frank called "gratuitous insults."[18]

Elsewhere, conservative groups clamored for the Justice Department to name an independent prosecutor to investigate allegations of congressional misconduct that were cropping up across the board—District of Columbia Delegate Walter Fauntroy for payroll irregularities involving his son; Speaker Wright's problems, and others.[19]

I am proud to say that I did my own small part of mud-throwing.

"Hey, I heard a good one," a source called me. This source was a member of an exclusive Capitol Hill secret society we called FLAC—Former Luken Associates Club—composed entirely of Hill rats who had worked for my old boss the Duke, U.S. Rep. Thomas Luken of Cincinnati. FLAC had tagged the Duke with bad press whenever possible over the years.

"Let's hear it," I said.

"Luken's Energy and Commerce subcommittee counsel quit in disgust and wrote a letter to the entire Committee about Luken's bizarre personal behavior."

"Let me guess . . ."

"I can get the letter."

Another FLAC agent delivered to me a copy of the letter, written by attorney David Colbert. I read it and laughed. Colbert had worked as counsel to Luken's Subcommittee on Transportation and Hazardous Materials for seventeen months.

"Seventeen months?" my original source asked incredulously. "Can you image putting up with that crazy bastard for seventeen months?"

Colbert leveled some serious charges. Luken's "tirades and

tantrums" had created problems "so grave in nature that I fear if left unchecked they will seriously impair the proper functioning of the subcommittee. . . . The manner in which Chairman Luken treats the professional staff of the subcommittee is nothing less than scandalous. In the time I have served the subcommittee as counsel I have been subjected to my share of the chairman's personal tirades and temper tantrums. I have witnessed behavior I would not condone in a two year old, much less accept in a professional setting."[20] Colbert also charged that Luken's interest in the Hazardous Materials subcommittee went no further than "today's headlines or tomorrow's honoraria."

I laughed again. "We're going to rock and roll with this one," I said aloud. I dialed the telephone and called a good friend at the Associated Press.

"I'll get it to our Ohio person," she said.

Thoughts of the Duke were in my mind as I called up the AP wire from my computer terminal the next day—Luken giving the lobbyist from Procter & Gamble control over his vote in the Energy and Commerce Committee when he instructed his young legislative assistants to clear proxy votes with the lobbyist whenever he, Luken, was not present to vote himself . . . the story of Luken so out of control while screaming at an aide that he started writing on the walls of his office to make his point . . .

The computer pulled up the story. "I'm tough and demanding," Luken admitted to the AP. "Sure I yell. I'm a yeller sometimes. Do I yell regularly? No."

No, of course not, he did not yell regularly. He shrieked, he screamed, he frenzied, he frothed, he gibbered, he jabbered, he accused, he tormented—but "yell regularly?" No way.

Heh, heh, heh. Roll up another one on the scoreboard for FLAC.

The strain was evident everywhere. Roll Call's Martin Frazier reported that the 101st Congress spent less time in legislative session and held fewer votes than any other recent Congress at the same point in time.[21] The House had spent only twenty-nine hours and forty-nine minutes in session, producing all of five votes. In the midst of this orgy of mud-slinging and excess, Annette Lantos, wife of California Rep. Tom Lantos, announced her personal crusade for more humane mousetraps in the House.

I pointed this out with gleeful malice to Paul Rogers, who muttered something rudely unintelligible and walked away. Paul kept a potted plant on his desk. For some time now, and to the delight of the staff, one of our very own office mice had been defecating in Paul's plant and kicking a nightly film of dirt and feces all over his desk.

It may not seem like much, but you have to find comic relief in this place whenever you can.

We were indeed edging toward stardom, but not in the way we anticipated. Congressman Coleman was becoming an increasingly noisy defender of Speaker Wright. On March 2, he took to the House floor to accuse Rep. Newt Gingrich and other House Republicans of behaving like "propaganda terrorists."[22]

When I saw that Coleman was the only one to defend Wright on the floor that day, I knew the Speaker was done for.

Unwinding at home that evening, I thought: thank God for the kids. Julia, so bright and quick, was developing a tremendous vocabulary and loved art. She was full of life and laughter and the energy of childhood. Robert was in the middle of that shimmering growth explosion of the newborn, sparklingly alert and gaining weight.

The next day was not nearly so pleasant. In the wake of the floor fight Coleman had touched off with the Republicans, my latest task was to prepare a "basic Jim Wright defense" statement that could be used for speeches, *Congressional Record* statements, press releases, and other political scat. Coleman, meanwhile, continued his high-profile attacks on the Republicans. On March 11, he told the press that "the entire issue is one of partisanship—part of the Republican effort to gain control of Congress and unrelated to the Tower situation." This statement was patently ridiculous— Washington was in a state of open revolt against itself over Jim Wright, John Tower, and a host of other potential scandals that were breaking out like measles. I knew it was ridiculous, but I remained silent. Congressman Coleman and Paul Rogers would work each other up about the

Wright case before Coleman would speak to the media or on the House floor, macho-juiced conversations along the lines of:

"Goddamn press is at it again . . ."

"With the help of the fucking Republicans . . ."

"No good sorry bastards . . ."

"Completely unfair . . ."

"Goddamn right!!!" Coleman would roar, face flushed and breath short, as he would storm out the back door to take on the world.

You cannot tell truth to politicians when the beast is in their eyes. You step aide, usually quickly, as they lunge forward into the fray, unencumbered by reason or balance. You write and you hope for the best; at times you cheer hooray for your side, and then you prepare for the inevitable cleaning-up that will follow. Those of us who work for politicians owe them not only our best judgment, but the best timing for delivering that judgment.

Losing your job, of course, is the worst timing of all.

Even as he led Wright's counterattack within the House, Congressman Coleman, loyal lieutenant of Jim Wright, was quietly taking steps to distance himself from his master. He may not even have done so consciously. Still, all contingencies had to be prepared for. While Coleman could not lose, ultimately, by defending Wright in Washington, loyalty only paid the bills so far.

Coleman arranged for House Majority Leader Thomas Foley—next in line to succeed Wright—to appear at a hometown fundraiser in Texas. Foley, too, benefited because the trip helped remove any possible questions about his own loyalty to Wright and the Texas delegation. As Coleman's press release pointedly stated, "Congressman Foley is the second ranking Democrat in the U.S. House of Representatives, following the Speaker, Jim Wright." Coleman had delivered Foley on the issue of twin plants, as he had done with Wright.[23] One Speaker passes and another Speaker comes, but the moneymen abideth forever.

Coleman had remained in Texas after Foley's appearance on March 16. We were shocked to learn that his daughter had been critically injured in an automobile accident on the afternoon of March 19. The days that followed were harrowing for him, I am sure . . . but I was continuing to distance myself not just from Wright but from the entire stinking mess here on the Hill. I wondered about Coleman the man. Would the experience of seeing his own child facing sudden death change him? Would it lead him to become more responsible? I kept looking for signs over the next several months that Coleman would reform, hoping desperately that he would change his grubby ways. There were none. Thankfully, his daughter recovered totally and rapidly. Coleman's behavior remained unchanged. I waited, and I was disappointed.

In the meantime, life would go on despite Wright and the ethics scandals, and we depended on congressional franked mail to sustain our political life. By the end of March, I had 15,000 letters in the works to veterans; 30,000 to senior citizens; 3,000 to Hispanic leaders; 15,000 to community opinion leaders; 2,000 to federal and military retirees; and 51,000 to Hispanic voters in South El Paso. At the same time, I was hawking a paper to the press explaining how the congressman had single-handedly obtained $89,335,000 for the district in the last year. This is one of the political beauties about a seat on the Appropriations Committee. That number was no exaggeration; if anything, it was conservative. Congressman Coleman *had* in fact obtained $89,335,000 for the 16th Congressional District of Texas. The appropriations oil was sufficient to calm the troubled waters stirred up by pay raises and ethics scandals. Our memorandum to Coleman about using this paper in an editorial board luncheon said with a certain ingenuousness: "Emphasize that this is not pork."

Back in Washington, the Texas delegation was on the run. After former Texas Sen. John Tower's nomination as President Bush's defense secretary was defeated, Russell Baker wrote in the *New York Times*, "Now we move on to the fight over Speaker Jim Wright's ethics. This could be really satisfying. He is another Texan."

The Texas delegation would never, of course, admit publicly that it was on the run. On April 4, with a decision on Jim Wright from the Ethics Committee looming closer and closer, Coleman denied to the press that the Texas delegation was under attack, but rather complained, "Not being able to assist those who help you politically is a problem for all of us. . . . It's okay to help your enemies but not your supporters." He was feeling sorry for himself again; it is difficult to lead and whine at the same time. When I read his remarks in the paper the next day, I recoiled. Not only were they pitifully self-serving, but he had inadvertently laid bare his conscience for all to see. He defined right and wrong in terms of his ego, as if the purpose of rules and laws was to legitimize whatever he happened to feel like doing instead of protecting the public or the national good.

Concern deepened as new reports filtered in hourly about the Ethics Committee. The search for enemies was in high gear. Congressman Coleman was convinced that because Ethics Committee Counsel Richard Phelan was from Chicago, he was "fucking Wright" as a favor to Danny Rostenkowski. The power of paranoia is strong indeed. It never occurred to any of Wright's supporters that an attorney like Phelan, Republican or Democrat, could be outraged Because of the truth. No discussions were heard in our office about the rights or wrongs of the Speaker's actions, no one weighed the man's judgment, not even privately. It was simply assumed that the charges were purely political.

On April 12, more damaging leaks appeared suggesting that the Ethics Committee would turn over its findings to the Justice Department. The *Wall Street Journal* reported that "there is an underlying bitterness in the Speaker's office that Mr. Wright is the victim of changing ethical standards in Washington." The great irony, however, was that Wright and the Democrats were largely responsible for this change by choosing to allege ethical difficulties by a host of Reagan administration officials from Attorney General Ed Meese on down. Democrats contributed to the crumbling of Washington's great unspoken agreements; that everyone, regardless of party, can snatch his own fair share if not too greedy or indelicate about the matter.

News reports became an important part of our discourse, forming the unknown factor in our daily political calculations. Television was an enemy, but its reports were ephemeral. Besides, Congressman Coleman and Paul Rogers never understood the medium. But newspapers . . . ah, newspapers were a splendid culprit because a clipping could be held in their hands and they could swear at it, put it down, and return thirty minutes later to continue the invective. They could see words that would not go away, words that painted a picture of Speaker Wright and the House of Representatives that was so antithetical to their political needs that they had no clue that each clipping represented one more count in the national indictment of the Capitol's culture of influence.

April 13 brought still more leaks, more unnamed Democratic defections from Wright's cause. Coleman neared despair. Defending Wright consumed all his energy. Letters would go unsigned, or we would sign them for him. The legislative staff performed heroics to keep our appropriations projects funded at each stage of the process. We took to signing Coleman's name on letters to keep Coleman "involved" in a host of other issues. We no longer debated our recommendations for Coleman but argued instead with Paul; he functioned as the *de facto* member of Congress from the 16th District of Texas, making member-level decisions hourly with the dispatch and arrogance of a John Sununu. Coleman had disengaged completely from his work. When he did show up at the office, he was alternately listless and frantic. I understood now what it must have been like to work with Colonel House and Mrs. Wilson following President Wilson's stroke.

One report claimed the Ethics Committee had voted to find Wright guilty of at least one major violation concerning a financial supporter and a direct interest in legislation.

"I wish they'd stop saying that every member has a George Mallick," Rogers complained. George Mallick was one of Wright's Texas moneymen with whom Wright had a complicated personal and financial relationship and, the independent counsel argued, an improper one as well.

I looked at him incredulously and thought of border crossings and Coleman's moneymen and the countless favors we undertook on their behalf. I started to say something, then decided to stew privately instead. I shook my head. *We learn nothing on this Hill*, I thought, *except to learn how to do it all over again.*

As the decision on Wright approached, Congressman Coleman and Paul Rogers continued to breathe contempt at every opportunity on the independent counsel, the Democrats who voted to find Wright in violation of the rules, the press, the public, and the whole idea of ethics. They constantly complained about "changing ethical standards"—a common refrain in the House—with members, naturally, the victims. Ethics regulations, in their view, should have the welfare of members as their overriding goal.

At the Democratic Whip meeting that day, Wright claimed emotionally that he never considered his wife's salary a gift. Coleman whined to me afterwards, "We've all decided there's no sense being a member of *this* Congress—goddamn standards being changed."

That same day, President Bush offered a proposal on ethics for the executive branch. Professionally speaking, it was a terrifically timed shot to make Congress look even worse by comparison. He called for a 25 percent increase in pay for federal judges, but not for Congress, an extension of the current one-year ban on executive officials from lobbying their former offices, and a ban on political action committee contributions. [24]

On April 17, the boom fell on Jim Wright. The House Ethics Committee publicly charged on April 17 that Speaker Wright had violated House rules on sixty-nine separate occasions by not disclosing tens of thousands of dollars in gifts and by laundering speaking fees through book sales. Even worse, the charges were bipartisan. The committee's six Democrats and six Republicans had unanimously found that Wright had received $145,000 in gifts that included the use of a condominium for free or at a cut rate, an $18,000 per-year salary for his wife, and the free use of a car. The committee hit the book sales even harder: ". . . seven bulk sales . . . demonstrated an overall scheme to evade the House outside earned income because honorarium payments were recharacterized as royalties." In other words, he had laundered the money. [25]

It was like the fall of Rome. Members looked at Indiana Democrat Frank McCloskey in amazement when he stated on the floor that day, "Hoosiers have not succumbed to the hysteria that has many asserting that Speaker Wright is doomed."

"Why the hell would he say that?" I asked a staff member.

"Remember? Wright gave him the seat by refusing to seat McIntyre. This is Frank's final installment payment."

Coleman was despondent and self-pitying while Rogers became frenetic, pacing about ineffectually.

"They out-and-out fucked him!" Rogers snarled. "Sixty-nine counts. Sixty-nine counts! That's what everyone's saying. But it wasn't sixty-nine, it was two—two areas. And the committee dismissed four of the six areas outright! So why aren't the goddamn headlines saying committee dismisses all but two areas?" It was no time to argue facts and morals. If we had only said the word "two" instead of "sixty-nine," Rogers thought the Speaker would have been salvaged.

Privately, we knew that Wright's fall had nothing to do with morals or number-shuffling. The members of the Ethics Committee were now armed with knitting needles. Wright's tumbril had been constructed. He had come to symbolize everything the public thought wrong with Congress, and the Democrats and Republicans on the Ethics Committee in turn had decided, and correctly, that the members of both parties would be better served if Wright were sacrificed. Not that he did not deserve it; but there was a growing side to the scandal that made members realize that yes, most of us do indeed have a George Mallick or a group of bordertown moneymen or whomever in our district for whom favors are granted in return for money.

Later in the day, Texas Rep. Charlie Wilson told the Associated Press in what I am sure he thought was a dangerous tone, "At some point we've got to start figuring out who's on our side and who's on the other side." He claimed Wright would win on the House floor by "losing a few cowardly Democrats and picking up some brave Republicans."[26]

I briefed Congressman Coleman on the committee's charges and received his reaction from Paul Rogers. "Jim Wright has not been found guilty of anything," our statement claimed. "We owe Jim Wright the benefit of the doubt. We're different from the communists—we have something in America called the presumption of innocence until proven guilty."[27]

All of a sudden Jim Wright was different, we were arguing— he alone deserved to be judged by a set of political rules different from those launched at Ed Meese, John Tower, and the rest of the Republicans accused in the 1980s. This was not a good sign. Anyone in Washington whose principal argument is injured fairness is almost certainly about to lose.

My phone rang. "Yeah?"

"You in?" It was my Democratic buddy who helped run the football and basketball pools.

"In what?"

"The game! Time and date."

"Of . . ."

"Wright's resignation! What do you think I'm talking about?"

"Jeez," I groaned. Are we gambling for the robe already? Then I looked around the office—Coleman nowhere to be found, Paul Rogers pacing this way and that as he muttered threats at images of people on television, the computer going chunk-clap-snap, chunk-clap-snap as the laser printer churned out one targeted mailing after another as if this whole nightmare had never happened.

I sighed. "I guess I'm good for it."

"Great. Plus we have new rules. You're allowed three changes each day—this sumbitch's moving quicker than the Aztec Two-Step."


A second bomb exploded over Capitol Hill on May 4: the *Washington Post* ran a story revealing that John Mack, the Speaker's top aide, had attacked and attempted to kill a woman when he was nineteen. Mack subsequently served twenty-seven months in jail. I had a weird sinking feeling in my stomach. We all knew John, and my wife and I had met and talked with him on a number of occasions. He was the most powerful Hill rat of us all.

When I first heard sketchy elements of the story two years before, I had dismissed it as some kind of Republican-prompted rumor campaign.

It is fair to say that most people thought John a terrific guy: warm, friendly, courteous, smarter than hell. He never made junior members or lower-level staffers feel unimportant, always taking the time to talk and to encourage. So how do you reconcile what you know about the man from your own personal experience with the fact that in 1973 a woman entered a store he was managing and without warning or provocation, he tried to beat her to death with a hammer, stuffed what he thought was her dead body into a car trunk, and then left the scene to take in a movie?

I had far more sympathy for the victim, or even for Mack, than I did for the Hill's reaction.

"She put the reporter up to it," Paul Rogers claimed, trying to turn the woman into the perpetrator. He thought of himself and John as good friends and fellow political geniuses. "She just waited until he had made it big before going after him." Paul's reaction was shared by House Majority Whip Tony Coelho, who also defended Mack by saying, "Under our system of law John Mack owed his debt to society, not to this young woman." Part of the woman's resentment, according to the article, was that Mack had never bothered to tell her he was sorry.

*Hold on a minute,* I thought. According to published reports, Mack had hit her on the head over and over again with a hammer, ripping her scalp in five places, grabbed a knife and stabbed her five times in the left breast and shoulder, and then finished off by slashing her repeatedly across the throat. As the *Washington Post* described it, "It took a general surgeon, a plastic surgeon and a neurosurgeon to repair the damage. Her left lung had collapsed and her head was a mass of lacerations and exposed bone. She spent 24 hours in intensive care with a tube in her lung, five more days in the hospital, weeks convalescing with her own nurse, and more than a year undergoing surgery and hair transplants."[28]

Surely, revenge would be an understandable motive—especially since John had not only never made any restitution or apology for his heinous crime, but had apparently had his punishment eased by then-Congressman Wright because of family connections: Wright's daughter was married to John's brother. John served twenty-seven months in jail and was paroled to a clerk's job in Wright's office.

But the Hill is a tight crowd that takes care of its own. John Mack was, in fact, far more the insider than his boss the Speaker; Majority Whip Tony Coelho was godfather to one of his children, and they shared an accountant and invested in the same company. Besides, Tony Coelho will defend his friends—for a price. Press reports in the wake of his public defense of Mack revealed that in 1981 he wrote a letter asking for a lighter sentence for David Weidert, the son of the executive director of a group called California Westside Farmers, which had contributed $1,000 to his campaigns in 1980 and 1981. According to one account, David Weidert had been convicted of beating a slightly retarded young man with a baseball bat, torturing him, stabbing him, and forcing him to dig his own grave before burying him alive.[29]

I sat at my desk, shaken. Was the Hill going completely out of its mind? What if the son of a moneyman had murdered my little boy or girl? How many letters would Coelho or another member have written then? *No one thinks rationally up here anymore*, I thought. I listened to Paul Rogers attacking Mack's victim and I read about Coelho, and I despaired. Did the Hill find a price for everything? Could nothing escape its clutching demand to own one's soul? As one female Washington executive put it, "John Mack was every woman in America's worst nightmare—the man who comes out of the blue for no reason except to try to kill you."

After the *Washington Post* story, female members such as Reps. Patricia Schroeder (D-CO) and Olympia Snowe (R-ME) threatened to circulate a letter demanding Mack's resignation (Interestingly, they took no action in 1987 when the story originally broke in a Texas newspaper but did not attract national attention.)

John Mack resigned two days later, on May 6, but not before his story had outraged the country. His case personalized the whole Jim Wright episode in Perceptionland, adding a horrifying human face to the already shattered image of the Hill.

So I pray that the victim finds peace and that John Mack finds his peace too, but I cannot find it in myself to pray for the courtiers of the Hill who pose and pander, blind to the human consequences of their schemes. I hope, at best, that they change themselves first and learn to find their own way home.

Then, on May 26, the political world was turned upside down yet a third time. Amidst rumors that he would definitely seek the position of Majority Leader if Foley moved up to Speaker, Tony Coelho announced that he would resign.

Coelho had issued a statement on May 14 disclosing that a California S&L operator had bought and held $100,000 worth of junk bonds in 1986 from Drexel Burnham Lambert until Coelho could round up the cash to cover the deal. He then listed the bonds on his 1986 tax returns as a long-term gain when in fact he had not held them for more than six months, saving roughly $2,000 in taxes. As his attorney Robert Bauer said in one of the classic lines of all time, "We concede there may be a problem here."[30]

Congressman Coleman and Paul Rogers took turns looking shell-shocked and denouncing the press. I sat at my desk and let loose a low chuckle. Good riddance; and then I wrinkled my nose and thought—*hey, this doesn't add up*. Okay, so he had one shaky deal and a possible tax problem, about which some people thought he could make a good case. So what?

Time to talk to a seldom-used contact I'll call Deep Source, someone who is better connected than the phone company.

He sighed. "You really want to know?"

I said I did, that it was personal.

"Well, we're gonna avoid particulars because we're on the phone and everyone knows this town is wired for sound. But Coelho was actually pretty clean, as far as I hear, and his accountant almost assuredly fucked up on not reporting the loans."

"So why'd he resign?

He sighed again. "Everything else. Everything else he was into— and they got him on something clean." He laughed harshly. "Look, if you think the Wright case is messy, lemme tell you, Tony Coelho's deals would make Wright look like Mother Teresa. Things that happened when he was at the DCCC . . . using those S&L guys' airplane to go to Vegas with John Mack, things that happened there . . . what money he used in Vegas . . . other shit . . . look, all of a sudden he was staring down the biggest, blackest, black hole of them all. But Coelho's also a smart player. He simply cut his losses. Not being Whip and not being Majority Leader and not being Speaker was nothing compared to what could have happened if a sharp prosecutor started opening him up like a can opener to see what was inside."

I thanked him and hung up. Wow. Tony Coelho, the Appetite Who Walked Like a Man, had given up running the country—his life's burning, incandescent ambition—because of something on the dark side that dwarfed even *his* appetite.

I needed a cup of coffee. Was it true? I had no way of verifying the details, but they were not important. Truth in Washington is the truth of essence, not particulars. And the essence was that any prolonged examination of Tony Coelho's personal finances, campaign contributions, and relationships with moneymen would rip open a mortal wound too ugly and bloody to contemplate.

I would keep the conversation to myself. It had given me the same feeling I'd had as a sixteen year old in the Panama Canal Zone when a friend and I took out his trimaran sailboat from the port of Balboa on the Pacific side and went to some small islands just south of the canal channel. As we neared the first island, I looked down into the clear, God's blue-water and watched an enormous shadow pass right under me and the boat. The boat was twelve feet; the shadow was bigger. It did not return for a second pass. But the tropics had taught me a lesson that would apply later to politics: you do not dangle your legs carelessly over the side into the deep water; the big ones sometimes feed close to shore.

The mood of the Hill became increasingly surreal after the departure of Mack and Coelho. Ethical disclosures did not cease; they became more and more lurid. The *Fort Worth Star-Telegram* reported that Jim Wright had used the *Congressional Record* to promote a videotape made by a company that had placed his wife on the payroll at $30,000 a year.[31] Meanwhile, Congress's image problems multiplied. While on an industry-paid junket to the South Carolina resort of Myrtle Beach, Rep. Jim McCrery (R-LA) made the news by visiting a topless nightclub called the Dollhouse and donning a dancer's brassiere on his head. He was "not drunk," he reassured *Roll Call* afterwards. "A congressman still has the right to do anything he wants to do," he insisted, but then assured the nation that he "was not representing the Congress" at the Dollhouse. Still, lest he be misunderstood, he cautioned that he was "not going to live like a monk" while he was in Congress.[32]

The Associated Press reported that Ethics Committee Chairman Julian Dixon (D-CA), who investigated Jim Wright, was lobbied by a company with whom his wife had a lucrative financial arrangement. Dixon denied it, even though the company's own law firm admitted contacting him four times in 1986 and 1987.[33]

Our days became marked by ringing phones and flying rumors, while gossip about the latest revelations hung in the air like the humidity that precedes a summer storm. Everything had become fair game as the press and the public scrutinized the way Congress did its business.

May 31 began as yet another incredible day of witch hunts, rumor, and gossip; it ended as the day the axe fell. Speaker Wright had lunch with the Texas delegation and told them he would announce his resignation at 4:00 P.M.

I rushed to the phone. "Hey, it's me. How much money can I still put on the Time and Date pool?" I was thinking hundreds at least.

My buddy sounded apologetic. "Sorry, dude. Pool's closed. Another friend called in for the 4:00 P.M. time slot earlier this morning, and that's when Wright's going to announce it himself."

Shit. Then I thought: Hey, wait a minute. How did someone know the 4:00 P.M. time *before* the Texas delegation luncheon? If Wright had told anyone else before then, word would have leaked out immediately. Hmmmm. I would learn later that the chief suspect worked on Wright's staff, but nothing was ever proven conclusively and my buddy maintained his code of silence.

Sharply at 4:00 P.M., Jim Wright stood on the floor of the House, quivering as he spoke. There was no tragedy in his speech, just a point-by-point rebuttal of the charges. He would resign on June 6. "All of us, in both political parties, must resolve to bring this period of mindless cannibalism to an end," he implored.

It hurt to watch. "How much longer is this going to go on?" a staffer complained midway through the hour-long speech.

Wright was falling back on the so-called Whittemore defense, named after Rep. B.F. Whittemore in 1870. When he was found guilty of selling appointments to West Point, Whittemore's supporters argued that the sale of cadetships was so pervasive that tradition had legitimized the practice. In 1870, as today, survival ruled all, and the House voted 187 to 0 to censure him even though he had by then resigned.[34]

I was struck that Wright still could not admit that his actions were wrong. In the halls outside my office, his words boomed out of every door. Staffers and members crowded around televisions, transfixed by the parting words of this extraordinary fall from grace.

*They do not care about the children*, I thought, as he received his final round of applause. I looked at pictures of Bobby and Julia on my desk. *They do not care about the children.*

Congressman Coleman looked shell-shocked. I fended off a deluge of press calls, none of which Coleman took. He had spoken to some reporters at the Capitol and it had not settled well. "I was saddened," he had told them. "We never heard his side of the story before the full Ethics Committee." The reporters thought he was crazy. Coleman was feeling extraordinarily sorry for himself and did not want to deal with the outside world. I called him at home at 10:00 P.M. to urge him at least to call the El Paso newspapers. His girlfriend's son answered the telephone and told me that he was "playing Jeopardy with Ron." Coleman came on the phone. I asked him to call the reporter. Coleman said he was in the middle of something important and refused.

House Majority Leader Thomas Foley was elected Speaker on June 6 amidst all kinds of predictions of campaign and ethics reform.[35] And then another bombshell exploded: the Republican National Committee circulated a memorandum that implied Thomas Foley was homosexual. This rumor had been brewing for some time, a May 15 Evans and Novak column and analyst Horace Busby's political newsletter had made veiled allusions to the subject.

In retrospect, the Foley affair had its beneficial side: the Republicans had gone too far. The staffer at the Republican National Committee responsible for the memorandum was ritually fired, President Bush went through the motions of leashing Lee Atwater, the committee's chairman, and a mollified Foley began to pitch himself as a healer, a Democratic Gerald Ford.[36]

The lull did not last. Both parties "beefed up their dirt patrols," as one reporter put it.[37] Republicans leveled an ethics barrage on June 28 at Democratic Rep. Jim. Chapman, and the Democratic National Committee returned the fire the next day at George Bush.[38] But surprisingly, the attacks sputtered. Like all revolutions, real blood seemed to have satiated the crowd's appetite, at least temporarily. There were newer, more interesting things to do, and by the end of June, Republicans and Democrats alike welcomed the chance to return to the traditional pastime of attacking each other's patriotism.

Meanwhile, Congressman Coleman and I had *real* problems: our ace in the hole, the Appropriations Committee, was way behind schedule. Only seven-and-a-half working weeks remained between July 4 and the start of the fiscal year on October 1, but not a single one of the thirteen regular appropriations bills had been finished. Ranking Republican Silvio Conte (R–MA) predicted another continuing resolution. Last year, Congress did clear all thirteen by October 1, the first time since 1954 that not even a day- or hours-long continuing resolution had been necessary. This year was more complicated. The Budget Committee was bumping chests with the Favor Factory over who could spend what of this year's so-called bipartisan budget agreement. Jim Wright might have elevated our status in Washington, but we depended on a steady stream of announcements at each step of the funding process to guide us through the shoals of Perceptionland, especially in a time when politicians were being chased through the woods the way villagers armed with torches and pitchforks went after hunted animals.

# CHAPTER TWELVE

# WAKE OF THE FLOOD

How can I describe those terrible days in the summer of 1989? We were like soldiers who had lost a major battle. We were political DPs—displaced persons, shell shocked veterans, wandering about the unhallowed halls of the House. In the weeks and months that followed the fall of the House of Wright, we Democrats on Capitol Hill picked through the shattered ruins of our world, destroyed by the Speaker, Tony Coelho, and the rest. Any vision once there had been reduced to naked appetite; we had no message, no vision, no program. Our political existence had survived but our spirits had not. What remained now was to pick up the pieces as best we could.

Democratic members who privately criticized Speaker Wright felt fear. If it could happen to him, they worried, it could happen to anyone. Individual survival was now all that mattered. The single saving grace of the Wright scandal was that it had ended with more than a year and a half to go before the next election. Between the Favor Factory and franked mail, we reasoned, we had a fighting chance.

On June 28, I attended a meeting of the Democratic National Committee called "The Incumbent Protection Plan." Rep. Beryl

Anthony (D-AR) opened the meeting by introducing a Washington attorney named Bob Bauer, one of a new breed of legal specialist whose practice was devoted to helping elected officials with real or potential ethical problems.

Bauer, naturally, stressed the attorney's role. "There is a tremendous advantage in having lawyers' letters in your files before you do something," he cautioned. "It shows prudence and diligence. Today's ethical climate is a trend, not an aberration. Appearance can and is actionable now. There is an array of appearance standards that threatens to change this city's political landscape." Bauer went on to describe a host of situations that might or might not be ethical, depending on the member, the amount of money involved, whether the other party had an interest in legislation, and so on. Given the audience, Bauer refrained from mentioning that if a Member were simply to accept no gifts from anyone, all of these fine-line considerations would be irrelevant.[1]

Bauer stressed the role of record-keeping but warned, "There are some things you do not want on paper, some you do. If you are running for reelection, you ought to have a paper trail and regularly advise the staff about the laws and regulations separating campaign and official functions." He also counseled that "when the roof caves in," a Member should be 100 percent certain of everything he says to the press and public.

Besides learning how to look over its shoulders, the House by July was trying to drown its sorrows in hard work, an untried concept with much potential. Speaker Foley's new work ethic caused some members to grumble because he instituted a five-day work week in an institution where "fuck-off Friday" was almost as sacrosanct as the congressional mailing privilege.

Coleman took a different approach. Still shaken by the fall of Wright, his own work habits became even more erratic. On July 17 he did not bother to show up to "mark up," or vote on, the annual foreign aid bill in the Foreign Operations Subcommittee. There was no apparent fallout except among our staff, who agreed that Paul Rogers's basic question posed at the start of the year—was Coleman a prime-time player or backbencher?—had been answered once and for all. Resumes began to crop up in the computer alongside our memoranda.

Two days later, after we had conducted a press briefing on Mexico, Coleman and a legislative staffer went to the full Appropriations Committee markup of the foreign aid bill. When I returned to the office, Rogers asked me, "Where's Coleman?"

"He went to the Foreign Ops markup."

He scowled.

"Isn't that the right answer?" I asked.

Pause. "No, it's not. Is it office policy now to ignore what I say?" he demanded as he glared at me. I said I did not know and nor did I like his tone.

"Well, it can get real unpleasant . . ." he muttered as he stomped into Coleman's office and shut the door. Rogers had apparently issued an order to the legislative staffer that Coleman was not to go to the Foreign Operations markup without checking with him first. Coleman, the congressman, had other ideas, and the rest of the staff would bear the brunt of Rogers's rage.

Rogers's behavior had our staff near open revolt. Several days later, Rogers tried to make a staff member pick up his mother at the airport. (The staff member refused.) With Coleman more and more disengaged, Rogers was in full deputy congressman mode, complete with ego, ceremony, and insistence that underlings scurry about to do his bidding.

Meanwhile, we had already sent over one million pieces of mail during the year at a cost of over $200,000 to the taxpayer. The powers that be were happy. What difference did it make to the congressman if his staff director had a Napoleonic complex? In spite of Coleman's nonparticipation in the matter, I was able to announce to the press that as a result of the full Appropriations Committee markup, "the Congressman" had obtained $1 million for a veterans outpatient clinic in El Paso, $15 million for the *colonias*, and $250,000 for air pollution monitors in the El Paso–Ciudad Juarez airshed.

These particular plums could not have been produced at a better time. The nation was up in arms over all things Washington: James

Watt, Iran-contra, Jim Wright, the HUD scandals, and all the rest. Polls showed that no partisan edge had emerged from the scandals. Gallup polls conducted for the Times-Mirror Company showed that only 15 percent of Americans closely followed the Jim Wright scandal, while other polls pointed out that Perceptionland still differentiated between the sins of Congress as a whole and the merits of individual representatives.

We had, then, a window of opportunity, but Coleman continued to act erratically.

On July 21 he secured a $4.1 million appropriation for a strategic materials center at the University of Texas at El Paso. "Here's our headline for the press release," Coleman told me belligerently. " 'Coleman Does It Again.' Got to remind those sons of bitches [in the media] just who does what around here." It was the second year in a row that we had snagged an appropriation for the school; last year's prize was $3 million. I dressed up the deal with a bunch of high-tech rhetoric about competing in global markets, technology transfer, and industrial diversification, but I could hear the political beast snicker as my fingers tapped the keyboard.

Then on July 25 Coleman left a full Appropriations Committee markup early to pick up his and his girlfriend's children, missing a historic vote on reparations payments to Japanese-American internees in World War II. Two days later he was back in the saddle again to announce that the House Majority Leader Richard Gephardt himself, would attend Coleman's annual Democratic barbeque, a development that in his eyes represented a major political coup.

Which Congressman Coleman would show up at any given moment was the question of the day.

The Republicans tossed us a home-run ball on July 28. We were doing appropriations bills because Speaker Foley wanted us to finish all thirteen regular bills before the August recess. With the Democrats in open rebellion on the capital gains tax issue, U.S. Rep. Robert Walker (R-PA) led an attempt on the House floor to eliminate the $4.1 million appropriations project for the University of Texas at El Paso (UTEP) that we had placed in the Fiscal Year 1990 Treasury-Postal Service-General Government appropriations bill.

Walker's action was a godsend. We always win floor fights over the Favor Factory, and back home in Coleman's congressional district, we made it look like the entire city of El Paso was under siege from the Republicans.

You can always tell what kind of day it is going to be on the House floor by the One-Minutes. Rep. Larkin Smith of Mississippi had one titled "Through the Drug War Maze in 28 Days, Day 9: House Administration Committee." Wisconsin Rep. Steve Gunderson admitted paying bonuses for the last nine years in violation of House rules. Then the leadership called up the appropriations bill, and Rep. Jim Traficant (D-OH) stepped up to the microphone. People snapped to attention because he is capable of saying or doing anything. He announced an amendment to cut one hundred IRS agents because they had been going "into the kitchens of America and scared families." Traficant, called by his own local Democratic chairman "a nitwit, a lunatic, a raving maniac,"[2] did not mention that the federal government had tried him unsuccessfully on bribery charges (he admitted taking the bribes, but claimed he was conducting his own investigation and was acquitted), and then won tax evasion charges against him to the tune of $180,000. Traficant's response was, "I am going to kick the IRS's butt. The IRS can go to hell."

Traficant lost his amendment by a vote of 398 to 21.

Next, Rep. Robert Dornan (R-CA) held things up by complaining about a Postal Service cancellation stamp that read, "Celebrating 20 Years of Gay and Lesbian Pride."

The Speaker asked wearily, "Are there further amendments to Title II?" Dorman, satisfied, sat down.

Finally, it was Rep. Robert Walker's turn to offer his amendment to strike five university-related projects from the bill, claiming that " . . . lobbyists and members of the Appropriations Committee are not the best judges of the Nation's academic and scientific needs."

"Like hell," our Appropriations guys remarked.

Appropriations Subcommittee Chairman Edward Roybal, the manager of the Treasury-Postal Service-General Government appropriations bill, responded, "The committee did not put in the projects simply because they wanted to." People on the House floor laughed. Everyone in my office who was watching the floor proceedings laughed. Joe Skeen, an Appropriations Committee Republican from New Mexico, said briefly that the projects "should be carried out because they do make a contribution to basic science." In other words, the fix was in on our side, too, Walker, so pipe down. Coleman, who did not participate in the debate, voted to keep the projects and won, 293–114.

Even better, the matter had caught the attention of *Congressional Quarterly*, which used Coleman and the UTEP project to illustrate the support back in members' districts for pork barrel projects. In a pre-interview memorandum I warned Coleman not to screw up: "Keep in mind that this is the one article Capitol Hill will read about this project and this issue as we try to keep it in the legislation."[3]

Coleman could no more explain what our strategic material project did than could my three-and-a-half-year-old daughter. But he was in his element: back in the center of attention bashing Republicans. Better yet, *Congressional Quarterly* had used his picture.[4] Still, we were worried. Coleman liked to coast, and every political victory was usually followed by an "atrocity," as our staff came to term these incidents.

The next one was only a few days away. Coleman called Rogers from home on the morning of August 2 to complain that he did not want to attend a 1:30 P.M. meeting with constituents because his son Travis might have the mumps. "Well, what am I supposed to do?" he demanded peevishly of Rogers. "I can either bring Travis to that meeting and expose everybody or bring him to the office or have a staff person come here and babysit."

"I suggest you do what anyone else would do," Rogers snapped back. "Get a babysitter and deal with it!" He hung up, visibly angry.

Our staff was in a panic because we all knew he was crazy enough to bring his mumps-laden kid to the office.

"Maybe he's lying just to get out of the afternoon constituent meeting," someone suggested hopefully as we gathered around the office coffee machine for an emergency meeting.

"Can't take the chance. You know he'd do it," I said.

"Hell yes he'd do it," Rogers snapped.

"Is mumps contagious?" someone asked.

"What the hell's mumps, anyway?"

The WATS lines were ablaze as we called our mothers across the country to find out if we had had the mumps as children. But then again, if we had, we would be prime candidates to babysit.

"Hey, I hear if you get them when you're an adult they make your nuts rot off," someone mentioned slyly to Paul Rogers, who had a compulsive dread of disease. As we all snickered to ourselves, trying to hold in the mirth, Paul freaked out and ran up Pennsylvania Avenue to the local bookstore to buy *Merck's Manual* to check out the malady in detail.

The crisis eased when a staff member, who had definitely had the mumps, volunteered to go to Coleman's house so he could make the constituent meeting. The next morning, a rumor circulated that Coleman was actually going to take Travis to the doctor. We waited anxiously for confirmation.

In this turbulent time, both in our office and in the House as a whole, the death of Texas Rep. Mickey Leland hit the Hill hard. Leland had been in Ethiopia visiting refugee camps in his role as chairman of the House Select Committee on Hunger when his plane had crashed. Congressman Coleman and Paul Rogers were distraught; Coleman and Leland had been deskmates in the Texas legislature, and Rogers had begun his career in politics as an aide to Leland.

But sentiment notwithstanding, Capitol Hill's political hype machine ground into gear; it depicts every member who dies in office as a fallen hero, especially under tragic and unexpected circumstances. It lost no time to use the occasion to celebrate itself in the process. Mickey Leland would be mourned deeply and poignantly by people like Paul Rogers, but when confirmation of Leland's death arrived, Speaker Foley did not miss a beat. Choking back emotion, he told the television networks that the tragedy was an instructive lesson to critics who thought all congressional overseas trips were cushy junkets. The next day, when Sen. John Heinz of Pennsylvania lost his life in an unrelated plane crash, Foley reminded the nation that " . . . a life committed to public service can sometimes exact a terrible price."

But in our office the follies continued.

"Hey, we finally tagged Gramm," a Democratic friend called to tell me.

"Oh, did that story run?"

"Yeah. Listen to the headline: 'Gramm Grabs Credit From Others, Critics Say.' Not bad, huh?"[5]

Not bad, but we had still blown the big one. For some time now we had been trying to push a story—all of it true, making it one of the most dangerous kinds in politics—linking Gramm to an enormous scandal within the U.S. Small Business Administration. Federal investigators were focusing on Region Six—El Paso, Albuquerque, San Antonio, and Houston—concerning allegations that SBA officials had forced minority contractors to pay bribes in order to get federal contracts. The matter first surfaced when some disgruntled contractors came to Coleman's office to complain that they had paid their money and still had not received any contracts. Coleman smartly referred all the contractors to the Justice Department. More ominously, in a spinoff of the case, allegations substantiated by supporting evidence showed that some shady contractors were using SBA funds to build warehouses and undertake activities to facilitate the transshipment of cocaine and other drugs from Mexico. The trail quickly hit dangerous ground; several potential witnesses had died mysteriously, one of them in a plane crash the day before he was to testify secretly before a grand jury.

As a result, at least one Small Business Administration investigator in the Inspector General's office had been deputized and armed because the SBA did not feel the FBI could protect him. The FBI, in return, was ensnarled because of a noticeable reluctance to pursue a federal corruption case that led straight to White House appointees as well as leading Republicans such as Sen. Phil Gramm.

Senator Gramm had several links to the case. While no one could prove that he had anything to do with the actual corruption (and he most likely had not), many of the individuals involved had been placed by him in political appointee positions with the Small Business Administration because of their Republican connections. Gramm, in essence, had been using federal jobs to build a Republican Hispanic political infrastructure in Texas and the Southwest. One of the individuals already convicted, an Eddie Alvarez, had been personally appointed by Gramm.[6] And phone logs obtained by federal investigators showed that another top Republican figure from New Mexico, former U.S. Interior Department Deputy Assistant Secretary Rick Montoya, made daily telephone calls to Alvarez. Another Gramm appointee, Henry Zuniga, was embroiled in the Wedtech scandal in New York and as a result was transferred to Texas. Because of subsequent allegations of corruption in El Paso, the SBA tried to transfer him to another office in Dallas, but Senator Gramm personally interceded with a telephone call to SBA head James Abdnor. Abdnor sought the advice of his inspector general and blocked the transfer.

As one investigator termed it, "It would be difficult to substantiate direct criminal conduct on the part of the senator. All of the individuals involved were put there by Senator Gramm, but I don't know if it was anything more than the usual political payoffs. Besides, Democrats did the same thing under Carter."

Connections with the Wedtech scandal were strong; many of its figures had ended up in the SBA's El Paso office. And the entire story was spiced by allegations of rampant use of drugs and prostitutes and mountains of cash—in other words, a typical scene on the U.S.-Mexico border, and one we thought well worth trying to get Senator Gramm to explain.

But for reasons I still cannot completely explain, we blew it. The timing could not have been better—the smell of scandal was in the air. Or maybe it could not have been worse—perhaps the press and the public had had their fill. Besides, the matter was extraordinarily political within the Justice Department; the FBI just never seemed to get off the dime. We had even met earlier in the year with a reporter from a national newspaper and spelled the whole thing out to him, but he had strong personal connections to El Paso and, as it turned out, to many of the local figures involved. No story ever ran. I also detected a faint sense of unease in our own office over just where the trail would lead. If you went back far enough, you began to stumble across people appointed by Democrats under the Carter administration. For whatever reasons, Coleman had no enthusiasm for the case, and without his active participation, we could never sell the story.

As the summer blazed on, things were getting equally weird in Washington. You could smell it on the House floor. On August 4, 1989, Rep. Pat Schroeder (D-CO) made a point of personal privilege to denounce a "Dear Colleague" letter by Robert Dornan (R-CA) that called her, Rep. Barbara Boxer (D-CA), and Les AuCoin's (D-OR) tactics in a recent abortion funding debate "McCarthy-like" and "deceitful."

Dornan rushed to the House floor and soon became as emotional as Schroeder and AuCoin, prompting Schroeder to ask the Chair, "Must the gentlewoman from Colorado and the gentleman from Oregon refer to the gentleman from California if he is not being a gentleman?"

Dornan interjected, "No, you may call him the member from California. But then my gentlemanliness will return shortly."

Dornan continued to expound on the abortion debate until AuCoin asked, "Who is the gentleman referring to now?"

"Nobody in general," Dornan replied. "All of those who listened to the other side of the debate."

Schroeder asked, "The gentleman is calling us killers or is he not calling us killers?"

"I did not hear that," Dornan sputtered. "I tried not to hear it. I will continue!"

On August 13 Rep. Lynn Martin (R-IL) took to the House floor to call franked newsletters "taxpayer-paid birdcage liners." Republicans were also in a frenzy over the National Endowment for the Arts' funding of allegedly pornographic art, and Rep. Dana Rohrabacher (R-CA) used his time to worry that "our tax dollars could even again be spent for submerging a picture of Senator [Jesse] Helms in a bottle of urine."

At this point, Rep. Robert Walker (R-PA) rose and said, "Mr. Speaker, I have a parliamentary inquiry."

You could hear the "Ah, shits" ripple through the Democratic ranks. Walker is the Republican's floor gadfly, and is capable of anything.

"What would be the ruling of the Chair should these particular artworks be brought to the floor for display as part of the debate?" Waller added.

"Christ," someone in our office said, "he's got the Mapplethorpe exhibit in the Republican cloakroom!" He dashed to the telephone to call friends to make sure they were tuned in to the House floor proceedings; this one had some potential.

The Chair disappointed us. "It would violate the decorum of the House," he intoned. The Chair and Walker went back and forth for several minutes as Walker tried to pin him down to admitting that while the Mapplethorpe exhibit and other such artwork could quite legitimately receive federal money, they were nevertheless offensive enough to be prohibited from being displayed on national television. Sometimes none of this makes sense to the average viewer until you understand that, first, many members, including Walker, deliberately play to the national television office; personally, I wish the Democrats had the sense to do the same thing. And second, the tube is not the entire stage. Republicans are smart enough to force Democrats to say and do stupid things on the House floor, and then to send mass mailings and press releases into the districts of those who did them. Once in a while, the Democrats try and catch up, but three-day-old statements from the Democratic National Committee are at least equally effective as birdcage liners as Lynn Martin's newsletters.

The weirdness continued closer to home, too. In the absence of direction from Coleman, Paul Rogers exercised power as if he were the elected member of Congress. He had the partisan beast in his eye on September 23 when he ordered that we "go after" Georgetown's Center for Strategic and International Studies (CSIS) because it had had the temerity to involve Republicans as well as Democrats in its programs on Mexico. Republicans, in his view, had no legitimacy discussing the subject. The CSIS was not being bipartisan; it was participating in one of those dark anti-Democrat conspiracies that only Paul had the skill to ferret out. Rogers ordered the legislative staff to get the Mexican Embassy to back out of an upcoming program that Congressman Coleman had already agreed to chair. On another front, Rogers had wanted the staff to attack the director of the University of Texas at El Paso project for whom we had obtained the $7.1 million in the last two years—something Rogers did not admit had become personal between him and the director.

When Rogers learned the staff had not carried out the task—and a damn good thing, too, because the congressman would have taken the brunt of the criticism—he launched a tirade. I feared he was nearing the edge, even though he had just told me I would soon be getting a $300 a month raise. For some odd reason, Paul and I got along very well, perhaps because he generally gave me a blank check in my work and I had long since past the point of caring about the substance of what we issued in Coleman's name. But we were in a tangled web here—and it was feared that the director of the UTEP Institute had arranged a payment to go to former Sen. Dennis DeConcini staffer Bobby Mills to lobby for the project in the Senate, something the director had previously denied.

All this back-stabbing went on without the congressman's knowledge or consent; Coleman remained uninvolved and unaware. Paul had become the ultimate Hill rat: he had *become* the Member, and he wielded authority accordingly. He made policy decisions on his own, signed Coleman's name to documents and letters without consulting him, and issued orders in Coleman's name without constraint.

I thought to myself: I am thirty-four years old. I do not feel good about this. Ain't America great?

Issues materialized out of the air, coming right at us at high speed. On September 26, the House was in a jitter over the capital gains tax issue. President Bush was pushing hard to reinstate the exclusion on capital gains, which had been eliminated by the Tax Reform Act of 1986. Capital gains was now treated as ordinary income and taxed at a maximum rate of 33 percent. Before the 1986 changes, it was taxed at a maximum rate of 20 percent. The Democratic leadership opposed any new changes because in their view only the most affluent Americans would benefit and the federal deficit would massively increase, but their position was being undercut by six Democratic defectors on the Ways and Means Committee, including Texans Mike Andrews and John Pickle.[7] The action on the House floor—the debate, the tone, the atmosphere—was edgy. Overshadowing this particular debate were members' fears that they were running out of time, running out of gimmicks, that something real and bad might happen. It was the march to folly all over again. During general debate, the Members were not speaking—they were pleading, almost desperately, for someone to understand them. Coleman had told me the day before, "Hell, I was walking this morning when the Speaker came up to me and said, 'Hey Coleman, you're good on capital gains, aren't you?' or something like that. And I said, 'Mr. Speaker, I really don't know what the hell we're voting on. The rule's changing by the hour, all this extra crap is piling on . . .' "

The leadership and the defectors bickered publicly for weeks. Majority Leader Richard Gephardt on July 31 declared a "stalemate." Liberals muttered threats against the leader of the defectors, Georgia Democrat Ed Jenkins, for putting together a coalition of conservative Democrats and Republicans. In September, the leadership tried to buy off the timber industry with a version of capital gains only for them, but it did not work.

When they fought it out on the floor on September 28, the leadership got rolled like a drunk in an alley, losing sixty-four Democrats in a 329–190 defeat.

"Hey, Foley took it on the chin," a buddy said at lunch the next day.

"Up the ass, you mean," another added. "And Gephardt along with him."

"So maybe it was worth losing after all," the first person said. We all laughed.

Majority Leader Gephardt had been banking on making capital

gains the showpiece of his new "class warfare" theme, which his polls had told him was the public's issue du jour. The media, however, having correctly detected no outpouring of support for Gephardt's latest issue from the supposedly oppressed classes, quickly pronounced the strategy a failure. Gephardt's leadership career, in fact, was the story of a Search for the Issue, for that one magic pathway into the heart of the electorate. He had tried protectionism, class warfare, tax fairness, you name it—everything except principle and character. Gephardt was part of the new Democratic leadership team that had been too slow to react to the attractiveness of the proposal as it drifted about, rudderless, in what the *Philadelphia Daily News*'s Sandy Grady called the World's Longest Identity Crisis.[8]

My first buddy burped. "Well, we should have expected it. They've been fucking up left and right. They got snookered on holding two separate votes on Uncle Frank (Hill slang for Congressionally franked mail). Idiots. They were indecisive in the pissing contest over child care. They got stampeded into repealing Section 89." He looked at his watch and laughed. "It's 12:30—do you know where your Members are?"

We followed such things closely, you see, and exceptional interest in floor activities set our office apart from most others. We had no particularly driving issue, no burning cause. Our issue was the mechanics, the levers, the exercise of power itself and the relationships of powerful individuals to each other; we were tuned into the schedule, the talk of the cloakrooms, the Speaker's latest rumor, the moneymen back home. We attempted to divine intent on the part of the Majority Leader, the Majority Whip, and the top staff people, but it was becoming more and more difficult as Coleman continued to fail to appear at Whip meetings.

"This just ain't doing it," Rogers complained to me one day. "Can't get my fucking calls returned by ANYONE!"

"Maybe there's a direct correlation between that and the meetings Coleman doesn't attend," I suggested.

"Something like that," he muttered, and stared at the television.

In October 1989, our office was caught up in an uproar over a newspaper article about a new border crossing in an industrial development at Santa Teresa, New Mexico—the lair of Charlie Crowder, a Coleman moneyman and crony. In effect, the New Mexico congressional delegation had announced that after fifteen years of bickering, they had decided on a new U.S. government border crossing at Santa Teresa.

The collective blood pressure started to rise when Paul Rogers attached a nasty note to the clipping, asking why we had not known about the announcement (the short answer: we could not read minds). Actually, our staff had not only known about it, but had told Rogers, who had apparently forgotten.

Rogers exploded ("went apeshit," one witness said) because *he* had made a backroom promise to former El Paso County Judge Pat O'Rourke that Congressman Coleman could get the border crossing at Sunland Park, a rival development at the ASARCO plant near El Paso. But he had not told the rest of the staff about this little detail, nor informed the congressman. Sunland Park would in time—maybe within fifteen years—receive a border crossing, but Rogers, who received a significant portion of his salary from the Appropriations Committee and certified each month that he did committee work, had not been to a single associate staff meeting since Congressman Coleman had joined the committee years ago. Consequently, he had missed the entire debate over where the crossing would go.

When the deal over the Santa Teresa crossing was completed, Rogers's promises were out on a limb. New Mexico members had a good deal of clout: Rep. Joe Skeen and Sen. Pete Domenici were the ranking Republican members on the respective House and Senate Appropriations Subcommittees on Treasury, Postal Service, and General Government, which funded the federal agency that built border crossings; Democrat Jeff Bingaman was a United States senator as well. The three had cut their own deals with the barons of New Mexico politics; their own moneymen had been made happy. In fact, the Santa Teresa affair highlighted the growth of congressional power. The decision on where to locate the border crossing was not made by the administration, but by two United States senators and one congressman who had sat down and decided, all by themselves, whom the money would enrich.

Pat O'Rourke, as it turned out, was representing the powerful Kastrin family of El Paso, which was developing Sunland Park. The Kastrins also helped bankroll Coleman, who was on intimate terms with the family. He regularly provided them with detailed inside accounts of Appropriations Committee projects that could affect their business interests.[9] The congressman and Paul Rogers dined privately with the Kastrins at exclusive Washington restaurants when they were in town,[10] and Fred Kastrin served as Coleman's campaign treasurer.

In December 1984, Coleman negotiated an agreement to pay a $2,500 fine to the Federal Election Commission concerning "technical violations" of a federal election law that involved eleven promissory notes to obtain bank loans for Coleman's 1982 campaign. Problem: The $77,700 total exceeded federal limits. William Kastrin had signed five of the eleven notes for a total of $22,167, of which $21,167 exceeded federal limits.[11]

On one occasion, April 22, 1987, Congressman Coleman lauded Debbie Kastrin, a major campaign contributor, in the *Congressional Record* for being recognized by a business publication as a "Rising Star of Texas." His statement congratulated her for her business and civic achievement, but made no mention of their financial ties with the congressman. In 1989, the Associated Press reported that Debbie Kastrin and William F. Kastrin had guaranteed a loan to the Ronald Coleman Trust in the range of $50,000 to $100,000 (House reporting requirements do not have to be more exact). Paul Rogers instructed me to tell the AP they were "[l]ongstanding personal friends who had no interest in legislation."[12] Another guarantor on the note was the same Pat O'Rourke to whom Paul Rogers had made the promise about the border crossing.[13] According to Rogers, the guarantors signed the note but did not have to put up any money because the note had been duly paid off.

To complicate matters even further, Santa Teresa's Charlie Crowder *also* served on Coleman's Finance Committee, and had also loaned a substantial amount of money to Coleman. (See Appendix II)

Nothing produces as anguished a screech in politics as when a politician is caught in a conflict between two friends who are also major campaign contributors, and even more so when the clash is unexpected. Such close relationships do not always imply wrongdoing, but they do illustrate how members of Congress, especially those on the Favor Factory, have one foot in the heady atmosphere of the Hill's national politics and another in its back alleys of money and deals.

As Rogers lectured us through clenched teeth the next day: "You can assume the Kastrins are playing it straight. Assume O'Rourke is playing both sides of the fence. . . . It's just that O'Rourke is pissed because he wanted ten grand to lobby for Sunland Park. A private individual gave him five grand but the Border Trade Alliance turned him down. He stands to piss off the players—Coleman, Skeen, Domenici—all because he wanted . . . a lobbying job. Coleman has two meetings coming up and needs to know all this shit. You keep alleging that you're left out of things and it's not true. There are conversations and things you don't know about, not privy to, and believe me, you don't want to know about them. The trade association people need to understand that Coleman is on the team."

Rogers had to do some fancy footwork to make sure that the moneypeople who did not get the border crossing right away understood that it was anyone's fault but his own: the Appropriations Committee staff, the political players back in El Paso, the perfidy of the New Mexicans; the list was a long one. It worked. He convinced the El Paso moneypeople in the end that the matter had been beyond his or Coleman's control. And Coleman did stay "on the team" despite the fact that he was unaware he had ever been off: he had left town for a weekend at the Ashby Inn in rural Virginia and had no idea the entire mess had ever taken place.

Those on the Appropriations Committee understood what "getting things done" meant. Congressman Coleman himself once mentioned candidly to Dr. David Roadie, a visiting political scientist from Michigan State University, "The Republicans have a constituency in the House and try to help their colleagues. On the spending side, that's easy to do. They don't draw the lines with us and we don't draw the lines with them. [Republican Congressmen] Walker and Gingrich wouldn't work here. [Republican Minority Leader Robert] Michel has been on—he's a Tom Foley type. We don't fight over petty issues. If [New Mexico Republican] Joe Skeen needs a new airport at Ruidoso or he has some land he has to deal with, we do it. Appropriations tends to be the more responsible members."

Scenes from a democracy: it was 3:10 P.M. on October 4, 1989, minutes before the big vote on the Stark substitute to repeal the catastrophic health insurance legislation. The year before, the House had passed a catastrophic illness law that expanded three major Medicare benefits. The number of hospital days each year that would be covered increased from sixty to 365; a limit of $1,370 was set on out-of-pocket doctor costs; and a new prescription drug benefit was established. But many senior citizens protested the additional premiums of up to $800 per year, even though only 5.6 percent of the elderly would pay the maximum (because they were rich already), and three-fifths of all seniors would pay nothing (because they were too poor). Rep. Pete Stark (D-CA) had offered a substitute bill that would have killed the premium increase but kept the prescription drug and other benefits.

Coleman sat at his desk. Alternately angry and fearful of the public reaction to voting for the Stark substitute, he argued against it, even though he personally believed it was the right thing to do.

"As far as I'm concerned, they can all go to hell," Coleman snapped at us. "You go to Town Hall meetings. They'll be yelling at you: You raised my premiums! You raised my taxes!" Coleman was prescient: after the vote, Ways and Means Committee Chairman Dan Rostenkowski was chased through the streets of Chicago by angry citizens.

"But it's only $2 a month," Paul Rogers contended. Despite his management style, his compassion for the impoverished elderly was genuine.

"Yeah, $2.40 a month, and they'll be screaming as soon as they get their premium increases," Coleman countered, leaning back in his chair. "It's a premium increase, a tax increase, and you can't tell the leadership that. What's the use of a leadership that can't win a vote?" Coleman was very good at working up a self-pitying lather. Today was a good performance.

Coleman called the legislative staff in the middle of the vote. "It's going down big," he said, referring to the Stark amendment. "Do you think I should vote for it now that it's going down?"

What courage! What backbone! What horseshit! Coleman voted against it in the end, and the law to protect elderly people from the costs of catastrophic illness was repealed; 242 members switched their votes from their 1988 vote. In the unsettled political times of 1989, they were taking no chances.[14]

Some issues were less contentious than others; on Gramm-Rudman sequestration day, Capitol Hill yawned. Coleman, Rogers, and former El Paso County Judge Pat O'Rourke went out to a long lunch from which they did not return. Coleman cackled to Rogers the next morning, "What do you think of sequestration, Rogers? Two lunches in a row—not bad, eh?" Not bad at all, especially when you're flooding your congressional district at the same time with press releases blaring, "Bush Administration Should Put Interests of Nation Ahead of Politics."[15]

The next day, the House-Senate conferees approved the $4.1 million project for UTEP. Sequestration be damned.

But tempers were still running high. One of our local newspapers had not given what Paul Rogers considered to be proper credit for $16.25 million in appropriations projects. It turned out that the original story did mention the congressman, but the quotes were edited out by a copy editor.

"This is still chickenshit," Rogers replied. "And I want a letter drafted to Tom King [publisher of the *El Paso Herald-Post*] pointing this out—to be signed by some big advertisers." I yeah-yeahed him but did no such thing. Rogers was beginning to see enemies everywhere again, especially in the press. He seemed bedeviled by adversaries wherever he turned, enemies who plotted Conspiracies the substance of which only he could divine.

Yeah, buddy.

Even leadership stalwarts such as Vic Fazio of California take their lumps occasionally, like the time in October 1989 when, as an Appropriations staffer put it delicately, "he got his nuts stoved in."

The Appropriations Committee has been chaired since 1977 by Rep. Jamie Whitten of Mississippi, the longest-serving member in Congress today. He has been the chairman of the Subcommittee on Rural Development, Agriculture, and Related Agencies for all but two years since 1949. He and his staff essentially run the Department of Agriculture. When he addressed the 125th anniversary celebration of the department, he candidly pointed out, "All anyone ever wants is a special advantage over the next fellow. Understand that, and you've understood the intent of every law ever passed."[16]

Whitten's love for agriculturally related appropriations was so strong that in a June 1985 conversation, Lt. Col. Oliver North told the CIA's Alan Fiers that Whitten's crucial support for a contra aid compromise depended on some water legislation, or, as North put it, "The key to the whole thing is giving some Mississippi and Alabama water projects money to Whitten."

Chairman Whitten had promised the Republicans that the continuing resolution (a catchall spending bill) would be "clean"—no political "pork" projects—and then turned around and tacked on $2.85 billion, plus "favorable consideration of other sums as necessary" for disaster relief, including the recent California earthquake. Gambling that Whitten would find a way around his promise to the Republicans, Fazio worked all weekend to draft a fifteen-page amendment, and when the committee convened asked for unanimous consent not to have it read. Whitten objected.

But Mr. Chairman," Fazio complained, "the amendment's fifteen pages long."

"That's why ah want it read," Whitten replied in his Mississippi drawl.

So the clerk took an hour to read Fazio's amendment, which, among other things, would have added another billion to Whitten's $2.85 billion. White House operatives skulked around the committee room all day, working the Republican members and telling the

California Republicans not to support Fazio. The White House threats worked; Republicans Jerry Lewis and Bill Lowrey refused to lift a finger for California's share of the pot.

At one point, after Fazio had introduced his amendment, Rep. Robert Livingston (R-LA) pointed out that Fazio's amendment included waivers to fix private beaches with public funds. Fazio backed off immediately and put the blame on Ron de Lugo, the delegate from the Virgin Islands, whose territory also needed hurricane relief assistance. Fazio contended that he thought de Lugo had taken care of it, and if he hadn't taken care of it, then he Fazio didn't care and we could take care of it *right now* if that's what had to be done to take care of it.

The Virgin Islands, devastated by a hurricane, indeed needed help. De Lugo had previously asked Coleman for an acceleration of some appropriations projects, which was within our power. As Rep. Mickey Edwards (R-OK) put it, "Appropriations is the key spot. Members need you and come to you for help. If you're not on Appropriations, you're at the mercy of other people."[17] But Paul Rogers counseled caution. "Check with the subcommittee," he said. "The governor and the lieutenant governor are known as 'rum and coke' because they're so corrupt. Make sure it's okay [for us to help]. Tell the subcommittee that we want to help, that there's a lot of Texans who own property there, but make sure de Lugo's not using the hurricane as an excuse to pile on a bunch of shit."

Our staff commented that maybe there would not be enough money anyway to accelerate the projects.

"Well," Paul said with a sly smile, "there *will* be a continuing resolution, you know."

Now here was the continuing resolution, and Fazio and the leadership were terrified privately that de Lugo and his cronies down in the Islands would steal all the money if it went en bloc to the Virgin Island government. Fazio tried to finesse the problem—de Lugo supported the Democratic leadership—with nonspecific legislative language that would address the relief need in such a way as to preclude Lugo getting his fingers on the money. Livingston unwittingly spoiled the plan, and sources later reported that he regretted doing so because the potential payoff to Louisiana in the aftermath of a future hurricane could have been enormous.

And to add to the chaos, Rep. Bill Hefner from North Carolina, figuring what the hell, tossed in an amendment to Fazio's amendment to add $100 million for reforestation in North Carolina. Chairman Whitten got sick of the whole thing and offered a motion to put Fazio's amendment into the bill as report language, which probably did not carry the force of law. The continuing resolution then passed. Whitten's extra $2.85 billion became statutory language in the law, which meant that it would have to be spent. Fazio's billion got stuck in the committee report, which meant it would never be spent. And the Virgin Islands, in the end, were left high and dry. The entire House approved the $2.85 billion measure on October 24, 1989, by a vote of 321 to 99.

On October 25, I attended an 8:00 A.M. budget crisis meeting called by the Democratic Study Group and chaired by Representatives Penny, Olin, Price, and Moody. Guest stars included Majority Whip Bill Gray, Budget Committee Chairman Leon Panetta, and Majority Leader Richard Gephardt, who should have been muzzled. He walked through the crowd after he had finished speaking, a glazed stare plastered onto his expressionless face. Gephardt exuded a cultivated earnestness that could turn your stomach worse than a room full of policy wonks getting hallucinogenic over yet another number-clogged "process." Gephardt was at home; he was a man who never met a process he did not like.

The next day I complained about all things disgusting to a former Hill rat who was now a downtown lobbyist. "At least it's more honest where you are," I said.

"Yeah," he laughed, "everybody knows we're whoring."

"Perhaps," I said, "but up here it's supposed to look like we're doing it for love."

I became bolder about confronting Coleman with the need to start participating in the job of being a member of the U.S. House of Representatives. We had mailed nearly a quarter-million questionnaires to every household in Coleman's congressional district, and in my report on the results, I told him that people were starting to criticize him for not being visible enough in the community—people don't "see you around" like they used to. There had, moreover "been a significant number of questions on the subject of ethics, junkets, lobbyists, the pay raise, special interests, and congressional perks."[18]

But warnings had no effect. By early November, Coleman was refusing to come to the office at all, and on the sixth the legislative staff had to go to his house to brief him on the Foreign Operations bill. The staff found him playing the computer video "Tower of Doom." He would not listen to the briefing, which included the extremely touchy subject of Israel's request for a "drawdown" of interest on loans from 10 percent to 8 percent. "Can't you see I'm almost to the Sixteenth Level?" he complained. He appeared at the House-Senate conference, listened to the back-and-forth, and said he would oppose the drawdown request. Rogers went crazy and tried to blame the legislative staff, but this time I think even he realized it was Coleman who booted it. By the end of the day, it was clear that Israel and the American-Israel Public Affairs Committee were going to win in conference. Coleman voted for the drawdown. Afterwards, we discovered he had actually promised AIPAC some time ago that he would support the drawdown. He had simply forgotten.

On November 20, 1989, the weird turned pro again.

The day started off with a staff meeting at which we received the usual marching orders: statements to be written, cosponsors called in on our bills, floor action to be followed. These meetings are chaired by our staff director. Congressman Coleman, lethargic as ever, failed to show up.

The main question of the day was the foreign aid appropriations bill and El Salvador. Rebels had launched a massive urban offensive on November 10. According to U.S. government investigators, shortly before midnight on November 15, 1989, Salvadoran Colonel Guillermo Alfredo Benavides ordered the execution of six Jesuit priests, including Father Ignacio Ellacuria, a critic of the government and a prominent liberal (some said leftist) intellectual. The executions sparked international uproar and threatened American aid to the Salvadoran government.

President Bush had vetoed the foreign aid appropriations bill over the weekend, and Appropriations Foreign Operations Subcommittee Chairman David Obey brought a rule to the floor on November 20 that would have allowed a vote on an amendment to delay 30 percent of El Salvador's aid until investigators got to the bottom of the Jesuit murders.

The Republicans went berserk, of course, and lined up one after another to speak out against the rule. But at the office, we, the staff, outraged by the murders, figured that Congressman Coleman would vote the right way—that is, to delay the aid—because he had always taken a tough stand on human rights in Central America, an important issue for El Paso's Hispanic community.

We were wrong. He decided to vote *against* the rule because of some tortured political logic involving agreement by the conferees on the bill to drop the family planning provision, which had prompted President Bush's veto in the first place.

No one on the staff believed him, however, because aid to El Salvador was an extremely emotional issue with Hispanic voters. Besides, Coleman was a tricky man to read. He would let off a lot of steam in private, arguing one way and then another as he went about deciding which path to choose. As his press secretary, one of my major responsibilities was to make certain to remember the last thing he said.

The congressman stormed around the office, pacing and shouting; I was afraid he was going to knock the decorated birthday cake from the Sears & Roebuck lobbyist off his desk. "I voted against the rule, all right. It was ridiculous. Ridiculous! We caved on family planning. Caved! We had the opportunity to stick it to 'em and we dropped it." Caught up in raw partisan emotion, he displayed no recognition that the central issue of the foreign aid appropriations bill was El Salvador and the Jesuit murders, not family planning.

Then he vented his wrath on David Obey. "It's Obey's bill. He allowed it just to get a bill because he didn't want to be in session for one more day. I wanted to kick George Bush's ass on the [abortion] issue! It was politics, just stupid politics, just to pass a bill." He began to whine about his ever having gotten on the Foreign Operations Subcommittee to begin with.

Rogers, who with the rest of us had urged Coleman to vote the other way, immediately dropped his conscience by the wayside and ordered a defense to be written up of Congressman Coleman's vote. The problem, of course, was that this was *the* El Salvador vote of the year, and Coleman had booted it. We prepared a defense nevertheless that turned a mistake into a stand on principle. A "no" vote on the rule became a "vote to insist on doing something meaningful on El Salvador." That meaningful something was not spelled out and the congressman offered no subsequent proposals—nor had he contributed to the defense itself. That was our job as Hill rats: to follow the political beast with our gilded shovels, turning its scat into something more palatable.

My conscience was troubled as I drove home that evening. It would have been one thing if Congressman Coleman had *believed* that aid to El Salvador was so vital to the United States that it outweighed the murders, horrible as they were—the honest position of many members during the floor debate. But true belief was not present here, only cheap emotion. Images began to appear to me, first of the congressman, completely imprisoned by his inability to resist scoring cheap political shots against the president, no matter what the cost, then of Paul Rogers's coldness. And the defense he ordered of Coleman's vote kept flashing in my mind against the newspaper pictures of the Jesuits, their cook, and her daughter, dead in a puddle of their own blood and brains. I do not know how the congressman or his staff director slept that night, but I was troubled deeply.

On November 16, the House raised congressional pay from $89,500 to $120,489. The leadership had learned its lesson from the Jim Wright fiasco at the start of the year and refused to release any of the details until the day before the vote, thereby preventing organized public opposition.[19]

The leadership allowed no One-Minutes before the vote, and the bill was handled by chief fixer Vic Fazio of California, the mayor of Capitol Hill.

"The word bipartisan will be mentioned many times today," he stated at the outset, "because this is truly an historic occasion." Fazio was right; the fix was in. Republican Minority Leader Robert Michel, ethics crusader Newt Gingrich, and Republican Conference Chairman Jerry Lewis had appeared earlier in the day before a meeting of all House Democrats; and Speaker Foley, Majority Leader Gephardt, and Majority Whip Bill Gray had spoken in front of House Republicans. The messages were the same: we will not go after you for supporting the pay raise. Even the Republican National Committee's Lee Atwater and the Democratic National Committee's Ron Brown got into the act, signing a "communication" which, according to Fazio, stated they had "no intention of making it [the pay raise] part of the dialog and debate during the next election cycle."

The fix was in, Fazio warned, and it was time to jump aboard the train. "Recently, we have even seen this kind of criticism [Congress-bashing] institutionalized and brought on to this floor. It has simply been to further destroy trust in this institution."

"Which a $31,000 pay raise will not do," a legislative assistant next to me cracked.

After Fazio, Republican Lynn Martin, who had accepted $186,532 in political action committee contributions in 1987–1988 alone, claimed that the legislation "removes the stigma that this House, this noble body, can be used or misused by outside interests. . . . It was a genuine concern for the future of this House and our own reputations that drove this ethics reform process."

New York Democrat Tom Downey was blunter: "We should be paid properly."

Near the end of these mouthfuls of self-congratulation, Majority Leader Richard Gephardt stood up and said, "Today is the day for us to be leaders, to have the courage to do what is right for this body, for this institution, for this country and its people," to which Vic Fazio replied, "I am excited. I am grateful."

How eloquent these thieves become when the fix is in! Lynn Martin, Vic Fazio, Richard Gephardt, and now Robert Michel, major league warhorses all, bellowing and grunting for money while brandishing "ethics reform" as their banner.

*Pay us not to take the bribes*, they demanded. *Stop us before we kill again.* The pay raise passed, 252 to 174.

As I stood outside the Rayburn Room in the Capitol Building a short time afterwards, a member turned to Rep. Albert Bustamante (D-TX) and said gleefully, "Well, we got our pay raise!"

"Yeah, they handled it right this time," Bustamante responded, referring to the quick-hit, last-minute, close-to-the-vest method used.

As Bustamante spoke, Rep. Bill Richardson listened to a group of Native American schoolchildren singing patriotic songs in the back of the Rayburn Room. At a larger table in the middle of the room, another member, his staff, and visitors could barely hear themselves over the din of "God Bless America."

Congressman Coleman, knowing that the pay raise would pass, voted against it. He hailed the banning of honoraria but criticized the 25 percent increase in member's pay as "too much."[20] He took the money anyway.

At the end of November 1989, Paul Rogers was complaining loudly about a newspaper story on Coleman in which Coleman was quoted as saying that he was not involved in national issues. "You ought to tell him [the reporter] that it was chickenshit to write that Coleman was not involved in national issues," Rogers suggested.

I looked at him. "Coleman told her that," I said evenly.

Rogers's face took on a look of amazement. "Well, I'll be dipped in dogshit," he observed sagely, and uncharacteristically let the matter drop.

I had another view of the story, one I was not about to share with Rogers. I looked down at the clipping. The front-page headline blared in bold-faced type: "COLEMAN BRINGS HOME PLENTY OF FEDERAL PORK."

I continued to stare. There it was, in plain black and white. The actual words. The one we had all been waiting for. Perceptionland had been seized.

My mission was complete.


December 20, 1989. Five-and-a-half hours after the first wave of U.S. paratroopers went into battle in Panama, my sister Jill in Atlanta called me at 6:30 A.M. to tell me that the invasion was in progress. I groaned and rolled back under the covers.

My family had lived in the old Panama Canal Zone for a number of years, but sorting out emotions would have to wait. The deployment of U.S. troops anywhere means only one thing to those of us who work on Capitol Hill: another react day.

React days are frenzied. News feeds on itself, and reporters on the Hill scramble to file a local angle on the story. That means they want a "react," or reaction, from the members of Congress they cover.

The seemingly off-the-cuff react you see on the six o'clock news is the product of a complicated choreography. It's finger-in-the-wind time. What's the Speaker saying? More importantly, what's our political ally, Majority Leader Richard Gephardt, saying? The former presidential candidate is known by many on the Hill as the "Cheese Weasel" for his ability to make the least offensive, most defendable, mush-mouth comment possible in any given situation. It is a rare talent. He is dependable, too; his actions are so finely tuned by public opinion polls that you know he will be right on target. With his glazed-eye stare and impassive countenance, he has the personality of a Boy Scout on Quaaludes. Besides, anyone who can single-handedly raise $610,107 from political action committees in one year is worth listening to. We count on him in times like these.

It doesn't stop there. Emergency briefings are going on all over the Hill; you can almost smell the cordite in the air. Whaddya hear? You call your buddies, friendly reporters, anybody. Noticing small signs is a good habit when you take your living from wild land.[21] What's the word from other members of the Texas delegation? And by the way, are we winning or losing? We become transfixed by

CNN. Members of Congress are herd creatures who head for foxholes when bullets begin to fly. Oh sure, you want to sound bold and informative in your home district, but you really want to say as little as possible until you figure out what's going on, *especially* if we're winning or losing, and at what price. We never forget that the public rabble that wants to grease the bad guys in the first twenty-four hours of any engagement are the same ones who call for the president's head when the butcher's bill arrives. In these critical early hours, there's no room for conscience or principle. Only fools try to lead the public, something we never do.

I began to compose lines of Cautious Support in my head while I waited for the baby to wake up.

The phone rang again during my first cup of coffee. Joe Old, city editor of the *El Paso Herald-Post*, wanted a statement from Coleman.

To buy time, I hurriedly told Old that we would have something from the congressman in time for the paper's metro edition deadline. I was ready to head for the Hill, so I called the office and found Rogers. "I'll talk to Coleman right away," he said. That was our system. Paul rarely allowed anyone to consult with the oracle himself.

The halls were lonely and empty as I walked to the office. We were out of session, and it was right before Christmas. The solitude was the principal legacy of the new Speaker, Tom Foley, and it had earned him our eternal gratitude. The hell with national stability in the post-Jim Wright era. Tom got us out before Thanksgiving.

I found Rogers in his private office. The word was already in: Coleman had no intention of getting out of bed to speak to the press. He was claiming illness, the old excuse, and it annoyed me; a lot of those GIs in Panama must be wishing *they* could be home in bed with the flu, real or imagined, right about now.

"He doesn't have to get out of bed," I protested. "It's only a phone call."

But there was no recourse. This is what the congressman had become: a disembodied voice on the phone, an entity, suspended somewhere out of sight, against which we hurled information through Paul.

Paul jotted down a draft to be issued in Coleman's name. The content was good but I thought it sounded as if Coleman were opposed to sending troops, a big no-no this early in the game.

So I reworked it to achieve Cautious Support:

At this time, with the limited information at my disposal, I will not try to second-guess the President and will stand behind his actions unless I have reason to feel otherwise. The U.S. does have a vital interest in Panama, and does have the right to protect the lives of American citizens.

There is no question that Noriega was an international narcotics trafficker and hoodlum who had to be deposed, but we all wish that it could have been done without the use of force. U.S. troops have not been used wisely in Central America in the past, and it will cause us political difficulties throughout the region. But given Noriega's declaration of a state of war last weekend following the shooting death of an unarmed U.S. officer, it appears the President had no other choice but to protect American lives and the security of the Panama Canal.

The statement had a little of this and a little of that. Better yet, it bought us time and protected us from criticism no matter how the battles went.

Rogers had no problem with it. He also had no choice. We had spent the previous afternoon at the Democratic Club and, after a few Grand Marniers, Paul had lectured a visiting Marine officer at length about how George Bush "didn't have the nuts" to do anything about Panamanian strongman General Manuel Noriega. In the intervening ten hours, of course, George Bush had sent the 82nd Airborne Division along with twenty thousand other troops. Paul was in no position to play games with my statement, and we both knew it.

"Why don't you call Coleman at home and run it by him before you put it out?" he suggested.

"If the son of a bitch can't get out of bed to call the paper, he's sure as hell's not going to want to hear from me," I said. I knew what had to be done, and it didn't include Coleman. I telefaxed the statement to our district office in El Paso for the staff to use when constituents called. Since the congressman had made himself unavailable for the day, I did not issue the statement to the press other than to the one reporter who had called. No sense stirring things up when you couldn't deliver the body. We'd just wait for press calls to dribble in on their own, and offer them the statement then.

Ten days later, Coleman was invited to join Majority Leader Richard Gephardt's trip to Panama. Hesitant to go, he asked Rogers, "You *sure* I don't have an opponent this time?"

"You do not have one, and even if you did, it would be all the more reason to go," Rogers told him, somewhat exasperated. "And if you really want to get on the Intelligence Committee, the campaign starts here."

When Coleman returned from the classified briefing on the trip, he announced he had decided not to go. "There wasn't anything top secret about it," he complained. "And why should I go? All I'd get is a bunch of press and publicity, and I don't need that for another two years."

Coleman's refusal to play congressman on the day of the invasion did have one major benefit. It allowed me to focus on the real mission of the morning: delivering Christmas whiskey to his political cronies in the Capitol. I had put it off repeatedly, but today was Wednesday, three days before Christmas Eve, and Paul was worried that war in Panama or not, people would start leaving town for the holidays. I could not dispute his point.

"What about Panama?" someone asked me over the din of TV reports on American casualties as I dragged the dolly loaded with two cases of spirits.

"You're confusing us with someone who gives a shit," I replied.

With a list in my pocket, I went through the underground tunnel between the Cannon Building and the Capitol to hand-deliver gaily wrapped boxes of Christmas whiskey to the leadership offices, the Appropriations Committee, the House postmaster, the guy who shined Coleman's shoes in the Democratic Cloakroom, and other such notables. The Sergeant-At-Arms was very important because he handled the members' personal checking accounts and never bounced their checks. If a check had insufficient funds, the sergeant would hold it for a reasonable time until the member could come up with the cash, a neat little arrangement that amounted to a taxpayer-subsidized, short-term, interest-free loan. The boys in the House garage received bourbon, but the Sergeant got good scotch.

# CHAPTER THIRTEEN

# HOGS IN THE TUNNEL

THE YEAR 1989 had been a hell of a bad year. Not only had Wright and Coelho gone down as the House staggered from one fiscal crisis to the next, but the institution had seen ethical "incomings" from every direction imaginable.

These incomings could not have come at a worse time. They had no rhyme nor reason. Like Scud missiles aimed toward Washington, they fell on Republicans, Democrats, House leaders, and junior members alike.

I sat at my desk early in the year, doing some private thinking on how to pilot the good ship Coleman through the ethics swamp that lay ahead of us. Each new congressional scandal, even though it did not touch us directly, lowered the public's opinion of the House and, by extension, of each member.[1]

When I was in college at Washington and Lee University, I'd sit at night with friends on the front porch of a Virginia farmhouse near the Maury River, flashlight in hand, sipping corn whiskey from jars and plugging water rats with .22 rifles when they'd scurry over the top of the embankment. Ahh . . . there's one. Crack! 'Nother sip? Sure thing. Got that sucker . . .

Where do I begin?

278

• Majority Whip Bill Gray could still not shake a Philadelphia-based criminal investigation of allegedly improper benefits he derived from speaking fees he had assigned to his church as charitable deductions.[2]

• Republican Minority Whip Newt Gingrich had been exposed as having at best a questionable financial relationship with his daughter over the purchase of a house from funds obtained from a shady book deal.[3]

• Georgia Rep. Pat Swindall was already doing time for helping to launder drug money.[4]

• Questions still swirled around Rep. Barney Frank (D-MA) over hiring a homosexual prostitute as a personal assistant.

• Arkansas Rep. Tommy Robinson was under fire for hiring the twenty-two-year-old daughter of his business partner as his staff director at $60,000 per year, the most money earned by any Hill rat in the entire Arkansas delegation, including those who knew something about politics and government.[5]

• Tennessee Rep. Harold Ford's federal trial on bank and mail fraud was about to begin.

• Ohio Rep. Donald "Buzz" Lukens was convicted of having sex with a teenage girl, refusing to resign until his appeal was heard. Besides, his attorney argued, the girl participated willingly, and he claimed she had been a delinquent before meeting the congressman anyway.

• Illinois Rep. Gus Savage was sweating out Ethics Committee charges of sexual impropriety toward a Peace Corps worker in Zaire. Savage, who took to the House floor on February 1, 1990, to denounce those Democrats who had requested the investigation, made frequent use of racially derogatory terms (Savage was black, the other three Democrats white, his Peace Corps accuser was black). Savage derided the reports of impropriety because they had been written by a "white reporter." The story, he charged, "immediately exploded on white television and in white newspapers across this nation," including the CNN "Crossfire" show run by a "fraudulent white liberal and a belligerent white conservative." Savage claimed that *Post* reporter Jim McGee had been "tipped off" by a "government secret agent," and, furthermore, that the *Post* had given him a special assignment to discredit black political leaders.[6]

Under House rules, Savage was allowed to delete and tone down the worst of his remarks before they appeared in the *Congressional Record*.

The following week, Rep. Robert Walker (R-PA) introduced a resolution to have the House Administration Committee study the policy of allowing members to change their *Record* remarks before publication.[7] It was a good idea, but the last time anyone asked a committee that included Rep. Vic Fazio to study anything, he came up with a 25 percent pay raise for Members, so maybe Walker's idea was not so great. But the resolution passed, 373 to 30. Congressman Coleman, however, voted against it, calling it a "joke"; with his own political beast gnawing at his brain, he accused Walker of a partisan attempt to embarrass Gus Savage.[8]

"Now that was silly," a colleague told me. "Everybody knows Gus Savage needs no help whatsoever to embarrass himself." (In March, Savage would engage in some bitterly anti-Semitic remarks from which Majority Whip Bill Gray refused to distance himself, saying lamely, "I didn't hear the speech.")

• New York Rep. Robert Garcia resigned just before getting three years in prison for his role in the Wedtech scandal.

• Another New York Democrat, Rep. Elliott Engle, was reported by the *Village Voice* as having discussed fundraising for his election campaign with an alleged organized crime figure.[9] At the time, Engle was running against Rep. Mario Biaggi, who *was* organized crime, having been convicted on influence-peddling charges.

In reaction to the rainfall of corruption, the Ethics Committee asked to have its annual budget quadrupled. A number of former members, including prominent Democrats such as former U.S. Sen. James Abourezk and Reps. Donald Fraser, Ken Holland, Ron Mottl, and Ned Pattison, helped start a group called Americans to Limit Congressional Terms, which prompted the media to ask incumbent members for their reaction. The Hill, to a person, opposed term limitations on themselves. It would be "political euthanasia," intoned Illinois Republic Henry Hyde, a House member since 1974.[10]

"We already have term limitations—they're called elections," Congressman Coleman sniffed defensively to the Texas press. "The campaign is being coordinated by a Republican lobbyist in Washington, D.C. . . . West Texans resent the idea that some hundred-thousand-dollar-a-year Washington, D.C., lobbyist should pick El Paso's congressman instead of the voters."[11]

"Heaven forbid that should happen," someone remarked, pointing out that Coleman had only accepted $652,631 from lobbyists in the period 1983 to 1988, including more from labor lobbyists—$281,650—than any other member of the Texas delegation. But our position had been staked out.

Closer to home, Congressman Coleman did two interesting things with his girlfriend Amy during the week of December 18, 1989. He obtained a $30,000 a year job on the House Administration Committee for her. Then he married her. He should get her the job while she was still his girlfriend, his Capitol Hill reasoning went, because that way he could not be accused of nepotism. I came into the office on December 19, picking my way through what we jokingly called "graft and corruption"—Christmas gifts from lobbyists that filled the office with cheese, cans of nuts, and liquor. There is always a great rush for the RJR Nabisco box even though Amy had directed that all the booty go directly into Coleman's office "before the staff steals it all." I had walked into Coleman's office for precisely that purpose and saw the changing of the guard that had taken place swiftly and in the dark of night. The credenza behind Coleman's desk had sprouted pictures of Amy and her son.

We opened the New Year on January 3 at the Democratic Club. The talk at our table was generally light and good-humoredly stupid. A number of patrons stopped by our table to congratulate the newlyweds.

Amy mentioned that she and Coleman had gone to Rep. Gerald D. Kleczka's house for New Year's Eve where Rep. Chris Perkins and his wife got trashed and made fools of themselves. I was not surprised; Perkins has a party animal image second to none, and he and his wife were widely suspected of being the couple caught having sex on a stairway at the last Democratic issues retreat in West Virginia.

"She was making animal sounds all night," Amy complained about Perkins's wife. "I'd be rich if I had a video camera. We took pictures, polaroids. [Someone] was holding them up and saying, 'Now this one's worth $2,000 and this one's worth'—you know, that kind of thing." Coleman warned her to be careful. She dropped the subject.

Ritual pleasantries disposed of, our first legislative seance took place the next day; what one of our former legislative specialists called "making chicken salad out of chicken shit" was still our business. Paul Rogers, the ultimate Hill rat, sat in Coleman's chair to preside.

"Where's Coleman?" someone asked. Laughter followed.

"Who knows?" responded another.

"At home, I think," I offered, and added, "Who cares?"

No one could top that rejoinder, so we started to create the congressman's 1990 legislative agenda.

The Congressional Research Service had prepared an analysis of twenty-one major issues at the start of the second session of the 101st Congress. "These issues are likely to engage the Congress in important ways—holding hearings, debating legislative solutions, voting on specific bills or treaties, and informing constituent groups." The paper covered AIDS, budget deficits, civil rights, the environment, U.S.-Soviet relations, and much more.[12]

We took a slightly different tack. The basic approach was easy. As Paul Rogers put it, "We need to . . . mostly regurgitate the same shit as last year plus any new initiatives you might have."

No one responded.

The silence did not come from a dearth of ideas. Our legislative staff was talented and educated—everyone had either a masters degree or a law degree—and the possibilties for legislative initiative were boundless. But we were a beaten crowd in early 1990, exhausted from trying to keep Coleman afloat politically and legislatively in 1989 while receiving no help from him. Our party and its leadership also exhibited an exhaustion of the spirit. The soothsayers in Perceptionland were pessimistic; media pundit David Broder observed an "eclipse of this power-conscious city's clout in the country. . . ."[13]

And so the dark times seemed to settle on our House. I would come home to family and friends and wince. Capitol Hill was no longer something you advertised; for the first time anyone could remember, it was a source of chagrin instead of charisma. It was not that our legislative assistants had no initiatives; they simply had no hope.

Staff director Paul Rogers's agenda seemed limited to sending a message to the Southwestern Bell telephone company. Bell's new lobbyist in Texas was urging Coleman's financial supporters to write letters to him about the company's interest in Baby Bells. "We need to let the business community know we don't appreciate it," Rogers ordered. The letter writers were not people in and of themselves; they were "ours" because their contributions kept our congressman alive politically. The Southwestern Bell lobbyist's biggest mistake was not instigating the letters but neglecting to ask permission from our office.

The rest of the meeting was devoted to Border Caucus problems and degenerated into a near-shouting match between Rogers, who was trying to pin the blame on the legislative staff for declining attendance at these caucus meetings, and the legislative staff, which to its credit pointed out bluntly that the fault lay with Coleman, who did little or nothing to promote the caucus.

Such heated arguments could take place because the congressman now rarely attended the sessions where we decided his legislative agenda for the week, month, or year. This is unusual but not unheard of; earlier in the decade, when Rep. Clarence "Doc" Long hired a new staff director, he told him, "You can do anything you want in terms of substance. All I want is to be Queen of the May." Coleman appeared to be emulating Long. At one point, I placed a bunch of props in his office so visitors would think it was worked in. Someone donated an empty diet soda can, and we changed the memoranda on the desk regularly.

The years on Capitol Hill had not been kind to Coleman; he has added weight, and his hair had silvered. His thin, nearly invisible lips and the naturally downturned corners of his mouth were fixed in a perpetual whine. We spent hours in the House photography studio trying to improve the image, but met no success.

A staff member once placed what I thought was the best picture at the bottom of the heating unit by his desk.

"What's that?" I asked.

"Scares the mice."

Fortunately, my only assignment this day was to start easing the congressman away from his previous Cautious Support for the Panama invasion. "Start to redraft Panama with an emphasis on misgivings," Rogers ordered. "And add the cost angle, too." One of his Democratic Club cronies had probably told him that invasions cost a lot of money, but when a liberal Democrat makes an appeal to the taxpayer to justify a position, it is almost always an argument of last resort.

Coleman did not participate in formulating his 1990 legislative agenda, but he did stop by the next day to pick up all the Christmas liquor the lobbyists had brought during the holidays.

In the meantime, we decided on the usual strategy: flog the hell out of Uncle Frank's congressional mail and run a double shift at the Favor Factory. With no "leadership" coming from the leadership or the Democratic party as a whole, we had no choice but to try to survive on our own and hope for another day.

As a precaution, we jump-started Coleman's official campaign biography to spell out to potential moneymen and PACs the power of the Favor Factory, "arguably the most powerful in Congress because it has the power of the purse over the entire federal government." If that did not make our intentions perfectly clear, we added, ". . . U.S. Rep. Coleman uses the Committee to compel the executive branch to specific actions to improve Texas communities and interests including . . . the oil and gas industry . . . military construction . . . the supercollider . . . as well as Texas-based defense industries."[14]

Appropriations was important to others as well. Texas Democrat Greg Laughlin was facing a Republican opponent in 1990 who had set up a private Gulf of Mexico Foundation. Laughlin was also high on the White House political hit list for criticizing President Bush's handling of the crisis in Lithuania (where Laughlin's family originated). Laughlin wanted a federal project that he could bill as revitalizing the environment in the Gulf of Mexico to head off his opponent at the pass, and his emissaries came begging, hats in hand. We would help him as long as no problems arose for our own $57,145,000 in Favor Factory projects. Money continued to talk: Laughlin would beat his Republican opponent, but we would remain unopposed.[15]

Early in January I tried to push Coleman to do a Gannett News Service interview on his agenda for 1990. But the legislative staff had not finished their memoranda on the 1990 agenda—these papers take time—and Coleman had no agenda other than what the staff invented. He had become incapable of formulating one on his own.

I asked anyway: when could he do the interview? This kind of publicity opportunity is the dream of most politicians. Besides, as a skilled Hill rat, I could come up with a congressman's legislative agenda for any given year with my eyes closed. He would only have to repeat what I told him.

"No," he replied. He could not do it this week.

"What about next week?" I persisted.

Negative. He would return from a junket to Mexico on Wednesday. He would leave on a Florida junket on Friday. Paul Rogers, hearing Coleman end the argument by heading out the back door, ran to catch him. "Hey, Coleman, we're scheduling you for an hour next week in between trips," Rogers called.

Coleman stopped and looked at him. "Fuck YOU," he said with a grin, slowly and deliberately. He left. I carried the liquor on a dolly close behind him.


At the time, the *Washington Post* ran a story about drug czar William Bennett's draft strategy, which would have designated thirty-four border counties as high-priority areas to receive federal funds. Coleman had written Bennett last October urging the measure, and

Bennett had sent him a pro forma reply. Rogers now decided that we needed to send a response to that response to complete the paper tracks.

He put a letter on Coleman's desk. "Here's a draft of the letter you sent Bennett last Tuesday. Please approve it and we'll get it out today."

"Last Tuesday, eh?" Coleman chuckled. He glanced at it and said, okay, get it out.

I was also concerned about the developing political storm over Sen. Daniel Moynihan's proposal to reduce the Social Security payroll tax, a move that had upturned the standard political equations because a prominent Democrat had offered a tax cut; the Republicans, quite predictably, were going berserk.

"I think it's great," Rogers commented. "But we need to get some stuff out in advance to counter the argument that it would cut benefits. I guess we'll have to call the Republicans liars. Probably the editorial writers, too. We'll have to call them liars as well."

But Coleman said that he had told Majority Leader Gephardt that there was no strategy, that the Democrats were doing nothing, playing with Social Security.

"Let's not say that publicly," Rogers cautioned.

"I didn't say it publicly," Coleman barked. "I told it to the Majority Leader and to the staff here. Moynihan's crazy. I'm just telling you I'm not voting for any tax cuts. Tax-cutting is not what America needs now. It's crazy. Just crazy. And it's crazy to mess with Social Security. It shouldn't be used to mask the deficit, but what about the year 2005? Who's talking about that? Shit."

No way around it—Moynihan's Social Security tax cut proposal was dangerous. The Republicans were growing increasingly nervous, and President Bush was desperate. He led a coordinated attack against the Moynihan plan, charging that the tax cut would lead to a tax hike—interesting logic for a Republican.

Budget Director Richard Darman, in his essay introducing the budget document, put his finger on it: ". . . Social Security is a notoriously volatile subject when it enters the political domain; and whether rationality will prevail remains to be determined."

Darman was right. Social Security was the political equivalent of going nuclear, of punching the red button. We should know. We had gone nuclear on a number of occasions against the Republicans. And it worked—it worked every time. The Republicans usually helped; they always had some poor guy somewhere who just could not keep his hands off ideas that tinkered with Social Security. And when that happened, we're talking Hiroshima.

The air was full of predictions about a year of clashes between the president and Congress. All masks were down. The hogs swarmed in the tunnel. "It's elbows and assholes to the lifeboats," a friend said. I laughed because it made me think of one of Capitol Hill's better jokes.

Jimmy Carter, Richard Nixon, and Teddy Kennedy are on the Titanic when it hits the iceberg. "Save the women and children first!" Carter yells, stepping back. "Fuck the women and children!" Nixon snarls as he elbows his way into a boat. Teddy Kennedy glances at his watch and says, "You think we have the time?"

January 23. They're ba-ack!

The freeway traffic was ugly and you could tell it was opening day at the races on Capitol Hill. Cars whizzed around with gleeful, reckless abandon as Hill rats from all directions tried to get into the underground garages by 9:00 A.M. for the first time since Thanksgiving.

They're ba-ack! The first thing Speaker Foley did after the prayer was to read Rep. Robert Garcia's resignation letter. He did not mention—presumably out of propriety—that Garcia's absence had anything to do with his recent felony conviction in the Wedtech scandal and the fact that he was about to enter federal prison in a matter of days.

The Texas delegation welcomed a new member, Houston Rep.

Craig Washington, at a reception in the Cannon Caucus room. "What do you think they do for a new member when they welcome him to Mount Olympus?" I asked a fellow Texas staffer. "Anoint his feet with olive oil and give him a wreath of laurel?"

"No," he replied. "They give him an alarm clock that can't be set before 9:30 A.M."

"Oooh," I chuckled. "Bitter roots and herbs."

"Yeah, it's a problem," he conceded. He looked at his television screen and saw that five-and-a-half minutes were still left in a quorum call. "And they haven't even finished the first vote."

Texas Rep. Jack Brooks led the House in the pledge of allegiance. The Texans swarmed around Craig Washington on the House floor, a pack of bustling gray flannel that looked like cockroaches exposed to unexpected sunlight. Representative Washington took the oath and the House rose in applause to welcome yet another brought up through the clouds, another one of Us Who Has Become. Brooks thanked the House for sending cigars to the hospital when he was deathly ill with pancreatitis. Since Brooks had an opponent in both the primary and general elections, the extent of his illness had been carefully concealed by the Texas Democratic delegation to avoid giving his Democratic primary opponent an edge, especially in the critical fundraising months before the January 5 filing deadline.

Rep. Martin Frost had commented, "Extraordinary that he said he almost died, with a primary and a general opponent." Coleman had responded, "If we lose that seniority, we're fucked." Brooks returned from the hospital to a hero's welcome and told the press, "I arrived live with an automatic Browning shotgun, and the buzzards better keep their distance."[16] Brooks beat his Democratic primary opponent on March 13 by a vote of 72 percent to 38 percent.

Rep. Mike Andrews did not leave Craig Washington's side. Washington was calling the redistricting shots in Houston, and Andrews was "at risk," as Rep. Martin Frost put it.

On January 25, Paul Rogers called me into his office to tell me that the hunt for a seat on the Intelligence Committee was on once again despite the congressman's inaction on the Panama invasion. Coleman had Majority Leader Richard Gephardt's support, Rogers claimed, and hoped to have the Speaker on board soon. Rogers asked me to do a memorandum for him so he in turn could brief Coleman on Intelligence Committee issues.

What a hoot! With the Hill rat's concern for status, Rogers wanted *me* to give *him* the important information so *he* could brief the congressman. I had seen it all before; the two of them would talk with neither one having any conception what he was discussing. By the end of the meeting, they would have convinced each other of their brilliance. And Coleman—whom we still could not drag to attend routine Foreign Operations subcommittee meetings—wanted to oversee the nation's most sensitive programs and activities. Richard Gephardt was a lot stupider than even I had thought.

"Son of a bitch!" Congressman Coleman yelled on January 26, 1990. "Can you believe the nerve? This just can't be allowed to happen!"

The subject of this particular tantrum was Vernon Green, an employee at the House bank whose thankless task was to inform members of Congress that their checking accounts were potentially overdrawn—by a mere $8,000 in this case.

What should not be allowed to happen, Coleman barked in the same tone reserved for ordering his parking tickets to be fixed, was being asked to come up with the money. After all, he had sent the obligatory bottle of expensive Christmas scotch the previous month to Sergeant-At-Arms Jack Russ, who ran the House bank.

This was not something new. On September 15, 1989, the House bank had told Coleman it would no longer hold $4,000 in overdrafts. The hunt was on. No honoraria were available. All of his bagmen back home in the congressional district were turning deaf ears to his desperate pleas until one of them finally took pity and scrambled up another $10,000—and a stern lecture.

(In the meantime, Congress voted to exempt its pay from the across-the-board Gramm-Rudman budget cuts in October 1989, and the next month increased its annual pay from $89,900 to $120,000.)

But neither the pay scams nor the moneyman's lecture did any good. Three months later, on April 17, 1990, Coleman was told that he had bounced so many checks—$5,765—he would be $1,700 short *even after* Coleman's entire paycheck of $4,000 had been deposited at the end of the month.

True to form, Coleman arrogantly demanded from the House bank the same kind of interest-free loan that outraged the nation when it all came to light in the fall of 1991: He would make good on the checks when he could.

He received his dispensation. Had he not, Vernon Green would have lost his job.

The congressman did not report any of that free interest as income to the Internal Revenue Service.

The next year, when the House checking scandal dominated the headlines, the leadership decided to blame the bank instead of Members like Coleman. The fix was in. Coleman received a letter on October 17, 1991 from Jack Russ, the House Sergeant-At-Arms, stating that

> "Our records show that four of your checks for a combined total of $285 were held by the bank for brief periods, usually one to three days, until they were covered by a deposit at the end of the month. Further our records show you were *not* notified on the occasions that these overdrafts occurred. You were not notified of the overdrafts because they were isolated instances in an account that otherwise maintained healthy balances. We regret any inconvenience this may have caused you."

Coleman's public statement took the offensive, blaming the Sergeant-At-Arms by claiming that "Contrary to my personal check register and without my knowledge, four (4) checks were presented against insufficient funds. . . . One of the weaknesses in the system, however, was apparently the bookkeeping methods used by the disbursing office. . . . I have been surprised at this shoddy bookkeeping and I, as most Americans, want to know why it occurred. . . . I should have been aware of this situation at the time it occurred."[17]

National budget concerns loomed, too. But without a quote from Richard Gephardt to use on the budget, we were in uncharted waters. Then I hit pay dirt: " . . . I question whether his [Bush's] priorities are right for the times." Gephardt finally did come through with the award-winning, "Democrats are actively working to find solutions to the problems experienced by American families . . ." Bravo! Hooray! Oatmeal triumphs again. It was a statement almost as stupid as Thomas Dewey's immortal line, "The future is ahead of us."

While we were in the process of looking for ways to kick the stuffing out of President Bush's budget, we were slipping in a little bit of our own. The Appropriations Committee slated itself for a 30 percent increase in its investigations budget, while overall, the House was getting a 27 percent increase, mostly for staff and members' salaries.

The news on the morning of January 31 was full of stories about Richard Darman's testimony on the new Bush budget. "People are just lining up to kick the shit out of him," a legislative staffer marveled. "The members are having to take numbers."[18]

Poor Darman. If the White House had any sense, it would wait a week or so after Congress had been in session to let these guys blow off some steam. But oh-no. They have to send up their emissary to the Hill on the first day Congress is back from a two-month recess and with a big head full of steam. Fools. Don't they know the members are so full of themselves that mirrors are breaking all over Capitol Hill on the first morning they get back? Most of them, unlike Congressman Coleman, are media junkies. They've been salivating for two months to get into the *New York Times*, the *Washington Post*, and the television networks. That means they're not only getting psyched up to batter Darman, but haunted by the fear that they have *to do it better than anyone else.*

We met later in the morning to talk things over. Rogers, for some reason sounding as if we were briefing the president instead of the congressman, said in stilted tones, "Mr. Coleman is speaking to the press tonight, commenting on the State of the Union speech. He needs specific, tough information." He turned theatrically to Coleman. "Tell me where the most helpful place is to start. Military construction?"

Try this, I said to myself: you are in Washington, D.C. You are a United States congressman. The president has sent us his budget. You get to vote on it. If you want more information, like dollars and numbers, read the document yourself.

"Military construction," grunted Coleman.

"It's a partisan game," a legislative staffer told him. "The latest numbers are that twenty-two out of twenty-eight bases to be closed are in Democratic congressional districts."[18]

"Les Aspin introduced legislation calling for a commission to do the closings," Rogers interrupted.

"Defense Secretary Cheney wants a bill next week," the other staffer added.

"I don't see why we have to do either," Coleman responded.

"Rep. Marvin Leath is fired up," the staffer explained. "He feels shot in the back. Congressman Pickle is angry." Both members from Texas faced base closings in their districts.[19]

The discussion continued until neither congressman, staff director, nor legislative staff could remember the total budget authority and outlays for Fiscal Year 1991. We moved on.

"He [Congressman Coleman] wants to rip Bush on education," Paul Rogers tried.

Coleman had had no such thought, but it sounded good to him, so he said, "Right. When I'm on TV tonight. Don't give Bush any credit. I'm going to have to run the risk of making moderates and Republicans mad at us. Need to say rhetoric is no good—can't get by with a pretty speech—a pretty speech is not enough." He was tasting the language for something usable, rolling the words around and listening to them as they came out.

"The Darman essay points to doom," someone said.

"I don't want to sound angry," Coleman countered. "You can't be angry on TV, but I want to hit him [President Bush]. . . . Our attitude needs to be to take him on."

"Brrgghhggh! Brrgghhggh!" Six year-old Travis Coleman, who had been crawling all over Coleman's office during the meeting, had a Teenage Mutant Ninja Turtle Warrior in each hand, and they began a ferocious battle for the future of the Universe.

Over the din of combat, Rogers half-shouted, "We're working on issues proposals!"

"They're good for targeted mailings," I said. "The more information we have, the more 499s we can do." These were mass mailings of 499 letters or fewer, which meant they did not have to be reported and cleared by the House Commission on Mailing Standards.

"Right," said Paul. "Don't worry about limits. We're just going to keep going."

"Don't ever worry about limits when it comes to mailings," Coleman added.

That evening, after finally tracking down an advance copy of the speech, I took it to his house. Coleman was still ready to "take on" President Bush until he saw a news report on television about Bush's "dramatic" troop reduction proposal for Europe. "Shit," he said, disgusted. "Bush is wiping all the crap he's talking about in the budget right off the table." I agreed. "And here we Democrats are," he pointed out, "whining and carping about programs." I had no argument there, either.

The next morning was constructive. I trashed President Bush's antidrug efforts for the *Houston Chronicle*, then I applauded the Bush troop reduction in Europe on Channel 4 in El Paso but pointed out that his budget did not reflect those changes. To top it off, I drafted a mailing to all the Democratic precinct chairmen in the 16th Congressional District that really kicked the Bush budget and detailed all the ways it would bring disaster upon West Texas.

Coleman slept in. What a great country!


Other times were less fun. Paul Rogers gave us the annual pep talk about Congressman Coleman's potential, a session that was so pathetic he did not even bother to try to get us liquored up at the Democratic Club to do it. "He's given me personal indications that he's going to get very involved," Rogers claimed. "The leadership's got its eye on him." Like a yellow jacket at a picnic, I thought. "He's in with Gephardt," Rogers continued. "Gephardt owes him because of Mexico. We've got some great opportunities here . . ."

Sure.

My immediate assignment was to write a paper on the separation of powers—"something Coleman can use to stand up for legislative government," as Paul termed it. For someone who spent most of the day watching television and reading newspapers, he showed little awareness that the pickings were pretty slim out there. "Point out the grand design by the Republicans to tear down the legislative branch in the public mind. The press has bought into this. The danger is that this greatest form of government in history could suffer. . . . It's bullshit that the president should propose and the legislative should dispose. Check the Federalist Papers. Add some one-liners."

Here is the ultimate Hill rat's mind at work: Congress's bad image would never have happened had it not been for the Republicans and the press. Jim Wright, Tony Coelho, honoraria, pay raises, perks and privileges, and the inability of the Democratic majority to govern—all this had nothing to do with it.

My next assignment was even better. "Sooner or later we'll be asked about the pay raise," Rogers told me. "Say that I voted against it, but I'm not about to suggest to the people of my district that I'm worth less—come up with some arguments for that." Once again we intellectualized of the political beast: shall it be philosophy today that we will wear, or is the beast moaning for a little history? If so, will intellectual history do, or should we swagger with a touch of diplomacy? No matter. These things were not thought through by anyone but me; if what I came up with sounded appropriately slick or musty, as the situation demanded, Paul would be for it.

Congressman Coleman did find the time to work on an incumbent's ultimate perk: picking his or her own voters, through "redistricting." The Texas legislature had informed him that if all the

Texas Democratic incumbents could agree on a plan to redistrict, the legislature would approve it. With Jack Brooks' support, Coleman had been appointed to chair a secret committee of Texas Democratic incumbents, including Reps. Martin Frost and John Bryant, to redraw the map. Both were from the Dallas area, and Frost would soon be named chairman of IMPAC 2000, the House Democratic leadership's national redistricting arm.

It was a tricky situation. A resurgent Republican party had turned Texas into a two-party state, at least where statewide races were concerned, and the Texas Poll of party affiliation showed only a faint Democratic edge of 32 percent to 31 percent.[21]

That meant only one thing to us: It was time to flex our political muscle.

"We have the potential to do something as a delegation this time," Frost said at the first meeting that only included him, Coleman, me, and Bob Mansker, Frost's top Hill rat.[21] "What is the most realistic way of getting the delegation to function as a group?" Frost asked. "[Rep. Mike] Andrews is at risk because of Hispanics," he continued, visibly nervous. "Johnny [Bryant] and I are at risk in Dallas [because of blacks]. There are problems with Republicans—for me and Bryant to get what we want, we have to screw [Rep. Joe] Barton. We can't do it without screwing Barton. I need to go south and west and Bryant needs to go south and east. We're going to take off the top part of his [Barton's] district where he lives and push him south towards College Station."

"The Republicans might oppose Barton getting screwed," Coleman reminded him. "They'll say, well, you're screwing Barton, so we're not going to cooperate. We're going to need an agenda for each meeting [with each Texas Democrat]. Run it all by [Jack] Brooks."

"At some point Bryant's going to have to go to [Rep. Jim] Chapman and ask, and he'll say yes or no," Frost commented. Bryant wanted Henderson County, which was then in Chapman's district. "I'll have to go to [Rep.] Stenholm. [Rep.] Bustamante wants out of San Antonio and [Rep.] Smith wants in. Andrews is in great danger because of creating a Hispanic district. [Rep.] Craig Washington is in the middle of it and it's going to be a big mess. And Charlie Wilson is looking to unload Nacogdoches."

"Why?" Coleman asked.

"They don't like his ass," Frost chuckled. "It's the Lufkin-Nacogdoches feud, goes way back to high school football or something like that."

Frost returned to his grand vision. "The best thing for Bryant would be for Ralph Hall to retire in 1992—that way Bryant could get some of those Democrats—but it doesn't look like Ralph will retire—Bryant's only hoping."

I loved it. The meeting was behind closed doors. Given that a congressional seat is a virtual lifetime appointment these days, what we were actually doing was deciding on the future congressmen of chunks of people (500,000 or so)—without their permission or knowledge.

How many counties do you want to screw Barton out of? "My" Hispanics. "Your" blacks. Ripping apart the body politic of the state of Texas and stitching it back together was heady stuff indeed. No, Johnny needs more Democrats than that. Not this county, *that* county. It was frank stuff, this planning of the execution of Joe Barton, (never mind that he was a whiny "sumbitch," as they say in Texas, who probably deserved whatever he got anyway).

Throughout the meetings on redistricting, Congressman Frost was clearly nervous; he took care not to seem too eager to stick his knife in. But facts were facts: the composition of Frost's district had placed him in a tenuous political position. A significant portion of his district's population was black—29 percent in 1980, far higher in 1990. And with a large increase in Texas's population since 1980, the state was slated to receive three additional House seats. Frost knew that legal standards under the Voting Rights Act would be more favorable to minorities than ever before, assuring that at least one district in Dallas would have a black majority population. Frost would lose black Democratic voters to the new district, but how many, from where, and who would replace them were questions up for grabs. Frost also knew a lot of hands would be reaching for the cookie jar, and he wanted his to be first. Frost himself would be supporting a black majority district by June, but not until he had figured out a way to save himself.

"I'd start with the tough spots," Coleman began at the next meeting on February 6. "Dallas—you and Johnny Bryant work out what you need to do. Then go east—Chapman, you and Bryant decide—then get Wilson and Chapman."

"Then you got Ralph Hall," Frost said, still hoping Hall would retire.

"You're assuming," said Coleman. "Brooks said he thought Ralph was going to retire but you can't count on it."

"So how do you approach each Member so we're saying the same thing?" Frost asked.

"What you do is ask them where they live, and tell them they're not going to live there anymore," Coleman laughed. "We need a standard press response. I think all you say is . . ."

"Barton is the chair of the Republican delegation," Frost interrupted.

". . . we in the Texas delegation . . ." Coleman continued.

"Barton's trying to screw me and Bryant," Frost interrupted again, desperately trying to get his point across.

". . . are working on a map that the legislature will approve. We must keep it confidential. Redistricting can get nasty. Sarlapius already has plans . . ."

"Plans out the ass," Frost interjected.

". . . and he wants to get rid of south Amarillo," Coleman finished.

"[Rep. Charlie] Wilson will be difficult because he thinks it; wired down there with his relationship with [Texas Comptroller Bob] Bullock, and he'll figure, why should I do what you want when I can do whatever I want?" Frost pointed out. "[Rep. Henry] Gonzalez won't talk to anyone. [Rep.] Kika [de la Garza] will be difficult because he's always difficult."

And so the conversation went. Frost wanted to know who would be the most uncooperative, then added, "I've made a pledge to Bryant, written in blood, that I'm not going to do anything in Dallas that he doesn't want done. I'll make that promise to him every day if I have to." Frost could have saved his breath. The Texas delegation had no problem with Frost's pledge, but they thought the blood he had in mind might be Bryant's.

"See what they want and we'll come back and add it up," Frost suggested. "[Rep. Bill] Sarpalius is already running numbers. He wants to keep Potter and Randall [counties]. Below the line is bad."

"Above the line ain't all that great, either," Coleman cracked, referring to Amarillo.

"Let's avoid a big room," Frost urged, wanting to keep the deliberations secret. "The Republicans are already doing it, but then there's less of them."

"And our goal is to keep it that way," Coleman responded with a laugh. "One district out of thirty is about right."

Coleman himself had no redistricting problems, but Rogers feared a primary challenge from the left in 1992, possibly in a redrawn district and probably from a Hispanic. So Rogers went to work: Nudge, nudge, nudge. Everywhere we turned, Rogers was nudging Coleman to the left. Rogers was even pushing Coleman to vote to cut the Strategic Defense Initiative, something he had never done before in deference to the Texas business community.

The latest nudge was on twin plants. Rogers told me he wanted a speech to "clarify" the congressman's position. Needless to say, Coleman had no real position; it would be whatever we decided it would be, which meant the winner of the eventual argument between me, Paul, and the legislative shop. Any outcome, of course, would be tempered by the realities of Coleman's moneymen in the twin plant industry. But Rogers saw an opening by which he could both please the moneymen and persuade Hispanics that Coleman was moving toward them.

"Make sure it contains legitimate criticism," he said, "but be sure to refute the claim that there's a loss of jobs."

"Okay," I said.

"Oh, and don't forget some shit about corporate responsibility, too; we need that."

"Ten-four." Twin plants are an emotional issue with the Hispanic community, liberals, and business. At the recent convention of the

League of United Latin American Citizens (LULAC), resolutions were passed calling for a moratorium on the plants. Rogers, sniffing the wind, tried to tug Coleman away from the edge.

"Let's start doing everything we can bilingual," he instructed, thinking ahead to future criticism from the Hispanic community. "That's where we're going to be hit in the next election. The Right's got nowhere to go and no one to do it with. We got to worry about the Left and we got to do something about this Coleman being anti-Hispanic crap." In short order, he would see the Great Hispanic Conspiracy everywhere.

And I mean everywhere. On one occasion, he launched full force into the conspiracy theory. "Everything has to be bilingual," he emphasized. "We need to flood those Hispanic boxes [precincts] with bilingual mail. The electorate is now 50 percent Hispanic, and if they're going to start going after us in primaries, we've got to be ready. Coleman's gonna get all the Anglo vote, and they're gonna need at least 70 percent of the Hispanic vote to beat him, and they don't have that now. They're going to say, well, Coleman is a nice guy, but he's not Mexican. And the Mexicans who have been receiving all this bilingual mail from Coleman are going to say wait, that's not true."

"Okay," I said, which was my usual response to the Hispanic Conspiracy theory. If I protested, he would order something done; if I waited him out, he would forget about it and go on to the next crisis.

"If we don't get out front with that frank[ing privilege] we're just going to be handing the seat over to them, just handing it over," he added.

"Okay," I said.

When this sort of craziness gets to the Member level, something, as they say, gets lost in the translation. We had decided to do public service announcements—in English and in Spanish—about the census. Coleman showed up fifteen minutes early at the House Recording Studio and immediately made cracks about his incompetent staff. I looked at the technician and said, "That's what he gets for showing up fifteen minutes early." The technician rolled his eyes, and we went into the sound room.

The English spots went fine. But Coleman began to stumble on the Spanish versions. Numerous takes later, we called a merciful halt. The final line in the script was: "Answer the Census. It counts for more than you think," or "Responda al Censo. Cuenta por mas de lo que imagina."

"Imagina" is pronounced "ee-mah-*hee*-nah." Let's just hope that "ee-*mah*-hee-nah" does not mean something embarrassing because the correct version just did not happen.

I had no sympathy for Coleman's accent. He had not been in the office for an entire week. I went to his house later in the day to have him do a press call, and brought a folder of material for his perusal, including a copy of Ralph Nader's Accountability Project questionnaire on keeping the pay raise. "Here's what we do with this one," Coleman laughed. He crumpled Nader's survey into a ball and shot a perfect jump shot across the kitchen and into the trash can.[22]

Back at the ranch we were fussing with the mail. I wrote "COMPLETE AND UTTER BULLSHIT" on a draft letter from the legislative staff to a constituent who was being "encouraged" by West Texas Utilities to oppose the Clean Air Act.

"I wanted to let you know I wrote 'bullshit' on one of your letters," I told a staffer. "After all, it was going to Coleman."

The staffer laughed. "Let me guess—the acid rain letter."

"Who's it to?" someone else asked.

"Some constituent being prodded by West Texas Utilities."

"I say fuck those people," the second staffer said.

"Yeah, really," I added.

"Okay," the first staffer said, still laughing, "you send the letter." There were no takers. We went back to work and the letter stood.

Vaclav Havel, the new president of Czechoslovakia, addressed a joint session of Congress on a fine morning in February, but Coleman skipped the joint session with President Havel to hunker down with Rogers and some appointments.

"Can the 12:00 come in?" the receptionist called from out front.

Coleman's secretary stuck her head in the door. "Can the 12:00 come in?"

"No," said Coleman.

"No," said the personal secretary to the receptionist. "He doesn't want to do it."

"He doesn't want to do it?"

"He doesn't want to do it."

Paul, thinking quickly, interjected, "But they already know you're here, Coleman."

"And how did that happen?" he snapped.

Paul, still dodging bullets, ad-libbed, "I guess the 11:30 people must have said something." Coleman grunted in dismay and the people were allowed in.

Paul and I had a brainstorming session later that afternoon on how to get Coleman some press over the recent death of a U.S. Customs agent in Texas who had been killed by a van that had crashed through a border checkpoint.

"I'm not exactly sure how to do this," Paul mused. The operative question was whether, and how hard, to pop President Bush for trying to cut back Customs, thus somehow holding him responsible for the agent's death.

"Well, it's worth a shot," I said wearily.

"Do we know it was drug-related?"

"The material from Customs said the van was suspected of being involved."

"Let's say we need more resources, more men, more protection. It's a Texas van, not Mexican. To follow it up with cuts in Customs inspectors! I promise you as a member of the House Appropriations Committee there will not be a cut but an increase. More resources for the front lines." He was savoring each phrase, tasting each word for its flavor and potential impact.

In the end I did a statement that laid the blame for the agent's death on the administration, but not on President Bush personally—that was taking it a little far even for us.

I called Coleman at home. "Do you want me to read it to you?" I asked hopefully.

"Actually not," he replied. So I summarized it.

He did not like the approach. "Well, that might sound good for later on, but we got the family still involved at this point," he said. "And President Bush might have called the family. Son of a bitch is capable of anything."

"So we'll make this one more of a glowing tribute, amber waves of grain, prayers for the family."

"Yeah, that sounds good." As I had known it would from the beginning. The way to beat Rogers, you see, was not to argue with him but to give his ideas verbatim to the congressman.

The Coleman touch was shown later on at a Border Caucus meeting on immigration. Coleman at one point turned to Reps. Howard Berman (D-CA) and John Bryant (D-TX) and asked flippantly, "You guys going to do any immigration this year?"

Berman and Bryant, who were on the Judiciary Committee and had been working on *the* huge immigration bill all year—they had, in fact, just finished two weeks of media-soaked hearings—could not believe their ears. Berman looked astonished; Bryant, Coleman's friend, nonplussed. The bill had been written up in every publication all over town. But what can you do? Coleman did not read, he did not study, he did not deal with the staff, he did not attend briefings or legislative staff meetings: in short; he made no attempt to learn the issues, surviving instead on the life-support system of his staff and damn little else.

Early in March, Congressman Coleman woke up to the fact that he had done very little since the 101st Congress convened. At a March 6 legislative staff meeting (hooray, he showed up!), he said, "There's some concern about legislation," as if it were someone else's fault. "We need a legislative program in place, even if not all of it gets passed. I want us to start drafting and introducing bills. In the Texas legislature, I wouldn't think of introducing something that wouldn't pass, but it's a different ballgame up here. We need to do it because it's a statement of something we care about." This was the same congressman, of course, who in February 1990 was in the office on four out of twenty working days for a total of six hours.

But Congressman Ron Coleman's problems at this point were

nothing compared to the Cheese Weasel's. Majority Leader Richard Gephardt had said on March 5 that the United States should give direct aid to the Soviet Union (it had not yet collapsed in 1990), and he was now running for cover from a firestorm of criticism.[23]

The reaction from most Democrats, particularly from the South, was dismay. "I think I'm gonna have Richard Gephardt come down to my district and give that speech to the Chamber of Commerce," cracked North Carolina Rep. Bill Hefner to the full Appropriations Committee the next morning. "Is he out of his fucking mind?" echoed down the hallways of the House office buildings. Republicans could not believe their good fortune, and they were elbowing each other out of the way to deliver One-Minutes.

In our own office, though, Paul Rogers endorsed the idea reflexively because it came from Gephardt. The thought of researching and actually thinking through something as important as U.S. direct aid to the Soviet Union was alien to him. He and Coleman approached my desk at 11:55 A.M.

"What's going on?" Coleman asked me.

Hell, I decided, let's give Rogers a jolt.

"Aid to the commies, that's what the Democrats are up to this morning," I told them. "Gephardt's catching hell left and right. Senator Bill Bradley just said, essentially, that Gephardt was on the planet Mars, or should be. So did Senator John Breaux and a bunch of other Democrats." Rogers was not pleased.

"Can you believe he said that?" Coleman asked. "Just amazing. I've always said: Never let a member back in his district. Nothing but trouble. Newt Gingrich jumped all over his ass this morning."

Rogers was no fool. "What a mistake," he added without missing a beat. "There go the Democrats again, digging themselves into another hole." He scowled at me as he and Coleman walked into the congressman's office.

Coleman subsequently introduced some of his vaunted "legislation"—to exempt El Paso from the Clean Air Act unless pollution from Mexico were taken into account. Since he was not around at the time, Rogers signed his name to the bill and another staffer took it to the floor to be introduced. When Coleman returned to the office, I put him on the phone with a reporter from *USA Today*. The conversation went well until she asked him if he were trying to exempt El Paso from the Clean Air Act.

He had no idea. Coleman, wild-eyed, began to flubber, waving his arms at me. I ran to his desk and wrote on a notepad, "The goal is to clean up both side of the border."

"The goal is to clean up both sides of the border," Coleman said authoritatively. He punched the speaker phone button so I could hear the questions.

"How will it be funded?" *USA Today* asked.

Notepad: "As part of the Clean Air Act, which authorizes activities but not new spending programs."

Congressman: "As part of the Clean Air Act, which authorizes activities but not new spending programs."

*USA Today*: "Will you do it separately or as an amendment?"

Notepad: "Waxman not opposed."

Congressman: "The subcommittee chairman is not opposed, so either in committee or on the floor."

*USA Today*: "And the role of Mexico?"

Notepad: ". . . clean up the air on both sides of the border."

Congressman: "We must clean up the air on both sides of the border."

And so it went until we all hung up. Coleman turned to me and asked, "Now who was that?"

But this farce did not touch the full blood-pressure alert at the end of the day. "Can you believe it?" Rogers asked me. "Gephardt wants Coleman to participate in the Gingrich special order, and the son of a bitch won't go over to the floor. He'd rather sit there and fuck with where his pictures are going to go." We were undergoing one of the periodic rearrangements of the decorations in Coleman's office, something that always captured his full attention.

"Why don't we tell him that Gephardt's office called again?" I asked. "He'll never know the difference and maybe it'll get him to do what he's already promised to do."

Paul laughed. "Why don't you tell him?"

I walked in. "Mr. Coleman, my buddy in Gephardt's office just called and wondered if you were still coming over to the special order."

"Okay," he said, surprising me, and got up and left.

After he had gone, Rogers, watching the House floor proceedings on television, chuckled again. "That special order might be over," he grinned. "I think they might be on to another one."

Moments later, we watched on television as Congressman Coleman walked onto the floor of the House and jumped into the middle of the fray, blasting Newt Gingrich and Republicans in general for having the temerity to question the judgment of Majority Leader Richard Gephardt.

Unfortunately, Gingrich's special order was indeed over and Rep. David Obey—Coleman's subcommittee chairman on Foreign Operations—was doing a completely different special order on national budget priorities and the economy. Coleman kept interrupting and talking about Majority Leader Richard Gephardt and foreign policy, which made hilarious nonsense in the context of Obey's special order. Obey could only give him one of those glazed unbelieving looks. Coleman finally left, totally oblivious but feeling great about having blasted Newt Gingrich.

But all was not lost. Coleman and I went to the Capitol on April 18 to do a thirty-second satellite feed for Earth Day. Sure, laugh if you will, but it was free television and made the tree-huggers happy (Hill slang for environmentalists). While we waited our turn to go in front of the camera, we watched Rep. Chris Perkins talk to a group of high school students. "Can you imagine having to sit in the sun and listen to Chris Perkins?" Coleman wondered. "And what do you do all day, Congressman? And he'd pull out his schedule card and say well, first I go to the Democratic Club for lunch, where I have a bloody and then order a hamburger, which a lot of people like to watch me knock down. [Perkins is reknowned for his atrocious table manners.] Then I have a glass of Parducci, and then I move on to the really serious Scotch."

Finally it was Coleman's turn in front of the camera. Rob Ambrose, an aide to Democratic Caucus Chairman Steny Hoyer, took Coleman by the arm. "Hey, Congressman, how you doing?" he asked. He and Coleman were good friends. Ambrose was the Coleman campaign aide who in 1982 had been embroiled in the bogus endorsement-letter-on-congressional-letterhead scandal.

"Fine, fine," Coleman said. "Gonna tag Bush's ass on this one."

"I heard the Speaker saying how good you were yesterday on taking on the Republicans," Rob said. "He was very pleased." Leadership staffers, even junior ones, practice their unctuousness at every available moment and their ability to pass on a word from On High.

"Hey John, see if you can't hold this up where I can see it," Coleman told me. I held up the script next to the camera but out of view of the picture. He kept peering at the script as the camera rolled and he repeated his lines.

"Great job, Congressman, terrific," Rob purred in hushed tones of praise.

"See you later," Coleman replied. We departed.


Boy, am I going to miss this place, especially after I heard about the joke Coleman told at last Friday's luncheon for Texas legislative directors and staff directors: "What's the definition of rodeo sex? It's when you come home from the rodeo and tell your wife you want to have sex. You get her naked and down on all fours, sidle up behind her, whisper in her ear 'This is how my girlfriend likes it,' and try to stay on for eight seconds."

The reactions of the female legislative directors and administrative assistants were not immediately available.


Budget Day, May 1, was one of the livelier days on the House floor. By the Hill's internal calendar, the day they vote on the budget officially marked the beginning of the Silly Season. Plus the budget resolution tells the Appropriations Committee how much it can steal from Treasury, so I suppose there is good reason to pay attention as well.

We were trying to figure out how best to launch Coleman's support for the Family and Medical Leave Act into Perceptionland.

"Does he want to do a satellite feed?" I asked Paul.

"You'll have to ask him yourself."

I walked in. "Whatcha got?" Coleman asked.

"Vic Fazio's office wants to know if you're going to do the satellite feed on Family Leave."

"Well, what do you think? I'm not so sure. The ones who are for it know where I am and it's got the business lobby madder than hell. I'm not sure."

"It's got the protections," Rogers added.

"Yeah, you're right, fuck 'em," Coleman said. "There's a fifty-employee exemption." He continued to talk around the issue but I could tell his heart was not in it, so I suggested, "Well, you know, we can reach those people by mail. I've got all the women in the computer, Democratic activist women, that kind of thing."

Coleman liked the idea. "Yeah, let's do that," he said. "No sense stirring up the pot."

Public relations aside, we had real problems on El Salvador. Coleman had voted in November 1989 *not* to cut off aid after the murder of six Jesuit priests, and local Hispanic groups were beginning to pressure him. If, as Rogers claimed, a Great Hispanic Conspiracy was underway to unseat Coleman, it had to be coopted. And after a public demonstration at our local office in El Paso against military aid to El Salvador, it was time to jettison the junta.

Reinventing the congressman as a "moderate who in the past has supported limited aid with tight restrictions," I wrote a fairly plausible explanation of why he had decided to vote against any additional miltary aid: death squad activity was on the rise. (With that country, you can always claim with absolute certainty that death squad activity is on the rise, and you can use it to justify any move whatsoever.)

The House voted on May 22 to cut aid to El Salvador by 50 percent, derailing the Central American aid package in the process. But who cared? This was 1990, a far cry from our early years. It was, in fact, the exact reverse: as Paul Rogers had predicted, our left was now covered and our right had nowhere to go.[24] (Two days later, the House reversed itself and passed a foreign aid bill with the

El Salvador money intact, but Coleman had the sense not to change his vote and we kept the left covered anyway.)

Just to make sure, though, we turned to Uncle Frank for a little assistance. The computer identified over 50,000 voters in the congressional district who were Hispanic voters or leaders, or Democratic liberals. We sent each of them a first-class, individually addressed, personally signed (by the computer) letter announcing the congressman's opposition to all military aid to El Salvador.

The summer was starting to play itself out early. I drove to Coleman's house in June to help him do a telephone interview on the U.S.-Mexico border region. We stood in the kitchen while he scanned my script. I placed the call. Coleman immediately launched into a near-verbatim recitation of my memorandum. When he reached the end, he was caught off-guard because he had not previously read it through. He looked at me, eyes raised in surprise and consternation. I shrugged. He was silent. And that is where Congressman Coleman all too often ended—at the margin of my talking points.

I sighed. It is so hard to keep politicians afloat.

Coleman was in the back office on June 5, woofing at Paul Rogers and the legislative staff about the United Auto Workers and the B-2 Stealth bomber. He had run into a UAW lobbyist in the hall on his way to the office, and the unplanned encounter had thoroughly irritated him. "The B-2? What B-2? And now they want me to commit to the B-2? They can kiss my ass," he bellowed. "We'll play that game. Let's see how they've been treating us on our fundraising the last six years. Shit. Fuck 'em." Meanwhile, a legislative staffer, who had been busily copying material for a meeting with the ambassador from the Philippines to avoid a repeat of an earlier meeting with the ambassador from Tunisia, entered the room. (Coleman had turned to the globe to see where the country was just as the ambassador arrived.) The UAW was forgotten.

Some of us were wondering about our own country. The *Dallas Morning News* called on June 13 to do a poll of the Texas delegation on the constitutional amendment to ban flag burning. The U.S. Supreme Court had ruled in 1989 that the practice was a form of political speech that fell under the protection of the First Amendment, a political uproar had ensued, and President Bush had announced his support of a constitutional amendment to prohibit flag desecration.

The battle turned ugly immediately.[25] The Democratic leadership's point man was Judiciary Committee Chairman Jack Brooks of Texas, a former Marine who fought in the South Pacific in World War II. Newt Gingrich typically opened the Republican salvo on behalf of the constitutional amendment by questioning the Democrats' patriotism. Brooks told the press that if anyone wanted a test of patriotism, he should look at draft deferments. Reporters asked if he was referring to Newt Gingrich, who had avoided the Viet Nam war draft with college and marriage deferments. Brooks replied sarcastically, "He had a deferment? Gingrich did? That big strapping son of a bitch?" (Gingrich is short, pudgy, and has an oversized head.)

In October, House Democrats had pushed through a bill to ban flag burning, which passed 371 to 43. Although most experts agreed privately that the legislation would probably be struck down by the Supreme Court, its purpose was to give Democrats and liberals something to be *for*—they could tell their voters they had voted to outlaw flag burning. Opposition to the constitutional amendment would be portrayed as simply a disagreement over the best means to accomplish a shared end. And besides, it would be years before anyone challenged the new law all the way up to the Supreme Court—well after the 1990 elections.

Now, however, we faced a vote on the issue.

"Listen," Coleman said. "I think I have to be for it. The Republican National Committee's [TV] spot is easy to visualize. They'll have some long-haired fool burning the flag, then pan to Arlington National Cemetery, or here locally, or maybe the Tomb of the Unknown Soldier, with the flag on the graves. Then they'll go close up to the name on the stone, or something like that. It's a disaster. We lost. What do you think?"

I had long given up trying to inject any note of conscience into the congressman's deliberations, particularly the first time around, so I reverted to a professional approach. I decided just to listen, and speak to Paul later to see if he could talk him out of it.

"You're right, I guess," I said.

"The Supreme Court wants to fuck with the Bill of Rights. Five guys want to fuck with it. Ronald Reagan won," Coleman continued. "Don't complain to me, bellyaching. Talk to the Supreme Court. Every Supreme Court has been able to avoid it, to find ways not to take it up. All kinds of reasons. Fuck 'em. Ronald Reagan won. He doesn't like the Bill of Rights, so we're going to amend it for the first time in two hundred years. Fucking *Dallas Morning News* doing a poll. Screw 'em."

"Okay, " I said. We hung up.

Paul had been on his way to El Paso and I reached him after he arrived. "The newspapers are calling about the flag amendment," I reported. "Coleman went ballistic but said he might go for it. What do you think?"

"I think he has to, too. You can tell them it's asinine but it'll probably get voted on quickly."

The flag issue went on hold for a few days, but the press from Texas kept calling us about another matter—car theft rings that were operating out of Mexico.

"What am I going to say?" Coleman asked me before an interview on June 20.

"Tell them you're going to work out a deal with the Mexicans and open up a dealership in El Paso."

He glared at me, so I tried again. "You were the one who set up the coordinating body between local, state, and federal authorities last year," I said. "And you brought up the subject again last week with President Salinas."

"What about Scagno [El Paso police chief]?" Coleman demanded. "He's said the Mexicans are all a bunch of crooks, liars, and thieves. It's been playing real well in Paso. I guess I gotta be for that."

Courage, Ron, courage.

When the flag issue reemerged, Coleman and I huddled. "We're getting a lot of calls from the district on the flag amendment, and the district staff needs a position for the callers," I opened.

"So what are the calls saying?"

"We're doing a tally now, but it appears they're overwhelmingly in favor of the amendment."

"Well, I'm going with my district on this one."

I called the district staff to let them know Coleman was going with the amendment.

"Oh," one of them said, "all the calls are *against* the amendment."

"Against the amendment," I repeated in disbelief.

"Yeah, let me check . . . seven, ten. Ten calls against, none in favor."

"Why the hell would I be told that they were all in favor when they were against?"

"Who knows?"

"OK. Hold off on telling people that Coleman's for the amendment. I need to try to find some way out." I checked with the legislative staff and discovered that the calls were running 5 to 1 against the amendment. Terrific.

I called Coleman. "I want to give you a revised tally on the flag amendment," I said. "I added them up from the last five days or so and the count is 17 to 6 *against* the amendment."

"What?"

"Yeah."

"So we had a last minute rush of calls?"

"I added them up from the last five days to double-check."

"Well, we better not tell people I'm for it anymore."

"Right. You're listening to the district, hearing views from all sides, giving everyone the opportunity to make their voice heard."

"Bet your ass."

We hung up. Back to the starting point.

The next day I walked past the Republican National Committee building on my way to the liquor store. The building had American flags hanging from every window.

Coleman called me again at 4:00 P.M.: "What do you hear on the flag?"

"Same thing. Most of the calls in the district are against the amendment."

"Shit. I know what I should do . . . but in the short term, it would be so much easier to go for the damn thing. Know what I mean? The veterans."

"Well, it's a tough one. The conservative columnists are against it."

"George Will is for it."

"Kilpatrick's against it."

"It's going to fail, that's for sure. It's going down. They don't have the votes. I just don't know what I'm going to do."

I took the day off on June 22, the day of the vote, to visit with an out-of-town friend from college who was a reporter for United Press International. It was mid-afternoon, and we were drinking tropicals (two shots Myers's Rum, two slices lime, Coca-Cola). Hell, I didn't care. I had turned in my resignation back in April and was preparing to move out of Washington, D.C., and permanently to Portland, Oregon, to be a full-time writer and earn a master's degree in intellectual and diplomatic history.

But Coleman suddenly got a case of the jitters about the impending vote, and called me at home.

"So what are you going to tell the press?" I asked, taking a long swig of my tropical.

He hemmed and hawed and finally said, "Well . . . I don't know, well, what are *you* going to tell 'em?"

"Well, how about . . . hmmm. Let's see. We're not going to let a few flag-burning extremists provoke us into tampering with the Bill of Rights . . . as a former army tank commander, you understand the frustration of those who fought for the flag . . . the statute you voted for is constitutionally sound. . . . Bill of Rights is one of those things America has fought for . . . and as a veteran, you share their abhorrence for those who would burn the flag . . ."

At this point, the UPI reporter was grinning at me and sticking his finger down his throat, making fake gagging sounds. I winked.

Coleman later told me privately: "Well, I did the right thing . . . if I'm going to get beat, so be it."

I thought: Will the real Ron Coleman please stand up?

Our statement was subsequently hailed in the local press in Texas; the *El Paso Herald-Post* applauded Congressman Coleman's vote and quoted me as saying Coleman was "determined not to let a few flag-waving extremists provoke us into tampering with the Bill of Rights. . . ."

It was a fitting end. The world as I had known it had been turned upside down—President Bush was supporting a tax increase and the Democratic leadership was defending the flag. I still had no answers, but I had finally run out of questions.

Nothing had changed, really, I suppose, except the degree of certainty of reelection for Coleman and virtually every other member of the House. Coleman did not say good-bye. He had no reason to; congressional aides are, by definition, extensions of the Member, and he was still there. I had some final beers at the office with friends and colleagues and packed up a few last things from my desk, including my laminated chunk of "Texas Bullshit" and a mahogany carving of the single-finger wave, symbolic pillars of our profession—bullshit and defiance. I wrapped them carefully in paper, and sealed the box.

Then I drove home to my wife and children.

# EPILOGUE

Near the end of June 1990, I went to the Democratic Club for the last time.

I did not go for the usual reason—to learn the fate of our heroes or to hear the political culture's high priests and fixers predict the future. I simply went to watch one more time. Besides, it did not feel right to say formal good-byes.

I walked in and I smiled. I took in the scene one last time: the bar talk crackled with the deals of the day and ribald jokes about the latest public disaster. The regular lobbyists at the bar were trying to convince the bartender to open the cash register so they could rifle through the dollar bills in preparation for a round of liar's poker. Another lobbyist walked into the dining area, his hand in the crook of a member's arm, guiding the way to their table.

I laughed. For the first time I could remember, I did not feel the need to learn the nature of the discussion between the lobbyist and the congressman. The political beast, for me, had finally been laid to rest. I gave them a small, unnoticed salute and walked out of the club's dim, shadowy light and into the bright sunshine. My eyes blinked and narrowed reflexively at the shock of the light. In a moment, though, they had adjusted, and I walked back toward the Capitol.

A few days before, I had walked near the same place with a friend. It was 10:30 at night. The lights of the Republican National Committee building were all on. Harried Hill rats in gray suits were heading home via the Metro, and summer interns were smooching in the shadows. The Capitol dome was lit, signifying that Congress was still in session.

"The Capitol Hill crowd is out tonight," my friend remarked.

"Yes," I replied, "they are." And "they" had become they now, no longer me or us or any other connection I might have retained.

My thoughts went unexpectedly to a friend named Michael Veon, a former Hill rat who had struck out on his own and won election to the Pennsylvania House of Representatives. He comes from a family famous for sports and civic involvement in Beaver Falls, and will no doubt become a member of Congress himself one day.

He had stopped by my office not too long before and told me that he was trying to get involved in something called "Young Political Leaders," a program run by a Hill rat named R. Spencer Oliver on the Foreign Affairs Committee. The program takes up-and-coming political leaders in the United States and puts them together with other nations' rising leaders.

Mike is a strong labor Democrat who has always believed in the party's mission both to defend working families and to foster organized labor. I listened to him tell me enthusiastically about the Young Political Leaders program (which involved a great deal of expense-paid foreign travel), and I asked myself: does he still believe or is he starting to get a whiff of the good life of perks and privilege? I knew him well, so I gave him the benefit of the doubt.

But we wait and we watch the next generation, and we wonder. Good luck, Mike, and godspeed.

Is there any hope for the rest of them? My family and I moved to the Pacific Northwest in the summer of 1990 shortly after I left the Hill, but smoke signals over the far horizon have not been too difficult to decipher.

The check-kiting and restaurant-tab scandals of 1991 have pushed Congress onto the defensive. Still, talk of change is in the air. When Rep. Rod Chandler (R-WA) announced his candidacy for U.S. Senator Brock Adams's seat, he pointedly stated, "I have never bounced a check. I have paid all my parking tickets. And I don't owe the House restaurant anything." On the other end of the ideological spectrum, former California governor Jerry Brown denounced what he termed Washington, D.C.'s, corrupt values when he entered the race for the

Democratic presidential nomination, and the U.S. Senate campaign of Rep. Les AuCoin (D-Or) suffered a major setback when AuCoin admitted bouncing seven checks in two days for relatively small amounts.

At the same time, the institution continues blindly to protect its own. The House Ethics Committee, charged with investigating the check-kiting scandal, requested only account numbers from the House Bank, refusing to look at the names of the abusers. And the chairman of the Ethics Committee, Rep. Louis Stokes (D-OH), had to step aside from the probe when his own check-bouncing was revealed.

A friend who still works on the Hill for the Democratic leadership recently wrote:

> Good positive things about the Hill? God, I don't know, John. It's such a circle of bad things, and I'm not sure how good things break into it. . . . [T]he more I work here, the more I find the excesses of constituents almost as offensive. We are deluged by requests by high school students to do research for their term papers. I guess we could ignore them, but Members are so scared that we don't. Special interest politics, and one-issue voters are so prevalent . . . So the mailings increase, the inquiries increase, the excesses increase, the money (oh God the money) increases, and where are we?

The notorious Rep. Thomas Luken retired, bequeathing his Cincinnati congressional seat to his son Charlie (who is normal, by all accounts). Former Representative Luken is now a Washington, D.C., lobbyist.

New Majority Whip William Gray (D-PA) resigned to become president of the United Negro College Fund. As one of my lobbyist buddies put it, "[U.S. Attorney General] Thornburgh had him dead to rights on laundering excessive speaking fees through his church. Gray was the only Democrat with a chance to beat him for the Pennsylvania seat. Thornburgh and Gray cut a very, very quiet deal. Gray will not run for the Senate seat. Gray will also not go to jail. Everyone will deny that a deal took place. There will be no way to prove it. Except that Gray will indeed not run for the Senate, and he will indeed not go to jail."

The money continues to flow. In the year that he brought down Speaker Jim Wright, Rep. Newt Gingrich accepted $67,491 in honoraria payments, pocketing $26,787 and taking a tax break on the rest—all from special interests, specifically in legislative matters in which he was involved.

In April 1991, *Time* ran an article on various pork projects that were slipped into various appropriations bills by members of the Favor Factory. My favorite was a "study" (which all but guarantees that it will happen) on a new exercise facility for Hill rats. The best for them may yet to come; $100,000 salaries are becoming more and more common.

The chairman of the House Administration Committee moved immediately to try to exempt the House from the Fair Labor Standards Act, which had been imposed recently through a minimum wage bill.

The 1989 Ethics in Government Act did nothing to deter members and Hill rats from accepting all-expenses-paid vacations from lobbyists and politicial action committees. And the 1990 "congressional mail reform" allowed more than 652 million pieces of unsolicited mail to be sent out at taxpayer expense.

Speaker of the House Thomas Foley plods along as if nothing were changing before his eyes. Foley is, above all, a defender of the existing congressional order, no matter the cost to the institution or his own party. We had written him on June 23, 1989, asking for expedited consideration of Congressman Coleman's legislation to provide running water and sewage service to the *colonias*. Because of a feud between Coleman and Rep. Kika de la Garza, chairman of the House Agriculture Committee and longtime Foley ally, Thomas Foley—at de la Garza's request—refused to act on Coleman's legislation.

Coleman wrote the Speaker again on April 4, 1990. This time we tried a political argument, stressing that President Bush was taking a tremendous political beating in Texas and the Southwest over his Health and Human Services Department's opposition to a $30 million loan program for the *colonias*.

"The issue has galvanized the Hispanic community," Coleman pleaded with Foley, "and we are missing a tremendous opportunity to show the difference between the Democratic Party and the Republican Party on an issue of crucial importance to the fastest-growing minority group in the nation. . . . [N]ow we have the opportunity to continue to pin President Bush and the Republicans into a corner. . . . "

Coleman again requested expedited consideration of his *colonias* assistance legislation.

Agriculture Chairman Kika de la Garza again told Foley not to do it.

And again Foley didn't do it.

Coleman did not push the matter further. The people of the *colonias* were one thing, his relations with the Speaker—and his career—were another.

So I sigh, and I think of the future. I am becoming increasingly convinced that change will come from the grass-roots level, not from the top. One of the chief fixers of them all, the powerful Rep. John Murtha of Pennsylvania, chairman of the Defense Subcommittee of the Appropriations Committee, nearly lost his seat in the 1990 Democratic primary to a challenger he had outspent by $368,849 to $7,010.

Change may come as well from individuals who nurture and maintain bonds with their communities as they rise to power, people like another Hill rat I worked with, Ken Bentsen, who also struck out on his own and won the election as Democratic chairman in Harris County (Houston), Texas. Ken was always the conscience of our office when it came to gut-level Democratic party issues— the First Nephew, we teased him, because his uncle is U.S. Sen. Lloyd Bentsen. His future is limitless as long as he believes in himself and strives to improve his community.

On the Hill, a handful of members keep the flame of belief alive: Robert Dornan, Vin Weber, and Robert Walker on the Republican side; Barney Frank, Ron Dellums, John Bryant and Tony Beilenson among the Democrats; and surely others in both parties whom I do not know. But the current Democratic leadership of Speaker Thomas Foley and Majority Leader Richard Gephardt is devoid of true belief. Like Newt Gingrich among the Republicans, their belief starts and ends with what they see every morning in the bathroom mirror.

As for Texas Cong. Ronald Coleman and his trusty sidekick, Paul Rogers, the ultimate Hill rat, he who became the word of the member made flesh? I hear of them only from afar now, and the news—if any, because I do not seek it—is blurry. I wish them nothing but the best of luck and success. Coleman's future is, as it has always been, limited only by obstacles he has placed in his own path. And he may well need the luck; I sighed heavily when I opened the *Wall Street Journal* on June 26, 1991, and found that one of its reporters had stumbled across a very small slice of the border crossing deal that involved Coleman's personal debt and one of the moneymen. Coleman had voted for a $12.7 million appropriations for one of the crossings, which was being developed by a man named Charlie Crowder, who had assumed a $65,000 debt for Coleman. Both admitted to the *Journal* that they had discussed the project, but assured it that no "lobbying" occurred.

As they say in Texas: Yeah buddy.

So let's roll up our sleeves and plunge in. Let's have more politics, not less, and the grubbier the better. Let's do more deals and better deals. Hell, let's celebrate the art of the deal as it is done on the Hill. But somewhere, somehow, in some way, rightly or wrongly, let's do it on behalf of something we truly believe in; good faith matters more than anything. I will trust a clash of convictions any time, any day, over bloodless, blow-dried, poll-driven talking heads like Richard Gephardt.

There is a final lesson from the children about what really counts in life: Marriage, children, books, sports, adventure, and truly believing in something and saying so. Maybe you throw in love and see if there's any room for your God. Then you shrug off the darkness and sling it down and slay it with knives, quickly, so you don't miss an hour or a day or however long the darkness tried to steal.

# END NOTES

CHAPTER ONE

1. For details on this controversy, see Karen Foerstel, "Staffer Dies of Heart Attack As Ambulance Stands Unused," *Roll Call*, 14 October 1991, p. 1.
2. "Dismissed," *Roll Call*, 5 October 1989, p. 4.
3. "Dellums adviser on Grenada tied to Marxist ruler," *Washington Times*, 22 October 1984, p. 1.
4. George Archibald, "Top Democratic aide wields sharp probes against GOP," *Washington Times*, 6 June 1989, p. A6.
5. Jonathan Yates, " 'Reality on Capitol Hill,' " *Newsweek*, 28 November 1988, p. 12.
6. Scalia quotes reprinted in Joan Biskupic, "Scalia Takes a Narrow View in Seeking Congress' Will," *Congressional Quarterly*, 24 March 1990, pp. 913–918.
7. U.S. Rep. Chuck Douglas, "Section 89: What Staff Hath Created, Congress Should Take Away," *Congressional Record*, 24 May 1989, p. E1853.
8. Henry Precht, "The Invisible Government in Washington," *Christian Science Monitor*, 14 July 1989.
9. "Working With Congressional Staff," advertisement by *Congressional Quarterly*.
10. Judy Schneider, "Minority Staffing: A Chronological History," *CRS*

*Report for Congress*, Congressional Research Service, Library of Congress, 19 March 1990, p. 1. Note that "Minority Staffing" means Republican, not an ethnic group.

11. Letter from Theodore E. Mathison, administrator of the Baltimore/Washington International Airport, to U.S. Rep. Ronald Coleman, 25 February 1987.

12. Hon. Jack Russ, Sergeant-At-Arms, U.S. House of Representatives, "Memorandum to Members, Delegates, and Resident Commissioner, Subject: Taxpayer Assistance," 6 February 1989, p. 1; Robert Burdette, "Special Tax Rules for Members of Congress," *CRS Report for Congress*, Congressional Research Service, Library of Congress, 13 November 1989.

13. Seth Kantor, "On Capitol Hill, the gravy trickles down to top aides," *Austin-American Statesman*, 20 October 1989, p. 1.

14. Charles Babcock, "Interest-Group Honoraria Plentiful for Top Hill Aides," *Washington Post*, 6 October 1989, pp. A1 and A20.

CHAPTER TWO

1. Federal Election Committee data in Michael Barone and Grant Ujifusa, *Almanac of American Politics 1990* (Washington, D.C.: National Journal, Inc. 1989), p. 1408.

2. Foley quote from Democratic response to State of the Union address, 31 January 1990.

3. Deborah Baldwin, "Compromising Positions: Novelist Ward Just Dissects the Ruling Class," *Common Sense Magazine*, March/April 1989, p. 38.

4. John R. Cranford, "Partisan Knives Are Drawn As Thrift Crisis Builds," *Congressional Quarterly*, 23 June 1990.

5. U.S. Rep. Terry Bruce, *Whip Notice*, 14 June 1990. This account is described in the confidential *Whip Notice*, which was published weekly by Bruce, a member of the House leadership organization, for those members within his area of responsibility to communicate what took place at the weekly Whip meetings. All quotes from this account are contained in the 14 June 1990 *Whip Notice* and were confirmed by the author.

6. "Democrats Call for More Investigators; Demand Prosecution of S&L Crooks," *Party Lines: Talking Points from the Democratic Party* (Washington, D.C.: Democratic National Committee, 19 June 1990), p. 1. See

also: "Never Again? Cost for the Bush Savings and Loan Bailout Continues to Mount," *Party Lines*, 7 March 1990; and "Neil Bush and Silverado," *Party Lines*, 23 May 1990.

7. "The Politics of the S&L Crisis," Democratic National Committee document distributed to Democratic House offices, 22 June 1990, fourth page.

8. For a detailed examination, see Frank Kuznik, "Public Figures, Private Eyes," *Common Cause Magazine* (Washington, D.C.: January/February 1990).

9. Federal Election Commission data in Tom Kenworthy, "Fighting Competition With Incumbency," *Washington Post*, 10 May 1990, p. A1.

10. Because it was so blatant even by Hill standards, copies of this letter were passed around to a number of House offices. Some excerpts ran in an untitled, no-byline article in the *National Journal*, 23 June 1990, p. 17.

11. Federal Election Commission data in Kim Mattingly, "Dems Now Resist Member-PAC Ban," *Roll Call*, 26 March 1990, p. 1.

12. Common Cause study reported in "Lawmakers assist colleagues with funds from 'member PACS,' " Associated Press, 29 March 1990. See also Richard L. Berke, "Incumbents Turn to Personal PACs," *New York Times*, 16 May 1989; and Clyde Wilcox, "Share the Wealth: Contributions by Congressional Incumbents to the Campaigns of Other Candidates," *American Politics Quarterly*, Vol. 17, No. 4., October 1989, pp. 386-408.

13. Roger Walker and David C. Huckabee, "PACs Sponsored by Corporations Partly or Wholly Owned by Foreign Investors," *CRS Report for Congress*, Congressional Research Service, Library of Congress, 14 November 1989 in "Summary" (first page of document, no page number given by CRS).

14. Charles Babcock and Richard Morin, "PAC-Man Pursues Hectic Schedule," *Washington Post*, 2 May 1990, p. A1.

15. "Lawmakers for Life," *Wall Street Journal* editorial, 14 April 1990, p. 22.

16. Barone and Ujifusa, p. 1410.

17. Susan Welch, "Congressional Nomination Procedures and the Representation of Women," *Congress and the Presidency*, Vol. 16. No. 2. Autumn 1989, p. [?]

18. Statement of Speaker Thomas Foley, *Congressional Record*, 6 June 1989, p. H2284.

19. David C. Huckabee, "Reelection Rates of House Incumbents: 1790–1988," *CRS Report for Congress*, Congressional Research Service, Library of Congress, Washington, D.C., 16 March 1989.

20. "Incumbents' edge: 'You have to be a bozo to lose this job,' " Associated Press, 29 May 1990.

21. For additional information, see Karen Forestel, "Clear Parking Stickers Invalid for Members," *Roll Call*, 26 March 1990.

22. See Jeff Bailey, "Housing Project Aided by Rostenkowski Defaults on a $170.8 Million FHA Loan," *Wall Street Journal*, 16 March 1990.

23. A good examination of Rostenkowski's financial practices can be found in Jay H. Hedlund, "Lobbying and Legislative Ethics" in *Representation and Responsibility: Exploring Legislative Ethics*, Bruce Jennings and Daniel Callahan, eds. (New York: Plenum Press, 1985).

24. U.S. Rep. Robert McEwen, "Home Rule in the District of Columbia Is a Disaster," *Congressional Record*, 21 February 1990, p. H398.

25. W. John Moore, "The Alumni Lobby," *National Journal*, 9 September 1989, p. 2193.

26. Letter of former Rep. Billy Lee Evans to U.S. Rep. Ronald Coleman, 20 September 1989.

27. Walter Pincus, "House Store Buys from Sergeant-At-Arms," *Washington Post*, 8 November 1989.

28. Timothy Burger, "Dining Bills in Members' Names Overdue," *Roll Call*, 26 October 1989, p. 9.

29. Rhoda Newman, "Grants Work in a Congressional Office," *CRS Report for Congress*, Congressional Research, Library of Congress, Washington, D.C., 5 December 1989, summary card attached to report.

30. For details, see Martin Frazier, "Ex-Rep Mica Stays on House Payroll," *Roll Call*, 5 March 1989, p. 1; and George Archibald, "Mica works for House and lobbyists," *Washington Times*, 16 March 1989, p. 1.

31. Advertisement in *Legal Times*, 21 May 1990, p. 13.

32. Rep. Lee Hamilton, "Reinvigorating Congress," *Washington Report*, No. 23, Office of U.S. Rep. Lee Hamilton, 7 June, 1989. Also published on editorial page of the *Washington Post*, 6 June 1989.

33. Letter from U.S. Rep. Lee Hamilton to author, 3 January 1991.

CHAPTER FOUR

1. See Mary Stone, "Facts on PACs: Political Action Committees and American Campaign Finance," League of Women Voters Education

Fund (Washington, D.C.: 1984); Joseph E. Cantor, "Campaign Financing in Federal Elections: A Guide to the Law and Its Operation," *CRS Report for Congress*, Congressional Research Service, Library of Congress, 8 August 1986.

2. Janet Hook, "The Influential Committees: Money and Issues," *Congressional Quarterly*, 3 January 1987, p. 19. For an overview, see David Huckabee and Joseph Cantor, "House Campaign Expenditures: 1980-1988," *CRS Report for Congress*, Congressional Research Service, Library of Congress, 20 September 1989; and Frank J. Sorauf, *What Price PACs?: A Report of the Twentieth Century Fund Task Force on Political Action Committees* (New York: The Twentieth Century Fund, 1984).

3. Arthur Sanders, "The Meaning of Party Images," *Western Political Quarterly*, Vol. 41, September 1988, p. 585.

4. Common Cause letter to all House members, 21 June 1990, p. 1.

5. Anne Reifenber, "Northern Democrats attack Texas' attitude on collider," *Dallas Morning News* 21 April 1990, p. A1.


CHAPTER FIVE

1. See U.S. Rep. Ronald Coleman, "Republican Publicity Power Play," *Congressional Record*, 24 January 1984, p. H50.

2. See Bob Duke, "Coleman disputes tactics used by Republicans," *El Paso Herald-Post*, 26 January 1984, p. A1.

3. See "Some dirty tricks," *El Paso Herald-Post* editorial, 2 February 1984.

4. Author memorandum to U.S. Rep. Ronald Coleman and Paul Rogers, "Voter Tape Mailing to Anglo Males in NE, EAST, and WEST El Paso," 26 June 1984.

5. Staff memorandum to U.S. Rep. Ronald Coleman, "Campaign Press Conference," 3 October 1984.

6. For background and discussion of the vote, see John Felton, "Reagan Wins Victory on Central American Plan," *Congressional Quarterly*, 12 May 1984, p. 1086.

7. This account and other additional details are from K. Larry Storrs, "El Salvador: U.S. Foreign Assistance Facts," *CRS Issue Brief*, Congressional Research Service, Library of Congress, 27 March 1989. See also "El Salvador, 1979-1989: A Briefing Book on U.S. Aid and the Situation in El Salvador," *CRS Report for Congress*, Congressional Research

Service, Library of Congress, 28 April 1989; and Robert E. Sanchez, "The Central American States and Panama: Country Background Reports," *CRS Report for Congress*, Congressional Research Service, Library of Congress, 18 September 1987.

8. "Hammond Blasts Democrats," a 27 July 1984 *El Paso-Herald-Post* story, carried our line verbatim: "Over the last two years I have voted for $31.5 billion less in deficits than the president requested."

9. See Edward Howard, "Stacking the Deck, *Common Cause Magazine*, January/February 1989, p. 25. Howard who ran against Democratic incumbent Peter Kostmayer in 1988, told Common Cause that he "discovered that my opponent had a 90 percent recognition factor, which is a phenomenal statistic, and a 74 percent approval rating—and that has to be the result of the franking privilege and computerized mail."

10. See Erin Ross, "Coleman slammed on crime bill votes," *El Paso Herald-Post*, 27 September 1984, p. C1.

CHAPTER SIX

For a detailed overview of appropriation bills' enactment, see Sandy Streeter, "Regular Appropriations Enacted Separately and in Continuing Appropriations," *CRS Report for Congress*, Congressional Research Service, Library of Congress, 16 October 1989. See also: Virginia McMurtry, "The President and the Budget Process: Expanded Impoundment and Item Veto Proposals," *CRS Issue Brief*, Congressional Research Service, Library of Congress, 28 December 1989.

1. It takes most members more than one term. See Mark Crain, "The House Dynasty: A Public Choice Analysis," *The Imperial Congress: Crisis in the Separation of Powers* (New York: Pharos Books, 1988).

2. Resume of John B. Howerton of the ASARCO Company, undated.

3. Appropriations is a leadership committee. According to a 25 October 1985 *Congressional Quarterly* study, 63 percent of its members had a lower presidential support score than the average House Democrat in 1987-88.

4. David S. Cloud, "For 'Mr. Rural Development,' Small Ideas Go A Long Way," *Congressional Quarterly*, 30 September 1989, p. 2548.

5. Lance Gay, "How the pork is parceled," Scripps-Howard News Service in *Washington Times*, 13 April 1989, p. F1.

6. "Official Policy Manual," Office of Congressman Ronald Coleman, January 1989.

7. "McCurdy Announces South America Trip," Press Release, Office of U.S. Rep. Dave McCurdy, 24 May 1985.

8. "Itinerary," McCurdy Congressional Delegation (Codel), 25 May-32 May 1985.

9. Craig Winneker, "Members Furious Over Travel Survey, Say Foreign Trips Are Critical to Jobs," *Roll Call*, 17-23 July 1989, p. 1.

10. See Ilona B. Nickels, "One-Minute Speeches: House Practice and Procedure," *CRS Report for Congress*, Congressional Research Service, 19 January 1990.

11. For background see "Schedule for the Week of May 22, 1989," Democratic Study Group, House of Representatives, 22 May 1989.

12. For background and contrast, see Kim Mattingly, "Moakley Rules the Rules Committee with Equity, Charm, in Sharp Contrast to Wright-Pepper Days," *Roll Call*, 12 March 1990, p. 1.

13. A standard discussion of rules is in Stanley Bach, "The Nature of Congressional Rules," *Journal of Law and Politics*, Vol. 5, Summer 1989, pp. 725-757.

14. The only reporter to catch on was Ralph Z. Hallow, "Congress Forces HUD to eat pork," *Washington Times*, 1 June 1990, p. A3; also "Talking Points: HUD SCAM," *Party Lines*, Talking Points from the Democratic National Committee, Washington D.C., 21 June 1989, p. 1.

15. See Dan Morgan, "House Panel Busts Budget . . . But Patriotically," *Washington Post*, 13 July 1990.

16. "MX Statement for Wednesday," author memorandum to U.S. Rep. Ronald Coleman, 13 July 1990.

17. "Draft Comments Re White House Lobbying on MX," author memorandum to Rep. Ronald Coleman, 25 March 1985.

18. See remarks of U.S. Rep. Ronald Coleman, *Congressional Record*, 28 March 1985, p. H1607; House debate, *Congressional Record*, 27 March 1985, p. H1569; "Draft MX Statement for Karen McPherson" (Scripps-Howard News Service reporter), author memorandum to U.S. Rep. Ronald Coleman, 27 March 1985; and Pat Towell with Steven Pressman, "House Gives President the Go-Ahead on MX," *Congressional Quarterly*, 30 March 1985, p. 563.

19. "Coleman Leads Congressional Efforts for Mexico Disaster Relief; Congressional Office to Expedite Information Requests through Department of State Concerning Status of Relatives," Press Release, Office of U.S. Rep. Ronald Coleman, 20 September 1985.

20. See Karen McPherson, "Coleman's 'protector' causes grumbling," *El Paso Herald-Post*, 6 December 1985, p. B1; Gary Scharrer, "Close-lipped office chief's latest to give notice to 'stunned' congressman," *El Paso Times*, 17 November 1985; and "Coleman Losing Touch With Key Staffers," *El Paso Times*, 23 November 1985.

CHAPTER SEVEN

1. David Broder, "Nation's Capitol in Eclipse as Pride and Power Slip Away," *Washington Post*, 18 February 1990, p. A1.

2. "First Gramm-Rudman of 1986 Vote Cuts House Committee Spending by $4 Million," Press Release, Office of U.S. Rep. Ronald Coleman, 6 February 1986.

3. See letter from Michael Sheehan to U.S. Rep. Ronald Coleman, 6 March 1986 for additional details.

4. Myron Struck, "New Right turns its attention to capturing seats in the House," *Washington Times*, 30 October 1986.

5. U.S. Rep. Tony Coelho, "Memorandum to House Democratic Incumbents/Candidates," in *Tactics and Ideas: A confidential campaign report for Democratic Congressional candidates*, Democratic Congressional Campaign Committee, Washington, D.C., 27 August 1984.

6. Nicol Rae, "Liberal Republicans in Congress," in *The Decline and Fall of the Liberal Republicans: from 1952 to the present* (New York: Oxford University Press, 1989).

7. "Coleman Votes Against Democratic Leadership Budget Because of Tax Increases, Inadequate Defense Increases, and Customs User Fees," Press Release, Office of U.S. Rep. Ronald Coleman, 15 May 1986.

8. Sandra Sugawara, "14 on Hill Given $2,000 Each to Tour Va. Company's Mines," *Washington Post*, 11 June 1986, p. A1.

9. Donald Baker, "Mine Tour Host Declined Honorarium," *Washington Post*, 12 June 1986.

10. Mark Nelson, "3 Texas lawmakers defend company-arranged mine tour," *Dallas Morning News*, 12 June 1986.

11. D'Vera Cohn, "UMW Raps Lawmaker 'Pay for Trip,' " *Washington Post*, 13 June 1986.

12. See "Aide denies Coleman received $2,000 for junket to coal mine," *El Paso Herald-Post*, 12 June 1986, p. B1.

13. "Letter to Down-District Media," author's draft approved by U.S. Rep. Ronald Coleman, undated.

14. Karen McPherson, "Coleman's talk not cheap; neither are liabilities," *El Paso Herald-Post*, 20 March 1986, p. B1.

15. Brooks Jackson, "Easy Money: U.S. Lawmakers' Take From Honorariums Hits $10 Million a Year," *Wall Street Journal*, 1 November 1988, p. 1.

16. All details and quotes from poll results are from "A Survey of Voter Attitudes In the Sixteenth Congressional District of Texas," Peter D. Hart Research Associates, Washington, D.C., June 1986.

17. For an in-depth discussion of campaign activities by Hill rats, see Jack Maskell, "Campaign Activities by Congressional Employees," *CRS Report for Congress*, Congressional Research Service, Library of Congress, Washington, D.C., 29 September 1989.

18. "Comments for—Re Take 10," talking points for U.S. Rep. Ronald Coleman for Scripps-Howard News Service interview, 30 September 1986.

19. Gary Scharrer, "For Coleman, it's no contest," *El Paso Times*, 5 November 1986, p. A1.

CHAPTER EIGHT

1. For immediate background, see John Felton, "Fresh Charges of Funds Misuse Fuel Debate on 'Contra' Aid," *Congressional Quarterly*, 14 June 1986, p. 1320.

2. "Statement of Speaker Thomas P. O'Neill, Jr.," Speaker's Rooms, House of Representatives, 23 June 1986. See also Richard Whittle, "O'Neill rebuffs Reagan's bid for House talk on contra aid," *Dallas Morning News*, 24 June 1986, p. A1.

3. North had surfaced in a few earlier news accounts such as Joanne Omang, "McFarlane Aide Facilitates Policy," *Washington Post*, 11 August 1985, p. A1.

4. A compilation of congressional debates on the various contra aid restrictions can be found in the *Congressional Record*, Vol. 33, No. 97, 15

June 1987. See also: Nina Serafino and Maureen Taft-Morales, "Contra Aid: Summary and Chronology of Major Congressional Action, 1981-1989," *CRS Report for Congress*, Congressional Research Service, Library of Congress, 1 November 1989.

5. "Statement of U.S. Rep. Ronald Coleman of Texas," News Conference, House of Representatives, 24 June 1986. See also "Coleman/ Barnes Announce Probe of Alleged Illegal Assistance to Contras by Administration and National Security Officials," *Press Advisory*, Office of U.S. Rep. Ronald Coleman, 23 June 1986.

6. "Statement of U.S. Rep. Ronald Coleman," *Congressional Record*, 25 March 1986.

7. "Coleman to Meet with Contadora Ministers, Visit Nicaragua As Progress Toward Peace Treaty Develops," Press Release, Office of U.S. Rep. Ronald Coleman, 2 June 1986.

8. See Richard Whittle, "Lawmakers return from Central America," *Dallas Morning News*, 6 June 1986, p. H-2; also "Looking for a Bipartisan Deal on Touchy 'Contra' Issue," *Congressional Quarterly*, 7 June 1986, p. 1266.

9. Memorandum to U.S. Rep. Ronald Coleman from Victor C. Johnson, Foreign Affairs Committee, "Proposed Resolution of Inquiry on Boland Amendment Violations," 18 June 1986.

10. Johnson based much of his claims on Robert Parry, "Reagan Administration Said to Manage 'Private' Contra Aid," Associated Press, 10 June 1986.

11. See Joe Pichirallo, "Poindexter Convicted on All Iran-Contra Counts," *Washington Post*, 8 April 1990, p. A1, for typical national press coverage of verdict. Also: Michael Wines, "North Subpoenas 2 Democratic Congressmen," *New York Times*, 26 January 1989, p. A19.

12. Robert Parry, "Contras-Congress," Associated Press, 21 June 1986.

13. The key part of the debate is found in the *Congressional Record*, 25 June 1986, "Amendment Offered by Mr. Hamilton," pp. H4278-4288.

14. For details see John Felton, "For Reagan, A Key House Win on Contra Aid," *Congressional Quarterly*, 28 June 1986, p. 1443.

15. See Richard S. Beth, "Resolutions of Inquiry in the House of Representatives: A Brief Description," Congressional Research Service, Library of Congress, 22 April 1987.

16. Robert Parry, "White House Balks at Releasing Contra Documents," Associated Press, 25 July 1986.

17. "Comment for RDC to Bob Parry," author memorandum to U.S. Rep. Ronald Coleman, 24 July 1986.
18. Author memorandum to U.S. Rep. Ronald Coleman, "Background Memorandum RE Press Accounts Relevant to Resolution of Inquiry," 24 July 1986. Reprinted in Appendix III.
19. Author memorandum to U.S. Rep. Ronald Coleman, "Questions for House Intelligence Committee to ask Lt. Col. Oliver North," 5 August 1986. A copy was sent to the Intelligence Committee via House Inside Mail and Rep. Coleman gave a second copy to Chairman Hamilton. Reprinted in Appendix IV.
20. Letter from U.S. Rep. Lee Hamilton to U.S. Rep. Ronald Coleman, 12 August 1986. The letter was drafted by the author, approved by Rep. Coleman, hand-delivered to U.S. Rep. Hamilton's office by the author, and mailed back to Rep. Coleman by Rep. Hamilton.
21. See Author memorandum to U.S. Rep. Ronald Coleman, "Increasing Media Questions About U.S. Rep. Hamilton and the Resolution of Inquiry," 23 February 1987.

## CHAPTER NINE

One of the best guides to the tortuous legislative maneuvering over contra aid is "Contra Aid: Summary and Chronology of Major Congressional Action, 1981-1989," *CRS Report to Congress*, 1 November 1989. See also:

Larry M. Eig, "Contra Aid: Analysis of Whether the National Security Council (NSC) and the NSC Staff Are An 'Agency or Entity Involved In Intelligence Activities' Covered By Section 8066(A) of the Department of Defense Appropriations Act, FY 1985 (Boland Amendment)," *CRS Report for Congress*, Congressional Research Service, Library of Congress, 11 May 1987.

Larry M. Eig, "Chart of Unclassified Legislative Restrictions Regarding Support for Military or Paramilitary Operations in Nicaragua, 1982-1986," Congressional Research Service, Library of Congress, 10 March 1987.

Nina Serafino, "Congra Aid: 1981-March 1987, Summary and Chronology of Major Congressional Action on Key Legislation Concerning U.S. Aid to the Anti-Sandinista Guerrillas," *CRS Report for Congress*, Congressional Research Service, Library of Congress, 21 July 1987.

1. Text of H. Res. 658, *Congressional Record*, 14 July 1977, p. 22932.
2. For more background, see Loch Johnson, "The U.S. Congress and the CIA: Monitoring the Dark Side of Government," *Legislative Studies Quarterly*, Vol. 4, November 1980.
3. *Congressional Record*, 25 June 1986, pp. H4280-4281.
4. Notebooks of Lt. Col. Oliver North as released by the National Security Archive. (See Appendix V)
5. Roger D. Hansen, "The Reagan Doctrine and Global Containment: Revival or Recessional," *SAIS Review*, Vol. 7, Winter–Spring 1987, p. 1. For historical context of the institutional considerations of the Reagan Doctrine, see: Frederick M. Kaiser, "Congress and National Security Policy: Changing and Varied Roles for a Shared Responsibility," *Comparative Strategy*, Vol. 9, No. 1, 1990, pp. 67-84; Ellen C. Collier, "Foreign Policy Roles of the President and Congress," *CRS Report for Congress*, Congressional Research Service, Library of Congress, 16 September 1986; Sherry Shapiro, "President and Foreign Policy: Selected References," *CRS Report for Congress*, May 1987; and Ellen C. Collier, "Bipartisan Foreign Policy and Policymaking Since World War II," *CRS Report for Congress*, 9 November 1989.
6. John Horton, "Mexico, The Way of Iran?" *International Journal of Intelligence and Counterintelligence*, Vol. 1, No. 2, Summer 1986.
7. Private source.
8. House Report 98-1196, "Report on the Activities of the Permanent Select Committee on Intelligence of the House of Representatives During the 98th Congress," 98th Congress, 2nd Session, 2 January 1985.
9. John Felton, "Intelligence Panels: Fresh Faces, Familiar Issues," *Congressional Quarterly*, 19 January 1985, p. 118.
10. U.S. Rep. Robert Dornan, *Congressional Record*, 25 June 1986, p. H4286.
11. Alfonso Chardy, "Contra backer offered to help Mexicans, notes show," *Miami Herald*, 27 March 1987, p. 5A.
12. Alfonso Chardy, "U.S. Intimidation: Secret campaign targeted 5 latin countries in effort to shuttle peace talks, aid contras," *Dallas Morning News*, 10 May 1987, p. A1.
13. Letter to author, 1 August 1991.
14. Letter to author, 16 July 1991. While Representative Hyde's denials can be questioned, given the circumstances surrounding the 4 March

1985 meeting, he is one of the few House members with a true reputation for integrity. Accordingly, I have reprinted his 16 July 1991 letter in its entirety in Appendix VII.

See also:

Robert McFarlane to Max Friedersdorf, "Meeting with Members of the House Permanent Select Committee on Intelligence (undated) re the 4 March 1985 meeting." (Included in North trial documents)

Oliver North to Robert McFarlane, "Fallback Plan for the Nicaraguan Resistance," 16 March 1985, NSC Intelligence Document (Top Secret/Sensitive), U.S. Government Exhibit 143 A, declassified.

15. "Minutes," National Security Planning Group Meeting, White House Situation Room, 25 June 1984, 2:00–3:00 P.M.
16. Oliver North, *Under Fire* (New York: Harper Collins, Publishers, 1991), p. 322.
17. Michael Barone and Grant Ujifusa, *The Almanac of American Politics 1990* (Washington, D.C.: National Journal, 1989), p. 1380.

CHAPTER TEN

1. See Andrew Mangan, "Texans again moving to top of Capitol Hill," Associated Press story, 18 January 1987.
2. Author memorandum to Paul Rogers, "Conversation With Allen Jones, American Trucking Association," 3 October 1988.
3. Paul Burka, "The Wright House," *Texas Monthly*, December 1986, p. 238.
4. "Honoraria take is pegged at $766,000," United Press International story, 18 November 1989.
5. Author memorandum to U.S. Rep. Ronald Coleman, "Budget Comments," 8 January 1987.
6. See Richard Ryan, "Marvin Leath's Quest for Power," *Texas Observer*, 28 August 1987.
7. "Coleman: Mr. President, You're Wrong on the Pay Raise," Press Release, Office of U.S. Rep. Ronald Coleman, 27 January 1987.
8. "Coleman Pushes Anti-Pay Raise Legislation Before House Task Force," Press Release, Office of U.S. Rep. Ronald Coleman, 3 February 1987.
9. See also: Michael Pelrine, "Chapman says he's against pay raise for

congressmen," *News-Leader*, Sulphur Springs, Texas, 17 February 1987.

10. *El Paso Times* editorial, El Paso, Texas, 4 February 1987.

11. See: Ed Foster, "Wright says Reagan amiss on new bill," *El Paso Times*, 14 February 1987.

Also:

"Opening Remarks for Jim Wright News Conference," script for U.S. Rep. Ronald Coleman written by author, 13 February 1987;

"Memorandum: Dinner Speech," for Speaker of the House Jim Wright by author, 13 February 1987. This memorandum stressed the benefits of twin plants. The "Memorandum: Breakfast Speech" for a labor audience was considerably less enthusiastic.

12. Photocopy of handwritten letter with writer's name deleted as received. Literally hundreds of copies of this letter were circulated among Hill rats at the time.

13. "Sample After Dinner Remarks" and "Remarks In Taiwan," author memoranda to U.S. Rep. Ronald Coleman, 10 August 1987.

See also:

"The 76th National Anniversary of the Republic of China," statement of U.S. Rep. Ronald Coleman, *Congressional Record*, 23 September 1987; "President Chiang Chin Kuo," Statement of U.S. Rep. Ronald Coleman, *Congressional Record*, 26 January 1988, based on Nathan Mao draft statement "Sample 18" (undated); "October 10, 1988—Taiwan's 77th Birthday," Statement of U.S. Rep. Ronald Coleman, *Congressional Record*, 20 September 1988, based on Nathan Mao draft statement of 14 September 1988, "Taiwan's 77th Birthday." Nathan Mao wrote on the draft, "Paul [Rogers], please ask the Congressman to enter this in the Record as soon as possible. Feel free to make any change or use it verbatim."

14. Author cover note to Paul Rogers with draft letters to the editor attached; Rogers's initials "OK."

15. "Continuing Resolutions: Good, Bad, or Unavoidable?" *Special Report*, Democratic Study Group, U.S. House of Representatives, Washington, D.C., 25 March 1988.

16. Citizens for America letter (unsigned) to U.S. Rep. Ronald Coleman; also "The Pork Book: A Guide to Congressional Excess," Citizens for American Educational Foundation (Washington, D.C., 1989).

17. "The View from the Hill: Lawmakers on Congressional Reform," *Center for Responsive Politics*, Washington, D.C., 1989, p. 41.

18. See Macon Morehouse, "House Votes to Create Groundwater Research Panel," *Congressional Quarterly*, 5 December 1987, p. 2995. Also: "Coleman Wins Hearing on Legislation to Prevent Low-Level Nuclear Waste Dump Site in U.S.-Mexican Border Region," Press Release, Office of U.S. Rep. Ronald Coleman, 2 December 1987.

19. Mark Edgar, "Allies fly across Texas for Gephardt," *Dallas Morning News*, 1 March 1988; "Coleman will give Gephardt support," *El Paso Times*, 26 February 1988.

20. See author memorandum to U.S. Rep. Ronald Coleman, "Questions from UPI About Your Daughter's Summer Employment," 19 November 1987; and "Ursula Meese, and Others," *Wall Street Journal* editorial, 3 March 1988.

21. See Peter Brock, "Special interests help to fatten Coleman coffers," *El Paso Herald-Post*, 28 May 1988; and Jennifer Dixon, "House Finances," Associated Press, 26 May 1988.

22. "Congressional Hearings on the Colonias Crisis Scheduled for March 11 and 12 in El Paso and Brownsville," Press Release, Office of U.S. Rep. Ronald Coleman, 1 March 1988; Thaddeus Herrick, "Human misery illumined [sic]," *El Paso Herald-Post*, 11 March 1988; Statement of U.S. Rep. Ronald Coleman, 17 May 1988; Jennifer Dixon, "Texans introduce legislation setting up border commission," Associated Press, 18 May 1988.

23. Dan Morgan, "Congress and a Company: An Alliance Fed by Money," *Washington Post*, 13 June 1988; letter of Dan Morgan to Wilbur R. Schmitt, Jr., of Pirelli Cable Corp., 24 May 1988; letter of Roy Meyers, communications director, Cassidy and Associates, to Dan Morgan, 30 May 1988; "Draft Working Document," John T. Barteld of Pirelli Cable for a draft letter to Dan Morgan, 1 June 1988; letter from John T. Barteld to U.S. Rep. Ronald Coleman, 10 March 1988; "No More Honoraria," Press Release, Office of U.S. Rep. Ronald Coleman, 26 July 1988.

24. Richard Whittle, "Take me out to the honorarium," *Dallas Morning News*, 24 May 1989.

25. "Coleman emerges as leader," Associated Press (no byline), 10 June 1988.

26. "House Adopts $3 Million Coleman Provision to Pay for El Paso's Share of Constructing the Zaragosa Bridge," Press Release, Office of U.S. Ronald Coleman, 29 June 1988; "Guadalupe, Chamizal Memorial and Tiguas Highlight $3.78 Million Won By Coleman in Appropriations Legislation," Press Release, Office of U.S. Ronald Coleman, 16 June 1988.

27. Typical of the coverage was Juan Palomo, "Texas lawmaker attacks Quayle's value in drug war, saying he 'sat out last war,' " *Houston Post*, 18 September 1988.

28. See: Gary Scharrer, "Coleman's yearly barbecue grows into a Texas tradition," *El Paso Times*, 15 September 1988.

29. John Elvin, "Burp. What Sleaze?" *Washington Times*, 29 June 1988, p. 6.

30. For additional information, see Martin Frazier, "House Rejects A Pay Hike, So Rosty Offers A Do-It-Yourself Plan," *Roll Call*, 28 June 1988.

31. Typical of the coverage was James Pierobon, "Wright denies wrongdoing in CIA case," *Houston Chronicle*, 23 September 1988; see also "Statement by Speaker Wright," 23 September 1988.

32. Letter from U.S. Rep. Ronald Coleman to Rep. Louis Stokes, chairman, House Permanent Select Committee on Intelligence (letter drafted by author), 22 September 1988.

33. "Report: Unopposed candidates still raise money," Associated Press, 27 October 1988; "Incumbent lawmakers scare away opposition," Gannett News Service, 23 October 1988.

34. "Corporate PACs Which Have Contributed to Congressman Ron Coleman," appendix to Congressman Ron Coleman Biography" (campaign version), undated, Fall 1988.

35. Typical coverage was Charles Mohr, "Forget the Deficit; a Real Crisis is Looming: Raises," *New York Times*, 9 December 1988; Judith Havemann, "$135,000 Salary for Congress Urged," *Washington Post*, 14 December 1988.


CHAPTER ELEVEN

1. For additional perspective, see Donald Lambro, "2 GOP Groups in Congress fusing to redefine party rule," *Washington Times*, 3 March 1989.

2. See Paul E. Dwyer, "Salary of Members of Congress: Congressional

Votes, 1967–1990," *CRS Report for Congress*, Congressional Research Service, Library of Congress, 13 March 1990.

3. "Some Facts on Congressional Pay," *Special Report*, Democratic Study Group, House of Representatives, Washington, D.C., 1 February 1989.

4. Patrick Buchanan, "Pay Dirt on the Hill," *Washington Times*. 11 January 1989.

5. Martin Frazier, "Pay Hike Looks Like A Lock," *Roll Call*, 15 January 1989.

6. Walter Pincus, "Majority in Congress Already Make $135,000," *Washington Post*, 24 January 1989, p. A1.

7. For background, see typical coverage such as Susan Rasky, "No Vote On Raise, House Whip Says," *New York Times*, 25 January 1989, p. A17.

8. Study by the National Commission on Public Employee Pension Systems reported by George Archibald, "Hill pay raise to create millionaire pensioners," *Washington Times*, 16 January 1989, p. A1.

9. Richard Morin, "Huge Majority in Poll Opposes 50% Raise for Top Officials," *Washington Post*, 17 January 1989, p. A1.

10. "Gold on Them Thar Hill," *Wall Street Journal*, editorial, 18 January 1989.

11. See Robin Toner, "Bush Endorses Pay Raise, Heartening House," *New York Times*, 5 February 1989.

12. Typical coverage was Mark Nelson, "Wright polls lawmakers on pay hike," *Dallas Morning News*, 1 February 1989, p. A1; and Tom Kenworthy and Don Phillips, "Wright Tests Support for Vote on Pay," *Washington Post*, 1 February 1989, p. A1.

13. Michael Greskes, "A Week in the Heat," *New York Times*, 5 February 1989.

14. See Tom Kenworthy and Don Phillips, "Democrats Singing the Blues," *Washington Post*, 4 February 1989, p. A4.

15. For additional background, see Janet Hook, "Pay Raise Is Killed, But the Headaches Persist," *Congressional Quarterly*, 11 February 1989, p. 261.

16. "The Speaker's Uncommon Courage," Statement of U.S. Rep. Ronald Coleman, *Congressional Record*, 8 February 1989.

17. John Elvin, "Democratic congressman willing to defeat liberals," *Washington Times*, 23 February 1989, p. A4.

18. See Tom Kenworthy, "Lawmaker Cites Gay Colleague as Example of Bias," *Washington Post*, 28 March 1989.

19. For more details, see Martin Frazier, "Justice Department Is Pressured to Name Outside Counsel," *Roll Call*, 27 March–2 April 1989.

20. Katherine Rizzo, "Ex-Aide Complain [sic] of Luken's 'Tantrums,' 'Tirades,' " Associated Press, 2 March 1989.

21. Martin Frazier, "Congress Lags Far Behind," *Roll Call*, 6–12 March 1989.

22. Jackie Koszczuk and Ron Hutcheson, "Ethics Committee week ends as GOP is accused of malice," *Fort Worth Star-Telegram*, 3 March 1989; "Coleman Claims GOP tampering with ethics committee on Wright," Associated Press, 3 March 1989.

23. "Your Visit to El Paso, Thursday, March 16, 1989," Memorandum to the majority leader from U.S. Rep. Ronald Coleman, written by author; "Majority Leader Introduction," Statement of U.S. Rep. Ronald Coleman, 16 March 1989; "Coleman Schedules News Conference with House Majority Leader," Press Release, Office of Rep. Ronald Coleman, 15 March 1989.

24. Additional details of the proposal can be found in Ann Devroy, "Bush Offers Proposal on Ethics, Pay," *Washington Post*, 13 April 1989, p. A1.

25. See "Ethics Committee News Conference," author memorandum to U.S. Rep. Ronald Coleman, 17 April 1989.

26. "Texans' View of Wright Probe," Associated Press, 18 April 1989.

27. "Statement Re Ethics Committee Report on Wright," talking points by author for U.S. Rep. Ronald Coleman, 17 April 1989.

28. Ken Ringle, "Memory and Anger: A Victim's Story," *Washington Post*, 4 May 1989.

29. Details from John Lofton, "Clues to Coelho's Empathy," *Washington Times*, 17 May 1989.

30. David E. Rosenbaum, "Coelho Saved About $2,000 in Taxes on '86 Bond Deal," *New York Times*, 17 May 1989.

31. Ron Hutcheson, "Sex, humor in chronicles of Congress," *Fort Worth Star-Telegram*, 3 May 1989. p. A1.

32. Jayne O'Donnell, "Rep. Explains Brassiere on Head: I'm No Monk," *Roll Call*, 1–7 May 1989.

33. A good analysis is in Joan Mower, "Rep. Dixon Denies Firm Lobbied Him," Associated Press, 30 July 1989.

34. Discussed in Richard Alan Baker, "The History of Congressional Ethics," *Representation and Responsibility: Exploring Legislative Ethics*, Bruce Jennings and Daniel Callahan, eds. (New York: Plenum Books, 1985).

35. For additional information, see David Rogers and John Yang, "Foley Steps In as New Speaker of House, Casting Himself as a Healer for 2 Parties," *Wall Street Journal*, 7 June 1989.

36. Ralph Hallow, "GOP squabbles over tactics after 'sleazy' smear of Foley," *Washington Times*, 8 June 1989, p. A5.

37. Steve Goldberg, "GOP, Democrats beef up dirt patrols," Scripps-Howard News Service, 27 June 1989.

38. "Talking Points: Bush's Fat Cat Protection Act," *Party Lines*, Democratic National Committee, 29 June 1989.


CHAPTER TWELVE

1. Author memorandum to Paul Rogers, "DCCC Incumbent Protection Meeting—Summary and Discussion, 28 June 1989.

2. Barone, Michael and Ujifusa, Grant. *Almanac of American Politics 1988* (Washington, D.C.: National Journal, 1987), p. 952.

3. Author memorandum to U.S. Rep. Ronald Coleman, "Congressional Quarterly Comment," 2 August 1989.

4. Paul Starobin, "Pork Perhaps, But Earmarks Popular . . . With Sponsors' Constituents," *Congressional Quarterly*, 5 August 1989, pp. 2026-2027.

5. Richard S. Dunham, "Gramm Grabs Credit from Others, Critics Say," *Dallas Times Herald* 10 September 1989, p. A1.

6. Joe Old and Keith Dubay, "FBI probe centers on ex-official," *El Paso Herald-Post*, 23 April 1987, p. 1; "Agents Seize SBA Records in El Paso Contract Probe," Associated Press story, 20 June 1987; Keith Dubay, "SBA director reassigned," *El Paso Herald-Post*, 25 June 1987, p. A1; Joe Old, "Contractor says kickback taken," *El Paso Herald-Post*, 30 May 1987, p. A1.

7. Cheryl Arvidson, "Tax fight splits 2 Texans from Democratic Leaders," *Dallas Times Herald*, 26 July 1989.

8. Sandy Grady, "Tax-break vote brings up memories," reprinted in *Fort Worth Star-Telegram*, 2 October 1989.

See also:

Janet Hook, "Rout of Democratic Leaders Reflects Fractured Party," *Congressional Quarterly*, 30 September 1989, p. 2529.

Tom Kenworthy and Dale Russakoff, "Timber Interests Crucial in Capital-Gains Fight," *Washington Post*, 27 September 1989, p. A4.

Robin Toner, "Democratic Strategy Faulted After Loss in House Tax Vote," *New York Times,* 1 October 1989, p. A1.

9. Staff Memorandum, "Bridges Mtg. with Veronica Callaghan, Friday," 24 June 1990.

10. Rep. Ronald Coleman Daily Schedule, 5 February 1987.

11. Letter from U.S. Rep. Ronald Coleman to William Kastrin, 18 December 1984; Coleman for Congress Committee Statement (undated) "Conciliation Agreement" between the Coleman for Congress Committee and the U.S. Federal Election Commission, undated, December 1984.

12. Untitled story on the Associated Press wire, 23 May 1989.

13. Ibid. Coleman's tortuous finances were relevant to the extent they involved persons with whom he conducted congressional business; two such notes as telecopied to the Washington, D.C. congressional office for Coleman's "blind" trust are reprinted in Appendix II. Additionally, Coleman had encountered this kind of problem previously when he wrote a "letter of introduction" for his Pecos, Texas campaign manager to the U.S. General Services Administration concerning land purchases for border crossings by the federal government. See Rick Brown, "Border bridge facility issue draws denial," *Odessa American* (TX), 24 October 1985, p. 1.

14. Spencer Rich, "House Votes to Repeal Health Plan," *Washington Post*, 5 October 1989, p. A1.

15. "Bush Administration Should Put Interests of Nation Ahead of Politics and Accept Bipartisan Compromise," press release from office of U.S. Rep. Ronald Coleman, 18 October 1989.

See also:

"The Coming Sequestration," *Special Report*, Democratic Study Group, U.S. House of Representatives, 11 October 1989.

"Effects of Sequestration," Dear Colleague letter to all House members from Rep. Leon E. Panetta, Chairman, House Committee on the Budget, 20 March 1989.

Leon E. Panetta, "Consequences of Sequestration," Dear Colleague letter to all House members from Rep. Leon Panetta, 2 November 1989.

16. John Hiram Caldwell, "Congressional Micromanagement: Domestic Policy," *The Imperial Congress*, p. 133.

17. *Congressional Quarterly*, 3 January 1987, p. 22. See also, Don Phillips and David Hoffman, "House Panel Approves $2.85 Billion Quake Relief Plan," *Washington Post*, 24 October 1982, p. A12.

18. Author memorandum to Rep. Ronald Coleman, "Preliminary Impressions from the Districtwide Questionnaire," 31 October 1989.

19. For details see "Ethics Reform and Pay Increase," *Fact Sheet*, Democratic Study Group, House of Representatives, 14 November 1989; and James P. McGrath, "Pay Raise Proposals for Members of Congress, Top Officials and Federal Judges: Issues and Outlook," *CRS Report for Congress*, Congressional Research Service, Library of Congress, 15 November 1989.

20. "Ethics Package, Pay Raise for Federal Employees Worthwhile Goals But 25% Member Pay Raise Too Much," press release from office of U.S. Rep. Ronald Coleman, 16 November 1989. "Coleman votes against congressional pay raise," *El Paso Herald-Post*, 17 November 1989, p. A1.

21. Peter Matthiessen, *Killing Mr. Watson* (New York: Random House, Vintage Edition, 1990), p. 167.

CHAPTER THIRTEEN

Voluminous accounts are available concerning the House of Representatives and ethics. The following relate immediately to this chapter, but I will gladly share my extensive bibliography on this subject upon request. In most instances, the references are supplementary for the reader. When working on the Hill, one did not need to wait for *Roll Call* to be published to know that the Ethics Committe had decided to drop various charges against him, but the subsequent article is a good reference for readers interested in more detailed information.

1. Steve Daly, "Sex scandals will cloud Congress' vision," *Dallas Morning News*, 9 August 1989.

For a view on how the new ethics climate was affecting the executive branch, see Terry Eastland, "Ethicshock," *Washingtonian*, August 1989, pp. 77–80.

For similiar effects on the legislative branch, see Jack H. Maskell, "Brief Summary of Changes in the Ethics Rules for the House of Representatives made by the Ethics Reform Act of 1989," *CRS Report for Congress*, Library of Congress, 4 January 1990.

2. Jeffrey Birnbaum and Edward Pound, "Rep. Gray Remains Dogged by Issue of His Ties to Church to Which He Donated Speaking Fees," *Wall Street Journal*, 26 June 1990, p. A20.

3. Kim Mattingly, "Ethics Panel Decides to Dismiss Charges Against Gingrich," *Roll Call*, 8 March 1990.

4. "Former Lawmaker Given Year in Jail," *New York Times*, 29 August 1989, p. A16.

5. Richard Dunham, "Some say Jerry Jones' feud knocked daughter off Hill," *Dallas Times Herald*, 1 February 1990, p. A-8.

6. Rep. Gus Savage, "Personal Explanations," *Congressional Record*, 1 February 1990, pp. H194-195.

7. "Privileges of the House—Relating to the Integrity of the Proceedings of the House of Representatives," floor debate of 7 February 1990, *Congressional Record*, pp. H330-332.
   Craig Winneker, "Task Force Will Examine Editing Policy for Record," *Roll Call*, 26 February 1990.

8. William E. Clayton, Jr., "Words of the House are suspect," *Houston Chronicle*, 8 February 1990.

9. Glen Simpson, " 'Village Voice' Charges Engel Asked Mob Help During 1988 Campaign," *Roll Call*, 1 February 1990.

10. Rep. Henry J. Hyde, Dear Colleague Letter, 21 February 1990. See also Mike Mason, "Old-timers, newcomers alike oppose term limits for Congress," *Dallas Times Herald*, 17 April 1990, p. A6; and Sula P. Richardson, "Congressional Tenure: A Review of Efforts to Limit House and Senate Service," *CRS Report for Congress*, Congressional Research Service, Library of Congress, 13 September 1989.

11. Author memorandum to U.S. Rep. Ronald Coleman, "Talking Points—Limiting Congressional Terms," 20 February 1990.

12. "CRS Major Issues for the 101st Congress, Second Session," *CRS Report for Congress*, Congressional Research Service, Library of Congress, 16 January 1990.

13. David Broder, "Nation's Capital in Eclipse as Pride and Power Slip Away," *Washington Post*, 18 February 1990, p. A1.

14. "Congressman Ron Coleman Biography," January 1990. Written by author at direction of staff director Paul Rogers.

15. Author memorandum to U.S. Rep. Ronald Coleman, "Gulf of Mexico Program," 16 February 1990.

16. Steve McGonigle, "Brooks says he has healthy desire to stay in House," *Dallas Morning News*, 17 February 1990, p. A1.

17. Private sources; Letter from House Sergeant-At-Arms Jack Russ to U.S. Rep. Ronald Coleman, 17 October 1991; and "Statement of U.S. Rep. Ronald Coleman," 17 October 1991.

18. Representative stories of this time include:

Jackie Calmes, "Bush Dealing from Strength As Budget Season Opens," *Congressional Quarterly*, 3 February 1990, p. 299.

Richard E. Cohen, "Defining the Democrats' New Message," *National Journal*, 10 February 1990.

Dan Carney, "Texas Democrats cool to Bush's budget plan," *El Paso Herald-Post*, 3 February 1990, p. B1.

"Ducks," *Washington Post* editorial, 1 March 1990.

Susan Feeney, "Democratic strategy to target middle class concerns," *Dallas Morning News*, 4 February 1990, p. 4A.

19. "The Great Base Closing Ploy: Creating a Political Tempest to Shield a Bloated Defense Budget," *DSG Special Report*, No.101-29, Democratic Study Group, U.S. House of Representatives, 24 March 1990.

". . . Heard It on The Grapevine: Pickle Sandbagged on Bergstrom," *Quorum Report: The Journal of Texas Politics*, Vol. 8., No.9, 23 February 1990.

Richard Whittle, "Base-Closing plan fuels defense debate," *Dallas Morning News*, 5 February 1990, p. 1A.

20. Sam Attlesey, "Democrats face reality of a two-party Texas," *Dallas Morning News*, 8 June 1990, p. A1.

21. All quotes are from verbatim transcripts secret Texas Democratic incumbent redistricting committee meetings.

22. Letter of Ralph Nader to all House members, 1 May 1990.

23. Tom Kenworthy, "Gephardt Says Bush Fails As a Leader—Democrat Proposes Direct Aid to Soviets," *Washington Post*, 7 March 1990, p. A1.

Susan F. Rasky, "Senator Makes Scathing Attack on Gephardt Over Criticism of Bush," *New York Times*, 10 March 1990.

24. See Mary Benati, "Coleman: El Salvador shouldn't get military aid," Gannett News Service, 30 April 1990. "Coleman to Oppose Military Aid to El Salvador," Press Release, Office of U.S. Rep. Ronald Coleman, 26 April 1990.

See also Tom Kenworthy and Dan Morgan, "House Vote on El Salvador Derails Central American Aid Package," *Washington Post*, 23 May 1990, p. 4.

Robert S. Kirk, "El Salvador: Bibliography-in-Brief, 1987-1989," *CRS Report for Congress*, Congressional Research Service, Library of Congress, January 1990.

Robert Pear, "House Amendment Would Halve Aid for El Salvador," *New York Times*, 23 May 1990, p. A1.

Nina M. Serafino, "Central American Peace Prospects: U.S. Interests and Response," *CRS Issue Brief*, Congressional Research Service, Library of Congress, 4 April 1990.

K. Larry Storrs, "El Salvador and U.S. Aid: Congressional Action in 1989," *CRS Issue Brief*, Congressional Research Service, Library of Congress, 13 February 1990.

————, "El Salvador Highlights, 1960-1990: A Summary of Major Turning Points in Salvadoran History and U.S. Policy," *CRS Report for Congress*, Congressional Research Service, Library of Congress, 13 March 1990.

Mark P. Sullivan, "Central America and U.S. Foreign Assistance: Issues for Congress," *CRS Issue Brief*, Congressional Research, Library of Congress, 15 May 1990.

James B. Wooten, "El Salvador: Status of the War and the Role of U.S. Aid," *CRS Report for Congress*, Congressional Research Service, Library of Congress, 4 April 1990.

For a good description of Salvadoran government counterinsurgency tactics, see Michael A. Sheehan, "Comparative Counterinsurgency Strategies: Guatemala and El Salvador," *Conflict*, Vol.9, No.2, 1989, pp. 127-154.

25. As with many other issues, extensive accounts are available of the debate over flag-burning legislation. See:

Richard E. Cohen, "Unfurling the Issue of Burning Flags," *National Journal*, 16 June 1990, p. 1496.

John Dillin, "Republicans Say They'll Take Flag Issue Directly to American Voters," *Christian Science Monitor*, 25 June 1990, p. 1.

"The Flag Amendment," *Fact Sheet*, Democratic Study Group, U.S. House of Representatives, 19 June 1990.

"Politicizing the Flag Debate," *Party Lines: Talking Points from the Democratic Party*, Democratic National Committee, 12 June 1990.

"Providing for Consideration of House Joint Resolution 350, Constitutional Amendment Banning Desecration of the Flag, and of H.R. 5091, Flag Protection Act of 1990," floor debate of the House of Represenatives, *Congressional Record*, 21 June 1990, pp. H3995-H4029; H4035-H4088.

"Research Materials on the Flag Debate," Democratic Study Group, U.S. House of Representatives, 12 June 1990.

# APPENDICES

LEE H. HAMILTON
9TH DISTRICT, INDIANA

COMMITTEES:

FOREIGN AFFAIRS

JOINT ECONOMIC

SCIENCE, SPACE,
AND TECHNOLOGY

**Congress of the United States**
**House of Representatives**
**Washington, DC 20515**

2187 RAYBURN BUILDING
WASHINGTON, DC 20515
TELEPHONE: (202) 225-5315

DISTRICT OFFICES:
107 FEDERAL CENTER
BUILDING 66
1201 EAST 10TH STREET
JEFFERSONVILLE, IN 47130
TELEPHONE: (812) 288-3999

CALL TOLL FREE
(800) 892-3232

January 3, 1991

Mr. John L. Jackley
c/o Wall Street Journal
    Opinion Page Editor
200 Liberty Street
New York, NY 10281

Dear Mr. Jackley:

I appreciated your interest in my statement in my newsletter of June 7, 1989, that Members of Congress who make distorted, demeaning statements about the Congress should face disciplinary action. I would like to explain in a little more detail what I had in mind.

The main task of the House Committee on Standards of Official Conduct is to determine what sort of actions by Members reflect discredit on the House. Rule 1 of the House Code of Official Conduct states: "A Member, officer, or employee of the House of Representatives shall conduct himself at all times in a manner which shall reflect creditably on the House of Representatives." A clearly false statement by a Member, such as saying to the press that Members of Congress are spineless, can be demeaning and reflect discredit on the House.

It is entirely within the purview of the Standards Committee to review these broader kinds of actions by Members of Congress. Many seemingly small, routine acts can reflect discredit on the House and undermine the perception of Americans in the integrity of government just as much as front-page sex or money scandals.

It should be noted that "disciplinary action" by the Committee can fall far short of reprimand or censure by the full House. The Committee could, for example, simply advise the Member that a particular statement reflects poorly on the House. Some past actions by the Standards Committee against Members have been taken solely on the Committee level (for example, admonishing Members for their handling of campaign funds). Obviously not any statement critical of the House would warrant disciplinary action-- especially when a Member is honestly trying to point up shortcomings in order to improve the House. But some which are particularly distorted and demeaning could. It would be up to the Committee to determine when the threshold had been clearly crossed.

I do not believe that such efforts by the Standards Committee to try to uphold the integrity of the House would be an unwarranted infringement on the free speech of Members. There are already rules on

the House books limiting the freedom of speech of a Member in making
distorted, improper attacks against another Member (such as Speaker
O'Neill being admonished for his statements on the floor critical of
Rep. Gingrich).  It is time that we started looking out to protect the
integrity and reputation of the House from unwarranted attacks as much
as we do individual Members.  It does not seem to be an unreasonable
demand on Members that they not be fundamentally unfair and demeaning
in their statements about the Congress.  Such a standard applies in
many occupations in our society.  A top ranking official in a private
firm, for example, who made false and demeaning public statements about
the company would no doubt hear about it from the company.

The broader point I was making in the article is that it is time
for us in the Congress to stop needlessly bad-mouthing the Congress.
We campaign for Congress by campaigning against Congress, and try to
tear it down in order to make ourselves look good by comparison.  The
vast majority of Members are honest, conscientious, and hardworking,
and it is time we started saying that.  Distorted and demeaning
statements about the House by Members take their toll in public support
for the Congress and undermine its ability to function properly.

I am enclosing a copy of my remarks in full, should you not have
seen them.  I would request that in future quotations of my statement
you quote it as I stated it, namely, that this is my view about
"distorted, demeaning statements".  I do not make this claim simply for
demeaning statements.

I appreciated your interest in my comments, and I hope that his
helps clarify my views.

Sincerely,

LEE H. HAMILTON, M.C.

Members of Congress like Rep. Coleman routinely engage in complex personal financial dealings with people who are political supporters and campaign contributors *and* for whom they assist in the form of federal spending projects and inside information. Such Members know exactly what they are doing; these Promissory Notes concerning Rep. Coleman's "Blind" Trust were faxed to him at his congressional office.

SENT BY:PERKINS COIE DC      ; 6-12-90 ; 10:02 ;      PERKINS COIE DC→        202-225-4061;# 2

## PROMISSORY NOTE

For value received, the undersigned promises to pay to the order of Deborah Kastrin, the principal sum of Fifty-five Thousand Dollars ($55,000), together with interest thereon at the rate of ten percent (10%) per annum from the date hereof. The entire unpaid amount of principal and interest on this Note shall be due and payable, without demand, on January 1, 2000 (the "Due Date").

Monthly installments of interest in an amount of $_____ are due and payable on the first day of each month and the balance of principal and interest accrued thereon remaining unpaid on the Due Date shall be payable in full on said date.

Payments shall be made at the place where the holder of this Note from time to time shall direct in writing.

At the option of the undersigned, all or any portion of the unpaid principal sum and accrued interest on this Note may be prepaid at any time without premium or penalty.

If the undersigned fails to make any payment due hereunder within ten (10) days after written notice of the default has been given by the holder hereof, interest shall accrue on the balance due, from the date the unpaid payment was due, at the rate of twelve percent (12%) per annum until paid.

DATED this _____ day of _____, 1990.

RONALD COLEMAN BLIND TRUST
Dated April 5, 1986

By: _____
William F. Kastrin, Trustee
not individually but
solely in his capacity as
Trustee under the Ronald
Coleman Blind Trust

## PROMISSORY NOTE

For value received, the undersigned promises to pay to the order of Charles L. Crowder, the principal sum of Sixty-five Thousand Dollars ($65,000), together with interest thereon at the rate of ten percent (10%) per annum from the date hereof. The entire unpaid amount of principal and interest on this Note shall be due and payable, without demand, on January 1, 2000 (the "Due Date").

Monthly installments of interest in the amount of $_____ are due and payable on the first day of each month and the balance of principal and interest accrued thereon remianing unpaid on the Due Date shall be payable in full on said date.

Payments shall be made at the place where the holder of this Note from time to time shall direct in writing.

At the option of the undersigned, all or any portion of the unpaid principal sum and accrued interest on this Note may be prepaid at any time without premium or penalty.

If the undersigned fails to make any payment due hereunder within ten (10) days after written notice of the default has been given by the holder hereof, interest shall accrue on the balance due, from the date the unpaid payment was due, at the rate of twelve percent (12%) per annum until paid.

DATED this _____ _____ day of _____, 1990.

RONALD COLEMAN BLIND TRUST
Dated April 5, 1986

By:_____
William F. Kastrin, Trustee
not individually but
solely in his capacity as
Trustee under the Ronald
Coleman Blind Trust

1787E

MEMORANDUM

TO: RDC
FROM: JOHN
DATE: JULY 24, 1986

RE: BACKGROUND MEMORANDUM RE PRESS ACCOUNTS RELEVANT TO
RESOLUTION OF INQUIRY

The following is a summary of press accounts (attached) and issues they
raise that are relevant to the consideration of your resolution of inquiry by
the House Intelligence Committee.

*Background of Lt. Col. Oliver North*

North graduated from the Naval Academy in 1968 and served in Viet Nam
as a platoon and company commander and was involved in unconventional
war tactics. He taught at the Marine Corps basic training school and the
FBI academy. From 1975 to 1978, he served as a planning officer at Marine
Corps HQ. He was detailed to the National Security Council in 1981, and
put in charge of counterterrorism contingency planning and crisis management. North also helped to coordinate the invasion plans for Grenada,
and directed the interception of the aircraft containing some of the hi-
jackers of the Achille Lauro.

As a result, his stock is still reported high with the President and Chief of
Staff Donald Regan. However, the Miami Herald reported on July 19 that
he was being reassigned, but it was not stated that the reassignment
resulted from attention on his activities or that management of the war has
been shifted from the NSC to CIA as a result of the House vote to provide
military and other aid.

*Allegations Regarding Secret and Illegal Assistance to the Contras*

In addition to the allegations in the Bob Parry/AP story, North also:

- intervened in October 1985 to negotiate a smooth flow of aid through
  the Honduran military to rebel units;
- coordinated the activities of Philip Mabry, a conservative Fort Worth

security consultant, to raise money for military assistance to the contras;

- worked with retired Air Force general Richard Secord to purchase short–take–off–and–landing aircraft from Saudi Arabia and then shipped to the contras;
- in early 1985, helped the contras obtain SAM-7 ground-to-air missiles.

By way of reference, the Boland amendment was in effect from October 1984 to November 1985. In November 1985, the House voted to authorize CIA to provide rebels with intelligence advice and communications equipment that automatically encodes transmissions so rebel leaders could relay CIA advice to troops in field without Sandinista interception. Military advice and tactics, however, were still prohibited.

### North's Other Accounts and the Resolution of Inquiry

One reason for the White House's reluctance to respond to the request for documents may be the fear of unraveling related operations.

In addition to the secret network of intermediaries to aid the contras during the congressional ban, North also had the political destabilization account designed to erode Sandinista support in the United States, Mexico, Europe, as well as within the Contadora group. This political destabilization program was ordered by a secret NSC directive signed by the President in February 1984.

This program was run as a separate account, but there have been no indications concerning any possible overlap.

Another concern might be that the resolution of inquiry includes the time frame during which the CIA could legally provide intelligence advice to the contras, an activity that North either coordinated or participated in since he was still the manager of the contra account at that time. Full compliance with the resolution of inquiry, then, could conceivably include documents of the highest sensitivity such as electronic intercepts, photo-reconnaissance and imagery intelligence, and sources and methods, since anything of that nature that went through North to the contras would be subject to the resolution.

From the Administration's point of view, and given the nature of North's job (not even including his other operations around the world), we have essentially asked them for the blueprints of supply networks in the Middle East, Europe, and Latin America for covert operations. The single issue of determining whether North broke the law in helping to obtain SAM-7s in early 1985, for example, would involve a discussion of the European suppliers, the transshippers and middlemen, the methods used to handle financial transactions for operations of this nature, and the intelligence information given to the contras concerning the vulnerability of Russian helicopters. A similar situation might be encountered during an investigation of the allegation that North helped obtain aircraft from Saudi Arabia for the contras.

As a result, I recommend that you continue to stress your understanding of the need for appropriate secrecy and for the involvement of the House Intelligence Committee, because it would not be beyond the Administration to accuse you of conducting a "witchhunt against vital intelligence operations" or something like they did with Senator Durenberger earlier this year.

*The Issue of Rivalry Within the Contra Leadership*

Although this issue is very murky, the issue of intense rivalry and jockeying for power within the contra leadership is connected to this story.

State Department moderates have been pressuring to reform the contras and to remove or reduce the power of Adolfo Calero and Enrique Bermudez, who have long been criticized for alleged ties to the Somoza regime. An added factor is the decision by moderate contra leaders Arturo Cruz and Alfonso Robelo to join forces to oust Calero or reduce his power.

The situation is also complicated because CIA Director Casey and Lt. Col. North are supporting Calero, whose group has long been backed by the CIA. State, on the other hand, is backing Cruz and Robelo.

Interestingly, it is North's alleged assistance to Calero that was the subject of Bob Parry's 6-10-86 story that really broke open the issue and prompted Bonior's 6/13/86 Dear Colleague. And it was former contra leader Edgar Chamorro—a Calero opponent—who said in a sworn statement quoted by Perry that North had assured the contras of continued support regardless of what the Congress might do.

As I mentioned earlier, this issue is murky and very little beyond the above has been reported by the press, but the coincidences are interesting nevertheless.

MEMORANDUM

TO: RDC
FROM: JOHN
DATE: AUGUST 5, 1986

RE:  QUESTIONS FOR HOUSE INTELLIGENCE COMMITTEE TO ASK LT. COL
     OLIVER NORTH

The following questions represent some key areas to be explored when members of the House Intelligence Committee question Lt. Col Oliver North later this week. As you and the committee members are well aware, one must ask precisely the right question in these kind of situations in order to obtain an accurate answer. North cannot be expected to answer, "No, I did not physically give an intelligence product to the contras, but my deputy assistant for contra affairs may well have described the document's contents to Robert Owen, who then filled them in." Each of the following questions, then, is a description of an area that should be explored by the committee members with various lines of questioning.

Given the limited information at hand, the most productive line of question would be to:

- establish the applicability of the Boland amendment to NSC activities relating to the contras;
- establish North's position within the NSC in terms of managing the contra account;
- establish North's position in terms of U.S. government activities concerning military and intelligence information regarding contra and Sandinista activities;
- within the above framework, establish North's ability to initiate actions on behalf of the contras, either personally or through intermediaries;
- determine if any legal parameters were set concerning his activities in light of the Boland amendment;
- pursue answers to specific allegations in light of his high access to and participation in national security information as established in previous questions.

## QUESTIONS FOR LT. COL. OLIVER NORTH

1. Is the National Security Council, in fact, involved in intelligence-related activities?

    *Note:* The answer is yes, but the question will establish for the record the connection to the Boland amendment.

2. Are you and were you aware of the Boland amendment restrictions on U.S. assistance to the contras, as passed by the Congress and signed by the President?

3. How did you become aware of the Boland amendment restrictions? Did the White House counsel or NSC legal advisers prepare any verbal or written analysis of any kind as to which activities were legal and which were not under the Boland amendment restrictions?

4. Did you ever seek any legal or policy opinion of any kind concerning your activities as they related to the contras during the time the Boland amendment was in effect? This questions concerns either general advice or guidance as well as specific activities for which you might have sought legal guidance.
    (If applicable)

5. Why did you never seek legal advice concerning your activities with contras, particularly given the restrictions on U.S. assistance? How were you so sure that your activities were legal when you've already stated that you never received any legal advice whatsoever on your activities concerning the contras during the time the Boland amendment was in effect?

6. After the adoption of the Boland amendment, did you receive any kind of verbal or written guidance or advice, legal or otherwise, concerning the legality of the activities included in the February 1984 directive signed by President Reagan to erode Sandinista support in Western Europe, the Contadora countries, and in other nations?

7. During the time of the original Boland amendment—October 1984 to November 1985—did you ever support in any way, directly or indirectly, military operations in Nicaragua?

    *Note:* This will put him on record as to compliance with the specific language of the Boland amendment. This response should be compared to the ones concerning the activities of Philip Mabry, Robert Owen, General Singlaub, General Secord, and others.

8. During that time frame, did you ever assist in any way, directly or indirectly, fundraising efforts for the contras?

9. (If "no" to above question) How, then, do you explain your activities as already publicly stated by Philip Mabry, Andrew Messing, and Teofilo Wilson?
   (If applicable)

10. What steps did you take to ensure that the funds raised by private groups you assisted did not in turn assist military operations in Nicaragua?

11. Describe your activities to assist Philip Mabry, a Fort Worth security counsultant, raise funds for the contras.

12. When contacted by Mabry, did you arrange for a meeting between Mabry and Andrew Messing of the National Defense Council?

13. How frequently did you meet with Messing? Please provide the Committee with the dates, times and subjects of those meetings.
    (If applicable)

14. Why do you believe that your assistance to private groups helping the contras, especially with fundraising, did not violate the Boland amendment ban on "directly or indirectly" assisting military operations in Nicaragua? Did you see no connection between their activities outside of Nicaragua and their military operations in Nicaragua?

15. Describe your activities to assist retired Air Force general Richard Secord to purchase aircraft destined for the contras from Saudi Arabia or any other sources.

16. To your knowledge, did the contras ever obtain SAM-7s or any other kind of surface-to-air missile capability during the time either version of the Boland amendment was in effect?

17. Describe your role in assisting the contras obtain SAM-7s.
    (If applicable)

18. How did the contras obtain the SAM-7s without your assistance or

knowledge, especially since you were in charge of the overall contra account?

19. Did you or any other NSC or U.S. official pass information to the contras on how to secure the SAM-7s through foreign arms dealers?

20. Did you or any other NSC or U.S. official give such information to Robert Owen, John Singlaub, or any other private individual associated with the contras?

21. Following the seizure of military supplies bound for the contras at the Tegucigalpa airport in October 1985, did you in fact travel to Honduras or at any other time to negotiate the flow of aid through the Honduran military to the contras? Did you participate in that effort in any other way?

22. What kind of prior arrangements had you made with the Hondurans regarding the flow of aid to the contras through Honduras?

23. Please provide the Committee with a copy of your memorandum and/ or plan to assist the contras with funding in the event Congress cut off aid.

24. To your knowledge, was President Reagan briefed on this plan to assist the contras?

25. According to Edgar Chamorro, you visited the contras in May 1984 and assured them of support regardless of Congressional action. Is that true? What did you tell them?

26. Did you obtain any kind of legal opinion whatsoever as to the legality of this plan after or before the Boland amendment was adopted?

27. Prior to the Boland amendment, who was responsible at the NSC level for military and intelligence tasking concerning intelligence community resources for the contra account? Who was responsible for coordinating the tasking?

    Note: The point is for him to establish where he stood in terms of the flow of national security information. Virtually all sources place him in charge of the contra account after CIA could no longer manage it directly. Once his relatively high position in the flow of national security information concerning contra activities is established, it then becomes extremely difficult for him to make the case that he did not know about and participate in major efforts to obtain military assistance for the contras such as detailed in this memorandum.

28. Did that change after the enactment of the Boland amendment?

29. Please describe the nature of your responsibility for handling the contra account. How and by whom were you tasked to handle that account?

30. Did you, or, to your knowledge, did any other U.S. official provide, directly or indirectly, military or intelligence information—not necessarily specific advice and recommendations—of any kind, including electronic intercepts, photoreconnaissance or descriptions of such intelligence, to the contras during the time the original Boland amendment was in effect?

31. Was any such intelligence information or descriptions of such information provided to Robert Owen or John Singlaub or any other private individual associated with the contras by you or any other NSC or U.S. government official?

32. To your knowledge, did they provide any such information to the contras or their allies? Did you expect them to? Were those private individuals authorized or cleared to handle such information?

33. Please describe your position in terms of intelligence community resources and the contra account during the time the original Boland amendment was in effect. Did you have tasking authority, and if so, what kind?

34. Did you have access to military and intelligence information concerning military and other activities of the Nicaraguan government that would have been useful to the contras?

35. During the time of the Boland amendment, did you ever meet with contra leaders? Can you give the Committee the dates, times and subjects?

36. Were these private meetings in relatively secure places?

37. How then can you expect us to believe that you did not provide information to the contras during this time that might have violated

the Boland amendment when you have already told us that you had no idea what was legal and what was illegal because you never requested or received such advice?

38. Please describe the working relationship between you, Robert Owen and retired General John Singlaub.

39. Was there ever an arrangement or understanding, either express or implied, to the effect that Owen and Singlaub would act as intermediaries for any purpose between you and the contras during the duration of the Boland amendment?

40. Did Singlaub or Owen at any time deliver any information of any kind obtained from you, and other NSC member, or any other U.S. official to the contras during the time the Boland amendment was in effect?

41. Did any information originating from you end up with the contras as a result of your relationship with Singlaub or Owen, even if you did not specifically instruct that information to be transmitted?

42. How often did you meet with General Singlaub? Please provide the committee with dates, times, locations and subjects.

43. How often did Owen meet with contra leaders in military-related meetings? Did he report the results to you? Did you meet with him before or after those meetings? How often did you meet with Owen? Please provide the Committee with dates, times, locations and subjects.

44. Did you meet with Miskito Indian leaders in June 1985 on the subject of their complaint that the FDN would not share military supplies? According to one of the participants in that meeting (Teofilo Archibald Wilson), you instructed them to "go to Miami" and that you would solve their problem. The Miami Herald reported that after they went to a Miami hotel room, Robert Owen appeared to discuss the issue, and upon their return to Honduras, Wilson said the CIA station chief in Tegucigalpa brokered an agreement that brought two plane-loads of ammunition. Is Wilson right?

4 Mar

☐ RCM meeting w/ Congressmen
   STUMP, Bob
   LIVINGSTON, Bob
   HYDE, Henry
   McCollum, Bill


McCollum - Hondurans believe that U.S. aid
            is essential to success in Resistance.

          - no obvious lobbying effort on bill.
            Gingrich
          - No "bargaining" going on.

       "   - O'Connor noty before public
             pronouncement

   Stump - Don't have votes for "covert"
           program.
H.H. - PRIVATE EFFORTS
       3d Countries - Taiwan, Saudi Arabia
 - RCM - PRES DECISION
          - USE FREEDOM FIGHTERS
          - CONSIDERED SIX OPTIONS

4 Mar 85

RCM MTG : Cont'd

- Plan _invader :. 825-SAM
          • 3d country support
          • CIA Intel
- Center the activity in W.H.
- Paul German to join          Themes.
McColm - Need list of swing voters.
       - Need to get marginals to region
Rcm - trips during recess.
Liv. - Collateral issues - release intel/drug trade, etc.

- CRUZ - needs to be able to speak on Hill.
- Hecse - needs to be a single party line on Contras
- Positive Indicators :
    = Poll by U.S.A. Today
    - Bermudez
Hrse - Boland Amendment expired.
     - Can gov. of Fla help. Fascell seored
Rcm - need to have input on who are targets.

TENTATIVE ITINERARY
FINAL FOUR
MARCH 27TH–MARCH 31ST

*March 27th, Friday*

5:30 P.M.    Welcoming Reception: Hospitality Suite Royal Orleans Hotel

6:30 P.M.    Assemble in front of hotel and board horsedrawn buggies for short tour of French Quarter

7:00 P.M.    Cocktail reception and dinner at the home of Congresswoman Lindy Boggs (music provided) Bourbon Street, French Quarter

10:00 P.M.    Depart Boggs home and walk one block to Lulu White's Mahogany Hall for jazz show "Dukes of Dixieland Band" 309 Burbon Street, French Quarters

*March 28th, Saturday*

8:00 A.M.    Optional continental breakfast in hospitality suite

10:00 A.M.    Optional guided Tour of Long Vue Gardens and lunch at the Windsor Court Hotel

11:00 A.M.    Official Brunch Meeting with Members, Pirelli and Ocean Spray executives, Banquet Room at hotel

1:45 P.M.    Mini Vans depart hotel for Louisiana Superdome for semi-final games for tournament

2:42 P.M.    Tournament semi-finals begin

8:00 P.M.    Depart Superdome by mini-vans for Royal Orleans Hotel

9:00 P.M.    Depart for two minute walk to K Paul's Kitchen for private dinner owned by world-famed chef, Paul Prudhomme (musical entertainment provided)

Optional post-dinner plans

*March 29th, Sunday*

A.M.    Optional Church Services

8:00 A.M.    Optional continental breakfast in hospitality suite

11:15 A.M.    Depart for short walk to Brennan's Restaurant

11:30 A.M.    Brunch at Brennan's Restaurant
Private Banquet Room, 417 Royal Street
French Quarter

2:30 P.M.    River Cruise on either "Creole Queen" or "Natchez" steam-
boats (2 hours)
French Quarter departure

8:00 P.M.    Depart hotel for short walk to Arnaud's Restaurant, 813 Bien-
ville Street, French Quarter

8:10 P.M.    Cocktail Reception and Dinner at Arnaud's Restaurant

Optional evening plans suggested such as Pat O'Briens, or
Preservation Music Hall

*March 30th, Monday*

8:00 A.M.    Optional Continental Breakfast in hospitality suite

10:30 A.M.    Group departs by Mini-van for Boatman House in the New
Orleans Garden District for brunch hosted by Bethany Boat-
man (string quartet will provide entertainment). Boatman
House is the home where Tennessee Williams wrote "The
Glass Menagerie"

P.M.    Optional guided tours and shopping in the antique district or
other sightseeing events

5:00 P.M.    Closing reception in the hospitality suite of the Royal Orleans
hotel.

5:30 P.M.    Official buffet dinner for Members, Ocean Spray and Pirelli
executives, Banquet Room at Hotel

7:15 P.M.    Depart Hotel by mini-van for Superdome Final game, Final
Four Tournament

11:30 P.M.    (approx.) Game concludes, vans return to Royal Orleans
Hotel.

HENRY J. HYDE
6TH DISTRICT, ILLINOIS

COMMITTEES:
JUDICIARY
FOREIGN AFFAIRS
INTELLIGENCE

2262 RAYBURN HOUSE OFFICE BUILDING
WASHINGTON, DC 20515
(202) 225-4561

# Congress of the United States
## House of Representatives
### Washington, DC 20515

July 16, 1991

Mr. John L. Jackley
2785 York Street
West Linn, Oregon 97068

Dear Mr. Jackley:

In reply to your letter of July 1, I appreciate your professionalism in writing me to check the information you have concerning my alleged relationship with some aspects of the Iran/Contra affair.

At no time was I ever present at any meetings, including one on March 4, 1985 at the White House with Mr. Robert McFarlane, where I was privy to "elements of a plan to erode the Boland Amendment." The implication from your letter was that I had knowledge of some illegal activity and failed to disclose it to the proper authorities. The essential purpose of that March meeting was to discuss legislative strategy for the upcoming committee markup and subsequent House floor action on an annual intelligence authorization bill which we fully anticipated would initially contain restrictions on aid to the Contras (See attachment 1, from the published Iran/Contra investigation records.)

The absence of any conspiratorial revelation of "illegal" activity is obvious from the declassified memorandum reporting on the meeting which Mr. McFarlane subsequently sent to Max Friedersdorf of the White House staff. Moreover, that memorandum, as well as Col. North's notes and other related documents, were widely circulated throughout the staff of the Iran/Contra committees.

Because the purpose of the meeting was to discuss legislative strategy, the $25 to $50 million probably was the amount we were proposing as an appropriation. Please do not forget that Congress appropriated $27 million in humanitarian aid for the Contras approximately five months after this meeting. An additional $100 million was authorized the following year. I remember a discussion about centering the lobbying activities for the appropriations vote in the White House which seems to be confirmed by North's notes. I think it is important to notice North's notations about what Mr. McCollum said: "Need list of swing votes." Clearly, we were all talking about an upcoming vote. My mention of third country contributions was a gratuitous suggestion which McFarlane said he rejected.

In addition, the leadership of the select committees knew of this information, as did some other committee members. Indeed, some of these very declassified documents were included in the appendices of the Iran/Contra committees' voluminous report (See attachments 1,2,3,4).

In the President's preeminent role in the conduct of foreign affairs, it is certainly legal and within his constitutional discretion to urge foreign nations to take steps as independent sovereign states which he believes serve the best interests of the United States. Those steps clearly may include, as in this case, urging foreign governments that by aiding the Contras they would be acting in the best interests of all freedom loving countries. Such diplomatic representations to foreign governments are certainly within the constitutional prerogatives of the President. Congress lacks the constitutional power to tell him who he can and cannot talk to, or to limit the subject matter of these discussions.

At the August 6, 1986 White House meeting, I am certain that I did not bring up any prior knowledge of the Contra resupply efforts which you say was outlined on March 4, 1985 because no such plan was discussed at the earlier meeting. I was as deceived as everyone else concerning the resupply operations because I believed the letters of denial from McFarlane and Admiral Poindexter.

I hope this letter, together with the enclosures, puts to rest the false notion that I knew about some illegal conspiracy and failed to disclose it to the proper authorities.

Very truly yours,

Henry J. Hyde

HJH:s

# INDEX

The only frustration that accompanies a book such as this one is the inability due to space limitations to include everything that ought to be covered. The world of Capitol Hill is vast, and its dealings over the last decade even more so. For questions or additional information about Capitol Hill, or readers' thoughts and comments about the book, the author can be contacted at P.O. Box 171, West Linn, Oregon, 97068. A personal reply is promised.